Disability, Criminal Justice and Law

Through theoretical and empirical examination of legal frameworks for court diversion, this book interrogates law's complicity in the debilitation of disabled people.

In a post-deinstitutionalisation era, diverting disabled people from criminal justice systems and into mental health and disability services is considered therapeutic, humane and socially just. Yet, by drawing on Foucauldian theory of biopolitics, critical legal and political theory and critical disability theory, Steele argues that court diversion continues disability oppression. It can facilitate criminalisation, control and punishment of disabled people who are not sentenced and might not even be convicted of any criminal offences. On a broader level, court diversion contributes to the longstanding phenomenon of disability-specific coercive intervention, legitimates prison incarceration and shores up the boundaries of foundational legal concepts at the core of jurisdiction, legal personhood and sovereignty. Steele shows that the United Nations Convention on the Rights of Persons with Disabilities cannot respond to the complexities of court diversion, suggesting the CRPD is of limited use in contesting carceral control and legal and settler colonial violence. The book not only offers new ways to understand relationships between disability, criminal justice and law; it also proposes theoretical and practical strategies that contribute to the development of a wider re-imagining of a more progressive and just socio-legal order.

The book will be of interest to scholars and students of disability law, criminal law, medical law, socio-legal studies, disability studies, social work and criminology. It will also be of interest to disability, prisoner and social justice activists.

Linda Steele is based at the University of Technology Sydney.

Part of the SOCIAL JUSTICE series

Series editors

Sarah Keenan, *Birkbeck College, University of London, UK*
Davina Cooper, *University of Kent, UK*
Sarah Lamble, *Birkbeck College, University of London, UK*

for information about the series and details of previous and forthcoming titles, see https://www.routledge.com/Social-Justice/book-series/RCSOCJ

Disability, Criminal Justice and Law

Reconsidering Court Diversion

Linda Steele

Routledge
Taylor & Francis Group
a GlassHouse Book

First published 2020
by Routledge
2 Park Square, Milton Park, Abingdon, Oxon OX14 4RN

and by Routledge
52 Vanderbilt Avenue, New York, NY 10017

A GlassHouse book

Routledge is an imprint of the Taylor & Francis Group, an informa business

British Library Cataloguing-in-Publication Data
A catalogue record for this book is available from the British Library

Library of Congress Cataloging-in-Publication Data
Names: Steele, Linda, 1981- author.
Title: Disability, criminal justice and law : reconsidering court
diversion / Linda Steele.
Description: Abingdon, Oxon ; New York, NY : Routledge, 2020. |
Series: Social justice | Based on author's thesis (doctoral - University of
Sydney, 2014) issued under
title: Disability at the margins : diversion, cognitive impairment and
the criminal law. | Includes bibliographical references and index.
Identifiers: LCCN 2020003176 (print) | LCCN 2020003177 (ebook) |
ISBN 9780815375265 (hardback) | ISBN 9781351240338 (ebook)
Subjects: LCSH: Offenders with mental disabilities--Legal status, laws,
etc.--English-speaking countries. | Mentally ill offenders--Legal status, laws,
etc.--English-speaking countries. | Pre-trial intervention--English-speaking countries.
Classification: LCC K5077 . S74 2020 (print) | LCC K5077 (ebook) |
DDC 345/.03087--dc23
LC record available at https://lccn.loc.gov/2020003176
LC ebook record available at https://lccn.loc.gov/2020003177

ISBN: 978-0-8153-7526-5 (hbk)
ISBN: 978-0-367-52058-8 (pbk)
ISBN: 978-1-351-24033-8 (ebk)

Typeset in Galliard
by Taylor & Francis Books

For Evan, Audrey and Jemima

Contents

Acknowledgements viii
Preface x

Introduction: Reconsidering court diversion 1

1 Introducing court diversion 23

2 Problematising court diversion 46

3 Theorising court diversion: Disability 74

4 Theorising court diversion: Carcerality and legality 97

5 The finer details of debilitation through law: Introduction to an Australian diversion scheme 119

6 Jurisdiction, disability and lawful relations 149

7 Choosing carceral control 164

8 Disability, criminal justice and law: Beyond court diversion 198

Conclusion 220

Bibliography 228
Index 259

Acknowledgements

I acknowledge the Gadigal people of the Eora Nation and the Wadi Wadi People of the Dharawal Country on whose unceded territories this book was written.

Disability, Criminal Justice and Law began as a PhD thesis undertaken at University of Sydney. I thank my supervisors—Arlie Loughnan, Leanne Dowse and Kristin Savell—for all of the encouragement, guidance and expertise they contributed. I am also grateful to my examiners—Peter Bartlett, Ben Golder and Tony Ward—for their insightful comments that have very much helped to shape the subsequent book. I am appreciative to Eileen Baldry for her assistance throughout the course of the PhD project in relation to the MHDCD dataset. I am also thankful for the patient assistance with the MHDCD dataset which I received from Julian Trofimovs and Melissa Clarence and for the assistance I received from a number of individuals, including from the court registries and legal organisations, concerning sampling and data access in relation to the Section 32 Court Data.

I am thankful for the feedback on drafts I received from colleagues: Thalia Anthony, Rachel Bolton, Louise Boon-Kuo, Terry Carney, Sara Dehm, Leanne Dowse, Ray Carr, David Carter, Chris Chapman, Brett Heino, Arlie Loughnan, Jess McLean, Amanda Porter, Lucy Series, Tess Sheldon, Alecia Simmonds, Anthea Vogl and Sheila Wildeman.

Thank you to the Social Justice series editors—Sarah Lamble, Sarah Keenan and Davina Cooper—for the generosity of time and thought apparent in the feedback and encouragement they provided throughout the process of writing the manuscript. I am also grateful for the thoughtful and encouraging earlier feedback from the anonymous book proposal reviewers.

I am thankful for the disability law and critical disability colleagues in Australia and abroad who have been a source of great inspiration and guidance. These include Eileen Baldry, Peter Bartlett, Fleur Beaupert, Jessica Robyn Cadwallader, Chris Chapman, Beverley Clough, Leanne Dowse, Gerard Goggin, Piers Gooding, Ameil Joseph, Ruth McCausland, Roxanne Mykitiuk, Lucy Series, Tess Sheldon, Claire Spivakovsky, Jill Stavert, Dinesh Wadiwel, Penny Weller and Sheila Wildeman. I also acknowledge the collegiality and support of many colleagues at University of Technology Sydney, including Thalia Anthony, Katherine Biber, Tracey Booth, David Carter, Sara Dehm, Maxine Evers, Beth Goldblatt, Brett Heino,

Isabel Karpin, Trish Luker, Elyse Methven, Jenni Millbank, Karen O'Connell, Anita Stuhmcke, Anthea Vogl and Ana Vrdoljak. Thank you to my mentors over the years: Rebecca Albury, Jenny Beard, Kevin English, Timothy Robertson SC, Nan Seuffert, Ana Vrdoljak and Sheridan Wilkins.

I acknowledge the research assistance of Iwona Accurso, Julian Trofimovs and Gemma Sentance, and copyediting by Matthew Sidebotham and Fliss Watts. I also acknowledge funding towards this book and the earlier PhD from UTS Law Health Justice, Endeavour Foundation, University of Wollongong and the University of Sydney.

Writing this book would not have been possible without my family. Thank you to Russell Steele for his constant encouragement and humour, and for always being able to help with childcare. Thank you also to Susan and Greg Gleeson and Suzanne and Ray Salmon for assisting with childcare. Thank you to Evan Salmon for his steadfast support and love. Thank you to Audrey for her thoughtfulness, kindness and curiosity and Jemima for her exuberance and laughter.

Preface

In 2006–2009 I worked as a solicitor at a community legal centre for people with intellectual disability. During my time there I represented clients in court diversion matters. This book is my attempt to grapple with many of the complexities and contradictions both with court diversion itself and lawyers' role in court diversion, which I observed during my time as a solicitor. This book, however, reflects only my personal opinions and not those of my former workplace or colleagues.

Introduction

Reconsidering court diversion

This book critically reassesses court diversion. Its central contention is that we need to reject the view that court diversion is a humane use of law specifically for disabled people who are in the criminal justice system. Instead, we must approach court diversion as part of a much bigger, systemic problem with law that we need to resist—the inclusion in legal doctrine and legal process of disability as a lawful and legitimate basis on which to circumvent equality for disabled people in the criminal justice system and to drastically shift the thresholds of permissible control, violence and injustice.

I argue that through the exercise of court diversion, legal doctrine and legal process are complicit in debilitating disabled people in the criminal justice system. Court diversion enables disabled people in the criminal justice system who might otherwise not be sentenced, or even convicted, to be subjected to coercive intervention through disability and mental health services. In so doing, court diversion provides legal pathways between otherwise disparate legal domains, spaces and modes of control and both sustains and serves to legitimise lifelong violence and precarity experienced by disabled people in the criminal justice system. Yet the language and logic of 'diversion' simultaneously serves to mask complicity of law in debilitation, portraying law instead as facilitating therapeutic and supportive interventions that are necessary, non-violent, non-colonial and just. Disentangling and laying bare law's (and relatedly legal actors') complicity in debilitation through disability is the primary purpose of this book.

The argument I have just set out might be unexpected and even unsettling and confronting for some readers, notably because court diversion's inclusion in criminal justice systems has at times been the result of the work of disability rights advocates and others committed to supporting and empowering disabled people. Certainly in proposing here that we reconsider court diversion I am not suggesting that instead we should retain the status quo of incarceration of disabled people. Rather, I am proposing that court diversion is part of what sustains that status quo through enabling the control of disabled people beyond the court house and prison which are often positioned as the conventional targets of disability criminal justice advocacy.

This chapter introduces the conventional approach to court diversion based in the overrepresentation of disabled people in the criminal justice system, and then moves to situate court diversion in broader issues of injustice associated with criminal justice and disability and mental health systems. The chapter then elaborates on the book's argument by reference to key aspects of an interdisciplinary analytical frame grounded in biopolitics which is used to critically reassess court diversion, drawing on theoretical ideas pertaining to disability, carcerality and legality.

The conventional approach: court diversion as therapeutic solution

This book defines 'court diversion' as a legal process whereby a judge is able to make an order that moves a disabled person appearing before them on criminal charges into treatment and support provided by disability and mental health services, in lieu of a sentence (and sometimes even a conviction). In light of the geographic development of court diversion (and my particular concerns with settler colonialism discussed below) this book is focused on court diversion in Anglo jurisdictions (England, Scotland, Northern Ireland, Wales, Canada, Republic of Ireland, United States of America, Australia and Aotearoa/New Zealand). Court diversion has its origins in England with the introduction in mental health legislation of hospital orders, as part of broader reform of mental health laws. Many Anglo jurisdictions with mental health laws modelled on England and Wales soon followed suit. A second wave of court diversion occurred in the late 1990s with the introduction of mental health courts in many jurisdictions in North America. Chapter 1 provides a more detailed overview of court diversion.

This book is focused specifically on court diversion of disabled people. 'Disability' is an umbrella term encompassing a broad array of diagnosed sensory, physical, neurological, mental and cognitive conditions. In contrast, when this book refers to disabled people in the criminal justice system it is referring specifically to people identified as having psychosocial disability or cognitive impairment. Psychosocial disability (also referred to as mental illness) includes a broad range of conditions, including depression, anxiety, schizophrenia and personality disorders. Cognitive impairment includes conditions such as intellectual disability and acquired brain injury. In criminal law, psychosocial disability and cognitive impairment are typically grouped together on the basis that these disabilities signal that an individual lacks mental capacity and rationality. This lack necessitates alternative doctrine and process because it would be unjust or ineffective to deal with these disabled individuals through conventional criminal legal doctrine and process, by reason of their incapacity and irrationality impacting on their ability to participate in trial, be found criminally responsible, or be deterred and rehabilitated through sentenced criminal legal interventions. Specific legal doctrine and legal process for people with these particular disabilities is, therefore, bound up with foundational aspects of criminal law (and, indeed, law more broadly) pertaining to mental capacity and rationality that traditionally have justified state coercive interventions in relation to individuals through criminal law. While people with other disabilities (such as physical disabilities or hearing impairments) might also be in the criminal justice system, they are not similarly subject to disability-specific legal doctrine and legal process in terms of the disposition of their charges and the basis on which they might be entitled to access treatment and support.

My analysis of court diversion focuses on diversion of individuals at court prior to conviction or prior to sentence. It does not include forms of diversion that *sentence* individuals to specific mental health treatment or move them into treatment from prison once they are serving a sentence. Similarly, I do not include diversion during trial to treatment where there is no possibility this treatment can be in lieu of sentencing. Nor do I include the application of laws ordering treatment or support after finding of unfitness to plead or be tried or not guilty by reason of mental illness (also referred to as 'NGMI' and the insanity defence)—these are not court diversion. This is because unfitness and NGMI follow a conventional criminal justice trajectory whereas the court diversion schemes I discuss relate to completely different considerations with no direct relation to criminal legal criteria for trial, conviction and sentence. Indeed, O'Mahony (2013: p. 91) notes the peculiarity of court diversion insofar as it relates to people who are 'considered neither wholly culpable offenders nor "wholly incapacitious" [sic] offenders'. This rather anomalous nature of court diversion vis-à-vis criminal law more broadly is what makes it such a significant site of analysis from a sociolegal perspective, something I return to in Chapter 2. It should also be noted that my analysis of court diversion focuses on adult criminal jurisdictions.

My argument about court diversion might seem counter-intuitive to some readers. At least prima facie, court diversion might be understood as law doing good in the lives of disabled people by facilitating access to beneficial and necessary treatment and support and creating an option that avoids the ultimate coercive intervention of imprisonment. This view is grounded in the conventional association of court diversion with the problem of overrepresentation of disabled people in the criminal justice system.

Concern with disabled people in the criminal justice system—their contact with police, criminal courts, prisons and community corrections—is frequently articulated in terms of *overrepresentation*—the overall number of disabled people in the criminal justice system is not proportional to their prevalence in the general population. Conventionally, this overrepresentation is attributed to disabled people not having access to disability and mental health services in the community. This is said to coincide with the failure of governments to ensure appropriate treatment and support in the community in the aftermath of the gradual downsizing and closure of large-scale asylums and disability institutions associated with deinstitutionalisation. Solutions to overrepresentation thus become focused on providing access to disability and mental health services for individuals when they are in the criminal justice system, on the assumption that this will reduce the likelihood of these individuals re-offending and, in the long term, reduce the overall number of disabled people in the criminal justice system.

Conventionally, as discussed in Chapter 1, court diversion is viewed by many scholars, disability advocates and policy-makers as a way in which law (legal doctrine and legal process) and legal actors (lawyers and judges) can play a positive role in addressing overrepresentation. Court diversion is conventionally considered beneficial because it provides judges a legal alternative to conviction and sentence and, therefore, can facilitate freedom from prison and access to disability and mental health services. As such, court diversion does not merely remedy individuals' untreated disability but, through embedding within the legal system pathways to services, also addresses systemic problems associated with the post-deinstitutionalisation failure of governments to ensure appropriate treatment and support in the community. In this conventional approach, there is an underlying assumption that disabled people's criminal offending is associated with a lack of access to services; that access to disability and mental health services can, and should, be facilitated by criminal courts; and that, in order to empower courts to do so, disability should be singled out as a separate category in legal doctrine and legal process.

The ascendancy of court diversion as a key disability criminal justice strategy can easily lead one to assume that court diversion is a self-evident good, resonating with the observation made by Richards (2014: p. 125) in the context of youth diversion that 'the taken-for granted nature of the concept of "diversion" is striking; it is a constant feature of criminal justice … discourse, but is rarely critically examined'. Yet, there is a body of scholarship that questions court diversion. As will be discussed in Chapter 1, this scholarship has drawn attention to coercive and 'net widening' aspects, its failure to address structural issues and its procedural limitations vis-à-vis criminal law. Taking note of the concerns raised in that scholarship, I propose that as court diversion becomes further embedded and normalised as part of how disabled people in the criminal justice system are to be treated by criminal law and criminal justice systems, it is timely to pause and subject court diversion to sustained critical scrutiny of its broader political implications and effects.

The need to reconsider: court diversion and disability injustice

Disability, Criminal Justice and Law's reconsideration of court diversion begins by focusing on problems associated with its coercive character and complex relationships to disability injustices associated with criminal justice and disability and mental health systems. These problems, which are set out in detail in Chapter 2, are generally overlooked or given insufficient weight in the conventional approach to court diversion.

Acute problems with court diversion

The fundamental problem is that court diversion still involves coercive (in the sense of involuntary) intervention, even though individuals avoid criminal legal intervention through sentencing laws. This intervention is facilitated by law through including disability (rather than criminal offending) as a basis for coercive intervention and occurs through disability and mental health services. Court diversion involves coercive intervention of disabled people in the criminal justice system who have not yet been convicted or sentenced and situates these people outside of the typical liberal legal limits on coercive intervention applying to non-disabled people in the criminal justice system. Therefore, court diversion demonstrates inequalities in the scope for legal coercion among people in the criminal justice system along lines of disability, because disabled people are subject to coercive intervention at a point in the criminal justice process when this is otherwise legally impossible. Court diversion also provides additional opportunities for perpetration of unlawful violence *and* legal violence against disabled people through disability and mental health services.

It is also problematic that access to disability and mental health services through court diversion is dependent on coercion, rather than being premised on choice, voluntariness and self-determination. This is indicative of inequalities in access to disability and mental health services among disabled people along the lines of criminality, because those who are diverted do not have choice in their access to services. Moreover, even though many disabled people in the criminal justice system are also poor, Indigenous or First Nations, or racialised minorities, court diversion's application to people on the basis of diagnosed disability can depoliticise people's circumstances and fail to acknowledge or seek to address the impact on disabled people of interlocking dynamics and forces of oppression.

Finally, court diversion applies only to a minority of disabled people in the criminal justice system; it does not address incarceration for the majority of disabled people in the criminal justice system, who continue to be incarcerated or subject to community corrections. Incarceration of disabled people, and the prison itself, continue. Beyond access to disability and mental health services, important structural issues—related to interlocking dynamics and forces of oppression shaping the experiences and lives of whole populations of disabled people in the criminal justice system—are not being addressed.

The problems I have identified here disrupt the conventional view of court diversion as beneficial and humane. These problems suggest that, through court diversion, the law is actually enabling injustice (in the sense of control, violence, precarity, discrimination, inequality) specifically of disabled people in the criminal justice system.

These problems lead to a series of novel questions about court diversion that drive this book. How is court diversion accommodated in law and politically tolerated? What is the significance of disability to control and violence through court diversion? To what extent does challenging oppression of disabled people in the criminal justice system require disruption of conventional understandings of disability political identity? How should court diversion be repositioned in our quest to end oppression of disabled people in the criminal justice system, and how can social justice be achieved for this group if not through court diversion? Can human rights provide the tools to challenge oppression of disabled people in the criminal justice system?

Court diversion through a prism of disability injustices

Appreciating the relevance and complexity of the new questions this book asks of court diversion requires viewing court diversion through a prism of disability injustices at the nexus of criminal justice and disability and mental health systems. These injustices are explored in further detail in Chapter 2. Viewing court diversion in this way connects the injustices arising from court diversion to broader dynamics and forces of oppression, including ableism, imperialism, colonialism, capitalism, patriarchal heteronormativity and white supremacy. While civil and criminal laws related to disability are a regular focus of law reform and government inquiries, the injustices of criminal justice and disability and mental health systems continue to be perpetrated, in part because institutionalisation and coercive intervention as well as the carving out of disability as a separate category endure in law. Indeed, the persistent orientation towards disability history in terms of the 'dark past' prevents us from seeing new or continuing forms of oppression.

Turning first to the criminal justice system, disabled people experience considerable discrimination, violence and other harms in prison (see Peters, 2003). This is exemplified by high-profile deaths in custody across a number of jurisdictions. These include the death of Ashley Smith, a young disabled Canadian woman, in her prison cell from self-strangulation while prison officers watched and videotaped her (Hannah-Moffat & Klassen, 2015). A further example is the death of Sarah Reed, a 35-year-old Black woman with mental illness in England; Reed died in her prison cell from self-strangulation while she awaited a fitness assessment (Coles, Roberts & Cavcav, 2018: pp. 5–10). The jury at the inquest into her death found 'unacceptable delays in psychiatric assessment, inadequate treatment for her high levels of distress, and the failure of prison psychiatrists to manage Sarah's medication contributed to her death' (ibid.: p. 10). Recently, international NGO Human Rights Watch documented first-hand accounts of disabled prisoners' experiences of verbal, physical and sexual violence, bullying, harassment and discrimination in Australian prisons (Sharma, 2018). Criminalised trans disabled people are particularly vulnerable to harm in prison, including through systemic transphobia and lack of provision of trans-specific physical and mental health care (Bassichis, 2007: p. 9). While court diversion does enable select individuals to avoid the violence of prison, it has no bearing on structural ableism and violence in the prison system to which those who are not diverted will continue to be exposed.

The violence of prison is particularly pronounced in relation to Indigenous and First Nations disabled people. This book's focus on Anglo jurisdictions captures numerous jurisdictions—Australia, Aotearoa/New Zealand, Canada, United States, Republic of Ireland, Northern Ireland—that were colonised (primarily by the British Empire). This book refers to these jurisdictions as 'settler colonial' nations (Veracini, 2010; Wolfe, 2006). At a very general level, and noting the considerable differences in experiences between jurisdictions, settler colonialism is an ongoing social structure involving occupation and exploitation of Indigenous and First Nations people's land and the dispossession, displacement and elimination of Indigenous and First Nation's people. Settler colonialism manifests in a variety of practices perpetrated on Indigenous and First Nations people including child removal, sexual violence, incarceration, massacre and enslavement, and these practices are facilitated and legitimated through imposition of settler legal and political systems. Wolfe identifies a 'logic of elimination' driven by 'access to territory' as the driving feature of settler colonialism:

> the primary motive for elimination is not race (or religion, ethnicity, grade of civilization, etc.) but access to territory. Territoriality is settler colonialism's specific, irreducible element.
>
> The logic of elimination not only refers to the summary liquidation of Indigenous people, though it includes that. ... settler colonialism has both negative and positive dimensions. Negatively, it strives for the dissolution of native societies. Positively, it erects a new colonial society on the expropriated land base—as I put it, settler colonizers come to stay: invasion is a structure not an event. In its positive aspect, elimination is an organizing principal of settler-colonial society rather than a one-off (and superseded) occurrence. The positive outcomes of the logic of elimination can include officially encouraged miscegenation, the breaking-down of native title into alienable individual freeholds, native citizenship, child abduction, religious conversion, resocialization in total institutions such as missions or boarding schools, and a whole range of cognate biocultural assimilations. All these strategies, including frontier homicide, are characteristic of settler colonialism.
>
> (Wolfe, 2006: p. 388)

Settler colonialism occurs in a context of Indigenous and First Nations people not ever having ceded their sovereignty and their ongoing resistance to settler colonial rule.

Criminal justice systems (notably policing and prison incarceration) have been and continue to be key ways through which settler colonial rule is enacted, and the law has a central role in shaping these practices as legitimate and just (see Cunneen, 2019b; Cunneen & Tauri, 2016; Cunneen, et al., 2013). Indigenous and First Nations people are detained in high numbers in police custody, prisons and juvenile detention throughout settler colonial nations and they have experienced considerable violence and premature death through policing and incarceration. Cunneen argues that in an Australian context institutional racism not only pervades the criminal justice system, but also social welfare policy (notably child welfare and social housing). While social welfare policy might appear prima facie equal in its application, Cunneen (2019a) proposes that it is instead structured to channel Aboriginal and Torres Strait Islander people into the criminal justice system. He states that: 'Paternalist policies which are based on coercion, by their very nature, require increased intervention and penalties for those who do not comply' (Cunneen, 2019a: p. 35).

The violence of criminal justice systems in relation to Indigenous and First Nations people is evidenced by high-profile reports such as the Royal Commission into Aboriginal Deaths in Custody (1991) in Australia and the more recent Royal Commission and Board of Inquiry into the Protection and Detention of Children in the Northern Territory (2017) in light of the torture of Aboriginal boys in juvenile detention. The recent National Inquiry into Missing and Murdered Indigenous Women and Girls (2019a, 2019b) in Canada has highlighted the gendered dimensions of settler colonial violence and death through criminal justice systems. Much of this conduct occurs in the course of routine, mundane policing, prison administration and summary court judicial decision-making exemplary of what is permitted by criminal legal doctrine and legal process. While in a minority of instances these harms are recognised through court decisions and government inquiries as unlawful and unjust, too often the very legal processes purportedly tasked with ensuring government accountability instead facilitate government inaction in the aftermath of outcomes of these processes and legitimate these harms variously as lawful, necessary, benevolent and just (see, for example, Razack, 2015). Bond (2017), who is an Aboriginal (Munanjahli) and South Sea Islander Australian, explains Aboriginal violence and death as central to the Australian settler colonial project:

> Where murder is not even considered manslaughter, where Black witnesses are deemed 'unreliable', where royal commission recommendations aren't implemented, where coroners refuse to exercise their power to make recommendations, and where White murderers of Black children enjoy the privilege of being unnamed for their own protection, it is blatantly clear whose lives really matter in Australia. …
>
> The settlers have long insisted that our death was destined, that our race was doomed, and that we, as a people, were vanishing. Our disappearance was inevitable because it was necessary to sustain *terra nullius*, the foundational myth of Australia. Black deaths rationalised White invasion and land expansion in Australia. …
>
> In our dying, rather than in our living, our bodies mattered most to the colonial project.

In the context of broader demands for self-determination and the fact that across many Anglo jurisdictions Indigenous sovereignty was never ceded, Cunneen points out that 'Indigenous peoples argue for transformation of criminal justice within the context of the collective right to self-determination—this is not a demand for the reform of justice but for its reconceptualization' (Cunneen, 2019b: p. 13).

Turning specifically to Indigenous and First Nations *disabled* people in the criminal justice system, it is important to note that many Indigenous and First Nations people reject diagnostic labels of disability. Individualised diagnoses broken down to specific internal characteristics do not reflect Indigenous and First

Nations cultural epistemologies and ontologies, nor do they capture the collective, intergenerational and structural nature of trauma experienced by reason of ongoing practices of white supremacy, settler colonialism and imperialism (for example, Avery, 2018; Raju & Penak, 2019; Westerman in Qadar, 2020). Moreover, as I elaborate in Chapters 3 and 4, disability diagnosis itself has a long history of being used to pathologise and dehumanise Indigenous and First Nations people and legitimate genocide and, in contemporary contexts, can be a barrier to collective self-determination and nation-building. Indeed, Million (Tanana Athabascan), writing in the context of Canadian First Nations, has argued that Western, medicalised discourses of 'trauma' and 'healing' that have structured reconciliation processes in Canada can fold back into rather than disrupt the very systems and practices of colonial control they are purportedly directed towards redressing (Million, 2013b). Some Indigenous and First Nations people instead propose a strengths-based approach to wellbeing. For example, Dudgeon and colleagues suggest an approach of 'social and emotional wellbeing', which is a multifaceted concept that acknowledges that a person's wellbeing is determined by a range of interrelated domains: body, mind and emotions, family and kinship, community, culture, Country, and spirituality (Dudgeon et al., 2017: p. 316; see also Avery's work on Indigenous culture as key to disability inclusion: Avery, 2018). Such approaches are situated in cultural safety work and collective self-determination rather than narrowly focused on individual diagnosis and coercive mental health treatment or disability case management, or even more purportedly progressive western ideas of individual empowerment and recovery.

With these caveats about disability in mind, research has noted that Indigenous and First Nations people who are disabled might be particularly exposed to violence and premature death. For example, a recent media investigation into ten years of Aboriginal and Torres Strait Islander death-in-custody cases in Australia found that:

> Mental health or cognitive impairment was a factor in 41% of all deaths in custody. But Indigenous people with a diagnosed mental health condition or cognitive impairment, such as a brain injury or foetal alcohol syndrome disorder, received the care they needed in just 53% of cases.
>
> (Allam, Wahlquist & Evershed, 2018)

Racialised minorities in Anglo jurisdictions—including diasporas formed from generations of slavery and indentured labour—are also subject to dynamics and forces of oppression pertaining to settler colonialism and imperialism including in the context of criminalisation and incarceration (Cunneen, 2019b). For example, disabled people who are Indigenous and First Nations people and other racialised minorities, including those not yet charged with criminal offences, are the target of discrimination, violence (including lethal violence) and harm by police officers (El-Enany & Bruce-Jones, 2015; Maqbool, 2018; Nicholson & Marcoux, 2018; Perry, 2017; Sins Invalid, 2016; Zhou, 2018). There are innumerable examples of activism and resistance in the aftermath of policing killings or deaths in custody, including activism against police violence by Black Lives Matter; the 'Justice For Tanya Day' Facebook site maintained by children of Tanya Day, an Aboriginal (Yorta Yorta) woman who died in police custody in Australia; Latoya Rule's activism in relation to her daughter Rebecca Maher, an Aboriginal (Wiradjuri) woman who died in police custody in Australia; and Marcia Rigg's activism in relation to the death in police custody in England of her brother Sean Rigg, a Black man diagnosed with schizophrenia. These demonstrate the resistance to state violence against Indigenous and First Nations people and other racialised minorities and the depths of the impacts of such violence on bereaved family members and communities.

While not a focus of this book, there are also important intersections between the criminal justice, immigration and mental health systems in relation to racialised minorities. While some progressive scholars and activists have argued for medical treatment as a basis on which undocumented migrants can be released from immigration detention or be granted residency or citizenship (such as the recent activism in Australia around 'Medevac' law reforms which would enable transfer of individuals from offshore immigration detention to Australia for medical treatment (Dehm, 2019)), some disability scholars have drawn attention to the ways in which the mental health system simply exacerbates racialised violence. For example, Tam states:

> … while liberal health advocates have secured more funding for specialized detainees mental health services, they have failed to comprehend how Black people are already subject to early detention and crisis intervention, a fact that has directly contributed to the criminalization, detentions, and deportations, and deaths of Black migrants in Canada. I argue that increased mental health assessment and treatment of immigration detainees is not only paradoxical but further exacerbates conditions of distress by contributing to the expansion, rather than abolition, of the detention and deportation systems.
>
> (Tam, 2017: p. 340; see also Joseph, 2015; Soldatic & Fiske, 2009; Ticktin, 2011)

My discussion here of Indigenous and First Nations people and other racialised minorities in the criminal justice system emphasises that the injustices of criminal justice systems and criminal law are not only apparent along disability lines but implicate interlocking dynamics and forces of oppression.

Before moving on, I pause to emphasise this book's ambition to forge new sociolegal connections between disability, law and settler colonialism. Critical disability studies scholarship outside of law, in the past decade, has increasingly engaged with settler colonialism (see Ben-Moshe, Chapman & Carey, 2014; Chapman & Withers, 2019; Chen, 2012; Puar, 2017; Tam 2013). This disability scholarship builds on the foundational work of critical race theorists in making apparent the colonial, racial and white supremacist dynamics of criminal justice systems and criminal law (see, for example, Davis, 2005; Roberts, 2017). In contrast, the scholarship on disability and law is marked by a relative absence of critical engagement with imperialism, settler colonialism and eugenics (see, however, Bielefeld & Beaupert, 2019; Steele, 2018d; see also Krishnarayan, 2017), including in relation to questions of redress for past injustices and how to support Indigenous and First Nations self-determination and nation-building. It is absolutely urgent and necessary for disability law scholars *across* Anglo jurisdictions to reflect on the settler colonial, imperial and racial dimensions of court diversion, and criminal and disability/mental health law more broadly. This is not only to address current oppression occurring through court diversion (and other areas of disability law) on Indigenous and First Nations populations and other racialised minorities. It is also to encourage tracing relationships between jurisdictions in terms of the form and reform of mental health law (noting that many settler colonies' mental health laws are based on those of England and Wales) and thus prompt scholarly debate about ongoing responsibility and accountability of settler colonial nations, *and particularly* imperial nations for injustice and violence that becomes possible and legitimate in law through disability (and related concepts of mental capacity, rationality etc.) over centuries.

Returning to the discussion of viewing court diversion through a prism of disability injustices in part associated with criminal justice systems, it is also important to note that the violence and deprivation characteristic of incarceration mean prison itself can disable individuals or exacerbate existing disabilities (Ben-Moshe, 2017: pp. 280–282; Ribet, 2010). As well as this material disablement, individuals become disabled through the criminal justice system in the sense of being officially categorised by police, courts or prisons as disabled. This recognition is typically contingent to legitimating specific interventions or outcomes, such as enabling solitary confinement or segregation in prison, or, alternatively, can sometimes be a basis for avoiding criminal justice intervention by shifting them from police responsibility to mental health systems.

Forensic mental health laws enable the transfer of disabled people in the criminal justice system between police custody and prisons into mental health facilities, and also provide for detention, coercive treatment, supervision and other forms of control of disabled people found unfit to be tried or not guilty by reason of mental illness. These laws have been criticised primarily because they enable indefinite detention of disabled people, including in prison and by reason of an absence of appropriate 'therapeutic' community options. In the Australian context, with state-based criminal law jurisdictions, forensic mental health laws in some states have been criticised for their particular impact on Aboriginal and Torres Strait Islander disabled people, including exposing them to violence and self-harm in prison and removing them from Country.

The preceding discussion demonstrates iterative relationships between disability and criminalisation and the indelible and harmful impacts criminal justice systems can have on disabled people who come into contact with police, criminal courts and prisons. For these reasons, from here on the book will use *criminalised disabled people* to refer to disabled people in the criminal justice system. As will become more apparent throughout Chapters 3, 4 and 5, this term more accurately reflects the deep entanglements of criminality and disability in terms of how control by law becomes possible and legitimate *through* disability for certain bodies marked as unfit and deviant (including those who are racialised, poor and/or Indigenous or First Nations), rather than 'disability' (as an *a priori* state of being) and 'criminal justice' being separate phenomena. This term also draws attention to the ways in which disability itself becomes criminalised (such as through civil mental health contact with police, altercations in group homes or public expressions of mental distress and trauma being categorised as public nuisance). Moreover, it is important to note that whether people are materially or institutionally/managerially/legally 'disabled' is very much interconnected with forces and dynamics of oppression discussed above. For example, disabled people who are of racialised minorities might be particularly targeted for discrimination and other harms in prison, including because of racialised perceptions of their behaviour that invite particularly punitive rather than therapeutic responses to their disability. One English study on racial minority women in the prison system suggests that 'mental health issues of women from minority ethnic groups may be classed as "anger management", as a result of racial prejudice and stereotyping, and a black woman is more likely to be sent to segregation than to be referred for appropriate treatment' (Prison Reform Trust, 2017: p. 29).

Based on this brief survey of the harmful impacts of criminal justice systems, it is certainly not an overstatement to say that policing, incarceration and other criminal justice interventions in relation to criminalised disabled people are significant political issues, with people's safety, health and, indeed, lives literally on the line. Yet, this survey also illuminates that the injustices for criminalised disabled people of the criminal justice system cannot be reduced to the absence of disability and mental health services, nor can they be solved by channeling criminalised disabled people through a framework of legal doctrine and legal process built purely on diagnosed disability. I say this because the oppression underscoring these injustices—control, violence, precarity, discrimination and inequality—engages interlocking dynamics and forces of oppression that cut to the heart of broader, structural political issues of social justice, and the law actually makes possible and legitimate (rather than counters) this oppression through disability.

Oppression of criminalised disabled people through criminal law and criminal justice systems—including through court diversion—is but one example of a range of ways in which oppression of disabled people is *politically tolerated and accommodated in law*. Mitchell and Snyder (2005: p. 628) note that '[o]ne of the primary oppressions experienced by disabled people is that they are marked as perpetually available for all kinds of intrusions, public and private'. Across society (and beyond the criminal justice system), disability is a lawful and legitimate basis on which to circumvent equality and drastically shift the thresholds of violence and justice. This is so whether it be immigration restrictions (Dolmage, 2018; Joseph, 2015; Soldatic & Fiske, 2009), negligible and exploitative wages in 'sheltered workshops' (Malaquias, 2019), non-consensual sterilisation (Steele, 2016), removal of children from disabled parents by child welfare services (McConnell & Llewellyn, 2000), prevention from bringing civil legal proceedings to seek damages for violence and other legal wrongs (ALRC, 2014: pp. 210–224), disqualification from serving as a juror (ALRC, 2013: pp. 234–242) and segregation (even caging) in schools (Steele, 2018b). In many of these examples, *perceived* criminality (often by proxy of 'race' or Indigeneity) provides further justification for different thresholds of violence and justice. Moreover, the rollback of the welfare state associated with neoliberalism has resulted in exposure of disabled populations to extreme precarity, including in relation to housing, income support, health services and legal assistance. Disabled people become increasingly constructed as pariahs and burdens on the state's finances. The significant impacts this has had are evidenced in the United Kingdom by the documented increases in disability hate crime and suicides of disabled people (Pring, 2017).

Disabled people experience higher rates of violence than non-disabled people (Hughes et al., 2012). While this violence pervades society, violence against disabled people in institutional settings (mental health facilities, large disability residential centres, nursing homes, group homes, supported employment) is a particularly significant issue (Cadwallader et al., 2018). This violence can be unlawful violence, such as physical or sexual assault by disability support workers or co-residents—the kind of violence we are familiar with in relation to non-disabled people (although disabled people, notably disabled women, experience higher rates of these forms of violence and institutional settings heighten vulnerability to such violence). Yet, as I discuss further in Chapter 2, this violence can also occur in ways only possible and legitimate for disabled people—what I first referred to (and other scholars and activists now refer to) as *disability-specific* lawful violence (see conceptual origins in Steele, 2013; Steele, 2014; and subsequent developments and applications in Steele, 2015; Steele, 2017b; Steele, 2017d; Steele, 2018b; Steele, 2018c). This violence consists of coercive interventions that are regulated by legal doctrine and legal process—including involuntary inpatient or community-based mental health treatment, involuntary detention in mental health facilities, non-consensual sterilisation and abortion, and restrictive practices (chemical, physical and mechanical restraint, and seclusion). Some might dispute my characterisation of disability-specific coercive interventions as a form of violence, on the basis these are done in people's 'best interests'. However, literature from survivor activists, Mad studies scholarship and critical disability scholarship supports this characterisation by emphasising the harms endured through the non-consensual interventions themselves and in the denial of autonomy and failure to acknowledge the worldview of disabled people (referred to as epistemic and symbolic violence). Indeed, some argue the harm of these interventions can far exceed that which the intervention was trying to prevent (for example, Daley, Costa & Beresford, 2019; Daya, 2019; Minkowitz, 2007; Roper, 2019). Often, violence involves an indiscernible mixing of unlawful and lawful violence, signalling the lack of legal oversight of these spaces. High-profile examples include the widespread abuse at a privately run assessment and treatment unit for disabled people with complex needs, 'Winterbourne View' in England (BBC News, 2012), and recently at another unit 'Whorlton Hall' (BBC News, 2019; Plomin, 2019); abuse at the Huronia Regional Center in Canada (Rossiter & Rinaldi, 2018); abuse, including through use of electric shock 'treatment' of young disabled people, at the Judge Rotenberg Center in the United States of America (Adams & Erevelles, 2017; Pilkington, 2018); and sexual and physical assault in Australian disability group homes (McKenzie, 2014). Legal doctrine and legal process is complicit in multiple ways in violence perpetrated against disabled people in disability and mental health systems, including by purposing particular sites as institutions, enabling confinement of individuals in institutional settings, enabling specific interventions to occur in institutional or community settings, and limiting the scope of available redress and the ability of disabled people to seek this redress. In a related vein, institutionalisation and control of disabled people outside of prison occurs through the various large-scale disability institutions across Anglo jurisdictions that have not yet been shut down *and* through their progressive, 'deinstitutionalised' community alternatives such as group homes and boarding houses. Institutionalisation remains lawful and legitimate by reason of legal frameworks that both purpose these places for institutional use and enable the confinement of disabled individuals within them.

Attention to violence and institutionalisation through disability and mental health systems is vital to understanding the acute problems with court diversion. This is because, while court diversion is conventionally understood as protecting criminalised disabled people from harm in criminal justice systems (notably prison), this assumption overlooks that diversion moves people into a system where violence and control is pervasive. What is missing in the conventional approach to court diversion is any critical reflection on the injustices of disability and mental health services and coercive interventions. It is deeply troubling that court diversion might not only heighten the exposure of criminalised disabled people to violence and control beyond prison but, in positioning law as facilitating a humane alternative to the criminal justice system, might on a structural level also mask the violence of disability and mental health services and of the law. Treatment and support is indelibly bound up in criminalised disabled people's oppression, and this troubles the conventional view that access to disability and mental health services through court diversion is desirable use of law.

Viewed through the prism of a matrix of injustices traversing criminal justice and disability and mental health systems, the overarching concern is that, far from being a necessary and benevolent solution to the problem of over-representation of disabled people in the criminal justice system, court diversion might actually be sustaining a much larger and deeper problem of disability injustice. Moreover, there are various ways in which law (legal doctrine and legal process) and legal actors might be complicit in disability injustice, not least because of the various disability-specific legal processes and outcomes available to enact coercive intervention specifically on disabled people. An inter-system survey across criminal justice and disability/mental health systems helps to show the interconnections across legal domains, sites and modes of control of and violence against criminalised disabled people. The book proposes that we need to disentangle disability from coercive interventions (whatever their proximity to the prison and even if they are in disability and mental health services) and be cautious about embedding disability as a special category in law.

An alternative approach: disability, debility and law

In light of the problems with and broader contexts of court diversion introduced above, this book critically reassesses court diversion through an interdisciplinary analytical frame. This frame is grounded in a Foucauldian approach to power in terms of biopolitics and, hence, is particularly attentive to how control and violence become possible and legitimate in law through disability—in the senses of diagnosed disability and disability and mental health treatment and support. It is vital at this point to emphasise that this book is not advancing universal claims about law's role in control and regulation of everyone in society. Rather, I will be making a very particular argument specifically about the nature of and justifications for control through law of criminalised disabled people. As I have already intimated and will go on to argue throughout the following chapters, this control, which is of a carceral, psychiatric and medical nature, is underpinned by assumptions about the inherent need for intervention in criminalised disabled people's bodies and lives and the assumed benefits of this intervention to the individuals and to society more broadly. It is in this context that I propose that the control that occurs through court diversion is violent, discriminatory and debilitating. I elaborate on the analytical framework in Chapters 3 and 4 through which I develop this argument. Here I introduce the primary moves in this frame that serve to set out this book's alternative approach to court diversion.

Disability

Critical disability studies scholars have challenged the conventional understanding of disability through a medical lens, or 'medical model', whereby disability is viewed as a diagnostic category that may be associated with the presence of conditions linked to genetic or structural conditions of the body. Viewed through a medical lens, characteristics of disability reside in the individual awaiting discovery through the expert process of diagnosis. In this medical approach, disability is something undesirable, a burden on carers and society. Disability evokes (at best) pity and (at worst) disgust and contempt. In this medical approach, collective efforts should be directed towards curing and rehabilitating individuals so they can try to live something approximating a non-disabled life. This medical approach does not comprehend disability in terms of political questions of power and oppression.

Disability activists have long argued that disability is a political issue and have contested segregation, discrimination, violence and inequality in public space, workplaces and schools and through disability institutions of confinement. Drawing on this activism and insights from other anti-oppression scholarship, such as feminist, critical race and queer scholarship, critical disability scholars have argued that disability can be understood by reference to constructed norms of ability that reflect what is socially, politically and economically valued in society. Some scholars who take a Foucauldian approach argue that disability is a biopolitical category through which individuals are controlled or 'disciplined' and populations divided, organised and governed. In this way, disability is instrumentalised in specific power relations to enable control of certain bodies and populations that is otherwise not possible or legitimate. In court diversion, disability enables judges to order forms of coercive intervention not otherwise possible in criminal legal doctrine and legal process and, in turn, empowers disability and mental health services to act on these individuals.

Control and violence through disability do not run parallel and separate to settler colonial control and violence. Rather, the legal system as a whole is founded on legitimating the white, fit, settler subject and nation, such that it is vital to appreciate that through court diversion disability becomes a way to invigorate (as well as mask) ongoing practices and impacts of settler colonialism and imperialism, contribute to oppression of racialised minorities, and obstruct Indigenous and First Nations self-determination and nation-building. Through court diversion the law vindicates the settler colonial project, insofar as its legal framework built around disability pathologises Indigenous criminalised disabled people and positions settler colonial society and criminal justice systems as rescuer (irrespective that Indigenous sovereignty was never ceded), while eliding the ways in which they are complicit in constructing those people as 'abnormal'. In so doing, a critical approach to disability illuminates how court diversion is implicated in settler-colonial nation-building in ways that might not otherwise even be contemplated.

Debility

This book moves beyond arguing that court diversion merely subjects individual criminalised disabled people to control, violence and precarity. Instead, it argues that court diversion actually has structural impacts on criminalised disabled people as a population. Criminalised disabled people do not reflect an even cross-section of the community. They are subject to what Dowse (2018) refers to as 'corrosive social disadvantage'. The positioning of criminalised disabled people cannot be explained by reference to hierarchies of ability alone, because criminalised disabled people are abjected *within* the category of disability. Their subordination cuts deeper and is messier than being attributable to a 'pure' disability.

The argument about court diversion's impacts on criminalised disabled people as a population draws on the concept of 'debility' (Puar, 2017). Ultimately, not *all* disabled people are equally entitled to the positive entitlements that can come from being recognised as disabled. There is a bifurcation of disability; for some, disability can be celebrated through access to individual disability rights that elevate one to a position of relative privilege; for others (including criminalised disabled people), disability is part of a messier combination of deprivation that positions individuals as undeserving of recognition of full citizenship and access to resources. This bifurcation matters because it challenges the assumption (which seems to underpin the support for court diversion) that explicit inclusion of disability in law can only ever be equally positive for all disabled people in giving them access to political and material entitlements. Debility is a process of positioning populations in an ongoing state of precarity *through* disability—of systematic deprivation and violence, 'the slow wearing down of populations'. This is contrasted to *capacity*, which is a basis on which disability becomes a means through which to realise individualised rights to freedom, equality and inclusion.

This book argues that law debilitates criminalised disabled people through court diversion. Court diversion can never 'capacitate' subjects into full citizenship because court diversion is premised on control and, in turn, violence and precarity. Moreover, access to resources through court diversion is conditional on subjection to control and violence and, hence, does not capacitate those who are diverted into free-market consumers exercising choice and control over their disability and mental health services and, ultimately, their bodies and lives. Thus, through court diversion law debilitates those who are diverted by subjecting them to control and violence and by giving them only conditional access to resources in an overarching legal framework explicitly based on situating them outside of criminal legal liberal citizenship. Court diversion debilitates all criminalised disabled people because it sustains criminal justice systems *and related laws* that enable the incarceration and control (in prisons and police custody) of criminalised disabled people who are not diverted. In a neoliberal context of self-directed funding and consumer choice, court diversion bifurcates disabled populations along lines of criminality and, in so doing, removes the opportunity for self-direction and choice from criminalised disabled people by coupling their purported access to liberty, resources and inclusion with carceral control outside the prison. Court diversion stratifies disabled populations in a deinstitutionalisation era to sustain the ongoing inequality and relative deprivation and precarity of those who are criminalised, even in the face of disability rights.

Carcerality

Understanding the full extent of the debilitating effect of law through court diversion requires moving beyond seeing court diversion as a standalone, isolated system of control to seeing how it serves to forge connections between criminal justice and disability and mental health systems and move individuals between them, effectively consolidating the oppression occurring in each of these two systems. Goffman's (2017) theorising of the 'total institution' highlights common features of control and degradation across a variety of places of confinement. Foucault's (1979) theorising of carceral (prison-like) control shows how control can exceed a specific place of confinement and, instead, circulate in power relations. My use in this book of the concept of *carcerality* makes apparent multiple modes and sites of control throughout society beyond the prison, and the *carceral continuum* explains the interrelationships of these and the way people are moved between them, including where they exceed the limits of control in any particular site or mode. Harcourt (2006: p. 1784) drew on these ideas in the US context to establish an empirical basis to 'rethink the category of confinement through the larger lens of institutionalization and to begin to trace that broader history of institutional incapacitation in twentieth century United States'. More recently, critical disability scholarship (for example, Ben-Moshe, Chapman & Carey, 2014) has given the carceral continuum a disability inflection in offering the concept of the *institutional archipelago*, which connects criminal justice, mental health, disability, child welfare, education and other sites, to show how disabled people are subject to multiple forms and spaces of control (both disability-specific and mainstream) and move between them.

Theoretical ideas about carcerality illuminate how court diversion relates to other modes of coercive intervention of criminalised disabled people. Moreover, these interrelationships mean that the prison legitimates more diffuse and 'therapeutic' forms of control in the community as being more 'humane', and these in turn provide a relief valve to prison. In having these connecting, transporting and legitimating roles, through court diversion law facilitates debilitation beyond the coercive intervention of court diversion itself to the longer-term impact of multiple systems of control on criminalised disabled people.

Legality

As well as law's role in enabling debilitation through court diversion, law is also vital in ensuring court diversion is viewed as humane and just. Theoretical ideas related to *legality* help to understand law's role in achieving political legitimacy. Court diversion is represented as non-violent, non-colonial and just through particular temporal associations about disability as requiring ongoing intervention that are harnessed in law to justify differential treatment of criminalised disabled people. Court diversion legitimates (white sovereign) law by positioning it as non-colonial because of the therapeutic and medical connotations associated with disability. Court diversion effaces acknowledgement of the structural injustice and violence to Indigenous and First Nations people from the criminal justice system, and prevents us from tracing *continuing* injustices across historical and foundational colonial acts of denial of sovereignty, land dispossession and genocide and contemporary incarceration in prison *and* mental health and disability systems. The relationship between court diversion and criminal legal intervention can be understood in terms of a 'psychological logic' that operates across these two forms of intervention. The notion of 'logic' directs us to understanding the ways in which different forms of intervention relate to each other to render coherent (and hence authorise) intervention in seemingly differential, unequal, inconsistent and even contradictory ways, because disability is seen as a natural and apolitical way to separate and hierarchise legal subjects.

Through these diverse theoretical ideas, we can understand how law, through court diversion, is complicit in debilitation of criminalised disabled people, and this not only impacts on those who are diverted but is implicated in sustaining incarceration of criminalised disabled people more generally, the existence of the prison, the legitimacy of criminal law and the fit, white, settler colonial and neoliberal nation.

Analysing court diversion through a case study: New South Wales, Australia

In order to explore the nuances of complicity in debilitation of legal doctrine and legal process that are inextricably connected to the specifics of particular pieces of legislation, jurisdictions and court processes, it is necessary for this book to home in on one case study of a particular court diversion scheme. This case study serves as the 'entry point' for broaching wider concerns about court diversion's political implications and effects, and about the very foundations of western legal systems. The focus of the case study is the court diversion scheme operating in New South Wales (the largest criminal law jurisdiction in Australia) under section 32 of the *Mental Health (Forensic Provisions) Act 1990* (NSW). Chapter 5 provides an overview of the legislative framework of section 32 and its development over time.

Before jumping into a close analysis of the legal framework of court diversion in New South Wales, Chapter 5 takes a step back and introduces the criminalised disabled people who are diverted pursuant to this scheme. The picture drawn in Chapter 5 of those who are diverted makes apparent a gap between the way in which disability and criminal law are presented in the text and jurisprudence of section 32 and the material conditions of the criminalised disabled people who are diverted, which are characterised by violence, deprivation, precarity, debility and state irresponsibility under conditions of settler colonialism. Having this 'bigger picture' is vital to then grappling with whether the centrality of disability—in the senses of diagnosed disability and disability and mental health services—to the legal framework of court diversion can address or exacerbate these dynamics. The chapter presents two hypothetical individuals whose institutional narratives have been informed by analysis of administrative data on the criminal justice and human service interactions of individuals who have been diverted pursuant to the New South Wales scheme. The institutional narratives of these two hypothetical individuals reflect a composite of different stories to protect the anonymity of the individuals in the data. These narratives capture some of the broader dynamics of social disadvantage, criminalisation, incarceration and targeting for violence criminalised disabled people are subjected to. I propose in Chapter 5 that while each of these hypothetical individuals was diverted at some point in their lives, provision of disability and mental health services cannot serve to capacitate them fully, if at all, but instead can simply fold back into debilitating carceral control and 'slow death'.

Chapters 6 and 7 analyse the New South Wales court diversion scheme by reference to the interpretation and application of the legal test guiding judicial decision-making within this scheme. This demonstrates how decisions to divert mediate a number of disability-related and criminal justice considerations that primarily relate to ensuring effective control of individuals, while also masking broader dynamics and forces of oppression. The analysis not only highlights the complicity of *law* (legal process and legal doctrine) in criminalised disabled people's debility, but also the complicity of *legal actors* (lawyers and judges). Laws enact violence, but they do so through people (including when people think they are doing the right thing or doing the best they can in a limited range of choices) and hence these chapters raise vital but complex issues of legal professional ethics and accountability which are revisited in Chapter 8. This analysis draws on court data on 14 individuals who made diversion applications in the NSW Local Court. The data do indicate that magistrates are concerned about the welfare and circumstances of criminalised disabled people appearing before them; yet, when they order court diversion, this concern is channelled into a carceral solution.

Chapter 6 introduces the first step in the New South Wales judicial decision to divert a criminalised disabled person—whether the individual has a diagnosed disability. This step demonstrates the significance of jurisdiction to law's debilitation through court diversion. Grounding legal authority to make a court diversion decision on disability is critical to the justness of debilitation, because it transforms the basis of lawful relations from consideration of past behaviour pertinent to a criminal offence to a concern with ongoing behaviour associated with internal, medical disability. Chapter 7 explores the second and third steps in the judicial decision to divert a criminalised disabled person under the New South Wales scheme. The second step of the appropriateness of court diversion exemplifies how court diversion's carceral control of criminalised disabled people is situated in a wider context of its structural role in shoring up the regulative gaps and legal legitimacy of criminal law. The third stage of the inquiry focuses on whether there are mental health and disability services available that will control the individual. This third step is vital to ensuring both that these services will set up ongoing dynamics of control, as well as representing these as humane and benevolent.

Disability justice beyond court diversion

If court diversion is part of a problem with law's debilitation through disability, then the solution cannot be to continue to craft disability-specific legal doctrine and legal process. Thus, the question arises as to what strategies and tools we might use to begin to address this problem of disability injustice and work towards greater social justice. Our thoughts might instinctively turn to international human rights law. Since the United Nations Convention on the Rights of Persons with Disabilities (CRPD) came into force, human rights have become the dominant political frame for understanding disability injustice. Indeed, the

CRPD has helped to shine a global political and legal spotlight on disability-specific coercive interventions that have for decades been comfortably accommodated within mainstream human rights instruments; these developments over the past decade mean this book contributes to a growing body of scholarship that is reinvigorating human rights as a particular political and legal strategy for contesting disability oppression.

Yet, the particular contribution this book makes to this body of scholarship and, in turn, to disability rights activist engagement with human rights can best be characterised as signalling the need for caution and apprehension in terms of the CRPD's utility in a criminal justice context. Through a survey of the CRPD's jurisprudence in Chapter 2, I propose that while the CRPD is useful in critiquing the disability-specific nature of court diversion, ultimately it is contradictory and ambivalent in a criminal justice context, principally because the CRPD and its jurisprudence focus overly on discrimination purely along lines of disability and stop short of broader engagement with interlocking dynamics and forces of oppression and prison abolition. The CRPD and international human rights law alone do not provide us with the tools to bring about the kind of structural change that my analysis suggests is necessary.

Instead, I find more compelling as a political framework the Disability Justice movement. Disability Justice activists see disability as interconnected with other dimensions of identity such as race, gender, class, queerness, geographic location and incarceration. They focus on the importance of challenging interlocking oppression and privilege including white supremacy, heteropatriarchy, colonialism and capitalism and other violent institutions (Bjornsdottir, 2017; Brown, n.d.; Mingus, 2011; Parker, 2017). Struggles for liberation involve collective efforts to bring about 'the end of oppressive systems' and 'the creation and the sustaining of just, equitable and life-giving, loving societies and worlds' (Berne & Sins Invalid, 2016; see also Parker, 2017). This involves dismantling multiple forms of coercive intervention—those pertaining specifically to disabled people and those applying to other groups, such as those detained in prisons or immigration detention—'in order to defeat the systems that incarcerate certain bodies and privilege others' (Withers, 2012b; see similarly in the context of trans and queer abolitionism: Bassichis, Lee & Spade, 2011: p. 19; Lamble, 2011; Mogul, Ritchie & Whitlock, 2011). US Disability Justice activists have noted that rights-based frameworks of disability equality are individualistic and only enable solutions within existing social and political arrangements (Parker, 2017; Berne, 2016; see more broadly Spade & Rohlfs, 2016).

Consistent with this book's rejection of a deficit approach to disabled people (and to other marginalised populations such as Indigenous and First Nations people) and instead seeing them as active agents of change, in Chapter 8, I draw on a breadth of existing transformative strategies directed towards dismantling the institutional archipelago (including prison) and supporting criminalised disabled people's individual and collective self-determination and flourishing, rather than making suggestions for introducing, expanding and finetuning court diversion schemes. It is important to pay attention to and support these collective initiatives and social movements that are already being led by disabled people, Indigenous and First Nations people and their allies. These existing practices confirm it is vital to challenge associations in law between disability, carcerality and legality, and to resist medicalised, or even more politicised, articulations of 'pure' disability that enable bifurcation and differential oppression of disabled populations in ways that perpetuate restricted access to liberty, resources and citizenship. Transformative strategies must contest, rather than reify, interlocking dynamics and forces of oppression that shape the conditions in which criminalised disabled people are situated. Specific strategies proposed include community-led support, safety and accountability systems, remedying violence and harm, critical disability approaches to legal pedagogy, creative engagement with law reform, strategic engagement with human rights, and jurisprudences of disability tracing endurance and evolution in law of degeneracy and the institution.

Chapter 1

Introducing court diversion

1.1 What is court diversion?

Disability, Criminal Justice and Law provides a sociolegal analysis of court diversion, with particular attention to the jurisdictional and legislative dynamics of court diversion schemes and the legal dynamics of judicial decision-making and enforcement of specific orders made under a scheme. In this chapter I depart from the existing court diversion literature, which focuses on the operational interface of the court system and mental health and disability systems, to home in on the legal dynamics of court diversion—notably, the legal criteria, forum and process through which court diversion takes place and the benefits and drawbacks of these dynamics.

I begin in Section 1.2 by introducing the problem of overrepresentation that court diversion is conventionally seen as addressing. Section 1.3 focuses on court diversion, which I define as a judicial order in lieu of sentence/conviction with treatment and support. It offers a legal taxonomy of court diversion that identifies two legal frameworks within which this diversion typically occurs, differing in process and forum. One framework is the statutory powers of involuntary mental health treatment and intellectual disability care available at all criminal court locations. The other is a new and separate mental health 'court' system, encompassing both standalone courts and separate 'lists' within (some) mainstream criminal courts.

I then turn to some of the arguments for and against court diversion. Section 1.4 discusses key points raised by scholars in support of court diversion—notably, that court diversion reduces recidivism by facilitating access to disability and mental health services that can address the underlying reasons for offending—while Section 1.5 discusses some of the concerns over the limits or negative impacts of court diversion, including its coercive and 'net widening' aspects, its failure to address structural issues and its procedural limitations vis-à-vis criminal law.

1.2 Overrepresentation of disabled people in the criminal justice system

It is widely observed that disabled people (those with cognitive impairments and psychosocial disabilities) are overrepresented in prisons across Anglo jurisdictions (see, for example, Fazel, Xenitidis & Powell, 2008; Jones, 2007). Correctional Service Canada (CSC) recently found that 79.2% of federally sentenced women met criteria for a current mental disorder (Brown et al., 2018: p. 14). In relation to federally sentenced men, CSC found that '[e]ighty-one percent of offenders (n = 899) met the diagnostic criteria for at least one mental disorder in their lifetime, whereas 73% of participants met the criteria for a current disorder (in the last month)' (Beaudette, Power & Stewart, 2015: p. 15). In the United States, a survey of 18,185 federal and state correctional inmates found that 41% self-reported as disabled, of whom 31% reported having a learning disability (Gonzalez et al., 2016: p. 109), and it has been reported that in California '45 per cent of state prison inmates have been treated for severe mental illness within the past year' (Steinberg, Mills & Romano, 2015: p. 1). In Australia, a survey of 1011 Australian prison entrants found that '[a]lmost one-half (49%) ... reported ever having been told they have a mental health disorder, including alcohol and drug misuse' (Australian Institute of Health and Welfare, 2015: p. 37), and a study of 1325 Queensland prisoners who were within six weeks of release found that 9% were identified as having an intellectual disability (Dias et al., 2013: p. 940). A study of 10% of the population of a major UK prison found that 7–10% had an intellectual disability (Hayes et al., 2007: p. 165). A study of 1209 prisoners in Aotearoa/New Zealand across 13 prisons found that '[n]early all (91%) prisoners had a lifetime diagnosis of a mental health or substance use disorder and 62% had this diagnosis in the past 12 months' and that this meant '[p]risoners were three times more likely than the general population to have a 12-month diagnosis of any mental disorder (62% compared to 21%)' (Indig, Gear & Wilhelm, 2016: p. v).

Noting our caveats in the Introduction about applying diagnostic disability categories to Indigenous and First Nations people, research suggests that Indigenous and First Nations disabled people are overrepresented in the criminal justice system. In Australia, 'Indigenous Australians experience higher rates of mental illness than other Australians and this appears to be mirrored in criminal justice systems' and 'Indigenous people with cognitive impairment are over-represented in criminal justice settings across Australia' (Baldry et al., 2015: p. 16). In Aotearoa/New Zealand, it is suggested that 'an unacceptable percentage of Maori are within the criminal justice system with a corresponding higher incidence of mental illness' (Toki, 2010: p. 440). In Canada, the CSC recently found that 95.6% of federally sentenced First Nations women 'met criteria for a current mental disorder' (Brown et al., 2018: p. 1). While racialised minorities are overrepresented in prisons across many Anglo jurisdictions (see Lammy, 2017: p. 3), there is scant research on the prevalence of disabled racialised minorities in prison

(Bradley, 2009: p. 21). This lack of data might reflect racial discrimination embedded in criminal justice and mental health systems rather than an actual absence of such populations (Prison Reform Trust, 2017: p. 29).

Criminalised disabled people in prison receive inadequate mental health and disability services and inadequate assistance from staff who lack the skills and knowledge about disability to support them (Sharma, 2018). Criminalised disabled people can also experience discrimination and other barriers in accessing legal assistance and participating in the court system (Australian Human Rights Commission, 2014).

According to conventional accounts, the overrepresentation of disabled people in the criminal justice system is attributable to a lack of mental health and disability services caused by the failure of deinstitutionalisation. Beginning in the 1960s and 1970s—dates vary between Anglo jurisdictions—governments adopted a policy of closing large-scale psychiatric hospitals and disability institutions, moving former residents into the community. However, this process was not accompanied by provision of sufficient community-based disability and mental health services, housing and other basic social supports (Ben-Moshe, 2017). Consequently, many former residents could not access the treatment and support they needed and ended up coming to the attention of police and being 'transinstitutionalised' into prison (Luther, 2016: pp. 283–284). In subsequent decades, the continued lack of disability and mental health services has resulted in many disabled people 'cycling' in and out of courts and prisons for low-level offences. While in prison, individuals might access (generally substandard) treatment. Some have proposed that for criminalised disabled people the prison has replaced the asylum and large-scale disability institution as a key institutional place of treatment and support (Harcourt, 2006; Richardson, 2016: pp. 3–4, 30; Schneider, Crocker & Leclair, 2016: pp. 304–305). Others go so far as to refer to prisons as 'de facto mental health institutions' (Redlich, 2008: p. 710), the 'new asylums' (Ben-Moshe, 2017) and the 'dumping ground for the seriously mentally ill who have not received adequate or successful treatment in the mental health system' (Bozza, 2011: p. 169).

In the North American context, some scholars have argued that an additional factor in the overrepresentation of disabled people in the criminal justice system was the reform of civil commitment laws in the 1970s and 1980s, which occurred alongside deinstitutionalisation. In the view of these scholars, 'dangerousness' replaced need for treatment as the basis for involuntary detention and treatment, making it more difficult to detain people in hospital who required treatment but were not considered a risk to the public. These reforms were made because the earlier criteria gave too much discretion and authority to the medical profession with little procedural oversight by the justice system. However, some argue that such reforms set the bar for involuntary treatment too high and left people untreated in the community, resulting in increased use of criminal law, or police powers under mental health laws, to access treatment (Schneider, Bloom & Heerema, 2007: pp. 14–18). What were purportedly improvements in civil liberties for disabled people in North America are viewed in retrospect as having the opposite effect, leaving many detained in prisons and police stations without adequate treatment, rather than in hospitals where they (presumably) were receiving the treatment they needed (Snedker, 2018: pp. 9–10).

Although some have questioned the causal relationship between deinstitutionalisation, criminalisation and criminal justice incarceration (see, for example, Ben-Moshe, 2017), narratives intertwining lack of treatment and support on the one hand with contact with and harm in the criminal justice system on the other have endured. Indeed, this grouping of disability, incarceration and treatment underpins the disability-specific strategies conventionally identified as a key means for preventing incarceration and recidivism of criminalised disabled people. These strategies focus on individualised treatment and services to address disability-related behaviour. Such solutions include enhanced mental health and disability services in prisons, community-based treatment and support alternatives to prison, disability screening at police stations, courts and prisons, police or pre-trial diversion and—the focus of this book—court diversion.

Decades on, in the twenty-first century, the introduction, improvement and expansion of court diversion schemes has become a key strategy for responding to the specific circumstances and needs of disabled people in the criminal justice system. This is evidenced by the attention given to court diversion in law reform and government reports across a number of Anglo jurisdictions.[1] For example, in England and Wales, Lord Bradley's (2009) 'review of people with mental health problems or learning disabilities in the criminal justice system' and Baroness Corston's (2007) earlier 'review of women with particular vulnerabilities in the criminal justice system' both recommended significant roll-out of court diversion and liaison schemes across all magistrates courts. In New South Wales (Australia), the Law Reform Commission has held two major reviews on disabled people in the criminal justice system, both of which recommended the enhancement of court diversion schemes (New South Wales Law Reform Commission, 1996; 2012b). The popularity and significance of court diversion is also evident in its support among disability, prisoner and human rights advocacy organisations.[2] Court diversion has also been seen as playing a key role in reducing deaths in custody (Prison Reform Trust, n.d.), including self-inflicted deaths of women (Corston, 2007: p. 13; Coles, Roberts & Cavcav, 2018: p. 20) and Aboriginal deaths in custody (Pyne, 2016).

1 See, for example, Australian Human Rights Commission, 2014; Corston, 2007; Garda Síochána and Mental Health Commission, 2009; Interdepartmental Group (Republic of Ireland), 2016; Law Commission, 2013; Law Commission, 2014; Mental Health Commission of New South Wales, 2017; New South Wales Law Reform Commission, 2012b; Northern Territory Law Reform Committee, 2016.

2 See, for example, Centre for Addiction and Mental Health, 2013; Edgar and Rickford, 2009; First People's Disability Justice Consortium, 2016; Intellectual Disability Rights Service Inc, Coalition on Intellectual Disability & Criminal Justice & New South Wales Council for Intellectual Disability, 2008; Irish Penal Reform Trust, 2001; John Howard Society of Ontario, 2015; Parsonage, 2009.

1.3 Court diversion

This book is focused specifically on court diversion, which I define as a legal process whereby a judge is able to make an order that moves a disabled person appearing before them on criminal charges into treatment and support provided by disability and mental health services, in lieu of a sentence and sometimes even a conviction.

In this part I draw readers' attention to the legal forms taken by court diversion in different Anglo jurisdictions. While there are some operational and service features which are generally common to court diversion schemes (which I will also set out here), schemes do differ in terms of their finer legal details. I take the time here to set out some of the legal features of court diversion schemes not only for the benefit of readers who are new to court diversion but also to orient all readers towards law in a context where existing literature on court diversion has tended to focus on disability and mental health systems' administration of court diversion orders. Awareness of the legislative, procedural and jurisdictional dynamics of court diversion is central to the book's exploration of the political complexities and implications of court diversion for criminalised disabled people, as will become apparent in my analysis of a New South Wales court diversion scheme in Chapters 5, 6 and 7. As a word of caution, the discussion in this part is of a largely descriptive nature—some readers who are more interested in the critical and analytical discussion that occupies the majority of this book might like to skip ahead to Section 1.4.

In the contemporary disability context, diversion is generally associated with moving criminalised disabled people into treatment and support in lieu of or during an individual's passage along the conventional criminal justice trajectory of charge, trial, conviction and sentence (Bartlett & Sandland, 2014: p. 285; Council of State Governments, 2002: p. 11; Laing, 2000: p. 45). Diversion of criminalised disabled people might be *informal* (through the exercise by police and prosecutors of their general discretion (Redlich, 2008: p. 710)) or *formal* (that is, pursuant to specific laws, policies or procedures). Formal diversion occurs at various stages of the criminal justice process: prior to police charge, prior to prosecution, at court but prior to conviction, at court after conviction and prior to sentence and after sentence (Richardson & McSherry, 2010: p. 250). This book's focus on court diversion encompasses diversion that occurs at court prior to conviction and prior to sentence.

In broad terms, I approach court diversion as the *legal process* through which criminalised disabled people move between the court and disability and mental health services, rather than seeing it as the end point of treatment and support itself. I adopt this focus because I am interested in the legal dynamics of court diversion and the way in which court diversion is a process through which coercive intervention is authorised as lawful and just—in short, law's complicity in both enabling and masking carceral control of criminalised disabled people. My legal approach to court diversion has two implications for the analysis that follows in subsequent chapters. One is that I focus on the role of courts and the judiciary in criminalised disabled people's coercive intervention (rather than focusing on disability and mental health service involvement in the aftermath of judges ordering court diversion). The second implication is that I am interested in the specific legal basis for coercive intervention through court diversion. The decision to divert is a discretionary one based on the appropriateness and availability of treatment and support because of an individual's disability (sometimes weighed against criminal justice factors such as public safety and seriousness of the offence). I am interested in how the legal basis for diverting an individual is distinct from criminal responsibility as a basis for criminal legal intervention through sentence.

Traditionally court diversion has primarily operated in lower courts or in relation to less serious and non-violent charges (James, 2006: p. 533; Schneider, Crocker & Leclair, 2016: p. 314; Slinger & Roesch, 2010: p. 260). Its fundamental purpose is to reduce future contact with the criminal justice system by facilitating access to disability and mental health services. It is assumed that these services can provide individuals with treatment and support to address the underlying causes of contact with the criminal justice system (Redlich, 2008: pp. 710–711; Stefan & Winick, 2005: p. 507). Court diversion might also link individuals with other services such as substance use, education, housing and welfare support (Redlich, 2008: p. 711).

Generally court diversion schemes share five features:

1 Court diversion schemes *apply specifically to people on the basis of disability*, defined in diagnostic or more loosely medicalised terms. Schemes differ in relation to the scope of disabled people included. Generally, court diversion schemes at a minimum apply to people with mental illness diagnoses; some might also include people with personality disorders, substance use disorders and cognitive impairments (e.g., intellectual disability).
2 Court diversion schemes *facilitate access to disability and mental health services*. Schemes differ in relation to the scope of support and treatment available. At a minimum, schemes generally provide referral to mental health treatment. Some schemes only provide access to mental health treatment in hospital for mental illness, others extend to mental health treatment in the community. Court diversion schemes might also provide access to care in secure or community settings for intellectual disability. Some schemes also include substance use treatment and social services such as assistance with housing and employment.
3 In court diversion schemes, disabled people are *dealt with by reference to different legal considerations* from those regulating conventional criminal legal intervention by reference to criminal responsibility for a specific offence and sentence by reference to that offence. Court diversion schemes are not dependent on individuals being legally unfit or not guilty by reason of mental illness. In court diversion schemes, the legal considerations relate to the appropriateness of treatment and support taking into account such factors as

the individuals' disability and need for treatment, as well as criminal justice factors such as the likely outcome of criminal proceedings, seriousness of the offence and public safety.

4 Court diversion schemes—at least those considered here—*involve coercion*. Individuals might no longer be required to participate in a trial, be detained in prison, have to pay a fine or be subjected to some other criminal legal intervention. However, court diversion is premised on diversion *to* rather than diversion *from*. As such, individuals are not free in the sense of being able to choose to live how they wish and what happens to their bodies. Instead, their freedom from criminal legal intervention is conditional on engaging with disability and mental health services and sometimes also attending court for review of their compliance with court orders or being subjected to supervision by justice or health professionals. Moreover, in some schemes criminal charges can be revived if people fail to comply with their treatment and support requirements (Redlich, 2008: p. 712). In mental health courts (where treatment occurs prior to discharge), discharge is not guaranteed and might not eventuate even if they successfully complete the treatment program.
5 Court diversion schemes involve *cross-system collaboration* by judiciary, court staff and lawyers working with community mental health and disability services, and possibly also social support services (Redlich, 2008: p. 712).

Court diversion schemes are extremely heterogeneous and it is, frustratingly, impossible to provide a succinct, universally applicable overview of such schemes (Redlich, 2008: p. 711; O'Mahony, 2013: p. 56). Nonetheless, it is possible to understand court diversion schemes at some level of generality by reference to their legal frameworks. This part offers a legal taxonomy of court diversion that identifies two legal frameworks within which court diversion typically operates, by reference to the legal process and forum for judicial decision-making. The two types of court diversion I introduce are legislation available across all criminal courts, and creation of separate mental health courts. In very general terms, court diversion in US jurisdictions occurs through separate mental health courts; in the United Kingdom, Republic of Ireland and Aotearoa/New Zealand there are legislated powers available in mainstream criminal courts; and Canadian and Australian jurisdictions have a mixture of both frameworks. In the course of introducing these two forms of court diversion schemes, I will draw on examples from these various jurisdictions but do not seek to provide an exhaustive review—which the sheer diversity of these schemes makes an impossible goal.

Legislated powers to criminal courts

The legal framework of some court diversion schemes empowers judges in criminal courts to order involuntary mental health treatment and, less frequently, intellectual disability care. These schemes are legislated and, hence, available in all geographical locations of a particular court. This type of scheme dates back to the

1960s in England and Wales, with the introduction in mental health legislation of hospital orders (Laing, 2000: pp. 60–65). These have continued, in modified form, through to the most recent iteration of mental health legislation—the *Mental Health Act 1983 (England and Wales)*. Section 37 of the Act provides that a judge in a Crown Court (for more serious criminal offences) or a Magistrates Court (for less serious offences) can order that an offender who 'suffers' from a mental disorder and is convicted of an offence punishable by imprisonment be detained in hospital or placed under guardianship. The orders can be made if hospital treatment is appropriate or guardianship is warranted and where such an order is 'the most suitable method of disposing of the case … having regard to all the circumstances including the nature of the offence and the character and antecedents of the offender, and to the other available methods of dealing with him [sic]' (s 37(2(b)). Where such an order is made, the judge cannot also order a sentence of imprisonment or a fine. In the Magistrates Court it is also possible to decide not to record a conviction. Court diversion in England and Wales is supported by court liaison and diversion schemes (CLDSs), ancillary mental health services that are 'integrated within the mainstream courts system' (O'Mahony, 2013: p. 56; see also Laing, 2000: pp. 60–81). Other jurisdictions—including Scotland (Scottish Association for Mental Health n.d.: p. 5) and Australian states and territories (Davidson, 2015: p. 5)—have similar services located at or with a formal relationship to the court.

Initial hospital orders in England and Wales can be for a maximum period of six months, during which time individuals cannot apply to the First Tier Tribunal (Mental Health) in England or the Mental Health Review Tribunal in Wales (i.e., 'Mental Health Tribunals') for discharge (Fennell, 2011: p. 254). The orders can be renewed at the request of the responsible clinician (O'Mahony, 2013: p. 301). Under section 40 of the Act, once a hospital order is made, the individual 'effectively becomes a patient under civil law' (Interdepartmental Group (Republic of Ireland, 2016: p. 33). According to James (2010: p. 242), 'all links between the convicted person and the criminal justice system are thereby severed. Treatment outside the criminal justice system therefore constitutes the sentence of the court'. Or, in the words of Mustill LJ in a Court of Appeal decision on hospital orders: 'The offender who has become a patient is *not kept on any kind of leash* by the court' (*R v Birch* (1989) at 210, emphasis added). Peay (2011: p. 105) states that this effects a legal shift away from the criminal offence: 'The conviction becomes a part of the patient's history rather than the event that will determine their future'. In contrast to hospital orders, guardianship orders are 'rarely' made (Bartlett & Sandland, 2014: p. 366). Rather, 'a community order [formerly a sentenced probation order] is likely to be preferred over guardianship, because conditions relating to the acceptance of treatment can be attached' and the individual can remain within the control of the criminal justice system (ibid.).

Crown Courts can also make 'restriction orders'. Restriction orders limit the circumstances in which individuals on a hospital order can be discharged from hospital. These orders are made on the basis of protection of the public from serious harm (*Mental Health Act 1983*, ss 41–45). Under a restriction order there is 'no time limit on the length of detention' (Interdepartmental Group (Republic of Ireland), 2016: p. 33) and the Justice Secretary has the power to override and veto the responsible clinician's decisions on release (Bartlett & Sandland, 2014: p. 365). Individuals under such orders are 'forced to comply with conditions imposed by either the Ministry of Justice or by a Mental Health Appeal Tribunal' (O'Mahony, 2013: p. 307). When they are released, they are usually released conditionally and required to '[attend a] psychiatric clinic, take medication, maintain regular contact with a social worker and live in a specified place' (O'Mahony, 2013: p. 307). Those who are conditionally discharged 'remain … liable to recall to hospital' (Bartlett & Sandland, 2014: p. 370).

Other UK jurisdictions have court diversion schemes with features similar to hospital orders in England and Wales. Courts in Northern Ireland can order hospital admission for an offender 'suffering from mental illness or severe mental impairment' or guardianship for an offender 'suffering from mental illness or severe mental handicap' (*The Mental Health (Northern Ireland) Order 1986*, s 44). Under Scots law, in lieu of passing sentence the court can make a 'compulsion order' (*Criminal Procedure (Scotland) Act 1995*, s 57A) or an order for 'hospital admission or guardianship' (s 58) in relation to an offender with a 'mental disorder' who has been convicted of an offence 'punishable by imprisonment' (*Mental Health (Care and Treatment) (Scotland) Act 2003*, s 328(1); *Criminal Procedure (Scotland) Act 1995*, s 307(1)). The Scots hospital admission or guardianship orders are similar to s 37 orders in England and Wales. The 'compulsion order' is broader and allows for coercive intervention outside of hospitals including treatment and residing in a care home. The Republic of Ireland does not have legislated powers of court diversion (for an extended analysis of this jurisdiction, see O'Mahony, 2013). However, an Interdepartmental Group recently recommended the introduction of 'hospital orders' similar to those of England and Wales (Interdepartmental Group (Republic of Ireland), 2016: p. 34) on the basis that 'they would reduce the number of persons with serious mental illness being committed to prison' (p. 33).

A number of Australian jurisdictions also have statutory powers of court diversion available in mainstream criminal courts. In New South Wales (the focus of discussion in Chapters 5, 6 and 7), magistrates in local courts (courts of summary jurisdiction) can dismiss the charges of a defendant who is 'cognitively impaired', 'suffering from mental illness' or 'suffering from a mental condition' and discharge the individual into care, assessment, treatment or support (*Mental Health (Forensic Provisions) Act 1990* (NSW), s 32). Under the legislation, magistrates also have the power to order a 'mentally ill person' appearing before them on criminal charges to be taken to a mental health facility and detained for assessment (potentially leading, in turn, to involuntary detention and treatment under civil mental health legislation), be placed in the care of a responsible person, or be subject to a community treatment order. The charges of a person under this order are taken to be dismissed six months after the order is made, unless the individual is brought back to court during that period (s 33). Similar provisions to New South Wales' exist in Australia's federal jurisdiction (*Crimes Act 1914* (Cth), s 20 BQ), the Northern Territory (*Mental Health and Related Services Act* (NT) s 78; see also ss 78A–78E), and South Australia (*Sentencing Act 2017* (SA), s 30).

In Aotearoa/New Zealand, instead of passing sentence on an individual who has been convicted, the court can make an order that an offender with a 'mental impairment' be treated as a patient under the *Mental Health (Compulsory Assessment and Treatment) Act 1992* or be cared for under the *Intellectual Disability (Compulsory Care and Rehabilitation) Act 2003* (*Criminal Procedure (Mentally Impaired Persons) Act 2003*, s 34). The court decides whether the compulsory treatment and care will be inpatient/secure or community-based (ss 36–37). To make such an order, the court must have sufficient evidence that 'the offender's mental impairment requires the compulsory treatment or compulsory care of the offender either in the offender's interest, or for the safety of the public or for the safety of a person or class of person' (s 34(2)) (see generally Brookbanks, 2013).

Key commonalities across legislated court diversion schemes are (a) an order for treatment (or guardianship or support) in lieu of sentence and sometimes also conviction, and (b) that the decision to make such an order is discretionary and is based on a combination of disability factors (presence of disability and benefit or need for treatment and support) and criminal justice factors (public safety, seriousness of the offence, likely criminal legal outcome).

Separate mental health courts

Sometimes the legal framework of court diversion schemes is a specialised mental health court. Mental health 'court' has a very loose meaning encompassing a separate court and specialised lists or programs within criminal courts. When such lists or programs operate in mainstream criminal courts, they are limited to only some locations of those courts.

Mental health courts 'are specialty criminal courts for persons with mental illness that mandate and supervise community treatment, offer encouragements and sanctions contingent on compliance, and are voluntary' (Redlich, 2005: p. 609). The core of mental health courts is a modified court process that integrates mandated engagement with mental health services (Council of State Governments, 2008: p. 8). Their emergence is associated with the therapeutic jurisprudence movement (discussed below in Section 1.4). Mental health courts fit within the wider category of 'problem-solving courts', which are 'committed to using the criminal justice system in a manner that addresses the underlying causes of, or contributors to, crime within defined segments of our population' (Schneider, Bloom & Heerema, 2007: p. 40). Problem-solving courts include 'prostitution courts, drug courts, juvenile mental health courts, domestic violence courts, child abuse courts, aboriginal courts, teen courts, handgun courts, and homeless courts' (ibid.). While traditionally applicable to people with mental illness, some mental health courts also extend to people with cognitive impairments.

Mental health courts are the dominant form of court diversion in the United States of America (Scott et al., 2013: p. 843). The first US mental health court was established in Broward County, Florida, in 1997 (Stefan & Winick, 2005: p 507). Since then mental health courts have grown in popularity across the US, increasing from four courts in 1997 to over 300 in 2019 (Council of State Governments Justice Center, n.d.). The early proliferation of mental health courts was aided by federal support and funding for their development under Clinton and Bush administrations (Bazelon Center for Mental Health Law, n.d.: p. 1; Redlich, 2008: p. 713).

There is 'enormous diversity' in mental health courts across the USA (Council of State Governments, 2005: p. 82), including in relation to 'target population, charge accepted (for example, misdemeanour versus felony), plea arrangement, intensity of supervision, program duration, and type of treatment available' (ibid.: p. 4). There is 'no uniform model' of mental health court (Slinger & Roesch, 2010: p. 261) and 'communities have largely followed their own paths in creating programs that will best serve local needs' (Steadman et al., 2005: p. 216). Indeed, Schneider, Bloom and Heerema (2007: p. 104) state that 'there do not appear to be two courts that are identical in the United States' and '[t]here is no blueprint that can be downloaded and implemented in every jurisdiction'. Moreover, their legal frameworks are diverse and not always legislated. Schneider and colleagues state that '[t]he rules of these courts are, for the most part, unwritten and are prone to evolution' (ibid.: p. 105). Some operate within existing legal frameworks, whereas others have specialised legislation or rules (Council of State Governments, 2005: p. 24).

US mental health courts are typically categorised in terms of whether they apply 'preadjudication' and/or 'postadjudication'. 'Preadjudication' means that the mental health court applies to people not yet convicted of charges, and their successful participation in the court can result in charges being dismissed or reduced, or—sometimes—a reduced sentence. 'Postadjudication' means the mental health court applies to people who have been convicted and are awaiting sentence. Participation in the court generally forms part of a probation order or deferred sentence. In general terms, only mental health courts that are 'preadjudication' sit within this book's definition of court diversion because 'postadjudication' treatment and support is not in lieu of conviction and sentence.

Common features of US mental health courts include a separate docket, specific judges, prosecution and lawyers attached to the court, multidisciplinary collaboration of criminal justice and mental health professionals, a non-adversarial forum and voluntary participation in the court. Mental health courts usually have relaxed procedures and more informal relationships between disabled persons and judges (to the extent that 'sometimes clients and judges will hug' (Redlich, 2008: p. 712)). They typically deal with people with mental illness, that is, people with 'a range of psychological disorders'. However, some might also 'accept individuals with a broader array of disabling conditions' including 'developmental disabilities, traumatic brain injuries, and dementias' (Council of State Governments, 2008: p. 5).

Participation in US mental health courts is structured around compliance with a treatment plan (including such aspects as medication, therapy, substance abuse counselling and social services) and periodic attendance at court to check progress and compliance (Schneider, Bloom & Heerema, 2007: pp. 104–105). Failure to comply with the treatment plan can result in sanctions ranging from 'admonishments from the judge' and 'increases in supervision and in the number of status hearings' through to overnight stays in jail (Redlich, 2005: p. 608). However, failure is 'anticipated' and thus sanctions are staged in severity and have a developmental purpose in order to 'enforce compliance and maximize motivation to change' (Hiday, 2008: p. 489). Where there is 'repeated noncompliance', participants can be discharged from the mental health court and returned to the mainstream criminal court system (Hiday, 2008: p. 490; see also Slinger & Roesch, 2010: p. 261). While participation is voluntary in US mental health courts in relation to an individual's initial consent to enter a program, once in the program the individual is mandated to undertake treatment; if they fail to do so, they are subject to penalties. James (2006: p. 536) refers to this as 'a form of "voluntary" coercion'. He argues that mental health courts 'can be seen as a creative way of enforcing compulsory treatment in the community in states where there is no legislative provision for this' (ibid.).

Once the treatment plan is successfully completed, the individual 'graduates' from the mental health court. Some courts even have a 'graduation ceremony' to acknowledge the achievement of completing the court program; others 'avoid the term "graduate" altogether, feeling that it suggests a false finality to the broader goals of ongoing treatment engagement and avoidance of future criminal justice involvement' (Council of State Governments, 2005: p. 74). At this stage, the court reaches a final decision on the participant, including whether to dismiss charges, end a probation period or pass a sentence (depending on whether court is pre- or postadjudication) (Hiday, 2008: p. 490; Redlich, 2005: p 607; Slinger & Roesch, 2010: p. 261; Winick, in Stefan & Winick, 2005: p. 521).

Mental health courts operate in a number of Canadian provinces (Slinger & Roesch, 2010). As in the USA, there are 'many models that claim the label of a "mental health court"' (Schneider, Bloom & Heerema, 2007: p. 3). Generally, in Canadian provincial mental health courts judges' decisions focus on reduced sentences (Schneider, Crocker & Leclair, 2016: p. 313), and thus do not sit within this book's approach to court diversion. Crown Prosecutors (rather than courts) decide on a stay or withdrawal of charges following successful completion of mental health court and a treatment plan, although in some courts the Crown might request the judge impose an absolute discharge (see, for example, Yukon Community Wellness Court, 2009: p. 11).

Mental health courts operate in four Australian states—Tasmania, Victoria, South Australia and Western Australia (Richardson, 2019: pp. 102–103; Richardson, Thom & McKenna, 2013: p. 188–189). Two of these courts sit within this book's definition of 'court diversion': the Assessment and Referral Court List operating out of some Victorian Magistrates Courts (*Magistrates' Court Act 1989*

(Vic), s 4S) and the South Australian Magistrates Court Diversion Program (Courts Administration Authority of South Australia, n.d.; *Sentencing Act 2017* (SA), s 30). Recommendations have been made in Northern Territory (Australia) to establish mental health courts and in New South Wales (Australia) to establish a specialised mental health court list (Northern Territory Law Reform Committee, 2016: p. 7; New South Wales Law Reform Commission, 2010: pp. xxxii–xxxiii).

There are no mental health courts in Aotearoa/New Zealand (Richardson, Thom & McKenna, 2013: p. 187). The New Zealand government has recently considered existing evidence on mental health courts but has not yet decided to establish one (Ministry of Justice, 2016). There are no mental health courts in England and Wales, although they have been piloted at a few locations (Bartlett & Sandland, 2014: pp. 337–338; O'Mahony, 2013: p. 262 fn 46; Rutherford, 2010: pp. 23–24; Ryan & Whelan, 2012).

Having provided an overview of court diversion, the discussion now turns to the scholarship in support of court diversion and that which expresses concerns about its limitations and negative impacts on criminalised disabled people.

1.4 Support for court diversion

Support for court diversion is often associated with the view that disabled people have been criminalised due to a lack of access to mental health and disability services in the aftermath of deinstitutionalisation (Schneider, 2010: pp. 201–202; Schneider, Bloom & Heerema, 2007: pp. 1–2; see also Ferrazzi, Krupa & Lysaght, 2013: p 51). For example, Schneider, Bloom and Heerema, in the specific context of North American mental health courts, state:

> [m]ental health courts have been created in response to the burden placed on the criminal justice system as a result of deinstitutionalization. Recognizing that a criminalization process has occurred, these courts attempt to redirect the misplaced responsibility they have for the provision of mental health care services back to the mental health care system.
>
> (Schneider, Bloom & Heerema, 2007: p. 2)

Those in support of court diversion do not necessarily see it as the *only* solution—they see it as a key and immediate solution to addressing more systemic problems with the civil mental health system (Schneider, Bloom & Heerema, 2007: pp. 227–228). There is a belief that court diversion can actually *remedy* the failure of deinstitutionalisation at an individual level because it can *return* criminalised disabled people to their rightful place in the mental health system. In the words of Schneider, Bloom and Heerema (2007: p. 29), '[o]ur objective as a society should be to return the mentally disordered offender to the status of "patient"'.

Scholars in favour of court diversion argue that it provides access to treatment and support which will prevent individuals reoffending by addressing the 'underlying cause of the criminality'—their untreated disability (Schneider, Crocker &

Leclair, 2016: p. 303). For example, Winick identifies the core problem to which mental health courts are responding as 'untreated mental illness' (Winick, in Stefan & Winick, 2005: p. 515). There is a sense that criminalised disabled people simply do not 'belong' in the criminal justice system and prison 'because they are mentally ill and their behavior is more a product of their untreated illness than of their criminality' (Winick, in Stefan & Winick, 2005: p. 514).

The scholarly support for mental health courts is generally grounded in 'therapeutic jurisprudence' ('TJ') (Scott et al., 2013, p. 843). TJ, 'a theory that is widely regarded as having its roots in common sense' (Schneider, Bloom & Heerema, 2007: p. 43), is 'the study of the role of law as a therapeutic agent' (Wexler, 1991: p. 8). TJ aims 'to determine whether legal rules, procedures and lawyers' roles can or should be reshaped to enhance their therapeutic potential while not subordinating due process principles' (Perlin, 2013: p. 196). TJ suggests that 'for accused with mental disorders, minor criminal acts in appropriate circumstances may more realistically be the manifestations of an untreated psychiatric illness and a crumbling mental healthcare system' than of free choice (Schneider, Bloom & Heerema, 2007: p. 47). For TJ, the *process* is the key focus. Improved outcomes are assumed to follow from a process that has as its primary concern an individual's mental illness (rather than the criminal charges) and that is integrated with mental health treatment.

TJ scholars consider that mental health courts 'apply principles of therapeutic jurisprudence to help to achieve the psychological well-being of those who appear before them' (Winick, in Stefan & Winick, 2005: p. 522). Mental health courts do this through the role of the multidisciplinary team, which provides 'a supportive culture that can meaningfully facilitate the defendant's restoration to mental health' (ibid.: p. 524). According to proponents of TJ, this restoration of mental health does not occur through paternalism or force; rather it must be premised on voluntariness and motivation on the part of the individual. The role of the court is to help the individual 'see the need for change', while 'the individual must take primary responsibility for solving his or her own problems' (ibid.). As such, '[t]he arrest and court involvement can function as a real catalyst for change, as a therapeutic opportunity for the individual' and, '[w]hen it works well, a real therapeutic alliance can be forged within the courtroom, one that can provide a significant measure of help for those who wish to accept it' (ibid.: p. 524). Although couched in terms of liberty and choice, TJ proponents might take for granted coercion underpinning the provision of mental health services. For example, Winick describes the benefits of 'assertive community treatment' attached to some mental health courts, arguing such treatment is simply bringing treatment 'to the people in the community in roving vans, *much the way a lending library brings books to the people* rather than requiring them to journey to the library building' (ibid.: p. 510, emphasis added).

In jurisdictions where court diversion takes the legal form of legislative provisions in criminal courts (as opposed to separate mental health courts), support for court diversion has been framed in terms of it being a 'humanitarian' option for criminalised disabled people. This is on the basis that these individuals require treatment and support to address the underlying causes of their offending. Additionally, court diversion is a humanitarian option because prison is a harmful environment for criminalised disabled people. O'Mahony notes that incarceration can cause deterioration of mental health, and that prison practices such as solitary confinement can be particularly harmful for criminalised disabled people (O'Mahony, 2013: pp. 64–66). Thus, court diversion is 'an important tool in mitigating the effects of imprisonment that are likely to have a disproportionate impact on persons with disabilities' (ibid.: p. 66). In a similar vein, Bartlett and Sandland (2014: p. 282) state that 'diversion is a humanitarian intervention, based on the fact that the person in question needs medical treatment, and that punishment can only make things worse', particularly when 'that person's treatment by the criminal justice system has caused or exacerbated the need for medical treatment'. Bartlett and Sandland also suggest that diversion can be understood 'in terms of citizenship'—that is, 'as the application of the principle that all public services, and particularly health services, should be available to all citizens irrespective of status or situation' (ibid.: p. 283).

Proponents of mental health courts reject the possibility that these courts are discriminatory. Instead, they see them as capable of realising equality through facilitating access to treatment. For example, Winick argues that mental health courts are not 'targeting' disabled people (in the sense of seeking out disabled people to charge and bring into the criminal justice system). Rather, they are responding to the needs of disabled people once they are already within the criminal justice system, that is, once they 'have been arrested because there has been probable cause to believe they have committed a criminal offense' (Winick, in Stefan & Winick, 2005: p. 514). Mental health courts do not constitute a mode of segregation in the way that 'Blacks in the South at an earlier time … [were] discriminated against and treated unfairly on the basis of their race or some other inappropriate consideration' because anyone who engaged in the conduct that mental health court participants engage in would be arrested (ibid.: p. 514). In a similar vein, Perlin (2013: p. 209) argues that mental health courts, far from treating people with mental disabilities as second-class citizens, reduce the likelihood of suffering on the basis of their disability in the criminal justice system, where they are 'likely to be treated as a third or fourth class citizen'. Perlin argues, pragmatically, that mental health courts—given that mental health law systems (which already treat people differently on the basis of disability) are not going to be abolished—are the best option available (ibid.: p. 210). Snedker (2018: pp. 270–271) suggests that any stigmatising effects of mental health courts could be addressed by removing references to 'mental health' in their name: 'Courts should consider alternatives such as Behavioral Health Court, Alternative Court Program, Therapeutic Court, or simply Treatment Court'.

Court diversion schemes involving legislative provisions in criminal courts are seen as beneficial because in enabling coercion they are 'a useful way for the court to gain leverage over treatment and service providers and may help to break down the silo mentality of some health agencies' (Richardson & McSherry, 2010: p. 255). Further, treatment providers can be more accountable for providing services because of the involvement of the court (ibid.: p 255). Laing (2000: p. 50) suggests that in court diversion, particularly where an individual is still prosecuted, 'principles of humanity, care, retribution, and punishment are not necessarily mutually exclusive'. O'Mahony rejects the view among psychiatric users and survivors that court diversion schemes can legitimise laws, process and systems related to involuntary mental health treatment, arguing:

> This position is at odds with the clear evidence-base and the need to address the over-representation of persons with MHPs in the prison population. This position also fails to see that diversion at its different points is a crucial mechanism for accessing community supports and services.
>
> (O'Mahony, 2013: p. 77)

Court diversion schemes are commonly identified as having benefits to the broader public. Reducing reoffending through court diversion reduces the costs to police, courts and prisons by reducing recidivism and improving public safety (O'Mahony, 2013: pp. 62–63; Schneider, Crocker & Leclair, 2016: pp. 303–304; Slinger & Roesch, 2010: p. 259).

Running through the literature supporting court diversion is an acknowledgement of the ongoing challenge of the absence of evaluation or poor methodologies in evaluations.[3] While this might be considered a basis on which to reject court diversion, instead there is support for *more* evaluation in the interests of *enhancing* court diversion. The benefits and necessity of court diversion are assumed.

The scholarship in support of court diversion is premised on five largely unquestioned assumptions. The first is an assumed relationship between untreated disability and presence in the criminal justice system as the core reason for criminalisation. The second is that court diversion schemes should apply specifically (and exclusively) to disabled people because of their particular need for treatment and support. The third assumption is that criminalised disabled people should engage in treatment for their disability. The fourth assumption is that the court is a legitimate forum for facilitating engagement and compliance with mental health and disability services. Finally it is assumed that court diversion is addressing an individual medical problem; any recognition of structural problems relates only to barriers in accessing mental health systems.

3 See, for example, Richardson and McSherry, 2010, p. 253; Schneider, 2010: p. 201; Schneider, Crocker and Leclair, 2016: pp. 316–317, 321; Slinger and Roesch, 2010: pp. 260, 262.

1.5 Critical concerns with court diversion

This section provides an overview of the key concerns about court diversion expressed by scholars. Some progressive, rights-oriented scholars have identified concerns with limitations and negative effects of court diversion, albeit not all are absolutely opposed to court diversion per se. These concerns include court diversion's coercive and 'net widening' aspects, its failure to address structural issues and its procedural limitations vis-à-vis criminal law. Additionally, Perlin notes criticisms about court diversion from the political 'right', which he describes as 'the usual dreary railing against "touchy-feely" judges acting as surrogate therapists or psychiatrist-wannabes, allowing criminals to escape punishment' (Perlin, 2013: p. 207; see also Bozza, 2011; Johnston, 2013; Wolff, 2002). While noting these concerns, the following discussion focuses on rights-oriented criticisms because these are particularly pertinent to the analysis of court diversion in subsequent chapters.

One of the overriding concerns expressed by some scholars is the coercive effects of court diversion (Bazelon Center for Mental Health Law, n.d.: p. 7; Stefan, in Stefan & Winick, 2005: p. 516). Mental health courts are said to be coercive because participation in mental health treatment is required by the court, rather than freely undertaken. In making this argument, some scholars have identified the similarities between the coercive effects of court diversion on the one hand, and the coercive effects of civil mental health laws (Kaiser, 2010: pp. 21–22; Seltzer, 2005: p. 582; Stefan, in Stefan and Winick, 2005: p. 519). Stefan suggests that 'mental health courts are outpatient commitment by another name, with perhaps more enforcement potential than regular outpatient commitment because there is a criminal charge hanging over the individual, even if it is only trespass or shoplifting a cigar' (Stefan, in Stefan and Winick, 2005: p. 519). Kaiser (2010: pp. 21–22) has argued that the centrality of coerced administration of medication in mental health courts 'effectively silenc[es] reasonable objections to their use and portray[s] the treatment-compliant accused as the ideal'. McSherry (2009: p. 573) has stated that there 'is little evidence available as to the effectiveness of treatment imposed under hospital orders where the person has refused such treatment and it would seem that the safest course is for such orders to be made with consent whenever possible'. In an early contribution to the debate in the context of England, Fennell (1991: p. 346) noted that while '[t]here can be little doubt that it is right to seek to divert mentally disordered offenders from the penal system', he was concerned about where people were being diverted given the greater availability of more secure places and the discretion available to move people between institutional spaces.

Court diversion schemes are seen as subjecting people to longer and harsher penalties than if they had simply gone through a conventional criminal justice process (Bazelon Center for Mental Health Law, n.d.: p. 11; Kaiser, 2010: p. 22; Quirourette, Hannah-Moffat & Maurotto, 2016: p. 375). Hospital orders in England and Wales enable indefinite detention, in contrast to specified periods of punishment under sentencing for criminal offences (O'Mahony, 2013: p. 59).

Faraci argues that the shift from 'punishment' to 'treatment' in mental health courts actually enables greater levels of coercion—'for who would disagree with the proposition that the treatment provider is acting benevolently and the treatment is desperately needed?' (Faraci, 2004: p. 853). She notes that individuals can be required to participate in treatment plans for indeterminate periods or for terms incommensurate with the charges against them, and may experience intrusions on their liberty and privacy that surpass those likely if they had been dealt with through conventional criminal legal process (ibid.: pp. 841, 853).

On a related note, some scholars have also raised concerns about the social control impacts of court diversion (Kaiser, 2010: pp. 21–22; Richardson, 2016; Richardson & McSherry 2010, pp. 254–255). For example, Kaiser (2010: pp. 21–22) suggests that mental health courts 'acquire the mantle of beneficence, but they function as another source of social control'. Various scholars have identified net widening as a concern in relation to diversion (McCausland & Baldry, 2017: p. 296; Richardson & McSherry, 2010: pp. 254–255). In an in-depth analysis of Australian and American mental health courts, Richardson draws on Stanley Cohen's work on social control—the idea that community-based and human service-based criminal justice interventions extend and deepen the net of 'social control' typically facilitated by the criminal justice system through incarceration (Cohen, 1985). Richardson argues that 'mental health courts can result in denser and different nets for offenders in a number of ways' (Richardson, 2016: p. 262). Net widening occurs through 'front-end' net widening, which 'result[s] in new and "wrong" populations of offenders coming into the criminal justice system through wider nets', including through 'the referral stage itself; the eligibility, screening and assessment of offenders; the issue of voluntariness and attaining informed consent from potential participants; and the magistrate's decision whether to accept a person into the mental health court program' (Richardson, 2016: p. 145). It also occurs through 'back-end' net widening—that is, through 'the length of the program, onerous and intensive conditions, monitoring and surveillance, the use of sanctions and rewards, and the lack of visibility of decision-making' (ibid.: p. 209). However, Richardson ultimately concludes that 'there are many positive aspects to these programs that mean that on balance they are a constructive development for offenders with mental illness' (ibid.: p. 345).

Some scholars are concerned that court diversion facilitates criminalisation (Bazelon Center for Mental Health Law, n.d.: p. 14; Seltzer, 2005: p. 585). Insofar as these schemes provide a pathway to accessing mental health treatment, police, lawyers and judges might be more inclined to channel people with untreated disability through the criminal justice system as a gateway to treatment and support (Stefan & Winick, 2005: p. 508; Winick, in Stefan and Winick, 2005: p. 518). This risk is particularly acute where criminalised disabled people are more likely to be denied voluntary treatment in the community than non-criminalised disabled people because they are perceived as difficult (Laberge & Morin, 1995: p. 399; see also Bazelon Center for Mental Health Law, n.d.: p. 12).

Some scholars have criticised mental health courts' use of incarceration to ensure compliance with treatment plans. Faraci notes the contradiction of mental health courts being premised on preventing people going to prison, yet using prison as a penalty for non-compliance (Faraci, 2004: p. 837).

Court diversion schemes might be seen as providing individualised 'solutions' that further entrench structural problems with mental health systems and criminal justice systems. Baldry, writing in the Australian context, has argued that court diversion schemes are 'individualistic and "at the bottom of the cliff" so to speak, and do not address the causal and cumulative factors argued to be associated with criminalisation of persons with disability' (Baldry, 2018: p. 58; see also Snedker, 2018: p. 283). Stefan proposes that if one of the rationales for mental health courts is that 'the mental health system needs to be fixed', then the 'solution is not to graft its responsibilities onto the criminal justice system' (Stefan & Winick, 2005: p. 515). In a similar vein, Seltzer argues that mental health courts signal an acceptance of the problems with the mental health system and simply facilitate accommodating these in a more efficient manner, with the perverse effect that '[t]heir very presence makes it more difficult to generate political will to address the root of the problem' (Seltzer, 2005: 570). The Bazelon Center for Mental Health Law (n.d.: pp. 8–9) identifies an irony in 'requiring an individual to follow a treatment plan developed by a mental health system with its own history of failures and which indeed may have placed the individual at risk of arrest in the first place'. Similarly, Richardson and McSherry note that, while the assumption is that diversion provides new opportunities to access services not otherwise accessible and or available, it might also be the case that many people are already involved with mental health services. They query whether 'the mental health court will be sending participants to treatment that has already failed the person' (Richardson & McSherry, 2010: p. 255). Concerns have been raised about the lack of accountability of mental health professionals to ensure provision of adequate services and support (Seltzer, 2005: pp. 573–581; Richardson & McSherry, 2010: p. 256). McCausland and Baldry (2017) suggest that disability services involved in administering community-based court diversion orders can contribute to a cycle of criminalisation if they set people up to fail and report their breaches to police.

Court diversion schemes which are focused on 'fixing' individuals do not attend to structural problems in the mainstream criminal justice system from which disabled offenders are being moved (Kaiser, 2010: p. 22; Seltzer, 2005: pp. 581–582; Stefan, in Stefan & Winick, 2005: p. 513). Writing in the context of mental health courts, Kaiser (2010: p. 22) observes an 'inherent contradiction' whereby 'advocates simultaneously contend that many persons with mental illness do not belong in the justice system but then argue for using the same cumbersome apparatus to address the multiple issues of accused persons.' Kaiser argues that the use of mental health courts is 'diversionary' because they 'discourag[e] research and investment in more propitious supports and services and creating the illusion that something positive is being done' (ibid.: p. 21; see also Stefan, in Stefan & Winick, 2005: p. 511). Stefan argues that if disabled people experience discrimination in the mainstream criminal justice system, the solution is to fix the criminal justice system rather than create a separate system to shore up failures in the mainstream criminal justice system (Stefan & Winick, 2005: p. 513).

Another set of concerns relates to the reduced legal safeguards afforded to disabled people who participate in court diversion schemes. Writing in the context of court diversion in England and Wales, Bartlett and Sandland suggest that:

> to divert a person may be to deny that person the same rights as other people to test the evidence against him or her in a court, and so can be seen as treating mentally ill persons as second-class citizens, and may amount to the denial of the ... right to fair trial.
>
> (Bartlett & Sandland, 2014: p. 288, discussing Carson, 1989)

Laing notes criticisms of court diversion 'plac[ing] too much discretion in the hands of the professionals without any legal safeguards or controls' because '[t]he decision whether or not to divert a particular offender is largely a matter of individual discretion' (Laing, 2000: p. 52; see further pp. 52–55). Similarly, Bartlett and Sandland (2014: p. 287) point out that 'diversion is not (subject to human rights law) a right that any suspect, accused, or offender has. ... [T]he treatment needs of offenders must always be balanced against the broader considerations of criminal justice'. Laing (2000: p. 50) has also raised concerns that court diversion will overlook the interests of the victims of the offender's crimes.

Some concerns have been raised about the informal process of mental health courts giving rise to a lack of legal safeguards, particularly in the US tradition of due process as a constitutional right (Faraci, 2004: p. 841; Redlich, 2005: pp. 606, 616). Moreover, the scope of judicial power to order coercive interventions in mental health courts might be less restricted than in the conventional criminal law trajectory, because in the latter context coercion is clearly contingent on laws of criminal responsibility and sentencing (Seltzer, 2005: pp. 573–581; Stefan & Winick, 2005: p. 508).

In relation to mental health courts, which are typically characterised by voluntary participation, a number of scholars have argued that the concept of 'voluntariness' has little meaning in a context of disabled offenders whose only alternative is a conventional criminal justice process and whose broader life circumstances are characterised by marginalisation and stigmatisation (Kaiser, 2010: p. 21; see also Baba, 2018; Faraci, 2004: p. 853; Seltzer, 2005: pp. 574–575; Stefan, in Stefan & Winick, 2005: pp. 512, 517).

Mental health courts have been identified by some scholars as having segregating and discriminatory effects. Stefan argues that mental health courts are segregating because they involve the creation of an 'entire alternative system ... created explicitly to separate a marginalized and powerless minority from the branches of government that serve the public in general'. She states that '[a]n inaccessible courtroom, however offensive, is less extreme than an entirely segregated criminal justice system with different judges, different (and fewer) procedural protections, and different practices' (in Stefan & Winick, 2005: p. 512). In a similar vein, the Bazelon Center for Mental Health Law (n.d.: pp. 2–3) argues that American anti-discrimination law applies to all courts, such that criminal courts should be made to comply rather than creating additional mental health courts for a specific group disadvantaged by the mainstream courts. Despite making these criticisms, both Stefan (in Stefan & Winick, 2005: p. 512) and the Bazelon Center for Mental Health Law (n.d.: p. 4) support additional diversion programs from mainstream courts.

Some scholars have argued that court diversion and mental health courts have stigmatising effects, given that disabled people are treated as a separate category in need of 'fixing' through therapy (Richardson & McSherry, 2010: pp. 254–255, see also Baba, 2018; Kaiser, 2010: p. 21; Stefan & Winick, 2005: p. 508). Hospital orders in England and Wales have been viewed as sustaining deeply stigmatising ideas of people with mental illness as inherently dangerous (Bartlett & Sandland, 2014: p. 396). Spivakovsky and Seear (2017) have argued in the context of Victoria (Australia) that the very notion of mental health 'problem' solving courts identifies disability as the 'problem', and that this sustains problematic cultural logics about disability, criminality, risk and regulation which legitimate coercive interventions of an ongoing nature, specifically in relation to criminalised disabled people (see also Quirourette, Hannah-Moffat & Maurotto, 2016: p. 374).

Court diversion overlooks or even sustains social inequalities along lines other than disability. In earlier work (drawing on the data discussed in Chapter 5), the author and colleagues suggested that court diversion in New South Wales reifies a medical approach to disability and fails to address social disadvantage, including that caused by the criminal justice system itself (Steele, Dowse & Trofimovs, 2016). Writing in the Australian context, McCausland and Baldry (2017: p. 296) suggest that diversion might be 'failing to accommodate some of the most vulnerable people with mental and cognitive disability such as Indigenous women'. They suggest two reasons for this underuse in the context of Aboriginal communities in New South Wales: the 'impact of the drive for efficiency in summary courts, as well as the application of the crime-control' model in court processes, and 'the stretched capacity of solicitors to represent their clients under the high-volume conditions and lack of viable options in the community' (ibid.: p. 300). Spivakovsky and Seear (2017: p. 466) also raise concerns with the 'sweeping generalizations' made through mental health courts about 'large, diverse populations of subjects such as "the mentally ill", without proper consideration of the many differences and distinctions between people who experience mental illness'. Some have noted that Indigenous and First Nations people might be under-represented in court diversion and mental health courts (Pyne, 2016: p. 40; Richardson & McSherry, 2010: pp. 255–256; Richardson, Thom & McKenna, 2013: p. 192). There might also be the problem of 'postcode justice' (Richardson, Thom & McKenna, 2013: p. 188) for those court diversion schemes that are specific to a particular geographic area.

Bartlett and Sandland (2014: p. 395) suggest that diversion results in the convergence of mental health and criminal justice systems, citing the work of Rutherford (2010). Rutherford argues that there are some benefits of convergence, including 'improvement to mental health treatment and care in the criminal justice system', improvement in 'information-sharing between health and criminal justice agencies' and 'cross-government, multi-department' policy reform (ibid.: p. 9). Yet there are also multiple risks associated with increased convergence, including that 'lines between prisons and hospitals may become overly blurred', 'a danger that convergence will increase stigma for offenders with mental health problems, who may receive a dual labelling of "criminal" and "mentally ill"', and exacerbation of the overrepresentation of black and minority ethnic (BAME) disabled people across criminal justice and mental health systems (Rutherford, 2010: p. 10; see further pp. 86–87). Bartlett and Sandland argue that diversion is typically understood as 'posit[ing] two entities, two separate systems, two disposal options, an either/or choice between punishment and treatment (albeit subject to a caveat regarding safety), when in reality it is not clear that there is such clear water between the two'. They suggest that the two systems might in fact be pursuing the same aim of control to achieve public safety and, hence, are perhaps 'different branches of the same system' (Bartlett & Sandland, 2014: p. 278). Resonating with Spivakovsky and Seear's (2017) argument concerning cultural ideas about disability that naturalise the control of criminalised disabled people, Bartlett and Sandland (2014: p. 281) note this drive towards control specifically of criminalised disabled people, as sitting at the intersection of two abjected categories—disabled and criminals. Despite these observations, Bartlett and Sandland argue that 'the most pressing issues' about court diversion relate to 'the chronic *underuse of all diversionary mechanisms* at all stages of the court, sentencing and penal processes' (ibid.: pp. 395–396, emphasis added). They attribute this underuse to:

> deep psychological attachment to the 'criminal lunatic', the offender who is both mentally disordered and culpable, both 'mad and bad', as a prime figure of the Other, the monster, the antithesis of normality, and therefore the mechanism by which the 'normal' is defined, and hence a comforting and reassuring figure, as well as a figure to be feared.
>
> (Bartlett & Sandland, 2014: p. 396).

The critical concerns with court diversion discussed in this section certainly provide grounds on which to challenge the conventional assumption, introduced in the preceding section, that court diversion is necessary, benevolent and beneficial. Yet, the scholarship still stops short of an in-depth critique of court diversion, with many of the scholars discussed here still supporting some form of court diversion. *Disability, Criminal Justice and Law* pushes beyond the existing critical concerns of court diversion by proposing that the problems with court diversion are not piecemeal nor are they capable of remedy. This is because court diversion is part of a much bigger, systemic problem of disability injustice—the inclusion in legal doctrine and legal process of disability as a lawful and legitimate basis on which to circumvent equality for disabled people in the criminal justice system and to drastically shift the thresholds of permissible control, violence and injustice.

Having set the background to court diversion and the existing currents in the scholarship, I now turn to articulate my concerns with court diversion that drive the analysis in this book.

Chapter 2

Problematising court diversion

2.1 Towards a reconsideration of court diversion

This chapter introduces a number of problems with court diversion and considers whether human rights law can provide the tools to address these. The discussion provides the foundation for the theoretical analysis of court diversion in the following chapters. Section 1.5 discussed a variety of concerns with court diversion raised by other scholars. This scholarship has informed the thinking in this chapter, but the following discussion goes beyond a focus on the immediate legal implications of court diversion for individuals diverted and instead looks to the broader political implications of court diversion for criminalised disabled people generally, the overwhelming majority of whom will not be diverted and will instead be dealt with through criminal legal intervention. What does court diversion mean for the structural conditions facing criminalised disabled people—in prison and in society more broadly?

Support for court diversion has focused on its humane and therapeutic aspects—that it can help people avoid prison and access mental health and disability services. What is often missing in these discussions (or is briefly touched on, as in Winick's odd likening of assertive treatment to a mobile library) is that coercion is at the very core of court diversion; liberty and resources come only through coercion. The problems with court diversion that I identify in this chapter and which drive the analysis in following chapters are centred on court diversion involving coercive intervention that *surpasses what is otherwise possible through criminal law* and compounds the disproportionate use of and harms caused by criminal legal interventions in relation to disabled and other oppressed groups (such as Indigenous and First Nations people and other racialised populations). Section 2.2 sets out some key features of court diversion's coercive intervention. These features include that it occurs in relation to criminalised disabled people at a point in their criminal legal proceedings where intervention pursuant to criminal law is legally impossible because they have not yet been convicted or sentenced. Another feature is that court diversion's coercive intervention applies only to criminalised disabled people because disability is an eligibility criterion and diversion involves disability and mental health services. Together, these observations lead to some preliminary conclusions: criminalised disabled people are being treated differently in law to non-disabled criminalised people and non-criminalised disabled people; violence against criminalised disabled people (both legal and unlawful) is being sustained through court diversion; important structural issues beyond access to disability and mental health services are not being addressed; and, ultimately, incarceration of criminalised disabled people continues.

Having set out the problems with court diversion driving the book's reconsideration of court diversion, I then turn in Section 2.3 to question whether human rights in the form of the United Nations Convention on the Rights of Persons with Disabilities (CRPD) provides a framework for exploring this problem. It is important to engage with the CRPD because it is increasingly becoming the routine political reference point for disability justice (particularly in Australia, the Republic of Ireland and the UK). I suggest that the CRPD is useful in critiquing the disability-specific nature of court diversion, notably by reference to rights to equality and non-discrimination, legal capacity, access to justice and liberty. However the CRPD cannot respond to the full complexity of court diversion. This is because the CRPD is of limited use in a criminal justice context, principally because the CRPD and relatedly its jurisprudence and the work of the UN Disability Committee stop short of broader engagement with interlocking systems of oppression, settler colonialism and prison abolition. I conclude that we must look beyond this existing human rights framework of justice to develop a novel theoretical framework capable of fully interrogating court diversion's political implications and, for that reason, then turn in Chapters 3 and 4 to set out an alternative analytical framework for reconsidering court diversion.

2.2 Court diversion, coercion and disability

Court diversion involves coercive (in the sense of involuntary) intervention through disability and mental health services, even though individuals avoid criminal legal intervention through sentencing. While supporters emphasise that court diversion can reduce incarceration of criminalised disabled people, critics of court diversion observe that individuals are by no means 'free' to move around the community as they like and make autonomous decisions about how they live their lives and what happens to their bodies. Rather, in court diversion criminalised disabled people are *legally required* to engage with disability and mental health services.

As was discussed in Chapter 1, for some who are diverted this coercion involves being detained and forcibly treated in a mental health facility or case managed in a secure care facility (as in UK and New Zealand court diversion schemes). For those diverted into the 'community', intervention can include being forced to take medication or engage in psychotherapy, being required to live at a specified address (possibly in a locked room or under 24-hour supervision), being case managed, having daily routines scheduled and being accompanied by workers when outside the home (as in Australian and US court diversion schemes). Significantly, and as discussed in Section 1.5, coercion through court diversion can extend well beyond what is possible through criminal legal intervention (particularly for the lower-level offences with which diverted individuals are typically charged). Intervention through court diversion can be ordered for longer durations than any sentence the individual might have received in relation to their charges. In some instances, such as court diversion in the UK, the intervention can even be indefinite (insofar as release is dependent on clinical or ministerial discretion); in jurisdictions that utilise guardianship or civil mental health laws, court diversion can set up ongoing coercive relationships that continue beyond the timeframe of the diversion order itself.

In many court diversion schemes (such as in Australia and North America, although not the UK), if individuals do not engage with the disability and mental health services specified in their diversion orders they can be returned to the criminal legal domain and potentially convicted and sentenced. Moreover, in some mental health court schemes individuals who breach their court diversion orders can be additionally penalised through short periods of incarceration.

Thus, while criminalised disabled people avoid criminal legal intervention (including incarceration in prison) through court diversion, they are by no means free from coercive intervention. Coercion instead occurs through disability and mental health services. Freedom from one coercive intervention comes at the cost of being subjected to a different coercive regime, and if individuals fail to comply with this coercion they can very well end up back where they started.

Coercive intervention without conviction and sentence

Court diversion might expand the range of legal options for coercive intervention of criminalised disabled people beyond those dependent on conviction and sentence. Attaining a state of absolute freedom is of course impossible for anyone, such that it might be argued that court diversion is but one of innumerable ways that people (irrespective of disability) are subjected to coercion across their lives both through and beyond judicial decisions. Thus, to be more specific, my concern with court diversion is not merely with its coercion but with the legal dynamics of this coercion. Court diversion enables coercive intervention in relation to criminalised disabled people who cannot be incarcerated or subjected to other criminal legal interventions because they have not yet been sentenced or sometimes even found guilty and convicted. That is to say, court diversion occurs in a criminal legal context where coercive intervention is otherwise legally impossible.

Generally, coercive intervention through criminal law can only occur in relation to individuals who come before the criminal courts charged with a specific criminal offence, and who are convicted and sentenced in relation to that offence. Even in relation to the large numbers of criminalised people on remand, their incarceration is premised on anticipation of trial in relation to the criminal offence. This criminal offence threads together the legal chain of events that ultimately results in the individual's subjection to criminal legal intervention and, moreover, is what provides the *legitimacy* of this intervention. The flipside of this is that without a criminal offence to tether an individual to criminal law, that individual is legally entitled to be free in the sense that in a positivist view of criminal law the state has no authority to justify criminal legal intervention (such as incarcerating someone in prison) and in turn legal options (such as the writ of habeas corpus, torts of battery, assault and false imprisonment) are available to enforce these rights to liberty and personal integrity.

Court diversion expands the legal options for coercive intervention specifically in relation to criminalised disabled people because court diversion is ordered *in lieu* of being sentenced and convicted. I see this as deeply troubling for a number of reasons. Court diversion is not constrained by the legal protections that on a positivist view of law are supposed to ensure the fair, equal and just application of criminal law, such as the principles of criminal responsibility or sentencing. Generally in court diversion, the period of compliance is not calculated by reference to the offence and is either an arbitrary period for all or is determined by reference to the individual's perceived treatment and support needs.

Consequently, court diversion casts criminalised disabled people outside of what I refer to as 'criminal legal liberal citizenship' insofar as criminal law provides a framework for the protection and enjoyment of political privileges of autonomy, liberty and personal integrity by providing very strict limits on when these can be denied in the criminal justice system. The fact that court diversion operates outside of the conventional terms of criminal legal liberal citizenship has potentially profound political implications for understanding the impossibility of criminalised disabled people enjoying equality to other subjects of criminal law, and the terms on which they can ever access 'freedom' in a criminal legal context—and thus is suggestive of the role of criminal law in excluding them from full political community and humanness (for similar concerns raised in the context of racialised migrant populations and immigration law, see Boon-Kuo, 2018: pp. 38–41).

There are two clarifications that need to be made. First, in emphasising that court diversion applies to non-convicted people, I am well aware of the moral and political affective dimensions of 'innocence' in legitimating violence through law (see, for example, Ticktin, 2017) and the structural factors that contribute to the conduct of individuals who are 'guilty' (Norrie, 2001). As such, I am not pinning the injustice of coercive intervention for criminalised disabled people on their innocence per se, but rather noting as problematic the utter irrelevance of their innocence in a positivist legal context where guilt is usually held up as a key justification for coercive intervention in criminal law.

My second clarification is that disabled people are not the only population to miss out on criminal law's positivist protections, but they are excluded in different ways and this matters. There is a wealth of philosophical and critical scholarship critiquing the limits of the criminal legal liberal subject, including that marginalised populations such as Indigenous and First Nations people, racialised people, trans people and poor people are routinely excluded from this subjectivity and, hence, can never fully enjoy the liberal protections of criminal law (Naffine, 2009; Norrie, 2001). As such, my criticism is not that we necessarily want to uphold criminal legal liberal citizenship for criminalised disabled people, or that it is even possible for criminalised disabled people to access criminal legal liberal citizenship. Rather, my point is that court diversion is one example of how criminalised disabled people are excluded from this citizenship and, in turn, from full political community and humanness in a very *particular* way—through a separate process for dealing with their charges that is embedded in the structure (jurisdiction, process and doctrine) of law itself, rather than in the construction and application of mainstream laws applicable to everyone.

Turning then to a further concern with court diversion, coercive intervention of criminalised disabled people who have not yet been convicted or sentenced marks a temporal shift from the retrospective outlook of criminal law. There might be the temptation to situate court diversion in the context of the broader preventive turn in criminal law: a shift in criminal legal temporality away from punishment only for past criminal conduct to detention in anticipation of possible future conduct (Ashworth & Zedner, 2015; Carvalho, 2017). Readers are likely most familiar with this in terms of detention of terrorists, undocumented migrants and sex offenders, as well as civil orders such as apprehended violence orders, anti-social behaviour orders and youth conduct orders. However, there is a much longer history of anticipatory coercive intervention specifically in relation to disabled people, one that has been overlooked in the temporal framing of the preventive turn as being a more contemporary invention, and that reaches back centuries to include civil mental health, forensic mental health, guardianship and *parens patriae* laws (see, for example, Steele 2017d; 2018c). Thus, court diversion appears to sustain a particular relationship between legality, temporality and disability that legitimates coercive intervention in court diversion irrespective of the conventional limits of criminal legal intervention, and this is naturalised so as to be politically unremarkable.

Coercive intervention only of criminalised disabled people

Court diversion might legitimate discriminatory, violent and unjust coercive intervention specifically of criminalised disabled people. Coercive intervention in court diversion is restricted to criminalised disabled people. In applying only to disabled people, court diversion runs counter to the positivist view of criminal law applying equally to everyone, irrespective of their particular circumstances. On a positivist view of law the possibility of being subjected to criminal legal intervention does not hinge on who an individual is but, rather, what they have done (in the sense of the particular convicted criminal offence for which they are being sentenced). Instead, who they are is relevant to the finer details of their sentencing. This is because in criminal law individuals' subjective factors (such as Indigeneity, gender and social disadvantage) are generally not acknowledged until sentencing, *after* an individual has been found criminally responsible and convicted (except where there is a psychological basis for these factors negating the *actus reus* or *mens rea* of an offence or where they relate to a specific defence).

While subjective factors are usually considered at sentencing, this goes to determining the length and form of the sentence, rather than doing away with the sentence and conviction altogether.

Court diversion is interesting because it makes one dimension of identity—disability—relevant in criminal law to a completely different form of coercive intervention through criminal law irrespective of the absence of conviction and sentence. Disability is singled out in criminal law as having different legal implications, as compared to other dimensions of identity. And yet court diversion is not, for this reason, seen as discriminatory and unjust. Of course, there are many populations in the criminal justice system that are unjustly subjected to greater coercive intervention through criminal law—as exemplified by the incarceration of Indigenous and First Nations and other racialised minorities, people from impoverished backgrounds and women who are victims of sexual and domestic violence. Yet discrimination on the basis of race, Indigeneity, class or gender arises largely from application of general criminal laws rather than (as is the case for criminalised disabled people) the existence of separate jurisdictions, legal processes and legal doctrine for dealing with them when they appear before the court on criminal charges, and dealing with their charges in a way that renders the offences underlying the charges legally irrelevant. This is not to trivialise discrimination against these other populations but, rather, suggests that a focus only on discrimination in the application of mainstream criminal law might overlook the structural embedding in the jurisdiction, process and doctrine of law itself of injustice and inequality for criminalised disabled people.

Furthermore, in applying only to criminalised disabled people court diversion sustains a deeply troubling relationship between disability and legality. In Anglo jurisdictions that claim to uphold the rule of law (that is, ensuring non-arbitrary exercise of power over individuals through adherence to laws regulating how that power is exercised), law shapes and constrains the exercise of state authority by providing specific circumstances in which, and procedures pursuant to which, the exercise of power can occur. When state authority is exercised in the confines of law, it might conventionally be considered just and humane (in the sense that the state derives its political legitimacy from the rule of law). However, whereas the criminal offence is central to upholding the rule of law in the context of criminal legal intervention, in court diversion it is *disability* that constrains the exercise of state authority and legitimates these coercive interventions as non-arbitrary and, hence, just exercises of power. Because disability is central to the non-arbitrary nature of court diversion (that is, it is what makes it humane and just) it is difficult to then criticise the coercive dimensions of court diversion as unjust because it applies only to disabled people. In being subjects of non-arbitrary and just state power when court diversion applies to criminalised disabled people by very reason of their disability, recognition in criminal law of disability is the realisation for these individuals of the liberal ideal of non-arbitrary justice. I suggest that our inability to see court diversion as unjust in its adoption of disability as the threshold of legality is compounded by the valorisation of disability and mental health services as beneficial for criminalised disabled people—as what can effectively save them from the harshness of the criminal justice system and prison. The relationship in court diversion between disability and legality results in a contradictory relationship between court diversion and injustice, whereby part of the very reason of what I argue renders court diversion unjust (its application on the basis of disability) is perceived by others as what makes it just.

As I have emphasised throughout this chapter, court diversion applies on the basis of disability. To be more precise, however, it applies to a particular sub-group of disabled people—*criminalised* disabled people. Thus, court diversion might be carving out criminalised disabled people as a specific disabled population subject to unique legal modes of coercion and granting them (at an individual and structural level) only a limited, qualified and insecure entitlement to 'freedom' and resources rather than simply endowing these as of right: situating them outside criminal legal liberal citizenship. This might create what Boon-Kuo refers to in the context of undocumented migrants as 'differential regimes of entitlements', which can constitute a contemporary form of segregation: 'Systems of apartheid are sometimes considered to be predicated on explicit ideologies of racial inferiority, but, in keeping with contemporary forms of raciality, are also articulated through differential construction of citizenship' (Boon-Kuo, 2018: p. 188). Court diversion does not hinge on denial of legal capacity but, instead, applies to disabled people irrespective of legal capacity on the basis of treatment and support being more appropriate than conventional criminal legal intervention. As such, court diversion might reflect an even wider basis for coercive intervention because it can apply regardless of recognition of legal capacity. This is particularly significant given that criminalised disabled people do not reflect an even cross-section of all disabled people—rather (as discussed in Chapter 5) more often they are also Indigenous, racialised, poor, have been in the child welfare system, and victims of violence.

Moreover, because in court diversion coercive intervention becomes the precondition for access to disability and mental health services, criminalised disabled people have unequal access to services compared to non-criminalised disabled people. Court diversion does not provide scope for individuals to access treatment and support voluntarily or, indeed, to make the decision they *do not* want to access treatment and support. This hierarchy of service access along the lines of criminality is particularly troubling in the current neoliberal dynamics of marketisation and privatisation of disability and mental health services: austerity cuts that have restricted eligibility for disability and mental health services, cuts to self-advocacy and user-led advocacy services, and broader precarity in relation to welfare payments and housing (see Pring, 2017). It is troubling that the coercive framing of criminalised disabled people's access to disability and mental health services tracks onto neoliberal hierarchies of 'deservedness' for disability services and, thus, might be unjustly tied to productivity, respectability and access to privilege (Chapman & Withers, 2019: p. 362).

One of the key concerns of scholars critical of court diversion discussed in Chapter 1 was that its application on the basis of disability stigmatises disabled people, positioning people as a problem or as deviant by reason of their disability. I agree with these concerns. However, the problems with court diversion's approach to disability go beyond this in two ways. First, court diversion schemes rely heavily on diagnostic frameworks and expert knowledge of disability. Court diversion might not merely sustain isolated stereotypes about disability, but an entire system of knowing disability (an epistemology of disability). As such, it might obscure other ways of knowing criminalised people who are diverted—both other ways of understanding disability and ways of seeing criminalised disabled people other than by reference to disability. Reliance on expert knowledge of disability might also invalidate how disabled people see themselves or how they choose to live their lives, thereby denying them the role of knower and agent.

Second, court diversion might be sustaining settler colonial violence through disability. The development of diagnostic and service frameworks about disability is inextricably related to notions of race, whiteness and Indigeneity and was used to justify dispossession and violence against Indigenous and First Nations people (see, for example, Avery, 2018; Bielefeld & Beaupert, 2019; Chapman, 2014b; Joseph, 2014 and 2015). Scholarship at the juncture of disability, eugenics and settler colonial histories has highlighted the interrelationship of Indigenous and racial settler colonial violence with disablement and medical epistemologies of disability (Avery, 2018; Hollinsworth, 2013; Joseph, 2014; Soldatic, 2015), as well as the role of disability diagnosis and disability-specific coercive interventions in rationalising enslavement, dispossession, child removal, disenfranchisement, incarceration, sterilisation and genocide of Indigenous and First Nations people and other racialised minorities (Chapman, 2014b; Chapman & Withers, 2019; Hollinsworth, 2013). In a context where science and biomedicine have been used to justify settler colonialism and genocide (TallBear, 2013), understanding Indigenous and First Nations criminalised people through prisms of disability and health might have particularly pernicious effects in settler colonial contexts by sustaining the myth of Indigenous and First Nations people as premodern and destined to disappear, which legitimises settler colonial rule through land dispossession and the death of Indigenous and First Nations people (Chapman, 2014b; Million, 2000 and 2013a; Razack, 2015; Voronka, 2013). Furthermore, Indigenous and First Nations scholars remind us that disability cannot be disentangled from the trauma of colonial violence sustained and genocide (Avery, 2018). All of this means that coercive intervention in court diversion might not merely happen to *incidentally* apply to criminalised disabled people who also happen to be Indigenous and First Nations or of another racialised minority, but actually be part of a bigger picture of settler colonial violence sustained *through* disability and disability law. Indeed, Million (2013a) suggests that attention to disability and health deflects attention and efforts from Indigenous and First Nations self-determination. Noting that across numerous Anglo jurisdictions Indigenous sovereignty has never been ceded, court diversion might not only sustain settler colonialism but also be a barrier to Indigenous and First Nations self-determination, recognition of sovereignty and reparations for dispossession and genocide.

The application of court diversion to criminalised disabled people is justified on the basis of the special disadvantage this group has experienced by reason of deinstitutionalisation. Yet, criminalised disabled people are not disadvantaged simply because they are missing out on services that can treat internal, biomedical conditions. Rather, they experience what Dowse refers to as 'corrosive social disadvantage' (Dowse, 2018) that is inextricably linked to dynamics and forces of privilege and oppression. While I explore this point in some detail in Chapter 5, here I flag that court diversion is problematic because it does not address these structural issues, which are not captured by diagnosis (Steele, Dowse & Trofimovs, 2016). Rather, it starts downstream (Wildeman, 2018a) or at the 'bottom of the cliff' (Baldry, 2018), in the aftermath of and in the midst of the flow of poverty, structural oppression and settler colonial violence.

Moreover, identifying diagnosed disability as the conduit for addressing overrepresentation in the criminal justice system through court diversion might arbitrarily remove a piece of the bigger puzzle of structural oppression—that which is perpetrated through the criminal justice system—and, in so doing, make it difficult for us to see connections between systems of oppression and broader conditions of settler colonial rule. If we look more broadly, the same categories of people—disabled, poor, Indigenous and First Nations and other racialised minorities—are incarcerated across different systems and over time, and despite social and policy reforms (Chapman, 2014b). And the history and ongoing logics of eugenics highlight that these are not mutually exclusive categories of individuals but, instead, capture many of the same people and, at a cultural level, gain their meaning from each other (Chapman et al., 2014; Joseph, 2015). Court diversion applying specifically to criminalised disabled people might sustain oppression of criminalised disabled people who are also Indigenous and First Nations, racialised, poor etc., while simultaneously preventing us from seeing court diversion as part of interlocking systems of oppression.

Finally, if court diversion does expand legal options for coercive intervention specifically related to criminalised disabled people, then this presents us with a conundrum—overrepresentation is being addressed through a legal process that sustains coercive intervention and inequality of criminalised disabled people. Moreover, the 'over' in overrepresentation is premised on some ideal level or normal rate of criminal justice representation spread equally throughout the population; in a perfect world, disabled people will be imprisoned at the same rate as middle-class white male executives. Yet, court diversion facilitating coercion specifically of criminalised disabled people and casting them outside of criminal legal liberal citizenship confirms the very unequal structure of criminal law that undermines the myth of equality underpinning the problematisation of overrepresentation—a point I return to in Chapter 4.

An additional set of problems with court diversion relate to the way it aids coercive intervention through disability and mental health services. Through these services, court diversion might further sustain the systemic harm and injustice that is perpetuated through disability-specific coercive intervention throughout Anglo legal systems.

Anglo legal systems have multiple legal routes (such as mental health legislation, guardianship legislation, disability service legislation, forensic mental health legislation, *parens patriae* court jurisdiction and the doctrine of necessity) for coercive interventions that are specifically and exclusively lawful in relation to disabled people (Steele, 2014; 2017b; 2018a). Through these laws, Anglo legal systems have multiple forms of *disability-specific* coercive intervention. These include involuntary inpatient or community-based mental health treatment, involuntary detention in mental health facilities, non-consensual sterilisation and abortion, and restrictive practices (chemical, physical and mechanical restraint, and seclusion). These are disability-specific because they apply only to disabled people. All of these are non-consensual in the sense that someone else decides when they should occur and the consent of the disabled individual is not sought. We do not generally hear of these types of non-consensual intervention occurring legally and routinely in relation to non-disabled people (and if we did, they would likely be criticised as massive impingements on people's civil rights to equality, liberty and personal integrity). Rather, for non-disabled people, non-consensual intervention is reserved for very circumscribed situations, such as criminal justice and immigration enforcement, public health protection or responding in acute emergencies. I am not here suggesting that there are not significant political issues with these circumscribed legal bases for intervention (for example these non-consensual interventions can apply disproportionately to Indigenous and First Nations people and other racialised populations). Nor am I suggesting that these situations do not themselves involve excluding individuals from liberal legal subjectivity (see, in the context of immigration, Boon-Kuo, 2018; in the context of public health, Carter, 2016). Rather, my point is that for disabled people, non-consensual intervention well beyond the narrow, circumscribed situations mentioned above is widely available and occurs in relation to disabled people in ways that can be routine and mundane and are diffused, normalised and invisibilised within the community. In part this is by reason of the way that jurisdiction, legal process and legal doctrine are structured along the lines of dis/ability and in/capacity, which in turn means that these interventions are specifically and exclusively *lawful* in relation to disabled people.

Disability-specific coercive interventions constitute a form of 'legal violence' (Cover, 1986) that I refer to as 'disability-specific lawful violence' (Steele, 2014; 2017b; 2018b; 2018c). Generally law protects individual autonomy and personal inviolability by rendering non-consensual physical contact or restriction of liberty unlawful, as assault or false imprisonment. However, while the absence of an individual's consent typically renders unlawful any violence against that individual, disability-specific coercive intervention is not recognised in law as *unlawful* violence, even though it is not consented to. To understand this contradiction, it is necessary to consider how criminal and civil law defines unlawful violence. Absence of consent is typically a defining element of unlawful violence (for example, criminal offences of assault, or torts of battery and false imprisonment). In very general terms, criminal law defines assault, and civil law battery, in terms of non-consensual interpersonal physical contact or the non-consensual threat of such contact (although consent does not always negate assault where the contact occasions actual bodily harm or worse). Pursuant to the tort of false imprisonment, restraint and seclusion is unlawful where it involves the non-consensual deprivation of liberty in a delimited space. Disability-specific coercive intervention does not constitute unlawful violence or imprisonment because of certain defences to criminal responsibility and tortious liability that operate to *exclude* certain conduct related to disabled people. These defences include third-party consent to medical treatment on behalf of an individual who does not have capacity to consent; the doctrine of necessity; and lawful authority (that is, where there is statutory or judicial authority for the intervention or confinement). The operation of these legal exceptions to unlawful violence means that restrictive practices and other such disability-specific coercive interventions do not attract liability under civil or criminal law. For individuals subjected to disability-specific coercive interventions, there is no access to remedies under tort law or victims' compensation statutory schemes, and no possibility of perpetrators being punished under criminal law. While there might be scope for imposing criminal or civil liability where the intervention or confinement is enacted negligently or contrary to law, this does not unsettle the fundamental legality of the intervention or confinement per se. The lawfulness of disability-specific coercive interventions means they are not per se capable of legal remedy, such that law is complicit in very particular ways with making possible and legitimate injustice and violence against disabled people (Steele, 2014; 2017b; 2018a), additional to the ways law is complicit in injustice and violence against oppressed populations through mainstream criminal laws. Court diversion, as one such legal route for disability-specific coercive intervention, might be considered to enact disability-specific lawful violence.

In this context, court diversion is not so much a legal anomaly as one example of a broader contemporary legal phenomenon of disability-specific lawful violence. Moreover, this contemporary legal phenomenon is but the latest iteration of a longer history of disability (sometimes framed as mental incapacity) being harnessed in law to enable oppression of disabled people (Bielefeld & Beaupert, 2019; Chen, 2012) as well as legitimating coercive intervention in the form of violence, dispossession and death of Indigenous and First Nations people and other racialised minorities (see, for example, 'civil death' in Dayan, 2011: pp. 39–70; see also Razack, 2015).

On a related note, it is problematic that court diversion contributes to violence against disabled people in institutional settings (mental health facilities, group homes, supported employment, day programs etc.). This can occur through the coercive interventions discussed in the preceding paragraphs or through unlawful violence. It is deeply troubling that court diversion might not only heighten the exposure of criminalised disabled people to violence beyond prison, but—in being positioned as a humane alternative to the criminal justice system—also on a structural level mask violence of disability and mental health services. While court diversion is conventionally understood as protecting criminalised disabled people from harm in the criminal justice system, notably prison, this assumption overlooks that it moves people into other systems where violence is pervasive. Moreover, noting that there are increasing demands being made by disability rights activists for accountability for violence against disabled people (see, for example, People with Disability Australia, n.d.), court diversion not only sustains perpetration of violence but might hinder realisation of redress and transformative change.

Applies to a minority of criminalised disabled people

Finally, court diversion might sustain the continued legitimacy of the prison. Court diversion applies to a minority of criminalised disabled people and it is not a routine way of dealing with the majority (Bartlett & Sandland, 2014: p. 396). My point here is not that court diversion *should* apply to all disabled people, but rather that its application to a minority of criminalised disabled people might be accommodating the continuation at a structural level of the criminal justice system, including prison. This is particularly worrying in a context of repeated concerns about rising prison populations across Anglo jurisdictions and ongoing instances of institutional violence and death occurring in prison. I am concerned that court diversion might be incapable of preventing incarceration of all criminalised disabled people (let alone all criminalised people) and it does not provide the basis for dismantling the prison system. Situating court diversion in the context of criminalised disabled people generally raises problems about how court diversion might legitimate their exposure to incarceration and harm in prison and the possibility that it divides and creates hierarchies of more entitled individuals within this population. Court diversion might stand in the way of more comprehensive, structural, radical reforms to the criminal justice system and to the rights and circumstances of criminalised people as prisoners (Bromwich, 2015; Dilts, 2014).

These concerns with the political implications of court diversion for criminalised disabled people who are not diverted are premised on three legal features of court diversion. One is that court diversion is subsidiary to or derivative of criminal legal intervention because it only operates once an individual enters the criminal court's jurisdiction via a criminal charge, and only captures those individuals for whom mainstream criminal legal intervention is not considered appropriate. As such court diversion depends on criminal legal intervention for its very existence and operation. No matter how many criminalised disabled people are diverted, incarceration in prison and other forms of criminal legal intervention still stay in place because court diversion has an exceptional relationship to criminal law. Court diversion might therefore function to legitimate and sustain, rather than dismantle or substitute for, the criminal legal intervention that applies to the majority of criminalised disabled people.

A second feature is that the legal basis for diversion in many court diversion schemes is the appropriateness of disability-specific coercive intervention over criminal legal intervention. This means that a particular decision to divert simultaneously (and seemingly contradictorily) sends the message that coercive intervention through criminal law is inappropriate for a specific individual while simultaneously moving that individual into an alternative mode of coercive intervention *and* keeps in place at a structural level the very criminal laws for incarceration that were considered inappropriate for that individual. Arguably, hinging coercive intervention through court diversion on 'appropriateness' is an instance of the state achieving the impossible by 'having their cake and eating it too': on the one hand it is denouncing criminal legal intervention for certain individuals (and subjecting those individuals to a different form of coercive intervention) while on the other keeping criminal legal intervention in place for all other criminalised individuals (including the majority of criminalised disabled people who are not diverted). Building on the criticism of court diversion, discussed in Section 1.5, that it does not 'fix' systemic problems with the criminal justice system, I would go further and suggest that court diversion might legitimate criminal legal intervention at a structural level and, as such, cannot be a vehicle through which to contest the structural injustices against criminalised disabled people that arise through criminal law and incarceration in prison. If there are reasons why coercive intervention is considered less appropriate for particular criminalised disabled people, then perhaps the system per se is inappropriate and unjust.

The breach aspects of court diversion are the third feature. While court diversion schemes operate in lieu of sentence and conviction, this does not mean it is impossible for those individuals who are diverted to be convicted and sentenced. As discussed in Chapter 1, many court diversion schemes are conditional. This means that as well as enabling coercive intervention through mental health and disability services, they also retain the authority to subject individuals to criminal legal intervention. While court diversion might shift individuals off the criminal justice trajectory, this movement is necessarily provisional and always subject to the possibility of return to that trajectory if individuals do not comply with the court diversion process.

The problems I have identified demonstrate court diversion must be reconsidered. Court diversion must be analysed in relation to criminal law and criminal justice systems *and* disability and mental health service systems and disability-specific laws. An analysis must explore inequalities for criminalised disabled people in relation to non-disabled criminalised people *and* non-criminalised disabled people. An analysis must also reconsider court diversion as it relates to embodied individuals who are diverted *and* the abstract legal subjects and legal concepts through which criminal law operates. It is vital to dig below the surface and engage with foundational liberal legal concepts such as freedom, liberty and equality, and core issues of legality and rule of law. Court diversion must be reconsidered in relation to ableism *and* other dynamics and forces of oppression, notably settler colonialism. I now turn to consider whether the CRPD provides a useful framework for exploring the full complexity of the political implications of court diversion.

2.3 Limits of disability human rights in a criminal justice context

The CRPD (UN, 2008)[1] is of limited use in relation to court diversion. The CRPD foregrounds equality of disabled people in society, against a historical backdrop of disability as 'legitimate ground for the denial or restriction of human rights' (UN, 2008: para 9, see also para 8). One effect of the CRPD has been that laws for disability-specific coercive intervention (which, by their very scope, can only ever apply to disabled people) are understood as discriminatory and, in turn, as violating rights to liberty and security of person (Art 14), integrity of person (Art 17) and legal capacity (Art 12).

Since coming into force in 2008, the CRPD has increasingly become a routine point of reference for scholars, law reformers and advocates for assessing the impact of laws on disabled people, including laws for disability-specific coercive interventions (such as mental health laws, forensic mental health laws, guardianship laws and sterilisation) (Minkowitz, 2007; 2010; 2014; 2017; Steele, 2016; 2017d; see also Plumb, 2015). Thus, it is important to consider the CRPD in the context of laws on court diversion. This is so even though the CRPD is not legally enforceable in Anglo jurisdictions and has had little to no impact on criminal legal reform (see Gooding & O'Mahony, 2016: p. 124). I am not interested here in the CRPD as a legal document but, rather, as a political document which can provide a prism through which to see anew the injustices of court diversion.

By drawing on the CRPD and relatedly its jurisprudence and work of the UN Disability Committee, I will show that the CRPD is useful in critiquing the disability-specific aspects of court diversion, notably in highlighting the discrimination and violence of coerced disability and mental health services. Yet, the CRPD is ultimately of only limited use because it does not provide the tools to grapple with the full complexities and contradictions of disability-specific coercive intervention in a *criminal legal context* and in relation to *criminalised disabled* people. I will suggest that the work of the UN Disability Committee and jurisprudence on the CRPD has predominantly focused on 'pure' disability discrimination and has not grappled with interlocking oppression and settler colonialism. Moreover, while the work of the UN Disability Committee and CRPD jurisprudence recognise the policing and incarceration of criminalised disabled people as a problem, these have not yet considered how to make sense of criminal incarceration itself as a human rights violation and to identify structural and systemic solutions.

I approach this discussion by reference first to the work of the UN Disability Committee on court diversion. I will then discuss the work of the UN Disability Committee and CRPD jurisprudence on disability criminal justice by reference to a select number of CRPD Articles. Finally, I turn to the UN Disability Committee's decision in *Noble v Australia*, which illustrates many of the limitations identified.

1 For the sake of clarity and brevity, the UN Convention on the Rights of People with Disabilities (UN, 2008) will be referred to here as the CRPD, and the UN Committee on the Rights of People with Disabilities will be referred to as the UN Disability Committee.

CRPD and court diversion

The work of the UN Disability Committee in relation to court diversion confirms the limited utility of the CRPD in the context of court diversion. The UN Disability Committee has only engaged with court diversion on a few occasions in its jurisprudence, principally in the context of Article 14 on liberty and security of person. Article 14 requires that States Parties ensure that disabled people, on an equal basis with others, '[e]njoy the right to liberty and security of person' and '[a]re not deprived of their liberty unlawfully or arbitrarily, and that any deprivation of liberty is in conformity with the law, and that the existence of a disability shall in no case justify a deprivation of liberty'. The UN Disability Committee stated in its 2015 Guidelines on Article 14 of the CRPD:

> The Committee has stated that deprivation of liberty in criminal proceedings should only apply as a matter of last resort and when other diversion programmes, including restorative justice, are insufficient to deter future crime. Diversion programmes must not involve a transfer to mental health commitment regimes or require an individual to participate in mental health services; such services should be provided on the basis of the individual's free and informed consent.
>
> (UN Disability Committee, 2015: para 21)

This statement by the UN Disability Committee brings together two separate comments made in earlier Concluding Observations in relation to New Zealand (the first sentence) (UN Disability Committee, 2014a: para 34) and Australia (the second sentence) (UN Disability Committee, 2016: para 29). The second sentence of the statement suggests that court diversion will breach Article 14 when it involves coercive engagement with disability and mental health services, irrespective of whether detention is involved. The first sentence is directed more towards incarceration and positions diversion as an alternative to incarceration (although the reference to restorative justice suggests that the diversion mentioned here is not disability-specific diversion schemes).

Recently, the Special Rapporteur on the rights of persons with disabilities identified 'detention as a result of diversion from the criminal justice system' as a 'common form' of disability-specific deprivation of liberty (UN Special Rapporteur, 2019: para 14, see also para 46). She went on to elaborate:

> [I]n these facilities, they will have less access to procedural guarantees than others in the criminal justice system and be subjected to forced interventions, solitary confinement and restraint. In such facilities, they are also subject to stricter regimes, and have less access to recreational, educational and health services than those available in mainstream prisons, as well as fewer procedural guarantees.
>
> (UN Special Rapporteur, 2019: para 20)

These comments suggest that court diversion that involves detention in the disability and mental health system, such as in the UK and New Zealand, breaches Article 14.

Taken together, these two statements suggest that court diversion is unjust when it involves detention or coercion through disability and mental health services because this involves coercion, and because individuals have less procedural protections than in relation to criminal legal intervention. The problem is one of discrimination along the lines of disability.

Scholars who have considered court diversion in the context of the CRPD have engaged with the CRPD in an instrumental fashion and argued that court diversion can comply if its coercive dimensions are removed, if it is focused on provision of support in the community and if it is more effectively integrated into mainstream court process and settings (Ferrazzi et al., 2013: pp. 53–54; O'Mahony, 2013: p. 149; Perlin, 2013). Unlike these scholars, I have strong reservations about the possibility of a 'CRPD' compliant court diversion and about the ultimate utility of the CRPD in addressing the problems I have identified with court diversion. In order to make these arguments, I now turn to the CRPD and disability criminal justice more broadly.

CRPD and disability criminal justice

The work of the UN Disability Committee on criminal law and criminal justice does not address the full complexity of political issues with court diversion that I have raised in Section 2.2. I argue that a reading of some key Articles of the CRPD (Arts 5, 12, 13, 14 and 19) indicates that court diversion *is* fundamentally contrary to the CRPD and is unjust by reason of its disability-specific aspects. However, I also argue that the CRPD is of little use in grappling with court diversion beyond its disability-specific dynamics and in addressing the full breadth and depth of problems raised in Section 2.2.

Equality and non-discrimination is a right in itself (Art 5) and a general principle governing the CRPD's operation as a whole (Art 3(2)). Indeed, the principle of equality and non-discrimination has been described by the UN Disability Committee as 'at the heart of the Convention' and running through all of the substantive rights in the CRPD (UN Disability Committee, 2018b: para 7). Article 5 places an obligation on States Parties to 'prohibit all discrimination on the basis of disability and guarantee to persons with disabilities equal and effective legal protection against discrimination on all grounds' (Art 5(2)). There are two separate categories of discrimination that the CRPD covers: disability discrimination and discrimination against disabled people on all grounds. Disability-based discrimination is defined in Article 2 of the CRPD as:

> any distinction, exclusion or restriction *on the basis of disability* which has the purpose or effect of impairing or nullifying the recognition, enjoyment or

> exercise, on an equal basis with others, of all human rights and fundamental freedoms in the political, economic, social, cultural, civil or any other field.
>
> (emphasis added; see also UN Disability Committee, 2018b: para 17)

The examples given by the UN Disability Committee of disability discriminatory laws, policies and practices include guardianship laws, mental health laws 'that legitimise forced institutionalization and forced treatment' and 'inaccessible housing and institutionalization policy' (UN Disability Committee, 2018b: para 30). Article 5 is useful in making apparent the unequal treatment of criminalised disabled people through court diversion, as compared to criminalised people in mainstream criminal legal process.

Article 12 provides for equal recognition before the law. The UN Disability Committee (2014a: para 9) has explained that '[t]he right to equal recognition before the law implies that legal capacity is a universal attribute inherent in all persons by virtue of their humanity and must be upheld for persons with disabilities on an equal basis with others'. The UN Disability Committee has called for abolition of practices that violate Article 12 (UN Disability Committee, 2014b: para 9, see also para 25) and introduction of supported decision-making models and associated resources and opportunities (ibid.: para 29). In its General Comment on Article 12, the UN Disability Committee states that to deny legal capacity on the basis of disability constitutes discrimination, as do subsequent restrictions on liberty or forced medical or psychiatric treatment based on denial of legal capacity (UN Disability Committee, 2014b: paras 40–42; see also UN Office of the High Commissioner for Human Rights, 2009: para 47). Article 12 is useful in understanding how court diversion is unjust because it denies criminalised disabled people the opportunity to choose what treatment and support they want (if any).

Article 13 provides that: 'States Parties shall ensure effective access to justice for persons with disabilities on an equal basis with others, including through the provision of procedural and age-appropriate accommodations, in order to facilitate their effective role as direct and indirect participants' (Art 13(1)) and that training of justice professionals is a key means through which Article 13 can be realised (Art 13(2)). In its 2017 report on access to justice under the CRPD, the Office of the High Commissioner for Human Rights (OHCHR) states that subsequent 'committal or forced treatment in mental health facilities under a regime of impairment-based detention' of those found unfit or not guilty because of mental illness is based on 'the individual's alleged "dangerousness" to self and others' rather than 'a finding of guilt' following trial and conviction (UN Office of the High Commissioner for Human Rights, 2017: para 39). As such, mental illness defence and unfitness regimes deny to disabled people the presumption of innocence and, in turn, their right to a fair trial (ibid.: paras 36, 39). This Article provides a basis for beginning to interrogate how inequality for criminalised disabled people might result from court diversion operating outside of the typical legal limits of criminal legal intervention.

The UN Disability Committee has described Article 14 as a non-discrimination provision because it is directed to ensuring deprivation of liberty and security of the person does not arise from discrimination on the basis of disability (UN Disability Committee, 2015: para 4). Thus, the Committee 'has established that Article 14 does not permit any exceptions whereby persons may be detained on the grounds of their actual or perceived impairment' (ibid.: para 6). The UN Disability Committee has stated that detention that occurs 'without the free and informed consent of the persons concerned or with the consent of a substitute decision-maker' constitutes arbitrary deprivation of liberty and violates articles 12 and 14 of the CRPD (ibid.: para 8; UN Disability Committee, 2014b: para 40). The Special Rapporteur has even argued that, at times, deprivation of liberty is caused by the absence of 'appropriate community-based support', such that disabled people are 'regularly deprived of liberty in order to access services that should have been delivered in the community' (UN Special Rapporteur, 2019: paras 29, 30).

Articles 5, 12, 13 and 14 are useful in drawing out unequal treatment of criminalised disabled people as compared to criminalised non-disabled people. Disability-based discrimination is useful in disrupting the self-evidence of court diversion as applying only to disabled people, and as politicising as a human rights violation the disadvantage criminalised disabled people experience by reason of being subject to coercive interventions on the basis of disability through court diversion.

The CRPD's ambivalence towards criminal justice

Ultimately, I argue in this section, the CRPD reflects an ambivalence towards criminal law and criminal justice. This ambivalence is exemplified by the focus on inequality along the lines of disability and its focus on disability institutions rather than additionally considering mainstream institutions of confinement such as prisons.

Not all disabled people are equally subjected to criminalisation, and many of those who are criminalised are subject to 'corrosive social disadvantage' (Dowse, 2018), which is associated with a messy coalescence of interlocking forces and dynamics of privilege and oppression which includes but is not limited to ableism. The CRPD is less helpful in addressing problems of inequality beyond those attributable solely to disability, such as inequality along the lines of criminality or inequality related to other systems of oppression or settler colonialism. This is evident if we turn to the second category of discrimination in Article 5—discrimination against disabled people on all grounds—to consider whether this can interrogate the complex discrimination at play in court diversion. The UN Disability Committee in its General Comment on Article 5 provides a lengthy list of 'all possible grounds of discrimination' (UN Disability Committee, 2018b: para 20) and has also noted that discrimination is not always related singularly to disability; it can be based on 'multiple and/or intersecting characteristics' (ibid.: para

19; see also para 32). Despite providing this overview, the General Comment's discussion of the relationship between Article 5 and other specific articles of the CRPD, which provides more grounded examples of discrimination, focuses nearly entirely on disability-based discrimination and does not specifically address intersectional discrimination that might emerge in the criminal justice context (ibid.: paras 10–17), nor how intersectionality arises in relation to 'abjected' categories of disabled people such as those who use drugs, are homeless, engage in sex work or have been in the child welfare system.

The General Comment on Article 5 also does not elaborate on discrimination in the criminal justice context, other than to note that law enforcement officers such as lawyers, judges and prison staff should be trained on the rights of disabled people, '[i]n order to encourage appropriate respect for and fulfilment of rights and obligations' (ibid.: para 55). Thus, while the CRPD does prima facie provide protection against discrimination on all bases, the UN Disability Committee has only considered intersectional discrimination in a cursory manner, reserving its more in-depth analysis for disability-based discrimination.

The failure to attempt to fully grapple with discrimination beyond disability discrimination is compounded by a near complete silence on settler colonialism. There is only one reference to Indigenous and First Nations people in the CRPD. This reference is in the Preamble in the course of noting concern 'about the difficult conditions faced by persons with disabilities who are subject to multiple or aggravated forms of discrimination' including on the basis of 'indigenous or social origin'. There are no references at all to colonialism, land dispossession or genocide. In reflecting on the absence of Indigenous and First Nations people from the text of the CRPD, Hickey (who is of Ngati Tahinga descent) notes that 'indigenous persons with disabilities were excluded from the Convention's early development because of a dearth of financial resources and their government's lack of support' (Hickey, 2014: p. 157) and that, ultimately, efforts to include specific references to and a separate Article on Indigenous and First Nations people were not successful (ibid.: p. 166). For Hickey, a key limitation of the CRPD is that it does not address cultural and collective interests that are central to Indigenous and First Nations people:

> While the discussions of persons with disabilities commonly depend on the notion of universalism and individual rights, regardless of any cultural-specific identity, the concerns of indigenous persons with disabilities are related to discussions of group rights and cultural relativism that are intertwined with collective identities.
>
> (ibid.: p. 158)

These critical observations made in the disability context also need to be situated in the longstanding critiques of human rights by Indigenous and First Nations people that identify tensions between recognition of settler state sovereignty in human rights and the demand for Indigenous and First Nations self-determination (see Watson, 2015). These limitations of the CRPD are reflected in the UN Disability Committee's discussion of legal capacity. While recognising the historical denial of legal capacity to 'ethnic minorities', the UN Disability Committee (2013: para 8) interprets the right to legal capacity as an *individual* right and, hence, does not explicitly address collective Indigenous self-determination, nation-building and sovereignty nor recognise that across many settler nations Indigenous peoples never ceded sovereignty, which are matters central to Indigenous and First Nations justice.

These limitations of Article 5 are compounded by limitations of Articles 12 and 14 in being unable to deal with violence and incarceration of criminalised disabled people that is not exclusively reserved for disabled people. The UN Disability Committee explicitly acknowledges that the state can have the power to restrict legal capacity on the basis of criminal conviction, but this cannot be done on the basis of a personal trait:

> *States have the ability to restrict the legal capacity* of a person based on certain circumstances, such as bankruptcy or *criminal conviction*. However, the right to equal recognition before the law and freedom from discrimination requires that when the State denies legal capacity, it must be on the *same basis for all persons*. Denial of legal capacity must not be based on a personal trait such as gender, race, or disability, or have the purpose or effect of treating the person differently.
>
> (UN Disability Committee, 2014b: para 32, emphasis added)

This is striking for four reasons. One is that it affirms the legitimacy per se of denial of legal capacity on the basis of conviction. Second, in permitting denial of legal capacity on basis of criminal conviction, but not by reason of a personal trait, this statement prevents criminality from being understood as a personal trait that can itself be the source of discrimination. The third is that it assumes that, at a structural level, the criminal legal system is premised on equality and only anticipates the possibility of inequality vis-à-vis specific individuals' (non-criminal) 'personal traits'. Fourth, on a related note, it overlooks the possibility of structural discrimination and oppression that gives rise to criminalisation but cannot be pinpointed to a specific individual's particular traits. While the denial of legal capacity following criminal conviction is theoretically capable of applying to all people, irrespective of disability, this overlooks the fact that disabled people (and people of other minority groups) are subjected more often to this denial of legal capacity and that this is not because of one-off, individual instances of discrimination but, rather, is embedded within the structure of criminal law and the criminal justice system. This odd deferral to the legitimacy of the criminal justice and prison systems is also evident in the context of Article 14, in relation to which the Special Rapporteur on the rights of persons with disabilities has explained:

> Article 14 establishes an absolute ban on deprivation of liberty on the basis of impairment. *While persons with disabilities can be arrested or detained lawfully,*

> *on an equal basis with others*, article 14 (1) (b) does not permit any exception whereby persons can be deprived of their liberty on the basis of their actual or perceived impairment. Any deprivation of liberty on such grounds would be discriminatory in nature and, thus, both unlawful and arbitrary.
>
> (UN Special Rapporteur, 2019: para 46, emphasis added)

And, indeed, the assumed legitimacy of criminal law and criminal justice systems is central to civil and political rights in international human rights and Constitutional rights law more broadly (see, for example, Dayan's critique of cruel and unusual punishment: Dayan, 2007), as reflected in the UN Special Rapporteur's explanation of the right to personal liberty in international human rights law:

> The right to personal liberty, as found in international human rights law, is *not an absolute right*. It can be *restricted in accordance with the law*, for example, in the *enforcement of criminal laws* or in the interest of public safety or public health. However, the right to liberty and security of person acts as a substantive guarantee that deprivation of liberty will not be unlawful or arbitrary. It is unlawful when it contradicts domestic or international human rights law, whereas it is arbitrary when it is imposed in a manner that is inappropriate, unjust, disproportionate, unpredictable, discriminatory or without due process.
>
> (UN Special Rapporteur, 2019: para 39, emphasis added)

There is some circularity at play here, whereby deprivation of liberty *can be* for the purposes of criminal law but not in an unjust manner, thus constructing these, at a structural level, as mutually exclusive—criminal law per se is not viewed as unjust. While I am not making universal claims in this book about criminal law's role in coercion and regulation, what does concern me about this circularity is that it shuts down any consideration of injustice embedded within the structure (rather than individual application) of criminal law and the very existence of prisons.

The work of the UN Disability Committee and jurisprudence on the CRPD has not engaged with the inequality and injustice inherent in criminal conviction or the prison system. The closest it gets to this is the consideration of 'access' in Articles 9 and 13, which provide that the process of criminal conviction and administration of coercive intervention following conviction need to be fair to and inclusive of disabled people, notably through training justice professionals and making reasonable accommodations to court procedure. For example, in its General Comment on Article 9 on accessibility, the UN Disability Committee has stated that States parties should 'identify and eliminate obstacles and barriers to accessibility' to, inter alia, prisons (UN Disability Committee, 2014c: para 17; see also UN Office of the High Commissioner for Human Rights, 2014). Yet all that this means is that the CRPD provides a basis for facilitating more 'equal' inclusion of criminalised disabled people *within* an arguably exclusionary, violent and unjust criminal legal system. The abolitionist and transformative approach to disability-specific coercive intervention that the CRPD does provide is completely lacking in the context of mainstream criminal legal intervention—and in this asymmetry, criminalised disabled people have the most to lose. In a recent report on deprivation of liberty, the Special Rapporteur notes that '[p]ersons with disabilities are significantly overrepresented in mainstream settings of deprivation of liberty, such as prisons and immigration detention centres' (UN Special Rapporteur, 2019: para 13). She also notes that 'criminalization of disability is a worrisome trend', including through 'penalizing atypical behaviours' and 'public displays of poverty and lack of support' (ibid.: para 34), as well as the broader criminalisation of homelessness that impacts on disabled people at the intersection of poverty, disability and homelessness (ibid.: para 33). This is a good first step in recognising the *problem*, but not in providing a nuanced, in-depth and sustained analysis of the human rights violations following from this and the transformative *solutions*.

A key example is the scholarship on fitness to be tried. Scholars arguing by reference to Article 12 of the CRPD that unfitness to plead is discriminatory have then relied heavily on Article 13 as providing an avenue for improving individuals' participation within the mainstream criminal legal process in the absence of the disability-regime of unfitness (see, for example, Arstein-Kerslake et al., 2017; Gooding & O'Mahony, 2016: p. 133). Arstein-Kerslake and colleagues, in their project on fitness to plead, have focused on procedural and technical changes within existing criminal legal and prison systems, such as ensuring equality in sentencing, disability-neutral rules and procedures and accessibility, and creating tailored supports (Arstein-Kerslake et al., 2017: pp. 418–419; see similarly Gooding & O'Mahony, 2016: p. 142).

Yet these kinds of solutions that try to enhance access to oppressive systems do not address structural inequalities. As Baldry (2018: p. 69) notes, the CRPD focuses on equality (in an individual sense) rather than considering equity (in a structural or collective sense). Baldry argues that '[a]ddressing individual circumstances and rights one at a time and when a person is already involved in the criminal justice system does not deal with the structural inequities driving criminalisation of disadvantaged people with disability in the first place' (ibid.: p. 69). She argues that the CRPD mirrors the individualised approach of criminal law, which serves to exacerbate inequity between criminalised disabled people such that:

> more advantaged persons with disability are likely to receive support early and have access to protective factors and resources and so be unlikely to be criminalised, and those from disadvantaged and racialised backgrounds are unlikely to have access to such resources and so be more likely to be criminalised.
>
> (Baldry, 2018: p. 70)

Perhaps some of these limitations go to the concentration of the CRPD—and its jurisprudence and scholarship—on civil and political rights at the expense of social and economic rights, a point made by Carney (2017) in the context of the scholarship on legal capacity. Touching on this, Baldry (2018: p. 68) argues that it is necessary to shift away from equal treatment in the criminal justice system to equality in life circumstances that will prevent individuals from being criminalised in the first place.

Ultimately, Articles 5, 12, 13 and 14 of the CRPD provide a compelling basis for abolition of court diversion by reason if its disability-specific nature but are completely silent on abolition of the prison, which is the primary site of incarceration of the majority of criminalised disabled people who are not diverted (and, if court diversion is abolished, might very well be those who would have been diverted). This tension is evident in the context of Article 12. In the civil justice context, abolishing disability-specific laws denying legal capacity leaves people free to choose whether they access treatment and support, or how they spend their money, or where they choose to live. In contrast, in the criminal justice context, as discussed in Section 2.2 court diversion is in a subsidiary relationship to criminal legal intervention, such that abolition of denial of legal capacity through court diversion simply shifts people back into criminal law as the principal system of intervention—noting that (as the UN Disability Committee itself states) criminal conviction is a valid basis on which to deny legal capacity (see similarly O'Mahony, 2013: p. 107).

Abolishing disability-specific laws for denial of legal capacity (such as court diversion) does nothing to address the structural issues inherent in the operation of laws that are grounded in recognition of legal capacity. In particular, such a strategy does not address how laws premised on legal capacity can apply in ways that unjustly impact on oppressed populations (such as disabled people and Indigenous and First Nations people and people of other racialised minorities), not least because 'legal capacity' provides a basis on which to justify imposing individual accountability and responsibility without recognising the social, economic and political forces that shape individuals' conduct. This has been observed by Bartlett, who has raised concerns about the extent to which the CRPD can address the treatment of disabled people in mainstream criminal justice processes and prison, suggesting that such issues can be marginalised if the focus is on rewording of laws from disability-specific to disability-neutral (Bartlett, 2012: p. 776; see also my critique of the 'disability-neutral' doctrine of necessity, in Steele, 2017d).

These limitations of the CRPD in a criminal justice context are exemplified by Article 19. Article 19 provides the right to live independently and be included in the community. States Parties are required to provide appropriate resources and supports to ensure that '[p]ersons with disabilities have the opportunity to choose their place of residence and where and with whom they live on an equal basis with others and are not obliged to live in a particular living arrangement' (Art 19(a)) and that they have access to support services 'necessary to support living and inclusion in the community, and to prevent isolation or segregation from the community' (Art 19(b)). Article 19 has been described by the UN Disability Committee (2018a: para 6) as 'one of the widest ranging and most intersectional articles of the Convention and has to be considered as integral to the full implementation of the Convention'.

The UN Disability Committee has rejected the possibility that institutions can provide independent living. This is by reason of their 'segregating character;' and their defining elements, including:

> obligatory sharing of assistants with others and no or limited influence over whom one has to accept assistance from; isolation and segregation from independent life within the community; lack of control over day-to-day decisions; lack of choice over whom to live with; rigidity of routine irrespective of personal will and preferences; identical activities in the same place for a group of persons under a certain authority; a paternalistic approach in service provision; supervision of living arrangements; and usually also a disproportion in the number of persons with disabilities living in the same environment.
>
> (ibid., para 16(c))

It is important to note that progressive alternatives to large-scale disability institutions such as group homes and supported disability housing can also share these features and hence are not seen as reflecting the ideals of Article 19 (and this is exemplified in the discussion in Section 7.7 below).

In turn, deinstitutionalisation has been identified as core to the structural change that is required for 'the systematic realization of the right to independent living in the community' (UN Disability Committee, 2018a: p. 41; see also p. 49; UN Disability Committee, 2018b). Deinstitutionalisation 'requires a systemic transformation, which includes the closure of institutions and the elimination of institutionalizing regulations as part of a comprehensive strategy, along with the establishment of a range of individualized support services' (UN Disability Committee, 2018b: para 58).

Article 19 is very useful in an analysis of court diversion because it highlights the ongoing pervasiveness of institutionalisation, including through the kinds of places used in court diversion (such as mental health facilities and group homes) and the practices of supervision and control used in these places in court diversion (discussed further in Chapter 7). Contrary to the claim that court diversion supposedly remedies the past failures of deinstitutionalisation, analysing court diversion by reference to Article 19 actually highlights how court diversion uses disabled people's lack of community resources as a justification for further institutionalisation. Article 19 is also useful in critiquing the lack of 'choice' and 'inclusion' for disabled people who are diverted on a conditional basis and subject to coercion.

However, Article 19 reflects the troubling hierarchy apparent in Articles 5, 12, 13 and 14 of privileging disability-specific injustices over injustices that occur in mainstream criminal justice settings or at the intersection of interlocking systems of oppression. It does this by implicitly defining the 'institution' in disability-specific terms and, thus, as excluding the prison from its understanding of both how disabled people are institutionalised and the scope of deinstitutionalisation. This is so even though prisons are places which reflect many of the 'defining elements' identified by the UN Disability Committee and are places where many disabled people are congregated. This oversight is apparent in the General Comment on Article 19, which makes no reference to prison or criminal justice systems when giving examples of institutions. This divide between prison and disability institutions is also evident in the 2019 Special Rapporteur report on deprivation of liberty, which focuses discussion on disability institutions as separate to its cursory mention of detention in prison. This then means that the radical and transformative end goal of dismantling disability institutions stops short of also dismantling the prison as an institution, and thus leaves criminalised disabled people locked up. The relative absence of the prison from the work of the UN Disability Committee (notably its work in relation to Article 19) and the organising of space along disability lines has dangerous political implications for criminalised disabled people, which might mean that the CRPD itself very well further entrenches the problems I have identified with court diversion.

Unfortunately, the majority of the CRPD legal scholarship has not engaged with the full breadth and complexity of criminal justice issues raised in this chapter, nor has it sought to reconcile the CRPD with the injustices inherent to the prison and criminal justice system. Ultimately, then, the CRPD does not provide the tools for thinking about transformative solutions that can address the complex structural conditions, including systems of oppression, settler colonialism and the prison system itself. I do not deny that it is important to realise equality within the mainstream criminal justice system (given that it is not going to be abolished any time soon), but it is surprising and deeply troubling that the CRPD does not even float the possibility of systemic and structural injustices in relation to criminal legal intervention and the possibility of abolition and transformation vis-à-vis prison and the criminal justice system.

Noble v Australia

The possibilities and limits of the CRPD in relation to an analysis of court diversion, particularly in relation to criminalised disabled people who are Indigenous or First Nations, are illustrated by the views adopted by the UN Disability Committee (2016) in *Marlon Noble v Australia*, a communication related to detention in prison through forensic mental health legislation following a finding of unfitness.

The author of the communication is an Indigenous Australian man with mental and intellectual disabilities who had been charged with child sexual offences when he was 19 years old. Noble was found unfit to plead in relation to these charges and was made subject to a custody order pursuant to sections 16 and 19 of the *Mentally Impaired Defendants Act 1996* (WA). Noble was then detained in prison for over ten years until released on a conditional release order (UN Disability Committee, 2016: para 2.4). Noble's conditional release was subject to ten conditions, which included undertaking supervision and drug testing, not spending unapproved nights away from primary residence, not having unsupervised contact with girls under 16 years of age and not consuming drugs and alcohol (UN Disability Committee, 2016: para 2.7).

Noble made a complaint to the UN Disability Committee in relation to violations of the rights to non-discrimination, equality before the law, liberty and security of person, and freedom from torture. Ultimately, the UN Disability Committee found breaches of all of these Articles. The Committee's reasoning reflects its interpretation of these provisions vis-à-vis disability-specific coercive intervention, as discussed earlier in this section. For example, its view that there was a violation of Article 5 was based on forensic mental health laws being differential laws with a disproportionate impact on disabled people. This was established in relation to Noble by reason of denial of his opportunity to enjoy the same procedural protections as non-disabled people, including by reason of a failure to provide him with 'the support or accommodation he required to exercise his legal capacity' (UN Disability Committee, 2016: para 8.4). The Committee concluded that the *Mentally Impaired Defendants Act 1996* (WA) 'fully suspended' Noble's 'right to a fair trial … depriving him of the protection and equal benefit of the law' (UN Disability Committee, 2016: para 8.4). In a similar vein, the finding that Australia had violated Article 12(2) and (3) and Article 13(1) of the CRPD was on the basis that the finding of Noble's unfitness to plead and the failure to provide him adequate support to participate in a trial meant that Noble 'never had the opportunity to have the criminal charges against him determined and his status as an alleged sexual offender potentially cleared' (UN Disability Committee, 2016: para 8.6), nor did he have 'adequate support or accommodation to exercise his rights to access to justice and a fair trial' (ibid.: para 8.6).

The UN Disability Committee decided that Noble's detention in prison through forensic mental health legislation after a finding of unfitness to plead violated Article 14(1)(b) of the CRPD. This was on the basis that his detention was ordered 'on the basis of the assessment by the State party's authorities of potential consequences of their intellectual disability, in the absence of any criminal conviction, thereby converting their disability into the core cause of his detention' (UN Disability Committee, 2016: para 8.7). The UN Disability Committee decided that his detention also violated Article 15 of the CRPD (freedom from torture or cruel, inhuman or degrading treatment or punishment). The violation of Article 15 was premised on 'the indefinite character of the author's detention and the repeated acts of violence to which he was subjected during his detention' (ibid.: para 8.9).

The UN Disability Committee made a series of recommendations to Australia in relation both to Noble and the legal system more broadly in order to prevent such breaches occurring in the future. In relation to Noble, it recommended Australia provide an effective remedy, revoke the conditions of his conditional release order and instead provide supports to enable community inclusion (UN Disability Committee, 2016: para 9(a)). In relation to structural preventive measures, it recommended that the *Mentally Impaired Defendants Act* (WA) be amended—along with all equivalent or related federal and state legislation—in order to make it compliant with the CRPD by providing 'adequate support and accommodation measures' so that disabled people can 'exercise their legal capacity before the courts whenever necessary', and ensuring provision to justice professionals of 'appropriate and regular training on the scope of the Convention and its Optional Protocol, including on the exercise of legal capacity by persons with intellectual and mental disabilities' (para 9(b)).

The UN Disability Committee did *not* acknowledge the 'overrepresentation' of disabled (and particularly Indigenous and First Nations disabled) people in the mainstream criminal justice system or in prison. Nor did it give any attention to the structural dynamics that contribute to criminalisation and incarceration of disabled people, let alone the dynamics of interlocking oppression and settler colonialism in the context of criminalisation and incarceration of Aboriginal and Torres Strait Islander disabled people nor the broader context of land dispossession and genocide in a context where Indigenous sovereignty was never ceded. These omissions resulted in a siloed focus on disability as somehow distinct to other systems of oppression. Moreover, while the UN Disability Committee recognised the violence in prison experienced by Noble, this did not prompt a consideration of whether prisons are inherently harmful and should be abolished, or connections to the long history of settler colonial violence through prisons, including deaths in custody (Cunneen, 2009). The recommendation of training overlooks the possibility of structural discrimination inherent to the very existence of prisons and the impacts this can have on criminalised disabled people who are subject to coercive intervention in mainstream criminal law and criminal justice systems.

The recommendations to amend the *Mentally Impaired Defendants Act* fall short of abolition of the fitness scheme in its totality; it is unclear how this legislation could be *amended* to comply with the CRPD (even on a narrow pure disability discrimination reading of the CRPD). Furthermore, while denial of legal capacity has been recognised as central to settler colonialism (as discussed in Section 2.2, above), the *Noble* decision did not in its recommendations include extending recognition of legal capacity to collective recognition of self-determination and sovereignty of Aboriginal and Torres Strait Islander people. Thus there is an odd asymmetry between the injustice through denial of legal capacity to Indigenous and First Nations people and the recognition of legal capacity as in some ways repeating (albeit through human rights) a western liberal understanding of legal capacity as individual in a consensual sovereign context, which thus re-enacts the founding colonial legal violence inherent in the denial of Indigenous sovereignty and the structure of settler colonialism.

To conclude, the CRPD is powerful in bringing forth the oppressive nature of disability-specific coercive intervention at the same time that it further entrenches the legitimacy of criminal legal intervention. Yet, ultimately, the CRPD cannot provide a framework for analysing court diversion by reference to the full suite of problems raised earlier in this chapter. The CRPD is anti-disability-specific in a narrow sense, but not 'anti-carceral' (Wildeman, 2018b) in a broader sense. Relying on the CRPD pushes analysis into a disability-specific wedge which results in us only being alert to political implications of court diversion that form part of a vision of freedom from pure disability discrimination. Reliance on the CRPD risks only further entrenching criminalised disabled people in the mainstream criminal justice system, rather than delivering us a world beyond prison. There is something profoundly disappointing in discovering the ambivalence of the CRPD regarding the criminal justice context and criminalised disabled people. I am left asking—is this the best international human rights law can offer? However, disappointment aside, in moving forward this exploration of the CRPD suggests that it is not useful for my analysis and a new theoretical framework is needed; and, secondly, that in the course of applying this framework to court diversion I should also, when opportunity arises, utilise it to make sense of these deep limitations of the CRPD—the problems with human rights (worryingly) might indeed be of the same ilk as those with court diversion.

Chapter 3

Theorising court diversion

Disability

3.1 Theorising court diversion

We should approach court diversion as a mode of biopower through which law debilitates criminalised disabled people. This way of approaching court diversion utilises an analytical framework that foregrounds key concepts of 'discipline', 'massification', 'scientific racism', 'slow death', 'inclusionism' and 'debility' which are articulated by drawing on aspects of Foucauldian theory, critical disability studies, critical legal and political theory and queer theory. The analytical framework moves beyond a focus solely on disability discrimination and instead situates court diversion in interlocking oppression and settler colonialism. Through this analytical framework, court diversion can be understood as having violent, discriminatory and unjust impacts at multiple scales—for the particular individuals who are diverted and for criminalised disabled people as a population (the majority of whom are not diverted). My analytical frame is important because it suggests that far from addressing the problem of overrepresentation of disabled people in the criminal justice system, court diversion instead facilitates and legitimates the continued oppression of criminalised disabled people through criminal legal, criminal justice and disability and mental health systems.

A key point to emerge from this analytical frame is that I argue that court diversion effects a shift in the legal subjectivity of criminalised individuals, from a criminal legal subject known and acted upon by reference to the criminal offence to a disabled legal subject known and acted upon by reference to their disability (as a medical phenomenon). Court diversion dispenses with the criminal offence and the associated liberal legal protections that purportedly limit the scope of criminal legal intervention. This connection between shifting legal subjectivity illuminates the significance of legal dynamics to debilitation of criminalised disabled people.

The framework developed in this chapter and the next is a response to the problems identified in the previous chapter (court diversion enables coercive intervention without the need for conviction and sentence, court diversion applies only to criminalised disabled people and court diversion operates through disability and mental health services that can be harmful and violent). The framework differs from existing scholarly and human rights approaches to court diversion which were incapable of interrogating the problems I identified because the existing approaches are too narrowly focused on the immediate disability-related implications of court diversion for specific individuals who are diverted and ultimately leave unconsidered many of the structural and intersectional dynamics that sustain criminalised disabled people's oppression.

In this chapter I draw on theoretical ideas about 'disability'. I bring these ideas to analyse court diversion as a mode of control, violence and debility of criminalised disabled individuals who are diverted. I begin in Section 3.2 by introducing the foundational ideas of the framework: Foucault's approach to analysing power relations, at the scales of the individual (an individualising disciplinary power) and population (a massifying regulatory power). Then, in Section 3.3 I build on these Foucauldian ideas in order to craft an analytical framework that can explore the significance of disability to court diversion. Critical disability studies scholarship on 'disability' disrupts the common medical approach to disability pursuant to which coercive intervention is benevolent and necessary. In contrast, critical disability studies scholarship illuminates how a medicalised approach to disability is harnessed in the legal framework of court diversion to enable control and violence through disability and mental health services. I then build on the analytical framework by drawing on scholarship on disability, illness and settler colonialism. This scholarship assists in showing that court diversion's control and violence through disability is not parallel to and separate from settler colonial control and violence. Rather, the legal system as a whole (including disability-specific laws on court diversion) is founded on legitimating the white, fit, settler subject and nation. As such through the legal framework of court diversion disability becomes a way to make possible and legitimate (as well as mask) settler colonialism and obfuscate the realisation of Indigenous and First Nations self-determination and sovereignty.

Having established that court diversion gives rise to control and violence, I then move on in Section 3.4 to explain how this control and violence amounts to *debilitation* specifically of *criminalised* disabled people (rather than all disabled people), many of whom are also poor, victims of violence, Indigenous and First Nations and racialised. This move from control and violence to a more ongoing, structural notion of debilitation is important to appreciating the very particular and profound ways in which criminalised disabled people are oppressed in ways that both engage interlocking systems of oppression and do not correspond to the oppression of criminalised non-disabled people and non-criminalised disabled people. I draw on Foucault's ideas of degeneracy and scientific racism, along with recent scholarship on debility. These tools are useful in going beyond asking whether court diversion discriminates against people on the basis of disability and sustains inequality and structural disadvantage for disabled people. Instead, the focus is on whether court diversion—as applied on the basis of disability—is 'capacitating' to criminalised disabled people in the sense of giving them access to the full rights and entitlements of liberal citizenship or 'debilitating' in casting them as a population outside of the political and material benefits of full citizenship, including access to the basic means for living and flourishing. Here I argue that through court diversion law contributes to criminalised disabled people remaining in a state of 'slow death' characterised by systemic deprivation and their gradual wearing down over their lives.

3.2 Starting point: biopower

Understanding court diversion as debilitating begins with an approach to power as 'biopower'. In this section, I briefly draw the foundational theoretical ideas of my framework from Foucault's approach to analysing power relations in terms of 'biopower'. These ideas enable me to analyse power relations at different levels—the individual and population—and to make sense of the purportedly benevolent and dispersed power that animates the criminal legal, mental health and disability systems at work in court diversion.

Foucault rejected the idea that power can only be analysed as operating over individuals in ways that are repressive, restrictive and violent. Rather, for Foucault, power can also be analysed as productive—that is, through guiding individuals' behaviour towards particular ends by structuring their choices, relationships, spatial location and self-perception, situated in an overarching framework of purportedly enhancing their freedom and self-realisation. Foucault refers to this alternative approach to power (or, more precisely, power relations) as 'bio-power'. Bio-power is 'the set of mechanisms through which the basic biological features of the human species became the object of a political strategy, a general strategy of power' (Foucault, 2004a: p. 1). 'Biopower' controls people through enhancing life and flourishing but in ways that shape and guide individuals and populations towards particular ways of living and behaving (Foucault, 2008b: pp. 138–139). Foucault rejected the idea of the 'individual as a sort of elementary nucleus, a primitive atom or some multiple, inert matter to which power is applied, or which is struck by a power that subordinates or destroys individuals' (Foucault, 1997b: p. 29). Rather, the individual 'is one of power's first effects' (ibid.: p. 30). Power does not operate by dictating in absolute terms how people must behave but, instead, structures a 'field of possibilities in which the behaviour of active subjects is able to inscribe itself' (Foucault, 2000: p. 341). Power thus operates *through* people's action—the choices they make and how they behave (ibid.: pp. 340–341). Individuals have an active role in the operation of power over their selves because they 'are never the inert or consenting targets of power; they are always its relays. In other words, power passes through individuals. It is not applied to them' (Foucault, 1997b: p. 29).

Bio-power is contrasted with the conventional model of power as 'sovereign power', which consists of the 'juridical edifice of sovereignty, State apparatuses, and the ideologies that accompany them' (ibid.: p. 34). There are four key characteristics that distinguish these two forms of power. The first relates to the relationship between power and life. Sovereign power consists of repressing action—

'the right to take life or let live' (Foucault, 1997c: p. 241; see also 1997a: p. 15). In contrast, bio-power consists of 'the right to make live and to let die' (Foucault, 1997c: p. 241) and the 'highest function [is] no longer to kill, but to invest life through and through' (Foucault, 2008b: p. 139). Individuals are controlled through structuring the field of possible action, rather than by providing only one course of action that must be taken under fear of death.

A second characteristic distinguishing the two approaches to power is the relative contingent nature of power. According to Foucault, in 'sovereign' approaches to power, power is an 'entity' that could be understood in the abstract from people and context (Foucault, 2000: p. 340)—it is something that can be held and exchanged. In comparison, bio-power is not 'a substance, fluid, or something that derives from a particular source' (Foucault, 2004a: p. 2). Instead power is a 'set of mechanisms and procedures' that only exist in relations and in action (ibid.: p. 2; see also Foucault 2000: p. 340; 1997a: p. 13).

A third characteristic distinguishing these forms of power is in terms of the status of law. Sovereign power operates through law (in the sense of rules prohibiting conduct). In contrast, law functions in bio-power to structure the range of possible actions that will guide people towards the norm. In bio-power 'the judicial institution is increasingly incorporated into a continuum of apparatuses (medical, administrative, and so on) whose functions are for the most part regulatory' (Foucault, 2008b: p. 144; see also Foucault, 1997b: pp. 37–38). This aspect of bio-power is particularly significant to an analysis of court diversion as a legal process.

The fourth characteristic is that in sovereign power, power is unidirectional and emanates from a central institutional source. In contrast, an analysis by reference to bio-power moves away from the functions of the institution to a more general technology of power that is more dispersed and circulates throughout society (Foucault, 2004e: pp. 116–118).

Foucault explains that bio-power began to emerge during the eighteenth century at two interrelated 'poles': discipline of individual bodies and regulatory control of populations. The first to emerge was discipline. Discipline 'centers on the body, produced individualizing effects, and manipulates the body as a source of forces that have to be rendered both useful and docile' (Foucault, 1997c: p. 249). Disciplinary power, the 'anatomo-politics of the human body', focuses on 'the body as a machine: its disciplining, the optimization of its capabilities, the extortion of its forces, the parallel increase of its usefulness and docility, its integration into systems of efficient and economic controls' (Foucault, 2008b: p. 139). Discipline exercises a 'microphysics of power' over individuals as subjects by separating individual bodies into various biological or psychological processes and performances, thus allowing control over the minutiae of the body (Foucault, 2004c: pp. 56–57). Discipline controls people by reference to 'a code of normalization' derived from 'the field of the human sciences' rather than 'a code of law' in the sense of sovereign prohibitions (Foucault, 1997b: p. 38). Noting discipline's function in guiding individuals towards the norm, this approach to understanding power relations directs attention to how individuals are divided by reference to the disciplines (or human sciences) in terms of being 'normal' ('that which can conform to this norm') and 'abnormal' ('that which is incapable of conforming to the norm') (Foucault, 2004c: p. 57). The process through which individuals become subjects whose conduct can be shaped and guided in certain ways is referred to as 'subjectification' (Foucault, 2008a: pp. 55–56).

The second pole of biopower—'regulatory controls'—emerged in the nineteenth century. I am going to provide greater details on this pole. I do so because it is fundamental to my argument about debility yet, in comparison to discipline (which readers might be more familiar with in relation to 'net-widening' critiques of court diversion), this pole of biopower has not been considered in the existing scholarship on court diversion or disability criminal justice more broadly. This pole focuses on 'the species body'. It is 'a bio-politics of the population' concerned with 'the mechanics of life' and 'biological processes' such as 'propagation, births and mortality, the level of health, life expectancy and longevity, with all the conditions that can cause these to vary' (Foucault, 2008b: p. 139). Regulatory control operates by taking as its target 'the mass effects characteristic of a population' (Foucault, 2003a: p. 249) rather than individuals within a certain territory (Foucault, 2004e: p. 129). For Foucault, the population is more than simply a sum of individual bodies or 'a collection of subjects of right differentiated by their status, localization, goods, responsibilities, and offices' (Foucault, 2004c: p. 75). Rather, it is a 'multiplicity of men [sic]', 'a new body, a multiple body, a body with so many heads that, while they might not be infinite in number, cannot necessarily be counted' which forms 'a global mass that is affected by overall processes characteristic of birth, death, production, illness, and so on' (Foucault, 1997c: pp. 242–243). Whereas discipline is 'individualising', regulatory control is a power that is 'massifying, that is directed not at man-as-body [sic] but at man-as-species' (ibid.: p. 243).

Regulatory control deals with 'the population as political problem' by reference to understanding and acting upon the overall biological processes through which the population exists and is reproduced (ibid.: p. 245). The aim of regulatory control is 'to achieve overall states of equilibration or regularity' (ibid.; see also p. 249; see the example of endemics, Foucault, 1997c: pp. 243–244) and 'improve the conditions of the population, to increase its wealth, its longevity, and its health' (Foucault, 2004d: p. 105). As such, regulatory controls do not seek 'to modify a given individual insofar as he [sic] is an individual, but, essentially, to intervene at the level at which these general phenomena are determined, to intervene at the level of their generality' (Foucault, 1997c: p. 246). One of the key features of acting through the population is the ability to divide the population into sub-populations. These sub-populations become identified by reference to their departure from the norm (that is, the average or accepted rate of a specified phenomenon) and are then differentially problematised and regulated.

Analysing power relations in terms of regulatory control provides ways to understand the structural status of sub-populations that resist normalisation.

Foucault offers the notion of 'degeneracy' to understand how regulatory controls operate to massify and then act differentially (and even violently) on individuals who are resistant to normalisation. According to Foucault (2003b: pp. 317–318), the 'degenerate is someone who is a danger. The degenerate is someone who cannot be reached by any kind of penalty. The degenerate is someone who, at all events, cannot be cured'. Foucault (1997c: p. 258) identified, criminals and people who are mad as examples of 'degenerate'. In the nineteenth century, psychiatry functioned as a 'hunt for "degenerates"' (Foucault, 2003b: p. 317). Psychiatry assumed a 'social defense' role in protecting society from the 'threat' posed by degenerates (ibid.: pp. 317–318). Thus, people considered abnormal or degenerate 'were not only problems for those whose intimate lives they shared but were threats to the general public and rightfully subject to surveillance and constraints imposed through psychiatry and other means by or on behalf of society as a whole' (McWhorter, 2009: p. 31). Those who are abnormal or degenerate impact on the overall fitness of the species or population and are not merely 'bad' or 'unfavourable'—rather, their degeneracy has a relational, depleting effect on the 'mass' in being wasteful, burdensome and dangerous to the generativity of the nation (for discussion in a contemporary context, see Voronka, 2003: pp. 20–31). Foucault argued that the concept of degeneracy gave rise to a new form of racism directed towards protection of the human species or 'racism against the abnormal' (Foucault, 2003b: p. 317). Thus, Foucault's approach to 'racism' is not drawn along ethnic lines and, hence, is distinct from racism as vindication of a particular ethnic racial group (as conventionally understood in contemporary politics and discrimination law) (ibid.: p. 316). Foucault explains this scientific racism as 'a way of separating out the groups that exist within a population' by 'establishing a biological caesura within a population that appears to be a biological domain'. This caesura then 'will allow power to treat that population as a mixture of races, or to be more accurate, to treat the species, to subdivide the species it controls, into the subspecies known, precisely, as races' (Foucault, 1997c: p. 255). Degeneracy provides a basis for physical exclusion (ibid.: p. 258) and violence, all of which is directed towards obliterating unfit individuals in order to shore up the overall fitness of the population (ibid.: pp. 255–256). Thus, we can understand the ways in which prejudice against a number of disparate groups is actually all positioned against the one, common, goal of preservation of the privilege of the white, fit subject and nation (McWhorter, 2009: p. 35). In this context, 'white' does not have a literal meaning of referring exclusively to people of particular ethnic backgrounds commonly associated with white skin colour but, rather, the sense of 'white supremacy' and as the 'colour of domination'. 'White' thus captures people who are in a position of privilege and domination in the context of interlocking 'systems of domination', including ableism, sexism, racism and heterosexism, that are situated in political conditions of patriarchy, capitalism and settler colonialism (Razack, 1998: pp. 10–16).

Discipline and regulatory control are not completely separate to each other but are 'superimposed' (ibid.: p. 249) and 'can be articulated with each other' (ibid.:

p. 250). As such, discipline of individual bodies should not be abstracted from regulatory control but, rather, should be understood as 'only exist[ing] insofar as there is a multiplicity and an end, or an objective or result to be obtained on the basis of this multiplicity' (Foucault, 2004a: p. 12). Conversely, 'managing the population means managing it in depth, in all its fine points and details' and hence relies on discipline (Foucault, 2004d: p. 107). The coherence of the two poles is derived from the norm which circulates between discipline and regulatory control (Foucault, 1997c: pp. 252–253). Power is thus triangulated—sovereign, discipline and regulatory control—and works in multiple ways through bodies (Foucault, 2004d: pp. 107–108).

From this brief introductory overview, three points are immediately apparent which speak to the problems with court diversion identified in Chapter 2. The first is that a Foucauldian approach to power enables one to consider power relations at the level of diverted individuals (by reference to discipline) and at the macro level of criminalised disabled people more broadly (by reference to biopolitical regulatory control). The second is that the 'productive' nature of power allows exploration of how power operates through purportedly benevolent and therapeutic disability and mental health services, while the dispersed nature of power allows a consideration of the relationship between court diversion and an array of modes of intervention through criminal justice and mental health and disability systems. A third point is that Foucault's approach to regulatory control provides a way to make critical sense of characteristics often correlated with criminalised disabled people—disability, sickness, drug use and addiction, homelessness, criminality, race, poverty—which in conventional anti-oppression theory might otherwise be viewed as distinct and unrelated (or even absent and incomprehensible) and which in legal terms fall outside discrimination law identity categories. This is useful in understanding why criminalised disabled people might be subject to particular forms of control and violence that set them apart from other disabled people and non-disabled people; they are seen as unable to be recuperated, even to contemporary disability identity politics. As such, Foucault's approach to regulatory controls is useful in interrogating how court diversion exacerbates (and masks) the broader social and political circumstances of criminalised disabled people, not simply as an end in itself but for the benefits this provides to the security of the whole population and to settler colonial nation-building.

Having introduced the approach to power relations that undergirds my analysis, I now build upon this approach by reference to theoretical ideas speaking more directly to 'disability' in a criminal justice context.

3.3 Disability, court diversion and biopower

Foucault's scholarship on biopower assists in understanding disability as a biopolitical category through which control and violence in court diversion are made possible and legitimated. Critical disability studies scholars have shown that disability is conventionally understood through a medical lens, or 'medical model', as an individual, natural deviation from 'a biomedical norm' (Allen, 2005: p. 94; see also Goodley, 2014: pp. 3–5). This is exemplified by diagnostic approaches to disability that break down a specific disability to particular characteristics residing in the individual, which await discovery through the expert process of diagnosis (Altermark, 2018: 21–44). In this medical approach, disability is something undesirable and a burden on carers and society. Disability evokes (at best) pity and (at worst) disgust and contempt. In this medical approach, collective efforts should be directed towards curing and rehabilitating individuals so they can try to live something approximating a non-disabled life. This medical approach does not comprehend disability in terms of political questions of power and oppression.

In critiquing this medical approach, critical disability studies scholars have drawn on Foucault's approach to power relations. Critical disability scholars, some of whom draw on Foucault's ideas of biopower, challenge the medical approach to disability and argue that disability can instead be understood by reference to constructed norms of ability that reflect what is socially, politically and economically valued in society (Altermark, 2018: pp. 37–47; Tremain, 2002). In this approach, diagnostic systems of disability 'create what they propose to represent' (Altermark, 2018: pp. 40) such that they actually constitute as phenomena that which they claim to discover (Tremain, 2005: p. 11). Rather than simply providing a retrospective and static description of individuals and populations as abnormal, with no consequences other than to stigmatise those so labelled or put up barriers to disabled people realising their rights, these constructed and contingent norms actually make possible ways of intervening in individuals and populations *through* disability (ibid.). In short, critical disability studies scholars argue, disability is a biopolitical category through which individuals are disciplined and population is regulated relative to the norm. Disability is then instrumentalised in specific institutional contexts to enable control that is otherwise not possible or legitimate.

Court diversion applies to *criminalised* disabled people—disabled people who have been charged with criminal offences. Typically, individuals appearing before the court on criminal charges are dealt with by reference to the criminal offence—any coercive intervention is dependent on trial for the offence (in the context of bail) or on an individual having been convicted of the offence. Drawing on ideas of biopolitical subjectivity, I argue that court diversion transforms criminalised individuals from criminal legal subjects known and acted upon by reference to the criminal offence to disabled legal subjects known and acted upon by reference to their disability (as a medical phenomenon). Court diversion subjectifies them as disabled legal subjects by classifying and knowing them by reference to their disability, such that acting on them through disability and mental health services becomes the natural and necessary response. This disabled legal subjectification facilitates criminalised disabled people's debilitation because court diversion positions them in a state of legal and material precarity. In so doing, court diversion dispenses with the criminal offence and the associated liberal legal protections that purportedly limit the scope of criminal legal intervention.

In general terms, this subjectification is evident in three consecutive features of court diversion that I identified in Section 1.4. First, individuals must have a specified diagnosed disability in order to apply for diversion—that is, court diversion classifies individuals by reference to disability. Second, judges, in the course of making discretionary decisions whether to divert a particular individual, will focus on the individual's disability in weighing up treatment and support as opposed to conventional criminal legal disposal—this can be understood as court diversion knowing individuals by reference to their disability. Last, if court diversion is ordered, individuals will be required to engage with disability and mental health services—that is, court diversion controls people through acting on their disability. Whereas the 'offence' threads together the legal process and ultimate outcome of criminal legal coercive intervention, 'disability' (in its medical form) threads together the legal process and ultimate outcome of court diversion. This 'threading' is possible because of the transformation of the individual from a criminal legal to disabled legal subject.

The decision-making process to order court diversion is generally dependent on professional knowledge of disability held by psychiatrists, psychologists and neuropsychologists. I refer to this as 'psy knowledge', drawing on the work of Rose (1996). This knowledge of disability is grounded in a medical approach to disability structured by diagnostic frameworks. Rather than seeing psychiatry as a scientific practice of discovering internal, pre-existing pathologies, we might draw on Foucault's idea of psychiatry as 'social defense' (discussed in Section 3.2 above) to argue that the role of psychiatry and psychology in court diversion is to know criminalised individuals who are resistant to criminal legal intervention as 'dangerous individuals' who can instead be subject to control through a medical framework of treatment. This is evident in court diversion, where diagnosis and psychiatric knowledge of the individual provides a basis for the necessity, not simply of their humane discharge from criminal law into some kind of state of absolute freedom, but, rather their subjection to an alternative therapeutic and ongoing mode of control premised on disability. As discussed in Section 1.5, Spivakovsky and Seear have argued that mental health courts sustain problematic cultural logics about disability, criminality, risk and regulation that legitimate coercive interventions specifically in relation to criminalised disabled people (Spivakovsky & Seear, 2017). They argue that in the parliamentary debates of the legislation introducing the Victorian Assessment and Referral Court List (discussed in Section 1.3), people with cognitive impairments or mental illness are portrayed as '"faultless" victims of a debilitating "affliction"' (Spivakovsky & Seear, 2017: p. 464) and that this then results in the assumption that 'a person's cognitive impairment or mental illness somehow *creates*, or at the very least, *facilitates* criminality' and that the person hence 'neither has a choice in how they behave nor the capacity to change; they are wholly controlled by their unrelenting medical condition, and for this reason, they become "faultless"' (ibid.). It follows that direct intervention on the disability itself (rather than punishment relative to responsibility for the specific crime) is required (ibid.), and this intervention needs to be of an ongoing nature because the core problem is their ongoing impairment (ibid.: p. 465).

Moreover, reliance in court diversion on psy expertise enacts 'epistemic violence' on criminalised disabled people by denying them status as 'legitimate knowers' who can give meaning to themselves and their experiences and by authorising others' decisions on what happens to their bodies and lives (Liegghio, 2013: p. 123; see further Altermark, 2018; Beaupert, 2018a; 2018b; Roper, 2018; Roper, 2019; Roper & Gooding, 2018). In turn, the epistemic violence through court diversion negates the status of these individuals as political actors, capable of exercising resistance to legal and medical authority (Beaupert, 2018a; 2018b; Joseph, 2014).

Some critical disability scholars have illuminated how disability and mental health services exert control by shaping disabled people's behaviour towards socially and politically desired ends (see Altermark, 2018; Drinkwater, 2005; Fabris, 2011; Levinson, 2010; Tremain, 2005; Yates, 2005). Altermark (2018) articulates a key tension in these services between freedom and control—control that is always directed towards a future freedom. Drinkwater argues that these services 'structure … the field of possible action' (Drinkwater, 2005: p. 231) and 'induce people to act normatively *of their own free will*' (ibid.: p. 238, emphasis in original). Levinson (2010, p. 38) refers to this tension in terms of services 'mobili[sing] individuals to act freely for themselves in specific ways'. This productive power operates in the group home setting through such techniques as daily routines focused on micro-practices of service users' bodies (their 'habits, behavior, conduct, hygiene'), surveillance through monitoring service users' diaries and record-keeping by staff, and eliciting compliance through persuasion (Drinkwater, 2005: pp. 235–238). These services are also framed in terms of discourses of freedom and self-realisation (ibid.: p. 232). On this basis, it can be argued that the use of disability and mental health services in court diversion is itself controlling (irrespective of the services' coercive quality by reason of being legally ordered, which I discuss below). While the individuals are not detained in prison, within the disability and mental health services they are instead regulated through intensive supervision and management in the community or, in the case of the UK and New Zealand schemes, confinement in treatment facilities. These services are ostensibly directed toward enhancing flourishing through an emphasis on treatment, support and working towards fostering independence and freedom.

Comprehending the disciplinary effects of disability is hampered by the dominance in disability policy of a linear representation of time—contemporary disability and mental health services are understood as being in a constant state of movement further away from a repressive past of large-scale institutionalisation from which they are completely separate. Writing in the context of intellectual disability, Altermark (2017: p. 2) argues that 'the developmental path of intellectual disability politics as a dark past of state institutionalisation … has been replaced by policies of community living and societal inclusion'. Altermark argues, however, that this 'idea that there is a break in history, between past and present, redirects our criticism to the repression of the past', thus causing us to overlook 'how power has transformed, rather than disappeared, after deinstitutionalisation' (ibid.: p. 1) and 'neglects more subtle and productive practices governing people with intellectual disability' (ibid.: p. 6). Court diversion is situated in these disability institutional temporalities, as evidenced by the common refrain among supporters of court diversion that it provides a humane alternative to the current institutionalisation in prison, which, in turn, is caused by the failure or unfinished work of deinstitutionalisation (I return to the rhetorical value of 'failure' in Chapter 4). The productive power that operates through court diversion is supported (rather than contested) by the very discourses that we might otherwise assume will empower disabled people in the aftermath of the repressive control and injustices that precipitated deinstitutionalisation. In Chapter 4, I reflect on this tension of the subversion of reform in the context of the 'institutional archipelago', in drawing connections between court diversion and a wider network of modes of control across criminal justice and disability and mental health systems.

However, seeing court diversion as disciplinary does not alone give us a sufficiently full, complex and rich understanding of the political implications of court diversion. As noted in Section 3.2 above, discipline is not an end in itself; it is directed towards normalisation. The norm is not only drawn along exclusively dis/ability lines. We need to understand the disciplinary effects of court diversion in terms of the more complex abnormality posited by criminalised disabled people. Moreover, we need to avoid an exclusive focus on discipline of the individual and instead extend our analysis to the biopolitical effects of court diversion on the population—how court diversion shapes and limits the circulation within society of criminalised disabled people *and* shores up the fitness of the settler colonial nation as a whole.

Court diversion as violent

Court diversion is a mode of biopower that results not only in control but also in violence. The effects of court diversion go beyond the mere gentle guidance of those who are diverted. This is because in court diversion disability and mental health services are not accessed voluntarily—they are mandated by a court order and hence are non-consensual and, thus, coercive. Coercion operates at the individual and population levels. While individuals might possibly make the choice to apply to be diverted, this choice is made in a structural context within which disabled people are carved out as the only population to whom diversion can apply; criminalised non-disabled populations are simply beyond coercive intervention if not subjected to criminal legal intervention (that is, this is not a choice they need even make in order to avoid criminal legal intervention). In Chapter 2 I raised the possibility that the non-consensual nature of court diversion meant it was violent. Here I pick up on this point by suggesting court diversion reflects a very particular form of violence against disabled people that goes beyond equating court diversion to an individual act of physical assault or false imprisonment. Instead, drawing on critical disability studies scholarship on violence and Foucault's ideas of 'scientific racism', I propose that court diversion enacts structural and settler colonial violence directed towards both sustaining the fitness of the population and negating the very humanity of criminalised disabled people by exposing them to a 'slow death'. Berlant describes 'slow death' as 'the physical wearing out of a population and the deterioration of people in that population that is very nearly a defining condition of their experience and historical existence' (Berlant, 2007: p. 754; see subsequent development in the context of 'debility' in Puar, 2017; see similarly the concept of 'social death': Bromwich, 2015). Gilmore, writing in the context of the Californian prison system has noted that: 'Racism … is the state-sanctioned or extralegal production and exploitation of group-differentiated vulnerability to premature death' (Gilmore, 2007: p. 28). Drawing on Berlant and Gilmore, we can consider how law, through court diversion, exposes individual criminalised disabled people to violence and control that can contribute to their precarity *and* sustains criminal justice and disability and mental health systems that provide the conditions for 'vulnerability and premature death' across and beyond particular legal orders.

Some critical disability scholars have argued that disability is a subject position that necessitates and legitimates violence. As I and others have argued, at a general level, material violence (non-consensual physical contact of an individual—that is, the meaning associated with the common usage of the word 'violence') is justified on the basis that disability is an unwanted existence and that disabled people cannot be 'grievable' subjects. Their pain cannot be comprehended because their disability renders their bodies and lives devalued and, hence, incapable of eliciting grief (Erevelles, 2011: pp. 95–120; Spivakovsky, 2018; Steele, 2017c, 2017d; Taylor, 2015). This tension is augmented in the specific context of coercive intervention through disability and mental health services, because these services are by their very nature directed towards negation of the disabled subject. Kafer argues that disability is situated in a temporality that casts it as necessarily outside of futurity, and attributes this to the temporal quality of disability—'a better life would of necessity require the absence of impairment', where disability is cast as 'pitiable misfortune, a tragedy that effectively prevents one from leading a good life' (Kafer, 2013: p. 2). Taken to its end, this means that a 'better future … is one that excludes disability and disabled bodies' (ibid.: pp. 2–3). Kafer argues that disabled people are commonly understood through a 'curative imaginary', which is 'an understanding of disability that not only expects and assumes intervention but also cannot imagine or comprehend anything other than intervention' (ibid.: p. 27). In this imaginary, 'the only appropriate disabled mind/body is one cured or moving toward cure', with cure involving 'the elimination of impairment' or 'normalizing treatments that work to assimilate the disabled mind/body as much as possible' (ibid.: p. 28).

Building on Kafer's work, Kim proposes the concept of 'curative violence' to explain the profound violence perpetrated on disabled people through medical intervention: 'the exercise of force to erase differences for the putative betterment of the Other', which 'occurs when cure is what actually frames the presence of disability as a problem and ends up destroying the subject in the curative process' (Kim, 2016: p. 14; see also Clare, 2017: pp. 23–31). According to Kim,

> [t]he violence associated with cure exists at two levels: first, the violence of denying a place for disability and illness as different ways of living and, second, the physical and material violence against people with disabilities that are justified in the name of cure.
>
> (Kim, 2016: p. 14)

Non-consensual medical interventions are positioned as beneficial and benevolent acts that alleviate harm (of one's disability), rather than as violent acts themselves capable of causing harm. Thus, therapy is inherently violent—even if not enacting an actual death, it sustains profound ontological violence. Kim's work on curative violence sits alongside the work of Mad studies scholars who have discussed the symbolic or ontological violence of non-consensual mental health interventions (see, for example, Beaupert, 2018a, 2018b; Lee, 2013; Roper, 2018). This violence is considered of benefit not only to disabled people, but also to others who are invested in securing a collective future without disability.

This approach to understanding violence perpetrated through coercive intervention is significant because it draws a connection between the immediate physical violence of the non-consensual contact to the disabled body and a deeper ontological violence that devalues disabled people's very existence as disabled. However, for our purposes of analysing court diversion and noting that court diversion applies only to disabled people who have criminal charges, this approach to disability and violence does not attend to the possibility for inequalities in how violence is enacted within the disabled population. In particular this approach does not engage specifically with the context of criminalised disabled people who are not only disabled but are additionally 'non-normatively' (Dowse, 2018) disabled due to also being poor, Indigenous and First Nations, racialised, homeless, involved in the child welfare system as a child or parent, addicted to drugs and so on. In this respect, we can return to Foucault to consider how violence against criminalised disabled people through court diversion might be understood in the context of scientific racism.

Even though bio-power is focused on 'the right to make live and to let die' (Foucault, 1997c: p. 241) rather than 'the right to take life or let live' (ibid.), this does not mean violence is completely evacuated from bio-power. Foucault argued that violence still occurs in bio-power through racism (in the species use of the term articulated by Foucault), insofar as violence becomes legitimate when perpetrated in the interests of overall fitness of the population. Foucault stated that 'race or racism is the precondition that makes killing acceptable'; it 'can justify the murderous function of the State' (ibid.: p. 256). 'Racism' in the sense used by Foucault introduces 'a break into the domain of life that is under power's control: the break between what must live and what must die' (ibid.: p. 254). The division of people into sub-species is a way to intervene differentially in order to ensure the overall fitness of the population as a whole and, at its extreme, this means enabling 'killing' of degenerates who have a depleting effect on the population. Foucault states:

> racism makes it possible to establish a relationship between my life and the death of the other that is not a military or warlike relationship of confrontation, but a biological-type relationship ... The fact that the other dies does not mean simply that I live in the sense that his death guarantees my safety; the death of the other, the death of the bad race, of the inferior race (or the degenerate, or the abnormal) is something that will make life in general healthier: healthier and purer.
>
> (Foucault, 1997c: p. 255)

There is an important relational aspect to this violence. As Foucault explains,

> racism justifies the death-function in the economy of biopower by appealing to the principle that the death of others makes one biologically stronger insofar as one is a member of a race or a population, insofar as one is an element in a unitary living plurality.
>
> (Foucault, 1997c: p. 258)

Historically, this violence is evident in the extreme in Nazi Germany, and in more mundane forms such as in the public hygiene and eugenics movements of the early twentieth century. Yet, Foucault clarifies that 'killing' in bio-power does not only mean murder but also 'every form of indirect murder: the fact of exposing someone to death, increasing the risk of death for some people or quite simply, political death, expulsion, rejection, and so on' (ibid.: p. 256). Not only can we understand the concept of 'slow death' developed by scholars such as Berlant and Puar in the light of scientific racism, but we can also appreciate the concept of curative violence developed by Kafer and Kim in the specific context of disability as part of a broader system of violence modulating degeneracy and fitness and integral to settler colonial nation-building. The violence of disability-specific coercive intervention in court diversion is implicated in this larger project.

Bringing these ideas of violence to the non-consensual intervention of court diversion, I argue that court diversion could constitute racist (i.e. species) violence under bio-power insofar as it works to exclude and segregate criminalised disabled people. I propose this because the acute acts of non-consensual intervention made possible through court diversion are situated in a broader context of exclusion of criminalised disabled people from conventional terms of criminal legal liberal citizenship and provisional entitlement to liberty and resources. This violence in court diversion as one piece in a larger puzzle of coercive interventions and other 'curative' acts directed towards eliminating disability might also be understood as 'slow violence' (Nixon, 2013). Nixon defines 'slow violence' as 'violence that occurs gradually and out of sight' and 'is dispersed across time and space'. Slow violence 'is typically not viewed as violence at all' by reason of the conventional understanding of violence as 'an event or action that is immediate in time, explosive and spectacular in space' (ibid.: p. 2). The concept of slow violence is particularly useful for understanding how legal and bureaucratic decision-making over a period of time and at a spatial distance from individuals' suffering can be implicated in the harm people experience, as is demonstrated by the application of the concept in recent Mad studies scholarship in the contexts of policy framing of mental health 'crises', randomised controlled trials for mental health services and prison segregation (Kilty & Lehalle, 2019; Sheldon, Spector & Birdsell, 2019; Van Veen, Teghtsoonian & Morrow, 2019; Voronka, 2019).

The critical disability studies and Foucauldian approaches to violence need to be considered in a settler colonial context, in order to understand how violence directed towards unfitness is protecting the modern, vindicated, settler colonial population (Razack, 2015; see also Chapman, 2014a). In discussing settler colonial violence, Razack (2015: p. 38) argues that Indigenous and First Nations people 'are not entitled to bodily integrity' and 'can be violated with impunity' (ibid.: p. 45; see also Bond, 2017). This violation is enabled by their association with decline—including by reference to discourses of disability, disease and addiction. In this context, 'vulnerability' then becomes a discourse that can mark both individual Indigenous and First Nations bodies and a whole population as destined for decline and in need of rescuing in ways that 'elide the colonial condition altogether' (ibid.: p. 56, see also p. 59; from a different theoretical position, see Chrisjohn, McKay & Smith, 2017). Million (Tanana Athabascan), writing in the context of Canadian First Nations, argues that the shift to 'healing' from self-determination (which is manifested through a focus on therapeutic services including physical and mental health services) becomes a biopolitical technique for maintaining colonial rule (Million, 2013a: pp. 5–6). As Chapman and Withers (2019: pp. 343–344) note in the context of reflecting on Million's work: 'Framing Indigenous people as desperately, exceptionally, and individually, in need of healing, but not as legitimately and collectively seeking justice, land, and sovereignty is only one way that Indigenous people's political resistance gets depoliticized and morally denigrated'.

In situating the violence of court diversion in a settler colonial context, I argue that legal subjectification of criminalised Indigenous and First Nations people as *disabled* legal subjects both extends and deepens settler colonial violence and masks its continuities with forms of state violence more readily associated with the colonial project, such as incarceration and child welfare, through the more diffused and benign pathological prism of disability (Baldry, Carlton & Cunneen, 2015; Blagg, Tulich & Bush, 2017: p. 345). Far from being a 'solution' to addressing Indigenous and First Nations overrepresentation in the criminal justice system, disability-specific coercive interventions are part of the problem. Court diversion vindicates the settler colonial project insofar as it masks the fact that across many Anglo jurisdictions Indigenous sovereignty has never been ceded by pathologising Indigenous and First Nations criminalised disabled people as a problem to be fixed *and* positioning settler colonial society and criminal justice systems as rescuer, while eliding the ways in which they are complicit in constructing them as 'abnormal'.

My analysis suggests the need for more careful consideration of how settler colonial violence harnesses disability in its ongoing adaptation, enduring through 'universal' and non-race specific legal measures (Baldry & Cunneen, 2014: pp. 285–286), such as court diversion. In tracing the history of control and violence perpetrated against Indigenous and First Nations people and disabled people in Canada, Chapman compellingly shows how 'disability, poverty, or indigeneity are conceptualized individualistically' such that 'oppressive acts are rendered individually necessary and historically discontinuous' (Chapman, 2014b: p. 38). Chapman argues, however, that 'political rationalities have changed since earlier periods of confinement and elimination, but there has been little change in who gets forcibly removed from their homes and communities' (ibid.: p. 38). It is thus important to analyse violence in court diversion as implicated in settler colonial destruction of Indigenous and First Nations peoples and a continuation of that biopolitical logic. Such analysis is vital in order to understand how court diversion is implicated in ongoing denial of sovereignty and self-determination, and in white, able settler colonial nation-building.

3.4 Moving beyond the (pure) disabled subject of discipline: degeneracy, debility and inclusionism

Court diversion enables biopolitical control and violence specifically of *criminalised* disabled people, in what amounts to 'debilitation' because court diversion exposes them to control and violence in very particular ways which are distinct from the oppression of non-criminalised disabled people and non-disabled criminalised people. In order to appreciate how this occurs, it is important to note there are other inequalities that are at work in relation to criminalised disabled people which my analysis has not yet addressed. As I intimated in Chapter 2, criminalised disabled people's oppression cannot be captured purely in terms of ability/disability, and court diversion makes possible inequalities *between* criminalised and non-criminalised disabled people in terms of the conditions on which they can access liberty, resources and inclusion. As such, I share the concerns of some more recent critical scholarship about the limits of understanding disability only in terms of constructed norms of ability—'a uniformly oppressed identity category or form of embodiment that lacks or is abnormal' (Fritsch, 2015: p. 28).

As I stated in the Introduction and Chapter 2, criminalised disabled people do not reflect an even cross-section of the community. They are subject to what Dowse (2018) refers to as 'corrosive social disadvantage'. Many have histories of victimisation, are homeless or are in precarious housing such as boarding houses and public housing, are unemployed, use drugs, have been in the child welfare system or had their own children removed from their care by the state, are socially isolated with little or no family support, have been excluded from schooling and have experienced abusive childhoods. Long-term cycling in and out of prison is a core characteristic of their corrosive social disadvantage and is entangled throughout their life rather than simply being an isolated event (Dowse, 2018). The disadvantage is not an individualised pathological characteristic but is instead associated with forces and dynamics of privilege and oppression. As such, the positioning of criminalised disabled people cannot be explained by reference to hierarchies of ability. Their subordination cuts deeper and is messier—it exceeds the category of disability.

Dowse proposes that the absence in critical disability studies of tools to understand the politics of criminalised disabled people is indicative of criminalised disabled people having 'transgressive' or 'non-normative' forms of disability which 'cannot be reconciled with contemporary claims that disability is an oppressed—yet normal and desirable—identity' (Dowse, 2018: p. 1). Speaking more broadly than the criminal justice context, Fritsch (2015: p. 33) has argued that '[n]on-normative ways of being disabled, forms of disability that do not fit into the neat packages of a highly mobile, young, wheelchair user working to be independently productive, are easily dismissed as not truly deserving of benefits or accommodations'. This 'non-normative' disability can be understood as an abjected disability—a form of existence 'cast into a zone of shame, disgrace or debasement' to be 'denied the warrant of tolerability, accorded a purely negative value' (Rose, 1999: p. 253). This notion of non-normative disability tracks on to eugenics logics of the deserving and undeserving disabled along the lines of neoliberal values—those who should be entitled to government support in order to be recuperated into (an approximation to) the normal, responsible citizen and those who are not entitled because they are completely beyond recuperation in constituting failures of self-governance. These ideas are useful in interrogating 'the ways bodies are differentially produced' (Fritsch, 2015: p. 33) and in turn how this results in 'differential inclusions and exclusions of disabled people who are not all equally oppressed' (ibid.: p. 38).

Ultimately, not *all* disabled people are equally entitled to the positive entitlements that can come from being recognised as disabled. There is a bifurcation of disability—for some, disability can be celebrated through access to individual disability rights that restore one to a position of relative privilege, whereas for others (including criminalised disabled people) disability is part of a messier combination of deprivation that positions individuals as undeserving of recognition of full citizenship and access to resources. This bifurcation matters because it challenges the assumption (which seems to underpin the support for court diversion) that explicit inclusion of disability in law can only be equally positive for all disabled people in giving them access to political and material entitlements. For those whose disability is abjected by reason of their criminality and other circumstances, invoking disability in law can actually be directed towards singling them out in order to subject them to control and violence, and the citizenship, liberty and resources they do access are utterly depleted in being provisional by reason of their coercive context.

McWhorter argues that sociological identity categories and related hierarchies distract us from a more complex analysis at the coalescence of circumstances that is positioned as degeneracy against the singular undifferentiated notion of fitness. Identity politics necessarily creates abjected undersides in all categories—such as, the degenerate queer, or degenerate black—those that cannot meet the terms of acceptance of those identities and whose conduct undermines political claims to entitlement based on normality (rather than more radical demands for acceptance of maladaptation (McWhorter, 2009: pp. 294–331)). Moreover, drawing on Razack's argument that Indigenous and First Nations people are necessarily positioned as unfit and, indeed, as waste which gets in the way of settler colonial modernity (Razack, 2015), Indigenous and First Nations criminalised disabled people are seen as exemplars of degenerates. In her genealogy of degeneracy in Anglo-America, McWhorter (2009) suggests that while terminology might change, over time the populations who are categorised as degenerate continue to capture the same groups of people—those who are from racial and sexual minorities, poor, disabled and criminals—and that individuals from these populations only come to escape degenerate status by approximating the normal rather than having their difference accepted.

I suggest that our starting point for making sense of this bifurcation in the context of court diversion is that criminalised disabled people can be understood in terms of Foucault's notion of 'degeneracy'—as individuals who resist recuperation not only into normative ways of being abled but also (recognised ways) of being *disabled*. In a contemporary context, criminalised disabled people continue to be seen in terms of degeneracy (see Erevelles, 2011; Joseph, 2014, 2015; see also Tam, 2017). In his analysis of deportation appeal cases from the Canadian Immigration and Refugee Board related to criminalised disabled people, Joseph refers to 'the ongoing reliance on notions of the biologically inferior or untreatable, the unrehabilitatable criminal, and the undeserving alien'. Joseph says that this approach to these individuals (which resonates with the Foucauldian notion of 'degenerate') 'redirects responsibility solely toward the individual, a notion of inherent criminality, dehumanized and deserving of punishment, and a reproduction of the Other represented in terms of lack, who is not "one of us" or deserving of our support or care' (Joseph, 2015: p. 16).

Understanding criminalised disabled people in terms of degeneracy then means that our analysis of court diversion is not limited to a siloed focus on disability but can begin to make sense of the very particular circumstances that criminalised disabled people experience as integral to their exposure to interlocking forces and dynamics of oppression, rather than merely incidental to or a by-product of pure disabled oppression. In turn, we are not so much focused on court diversion in terms of controlling criminalised disabled people's conduct as an end in itself but, rather, to how this control enacts a form of scientific racist violence (in the Foucauldian 'species' sense) directed towards reducing their threat to the population as a whole.

I suggest that degeneracy is also useful for understanding how oppression through court diversion is accommodated in law *and* politically tolerated in society. Because their circumstances sit outside identity categories, control and violence against diverted criminalised disabled people is not comprehensible in terms of identity politics and in terms of legal understandings of discrimination, and hence can be sustained even as we claim to be respectful of equality on the basis of disability, gender, race, sexuality etc. Contesting oppression of criminalised disabled people, including through court diversion, requires direct engagement with degeneracy (rather than a narrower focus on disability, or other identity categories).

Building on the Foucauldian notion of 'degeneracy', ideas of 'debility' (developed by Puar, Fritsch and Dowse) and 'inclusionism' (developed by Snyder and Mitchell) are useful in understanding how disabled people come to be bifurcated along the lines of criminality which in turn exacerbates criminalised disabled people's oppression. Critical race and queer scholar Puar challenges the binary divide of 'disability' and 'ability'. Instead, she argues that disabled people are subjected to 'differential and uneven precarity' (Puar, 2017: p. 73) by reason of processes of 'debility' and 'capacity' that modulate the impact of their disablement on their lives. In short, 'debility' is a process of positioning populations in an ongoing state of precarity *through* disability—of systemic deprivation and violence, 'the slow wearing down of populations'. In contrast, 'capacity' (which holds a very different meaning to mental or legal capacity as discussed in Chapter 2) refers to the process through which certain disabled individuals can enjoy individualised, disability rights-based identity. Puar argues that debilitation does not occur by chance or because of some inherent characteristics of certain populations, but rather is a deliberate practice that 'create[s] and precaritize[s] populations and maintain[s] them as such' (ibid.: p. 73). By reason of these two processes, Puar argues that 'disability is not a fixed state or attribute but exists in relation to assemblages of capacity and debility, modulated across historical time, geopolitical space, institutional mandates, and discursive regimes' (ibid.: p. xiv).

Situating disabled people in the context of these processes of debility and capacity, Puar explains that, for some, disability is an unexpected, isolated event: an accident that disrupts their identity rather than being part of who they are: an 'exceptional attribute of an otherwise fortunate life' (ibid.: p. xix). For these individuals, the impacts of disability can be mitigated because the individual can be 'capacitated' through access to white privilege and resources (ibid.: pp. 65–68). However, 'only certain privileged disabled bodies can occupy' this position of the capacitated disabled subject (ibid.: p. 14). In contrast, for other disabled people, 'disability is a product—not a by-product, but a deliberate product—of exploitative labor conditions, racist incarceration and policing practices, militarization, and other modes of community disenfranchisement' (ibid.: 65). For these individuals, disability is 'within the body by reason of other markers of race, class and religion' (ibid.: p. 65). This latter group of disabled people are 'sustained in a perpetual state of *debilitation* precisely through foreclosing the social, cultural, and political translation to disability' because their disability will never become a politicised identity of disability that comes with entitlements and full rights (ibid.: p. xiv, emphasis added). Puar argues that domestic legal and international human rights regimes stratify disabled populations by modulating access to resources and rights on the one hand and precarity on the other (ibid.: p. xx, see also p. 73). This then means that certain disabled individuals can achieve entitlements and rights in the context of a broader unexceptional—and, in fact, endemic—debility that affects the majority of disabled people, notably those who are racialised and criminalised (ibid.: p. xvi; see also Tam, 2013).

Whereas Puar explores bifurcation in terms of other identity positions and the material and geopolitical conditions in which disabled people live, Mitchell and Snyder consider bifurcation of disabled populations by reference to neoliberal values of productivity and self-regulation. They argue that inclusion of disabled people under conditions of neoliberalism is a form of 'grudging recognition' insofar as disabled people are conditionally included in contemporary society on the basis that they will conform to norms of 'ablebodiedness, rationality, and heteronormativity' (Mitchell & Snyder, 2014: p. 2). Mitchell and Snyder propose the concept of 'inclusionism'—that is, government rights rhetoric that prioritises 'inclusion' of disabled people in ways that ultimately continue to exclude and degrade disabled people who are not of value in neoliberal terms. They state (ibid.: p. 14): '[i]nclusionism requires that disability be tolerated as long as it does not demand an excessive degree of change from relatively inflexible institutions, environments, and norms of belonging' (see also in the context of access to disability group homes: Spagnuolo, 2016). These ideas of bifurcation, neoliberal recuperation, white privilege and abjection have also been taken up by queer scholars (such as Haritaworn, 2015; Spade, 2015; Spade & Rohlfs, 2016), who have argued that inclusion in neoliberalism privileges certain bodies capable of recuperation at the same time that these respectable identities are constituted by the abjection of others which reifies their structural deprivation and violence. Through these ideas we can begin to think about how 'rights' on the basis of disability for criminalised disabled people become qualified, depleted or conditional on attempts to recuperate into respectability. Indeed, this might even be useful in making sense of the ambivalence in the CRPD towards criminalised disabled people I discussed in Section 2.3.

Court diversion as debilitating

This chapter has provided an analytical framework for reconsidering court diversion, from which has emerged a new way to understand it in terms of biopolitical control and violence. Theoretical ideas of debility, capacity and inclusionism direct us to the possibility that criminalised disabled people are not simply in the criminal justice system by chance; rather, this is part of a larger picture of material deprivation and violence under structural conditions of settler colonialism, neoliberalism and capitalism. To this end, Puar (2017: pp. 80–81) identifies criminalised disabled people as one such population that is debilitated. Dowse (2018: p. 7) also sees criminalised disabled people as debilitated because they are 'largely understood to fall outside neoliberal expectations of self-management and self-reliance'. Dowse elaborates on this in the context of a close consideration of the circumstances of two criminalised disabled people—Jack and Casey. These individuals are 'simultaneously racialized, gendered, class and ultimately criminalised' but 'discourses of disability identity and empowerment are absent' (ibid.: p. 5):

> Jack and Casey are drawn in to 'disability' by institutional diagnostic designation while at the same time remain beyond the reach of an emancipatory politics of disability. Instead they are subject to a systematic and patterned regime of incapacitation linked to their transgressive behaviour and social disadvantage which draws them in to discrete sites of debilitation which extend from child protection residential care, to the school, the psychiatric hospital, the disability group home and ultimately the prison.
>
> (Dowse, 2018: p. 6)

Yet, pushing beyond the work of Puar and Dowse, the analysis in this chapter suggests that *law* has a particularly pernicious role in debilitation of criminalised disabled people. By effecting a shift in the legal subjectivity of criminalised individuals, from a criminal legal subject known and acted upon by reference to the criminal offence to a disabled legal subject known and acted upon by reference to their disability, the legal framework of court diversion opens up an additional mode of control and violence specifically of criminalised disabled people who are appearing before the court on criminal charges and who would otherwise be only exposed to the possibility of coercive interventions associated with bail and sentence.

The legal framework of court diversion can never 'capacitate' criminalised disabled people into full citizenship, because criminalised disabled people are necessarily viewed in terms of degeneracy that per se makes possible violence and precarity (Spivakovsky, 2018; Steele, 2017a; Voronka, 2013: p. 318). Moreover, access to resources through court diversion is conditional on subjection to control and violence in an overarching legal framework explicitly based on situating them outside of criminal legal liberal citizenship and, hence, does not capacitate those who are diverted into free-market consumers exercising choice and control over their disability and mental health services and, ultimately, their bodies and lives.

As well as its impacts on the individuals who are diverted, the legal framework of court diversion notably has biopolitical effects at a population level. One effect is that criminalised disabled people as a population can be moved into additional legal, material and bureaucratic spaces of control. Another effect relates to the legal framework facilitating service access via control and violence. In a neoliberal context of self-directed funding and consumer choice, court diversion bifurcates disabled populations along lines of criminality and, in so doing, removes the opportunity for self-direction and choice from criminalised disabled people by coupling their purported access to liberty, resources and inclusion with carceral control. Court diversion stratifies disabled populations in a post-deinstitutionalisation era to sustain the ongoing inequality and relative deprivation and precarity of those who are criminalised even in the face of disability rights.

I now briefly consider the implications of court diversion for criminalised disabled people who are not diverted. This is important because only a minority of criminalised disabled people are ever diverted. I argue that the use of diversion in special cases legitimates, or naturalises, the usual path of criminal legal intervention for others. Noting that, as Fritsch (2015: p. 14) states, '[b]odies are neither solely capacitated nor debilitated: there are graduations of debility and capacity', law also consolidates debilitation and slow death through retaining legal frameworks enabling the recurrent incarceration of the majority of criminalised disabled people. Court diversion legitimates criminal legal coercive intervention through the former's subsidiary relationship to the latter because it is only available to individuals who are lawfully within the criminal legal domain by reason of being charged with a criminal offence, and hence affirms the authority of the court per se to ultimately decide the individual should be subjected to criminal legal coercive intervention. The test for court diversion generally hinges on the appropriateness of diversion on an individual basis, thus, implicitly affirming the appropriateness of criminal legal diversion at a general and structural level. Last, individuals can be returned to the trajectory for criminal legal intervention if they breach their court diversion orders, thus affirming the legitimacy of criminal legal intervention even for those who were initially diverted on the basis that criminal legal intervention was less appropriate. I explore this further in Chapters 6 and 7.

A further political implication for criminalised disabled people more broadly is that court diversion does not transform at a structural level interlocking forces and dynamics of oppression. In general, even individual rights-based interventions do not disrupt structural disadvantage and violence (Spade, 2011: p. 29). Yet, this is even more impossible in a criminal justice context which will only ever deal with individuals' specific circumstances and within a framework that pathologises them as the problem and 'solves' this problem through intervention in and confinement of that individual. This problem was intimated by some of the criticisms of court diversion discussed in Chapter 2. However, I push further here and argue that court diversion cannot transform interlocking forces and dynamics of oppression specifically in a settler colonial context because it is premised on the pathologisation of Indigenous and First Nations criminalised disabled people and the vindication of settler colonial society and law as rescuer (Razack, 2015; see also Bond, 2017).

The argument I've developed in this chapter that court diversion is a mode of biopower through which law debilitates criminalised disabled people provides a strong basis for problematising the general lack of CRPD jurisprudence on court diversion and criminal justice issues beyond a focus on disability-specific issues, which I discussed in Chapter 2. The CRPD's focus on 'disability-specific' confinement and interventions arguably works to 'capacitate' disabled people who only experience pure disability discrimination, while leaving in a state of debility those criminalised disabled people whose experiences of discrimination, violence and inequality are part of broader structural conditions of deprivation and violence. The overwhelming focus on 'disability-specific' confinement in the CRPD and its jurisprudence creates a hierarchy of entitlement that privileges the liberty and safety of non-criminalised disabled people, while legitimating the confinement of and violence against criminalised disabled people, who continue to be confined in prison or subject to other criminal legal interventions. Ultimately, the prison endures the disruptive and transformative disability-specific abolitionist possibilities in the CRPD to continue to be a legitimate space of confinement and violence for disabled people. The (much celebrated) CRPD focus on abolishing disability-specific coercive confinement might have the contradictory effect of *sustaining* the (non-disability-specific) incarceration of criminalised disabled people in prison. Indeed, one could argue that the right to 'legal capacity' (in the CRPD sense of the word 'capacity') serves to 'capacitate' (in the Puar sense) those individuals who have relative access to white privilege. A focus on abolishing pure disability discrimination in the criminal justice context as might follow from the CRPD prevents a broader and necessary critique of the violence of the criminal justice system (see similar argument by Fritsch (2015: p. 39) in the context of workplace inclusion). My theorising of court diversion in this chapter thus has implications not only for how we engage with criminal law to contest disabled oppression, but also for how we engage with disability human rights, suggesting that these might very well be a source of oppression (or at least unhelpful in contesting oppression) for criminalised disabled people.

Chapter 4

Theorising court diversion

Carcerality and legality

4.1 Situating court diversion in a broader legal context

This chapter argues that the debilitation of criminalised disabled people (who may not be sentenced, or even convicted) through court diversion is represented in law as necessary, non-violent, non-colonial and just. The chapter makes this argument by moving beyond a focus on the inner workings of court diversion itself to situate it in broader dynamics of control, violence and injustice across criminal legal, criminal justice and disability and mental health systems. Understanding this wider context is vital to appreciating the full complexity of the political implications of court diversion, and to developing strategies that can address oppression of criminalised disabled people through and beyond court diversion (particularly oppression in which law is complicit). In making these arguments about law's role in controlling criminalised disabled people, it is vital to emphasise that I am not making universal claims about law's role in coercion and regulation. Rather, I am making a very particular argument specifically about the nature of and justifications for the carceral, psychiatric, and medical control of criminalised disabled people and highlighting the discriminatory, violent and unjust effects specifically of this control.

Section 4.2 introduces theoretical ideas about carcerality. These ideas disrupt the conventional view of prison as the primary site for control and infringement of liberal rights. Ideas about 'carcerality' refer to the exercise of power and prison-like control through diverse systems and sites (rather than exclusively through prison). The discussion begins with an introduction to the concept of 'carceral' and the carceral 'continuum' or 'archipelago' by reference to Foucault and disability carceral scholarship. I draw on these ideas to show how law through court diversion facilitates the movement of criminalised disabled people into the institutional archipelago and elides the violence and injustice of prison *and* disability and mental health services through the particular relation it sets up between them.

The chapter then shifts in Section 4.3 to situate court diversion more explicitly in a legal context. Here, I draw on theoretical ideas related to legality (that is, political legitimacy derived from law) in order to argue that law's debilitation of criminalised disabled people through court diversion is politically tolerated, even though it exceeds what is possible for non-criminalised disabled people and non-disabled criminalised people, and so clearly occurs outside of the conventional legal limits of criminal legal intervention. In this discussion, I foreground colonialism—a dynamic too frequently overlooked in scholarship on court diversion, disability criminal justice and even the CRPD—by arguing that court diversion renders debilitation through law 'non-colonial' because of its purportedly therapeutic focus, thus effacing acknowledgement of the structural injustice and violence to Indigenous and First Nations criminalised disabled people from the criminal justice system and pursuant to criminal law.

4.2 'Carcerality': court diversion at the nexus of disability-specific and criminal legal coercive intervention

Building on the argument that court diversion itself enables control, here I propose that court diversion additionally facilitates movement of criminalised disabled people between modes, sites and legal domains which contributes to their control (and thus debilitation) over the course of their life and beyond the specific term of the diversion order. By illuminating the role of law in sustaining criminalised disabled people's lifelong exposure to control, this chapter makes a novel contribution to the growing scholarship on disability and carceral control.

The chapter illustrates what is at stake in law's role in this movement by explaining the concept of the 'carceral', which recognises sites other than the prison as sites of control that constitute a 'continuum' or 'archipelago'. As such, court diversion can be understood as facilitating movement of criminalised disabled people *between* criminal legal and disability-specific modes, sites and legal domains of carceral control. Court diversion's debilitation extends to its kinetic quality in making possible and legitimating legal connections between otherwise separate systems and then moving individuals between these systems. This kinetic quality exemplifies how court diversion facilitates perpetration of 'slow death' in relation to criminalised disabled people by diffusing, fracturing and prolonging its effects across space and time.

For Foucault, power does not operate within the confined boundaries of a specific space of confinement (such as the prison). Rather, '[p]ower relations are rooted in the whole network of the social' (Foucault, 2000: p. 345). 'Carceral' refers to a quality of coercion which is prison-like but is not synonymous with the prison or with sentenced penalty (Foucault, 1979: pp. 296–297). These ideas are in contrast to a conventional approach, wherein coercive control is viewed in terms of a hierarchy that positions criminal legal coercive intervention (notably in prison) as the ultimate form of control. In the conventional approach, other modes of controlling individuals become incomprehensible or insignificant because, in their juxtaposition to the prison as the absolute form of control, they become associated with liberty.

Taking a historical approach, Foucault proposed that the carceral system was completed with the opening in 1840 of Mettray, a French institution for children that confined 'young delinquents condemned by the courts', 'minors who had been charged, but acquitted under article 66 of the code, and boarders held … as an alternative to paternal correction' (Foucault, 1979: p. 296). In holding diverse groups of individuals rather than convicted prisoners, Mettray was a 'punitive model' but was 'at the limit of strict penality'. Foucault proposed that Mettray was one of a 'whole series of institutions which, well beyond the frontiers of criminal law, constituted what one might call the *carceral archipelago*' (ibid.: pp. 296–297, emphasis added). Foucault argued that within nineteenth-century French society there was a 'carceral network' consisting of prisons and institutional spaces that adopted the 'prison model' but that also extended to mechanisms that use 'carceral methods' and 'all the disciplinary mechanisms that function throughout society' (ibid.: p. 298). The carceral archipelago 'transported the [penitentiary technique] from the penal institution to the entire social body' (ibid.). Foucault's concept of the carceral archipelago draws attention to the possibility that coercive control can occur within and across a variety of institutions of confinement, as well as outside of these spaces, and can permeate social relations more broadly.

Foucault identified some important effects of the carceral system. One of these effects is a 'carceral continuum' of 'diffused penitentiary techniques' across society enabling the seamless movement of individuals between spaces, modes and rationales of control: the carceral archipelago 'established a slow, continuous, imperceptible gradation that made it possible to pass naturally from disorder to offence and back from a transgression of the law to a slight departure from a rule, an average, a demand, a norm' (ibid.: p. 298) and brought together the 'multiple dangers of disorder, crime and madness' (ibid.: pp. 299–300). A second important effect of the carceral system which Foucault identified is that control does not reside in one specific institution. Rather, Foucault argued, 'there is no outside'. The carceral network:

> takes back with one hand what it seems to exclude with the other … In this panoptic society of which incarceration is the omnipresent armature, the delinquent is not outside the law; he is, from the very outset, in the law, at the very heart of the law, or at least in the midst of those mechanisms that transfer the individual imperceptibly from discipline to the law, from deviation to offence.
>
> (Foucault, 1979: p. 301)

A third important effect of the carceral system identified by Foucault is that 'the carceral system and … its extension beyond legal imprisonment … succeeds in making the power to punish natural and legitimate, in lowering at least the threshold of tolerance to penality' (ibid.: p. 301). Foucault argued that this occurred through the counterbalancing of 'the legal register of justice' (what we would see as criminal legal intervention in the form of sentenced incarceration) and 'the extra-legal register of discipline' (ibid.: p. 301). On the one hand, the disciplinary mechanisms receive legal sanction in being juxtaposed with prison, which in turn 'avoids any element of excess or abuse it may entail' (ibid.: p. 302). On the other hand, the 'subtle gradation of the apparatuses of discipline and of the successive "embeddings" that they involve' has the effect of negating the violence of prison, because the difference between prison and other forms of discipline becomes one of degree rather than kind (ibid.). The sum of this counterbalancing is a 'strict economy' of power that 'render[s] as discreet as possible the singular power to punish' (ibid.).

A fourth point raised by Foucault relates to the 'failure' of prison. Shifting from an analysis of the functionality of the prison to a 'general economy of power' (Foucault, 2004e: p. 117), Foucault states that 'the real history of the prison is undoubtedly not governed by its successes and failures of its functionality, but is in fact inserted within strategies and tactics that find support even in these functional defects themselves' (ibid.: pp. 117–118). This suggests that carceral control through court diversion emerges *against* and *through* the limitations—and, indeed, even perceived failures—of the prison (a point I explore in further detail in Chapter 7).

Drawing in part on Foucault's theorising, Harcourt (2006: p. 1784) has empirically studied the movement of disabled people in America between prisons and mental health facilities proposing that: 'It may be time, then, to rethink the category of confinement through the larger lens of institutionalization and to begin to trace that broader history of institutional incapacitation in twentieth century United States'. In a similar vein and particularly relevant for our purposes, there is a growing body of scholarship that has engaged with Foucault's concept of carceral in the specific context of disability institutions—what I refer to as 'disability carceral scholarship'. This disability carceral scholarship displaces the prison as the exclusive or primary site of control of disabled people and, implicitly (although this is not so clearly developed in the scholarship itself), displaces criminal law and sentencing as the only legal regime of control of criminalised disabled people. This scholarship illuminates the 'carceral' or controlling quality of a broader range of sites, such as disability group homes, mental health facilities and special education schools. Many of these sites are particular to disabled people and are typically viewed as therapeutic, benign and even empowering. This has been referred to as the 'institutional archipelago':

> We are nuancing [Foucault's term 'carceral archipelago'] slightly to call it an 'institutional archipelago', made up of diverse services and spaces that all trace back to undifferentiated confinement and its ongoing reform—in which penalty is no more or less central than medical care or the right to education.
> (Chapman, Carey & Ben-Moshe, 2014: p. 14; see also Ben-Moshe, 2011; Ben-Moshe & Meiners, 2014)

Carey, Ben-Moshe and Chapman explain that understanding the institutional archipelago is not only attentive to a pure focus on disability but rather to disability in a context of interlocking forces and dynamics of oppression:

> Disability, situated alongside other key lines of stratification such as race, class, nationality, and gender, is central to understanding the complex, varied and interlocking ways in which incarceration occurs and is made out to be normal, natural, politically necessary, and beneficial. Sites of incarceration, such as medical institutions, nursing homes, and prisons, emerge and take shape in interaction with each other as various populations are sorted, identified, and treated according to rationalities and practices which, while different in many ways, all mark certain people as deviant and thus justify controlling what they can and cannot do.
>
> (Carey, Ben-Moshe & Chapman, 2014: p. x)

The institutional archipelago is useful in illuminating the interrelationships of control and segregation between contemporary disability care and support and prisons and other mainstream systems such as child welfare, education and immigration detention (see, for example, Ben-Moshe, Chapman & Carey, 2014; Joseph, 2015). This scholarship shows that disabled people can be confined in a number of different sites. Some individuals are confined across a number of these, at times with a seamless legal and systems transition between them. These ideas of the institutional archipelago mean that carceral control of disabled people is not tethered to particular material architectural spaces—such as the prison or the mental health facility. Indeed, sometimes the control might reside in the disabled person's body. For example, Fabris argues that psycho-pharmaceuticals that act as 'chemical restraints' confine individuals from within their bodies (Fabris, 2011; Fabris & Aubrecht, 2014) and Hatch has argued that psycho-pharmaceuticals facilitate transinstitutionalisation (Hatch, 2019; Hatch et al., 2015). In earlier work, I have argued that the attribution of 'disability' itself becomes carceral, such that this possibility of control travels dormant in the individual across space, to be activated through different legal, material and institutional settings (Steele, 2017a; 2018d). This book draws on these ideas to trace the ongoing relevance of carceral control to disability law (as compared to Unsworth (1991) who argues we are now in a 'post-carceral' era).

Similar to the institutional archipelago, Disability Justice activist Mia Mingus has proposed the term 'medical industrial complex' (MIC) to capture the interrelationships of diverse sites and forms of control, as well as to draw out the significance of capitalism and profit to the sustenance and growth of this complex. As Mingus explains, the MIC:

> is an enormous system with tentacles that reach beyond simply doctors, nurses, clinics, and hospitals. It is a system about profit, first and foremost, rather than 'health', wellbeing and care. Its roots run deep and its history and present are connected to everything including eugenics, capitalism, colonization, slavery, immigration, war, prisons, and reproductive oppression. It is not just a major piece of the history of ableism, but *all* systems of oppression.
>
> (Mingus, 2015; original emphasis)

The MIC enables the 'systematic targeting of oppressed communities under the guise of care, health and safety' (Mingus, 2015). The various components of the MIC are interconnected and overlapping (ibid.) and it has included within it the 'mental health industry', 'state disability services and programs' and the 'prison industrial complex', which interconnects 'prisons, psychiatric wards, forced medicalization and institutionalization' as well as 'group homes' and 'public/private [mental health] institutions and services' (ibid.). Similar arguments have been made by queer scholars, who have explored the role of caring and psy professions in extending carceral reach beyond the prison, including in the specific context of trans people (Haritaworn, 2015; Spade, 2015). *Disability, Criminal Justice and Law* contributes to the scholarly and activist understanding of disability carceral control by highlighting the significance of court diversion *and law* to the exposure of criminalised disabled people to control across their life.

Chapman and colleagues argue that, across individuals' lives and across macro policy shifts, disabled people have been confined within and moved *between* sites of confinement, such that any 'freedom' from one site of confinement generally results in entry into and confinement in another (Chapman, Carey & Ben-Moshe, 2014). Resonating with Foucault's ideas of the productive possibilities of the failure of the prison, disability carceral scholarship shows how the 'failure' of prisons and of institutionalisation/deinstitutionalisation is used productively in the institutional archipelago to generate further modes of control, including through purportedly progressive solutions to the prison and the asylum (such as group homes or community treatment orders). Ben-Moshe has suggested that this endurance of disability control and segregation has occurred not simply irrespective of deinstitutionalisation but actually *through* deinstitutionalisation. This has occurred through the subversion of the *failure* of deinstitutionalisation. Disabled people are pathologised as the cause of deinstitutionalisation's failures and ultimately the solution is, perversely, a return to control and intervention of some kind, notably coercive mental health treatment and confinement (Ben-Moshe, 2017). I propose that my analysis of the legal framework of court diversion exemplifies these temporal dynamics of carceral control, in terms of justifications both for diversion of specific individuals and the necessity of the legal framework itself.

Recent scholarship has considered this institutional archipelago in the context of ideas of debility, suggesting that 'capturing' individuals in this network is itself debilitating. Referring to the MIC, Puar notes that for 'institutionalized, incarcerated, racialized' populations 'claiming the term and identity of disability is difficult given many are already stigmatized as nonnormative, and deemed in need of fixing by the medical-industrial complex' (Puar, 2017: p. 15). Dowse has observed in the context of 'Jack' and 'Casey' (see Chapter 3) that this institutional archipelago does not merely sustain people's control but also 'cumulatively and inexorably lead[s] to their incapacitation via protective, biomedical (physical and chemical), disability and carceral institutionalisation' and contributes to their debilitation, a 'slow death' (Dowse, 2018: pp. 4–5).

My argument on court diversion advances and enriches these theoretical claims about disability carceral control in three ways. One is that court diversion can be understood as facilitating movement of criminalised disabled people *between* criminal legal and disability-specific modes, sites *and legal domains* of carceral control. Often the diversion court order will enable longer term control through disability and mental health services by utilising civil mental health or guardianship legal systems (see, for example, hospital and guardianship orders in jurisdictions such as England, or diversion in New South Wales). Importantly, this movement around the archipelago through court diversion is not unidirectional. Court diversion also enables seamless movement of individuals from disability-specific back to criminal legal intervention, with many schemes having breach provisions that enable charges to be reinstated if individuals do not comply with the diversion order. Further, disability and mental health services might channel individuals back into the criminal justice system, either by reporting individuals for offending within the service (such as property damage) or by utilising police to 'retrieve' individuals who have 'absconded' or who are not complying with community treatment orders (while not a criminal offence in itself, contact with police can result in offences during the police interaction) (McCausland & Baldry, 2017; Steele, 2017a; 2018c). My analysis also contributes to advancing our understanding of the 'institutional archipelago' by suggesting the contribution of international human rights law to disability carceral control. I propose that the CRPD also sustains the criminal legal dimensions of the 'institutional archipelago' because it does not adequately attend to the prison and to the connections between mainstream and disability-specific modes and spaces of control. Indeed, Golder, in his analysis of Foucault's strategic use of human rights, proposes that Foucault did not deploy human rights in his opposition to the death penalty because even if abolition occurred this would 'stop … short of critically engaging the penal apparatus that nourishes it' (Golder, 2015: p. 143, see further pp. 143–146).

The second implication is that, to the extent that it provides a new legal basis for control of criminalised disabled people *and* creates new connections or conduits between prison and disability and mental health services, court diversion does not so much solve as maintain the systems that sustain disabled incarceration. On a related note, I would argue that the particular archipelagic relationship between prison and disability and mental health services in court diversion actually works to obscure the violence of each. Court diversion has been recommended as a way to prevent criminalised disabled people becoming victims of violence in prison. Yet, my discussion above of the violence of disability-specific intervention gives rise to an odd and troubling contradiction. Broadly, mental health and disability services are sites of coercion and violence, and yet these very sites are the protective, safe and therapeutic location to which diverted individuals will be delivered from the harmfulness of the criminal justice system and prison. There is a curious circularity at play here, where the answer to the injustice of prison rests in the very institutions which are perpetrating violence in a more concentrated manner specifically in relation to disabled people—any possible *injustice* in the use of coercive intervention in these other settings becomes erased in this circularity by reason of their 'rescuing' role vis-a-vis the prison. Moreover, in moving specific individuals out of prison, the violence and harm of prison becomes contained within specific individuals (who are moved) and thus cleanses the prison of any violence residing in its very structure.

Retrieving excess through court diversion

Disability, Criminal Justice and Law contributes to our understanding of the legal dynamics of disabled carceral control by illuminating that the legal framework of court diversion serves a very particular purpose in the institutional archipelago—it can retrieve individuals who are beyond control through both criminal legal coercive intervention *and* voluntary engagement with disability and mental health services in the community. This occurs through the process of 'doubling' that creates an additional legal basis for coercive intervention.

Foucault acknowledged that 'all disciplinary power has its margins' (Foucault, 2008a: p. 53). That is, necessarily, there will be 'the unclassifiable'; in other words, '[d]isciplinary systems ... which classify, hierarchize, supervise, and so on, come up against those who cannot be classified, those who escape supervision, those who cannot enter the system of distribution, in short, the residual, the irreducible, the unclassifiable, the unassimilable' (ibid.). Indeed, Foucault identifies the 'mentally ill' as 'the residue of all residues' (ibid.: p. 54). This barrier to discipline of residual individuals is overcome through the generation of further modes of disciplinary regulation, which classify this residue as a specific phenomenon (rather than being random and unknowable outliers) and, in so doing, transform this excess into its own disciplinary category.

And at this point, the relational quality of discipline enters the analysis. This is because, for Foucault (ibid.), discipline is 'isotopic', consisting of a number of supplementary disciplinary systems characterised by the limits of other disciplinary categories, which are capable of 'retrieving' residual individuals in order to make their disciplinary regulation possible—thus entailing 'the appearance of supplementary disciplinary systems in order to retrieve these individuals, and so on to infinity' (ibid.). Foucault describes this as disciplinary power's 'double property' of 'anomizing' by 'always discarding certain individuals, bringing anomie, the irreducible to light' and, on the other hand, 'normalizing' by 'inventing ever new recovery systems, always reestablishing the rule'. Disciplinary power is characterised by 'the never-ending work of the norm in the anomic' (ibid.).

Critical disability scholars have identified the 'excessive' nature of the disabled subject, both the excessive nature of the disabled body per se (Erevelles, 2011; Shildrick, 2009) and the recalcitrance of disabled people in relation to specific disciplinary systems (for example, in the context of education: see Erevelles, 2011; Goodley, Runswick-Cole & Liddiard, 2016: p. 776; Watts & Erevelles, 2004). We can draw on these ideas to understand court diversion as subsidiary to criminal law, because it is in an isotopic relation to criminal legal intervention. Court diversion applies only to some criminalised disabled people (noting only a minority are diverted) because it is only designed to capture those criminalised disabled individuals who will be more effectively controlled through disability and mental health services as compared to conventional criminal legal intervention. Psy knowledge and professionals play an important role in giving scientific validity to this 'excess' as its own disciplinary category, through the work they do in explaining this excess to criminal legal intervention in terms of individual pathology. Criminal legal intervention is the default and, if this will be effective, then court diversion is not necessary—ultimately, court diversion is a matter of effective control, not of humane relief. Moreover, the coercive nature of disability and mental health service use in court diversion might actually serve to retrieve individuals who have themselves resisted or been rejected from voluntary disability and mental health service use in the community, because there is now a court order in place requiring their compliance with services (see also Spivakovsky, 2014a; 2014b). In a similar vein, writing in the context of HIV/AIDS and public health orders, Carter (2016) has discussed the way in which subjects who do not conform to treatment and services can then be positioned as in need of legal regulation to coerce their engagement and can be confined or forcibly treated through public health legislation.

Foucault's ideas about 'doubling' *through* psychiatric knowledge are useful for understanding how court diversion facilitates movement around the institutional archipelago, that is, transformation of criminalised disabled individuals from a criminal legal subject to a disabled legal subject of court diversion. This is important because, once we shift our focus from the inner workings of court diversion itself to how it fits in the bigger picture of control, we must grapple with the fact that subjects of court diversion begin as criminal legal subjects, on the trajectory of trial, conviction and sentence. Foucault argued that psychiatric knowledge has an important role in the criminal context. In his lecture on expert psychiatric opinion in French penal cases, Foucault (2003a) discusses the ways in which psychiatric expertise is central to knowing individuals with mental illness in a manner that makes their criminal legal regulation possible. He makes this argument in specific relation to a provision of the French Penal Code that excuses criminal responsibility on the basis of madness at the time of the offence. He refers to these as 'doublings' of psychiatric expertise and criminal law. By 'doublings', Foucault (ibid.: p. 14) suggests that 'what is involved is not really a game of replacements but the introduction of successive doubles', that is, ways in which psychiatric knowledge provides new possibilities for criminal law to act on individuals that replace existing models of offender, offence and judge.

The first of the three doublings is the doubling of the offence with criminality (ibid.: pp. 15–16). Through this doubling, the actions constituting the *actus reus* of the offence are transformed into a general pattern of conduct or a 'way of being', such that it appears as the offence but in a generalised form (ibid.: p. 16). The second doubling, which Foucault (ibid.: pp. 18–21) argues occurs once the psychiatric expert has doubled the offence with criminality, is the doubling of the author of the offence with a general delinquent character. Psychiatric expert opinion achieves this through 'recount[ing] a series of what could be called misdeeds that do not break the law, or faults that are not illegal', with the aim of showing 'how the individual already resembles his crime before he has committed it' (ibid.: p. 19). In this way, 'a whole series of illegalities below the threshold [of the crime], of improper acts that are not illegal, [are piled up] in order to make them resemble the crime itself' (ibid.: p. 19). This then means that the object of coercive intervention by the judge is no longer the offence but, rather, the 'irregular forms of conduct that were put forward as the crime's cause and point of origin and the site at which it took shape' (ibid.: p. 17). The third doubling, doubling the psychiatric expert into a judge and the judge into a doctor, means that the judge has the role of acting on the individual's irregular forms of conduct rather than acting on a specific offence, and they defer to the views of the psychiatric expert concerning control of the individual. This represents a shift from coercive intervention by reference to a particular offence to the normalisation of the individual (ibid.: pp. 25). These ideas of 'doubling' help us in understanding specifically how court diversion as a legal mechanism facilitates movement around the institutional archipelago, from a trajectory heading towards one 'island' of criminal legal intervention towards other 'islands' of control through disability and mental health services.

Thus, through court diversion law does not only augment the institutional archipelago—it has a very specific role in retrieving individuals who exceed criminal justice and disability and mental health services within this archipelago.

Massification through 'overrepresentation'?

Court diversion is held out as a process that seeks to address the 'problem' of 'overrepresentation' of disabled people in the criminal justice system. How can we reconcile the debilitating effects of court diversion with its stated goal of reducing overrepresentation? Is it simply an unforeseen error of judgement in using court diversion to achieve this goal, or is it actually part of the very design of this problem? I ask this because reducing overrepresentation seems such a self-evidently important goal, one that even progressives are unlikely to challenge other than to critique the *methods* or *solutions* to achieve this goal. However, here I suggest that the framing of the problem itself is part of how the debility of court diversion becomes possible and legitimate. By this I mean that overrepresentation is not a natural, apolitical phenomenon that pre-dates what court diversion does; it is a constructed statistical problem and part of the larger way in which criminalised disabled people are subjected to biopolitical control and violence through law

The problem of overrepresentation, introduced in Section 1.2, provides that disabled people are in the criminal justice system at high numbers because they do not have access to disability and mental health services. Court diversion will provide access to these services for some who are overrepresented and, long term, will reduce overrepresentation as a collective phenomenon. Court diversion presumably then should have positive implications for criminalised disabled people beyond those who are diverted, insofar as it is widely understood as reducing overall numbers.

In contrast, I argue that overrepresentation constitutes 'massification' because all disabled people who are criminalised are brought together into one undifferentiated mass or group. If something is overrepresented, the problem is not that it exists at all or that it is a problem for each and every individual but, rather, that it is present at a level in excess of what is otherwise acceptable. In a context of a norm of criminality that is assumed capable of being brought to a state of homeostasis, criminalised disabled people become a 'problem population in need of normative intervention' (McGuire, 2015: p. 358). What is problematised (by reason of the 'over') is not that each individual is wrongly criminalised and incarcerated, or the existence of prisons per se, but rather that *too many* disabled people are criminalised (the implicit assumption being that it is possible to have an appropriate level of disabled people in the criminal justice system). In particular—recalling the discussion in Chapter 3 of massification as a strategy that makes people indiscernible as individuals—bringing overrepresentation down to acceptable levels of representation does not result in equal reduction of each disabled person's criminalisation and incarceration but, rather, will only have a positive impact on some while others will remain in the criminal justice system. Overrepresentation accepts incarceration per se so long as it is within acceptable limits (see similarly Foucault's discussion of illness and population: Foucault, 2004c: p. 62). Statistical analyses of criminality, then, enable 'development of policies that modify the conditions of life of the population in ways that manage criminality in the most cost-effective manner' (McLoughlin, 2012: p. 289), that is, 'within socially and economically acceptable limits and around an average that will be considered as optimal for a given social functioning' (Foucault, 2004a: p. 5).

Singling out disabled people as a particular group in the criminal justice system is not motivated by humanitarian sentiments of evacuating them en masse from the criminal justice system but, instead, may be understood as being motivated by a concern to single out those elements of the criminal justice population who are most out of line with the average: 'to try to reduce the most unfavourable, deviant normalities in relation to the normal, general curve, to bring them in line with this normal, general curve' (Foucault, 2004c: p. 60). Bringing individuals in line with each other does not eliminate the underlying phenomena of representation in the criminal justice system that they are being assessed against; instead, it just tries to ensure consistency between different groups (ibid.: p. 63). The 'ideal' outcome is to bring overall numbers in the criminal justice system back to an acceptable level.

Thus, court diversion as a response to overrepresentation can then be understood, at a population or systemic level, to be about regulating or managing the overall proportion of disabled people in the criminal justice system relative to their prevalence in the general population by moderating criminalised disabled people's presence in criminal legal processes and prisons, and access to disability and mental health services. Arguably, this equilibrating (Foucault, 1997c: p. 246) function of court diversion at the systemic level is reflected in the discretionary consideration of 'appropriateness' of court diversion that features in many court diversion schemes (discussed in Chapter 1), such that not everyone is diverted on the arbitrary basis of disability. Court diversion is one of a number of reform initiatives (including diversion at all stages of criminal justice trajectory, training of justice professionals, more services in prison) that, in combination, work to reduce overall numbers of those incarcerated but that ultimately, at the individual level, allow incarceration to continue (see, for example, the discussion of food scarcity in Foucault 2004b: pp. 36–43; see also discussion of Foucault's ideas in the context of population response to dead bodies in disaster in Johns, 2015: pp. 185–214).

The end result is that overrepresentation is premised on the (more efficient) continuation of the prison and criminal justice system *and* the more effective regulation of criminalised disabled people. The construction of the problem shuts down transformative possibilities of abolishing prisons because the focus is on what is excessive (in the sense of what is over, too much etc.), which confirms a baseline that will be tolerated (see similarly how 'cruel and unusual punishment' creates an economy of excessive and non-excessive state violence in prison: Dayan, 2007). Moreover, in the hyper-macro phenomenon of overrepresentation, the intricacies of the experiences and circumstances of specific individuals become lost and incomprehensible as sites of concern and intervention, thus circumventing accountability and ultimately dehumanising individuals (see discussion of deaths in custody as a statistical phenomenon in Razack, 2015: pp. 192–207).

As scholars and activists writing in relation to a variety of different contexts, including disabled, racialised and trans people, have highlighted, equality in a criminal justice context is impossible, because prisons and criminal justice systems are premised on and themselves generate inequality (Ben-Moshe, 2017; Ben-Moshe & Stewart, 2017; Dayan, 2011; Dayan, 2014; Lamble, 2011; Russell & Stewart, 2001; Ware, Ruzsa & Dias, 2014). Indeed, the concern with 'overrepresentation' is not matched by a concern with identifying privileged groups who are *underrepresented* such that these advantageous inequalities of privilege and white supremacy continue. This is alluded to by Wildeman (2018a) in the context of her discussion of the 'mental healthification' of prison. 'Overrepresentation' also hides iterative relationships between prison and disability. Overrepresentation of disabled people *in* the criminal justice system constructs 'disabled people' and 'criminal justice system' as separate and mutually exclusive phenomena, rather than as intertwined (Ben-Moshe, 2017; Puar, 2017; Ribet, 2010; Ware, Ruzsa & Dias, 2014). The 'problem' of overrepresentation is actually premised on a false assumption of equality within the criminal justice system (in the sense of equal representation). This premise is troubling insofar as it overlooks the structural inequalities of the criminal justice system as I have just outlined. It is also troubling insofar as overrepresentation is a key justification for court diversion laws, and thus this justification carries the myth of equality into the legal framework of court diversion itself.

Therefore, problematising disabled incarceration in terms of overrepresentation is not directed towards making everyone's life equally better by bringing about an end to, or even a reduction in, coercive intervention per se. Rather, as a form of massification, overrepresentation enables the multiplication and greater diversity of coercive options in the service of regulating criminalised disabled people more effectively. Massification through overrepresentation manages the equilibrium of the institutional archipelago at a population level while at the same time masking individual violation and injustice and sustaining the myth of equality.

4.3 'Legality': court diversion's relationship to criminal law and in/justice

The final aspect of my theoretical framework shifts to explore law's complicity in court diversion. While I have threaded an analysis of law throughout this and the previous chapter, in this section law takes centre stage. Here I squarely focus on how law accommodates control and violence through court diversion, specifically of criminalised disabled people, when this is so clearly outside of what is otherwise lawful and politically tolerated. This exploration of law in relation to disabled carceral control, violence and debilitation is a particularly significant contribution to disability carceral scholarship, disability human rights scholarship and advocacy, scholarship and Disability Justice activism.

In this section I show how court diversion is itself rendered through law as necessary, non-violent, non-colonial and just; how, conversely, court diversion shores up the legitimacy of criminal law; and how, ultimately, these two dynamics are inextricably entwined. In order to do so, I draw on ideas about 'legality'. 'Legality' has been defined by Golder and McLoughlin (2018, p. 2) as 'the particular type of political legitimacy that liberal states have traditionally drawn from the law'—recalling that, in Foucault's discussion, one of the key effects of the carceral network is to ensure nothing is outside of law, even if beyond sentenced penalty. Ideas about legality supplement this by focusing our attention on how legal authority is organised jurisdictionally, legislatively, procedurally and institutionally in order to politically neutralise, indeed valorise, the power and violence inherent in court diversion. There is, of course, a long and rich body of scholarship in political philosophy on legality, such as that by Schmidt, Benjamin and, more recently, Agamben (see McLoughlin, 2009; 2012). I am, instead, drawing on a more disparate range of ideas, drawn from different bodies of scholarship, because I find these more useful in exploring the relationships between legality, criminality and disability. Using ideas of legality, I interrogate how court diversion is positioned in law as *state-sanctioned*, and as apparently *non-violent, non-colonial* and *just*, and hence beyond the scope of *injustice* and remedy.

The existing disability carceral scholarship has not engaged in an extended way with the complexities of law. However, bringing to that scholarship a nuanced understanding of law's complicity is vital not only to comprehending how oppression through court diversion comes about, but also to the task of developing strategies to contest this oppression in full awareness of the (potentially limited) extent to which law is useful in articulating and remedying this oppression as injustice (and is, instead, part of what we need to work against and transform).

Court diversion as 'noncolonial' carcerality

Court diversion legitimates (white sovereign) law by positioning it as non-colonial. The institutional archipelago can expand *and mask* settler colonial control and violence of Indigenous and First Nations people and other racialised minorities because of the therapeutic and medical means through which it occurs. Chapman traces the histories of the carceral control of disabled people and of First Nations Canadian people, arguing that the material practices and associated ethical frameworks map onto each other. Chapman concludes that 'the same populations that have been rendered "eliminable" for five centuries continue to be disproportionately impoverished, incarcerated, institutionalized, apprehended, medicalized, and killed' (Chapman, 2014b: p. 41; see also Wadiwel, 2017). Chapman's work directs us to the importance of tracing connections and continuities across space and time between modes of disabled carceral control, and also considering how colonialism inflects these reformations of disabled carceral control and the lines along which they segregate disabled populations (in an Australian context, see, for example, Coleborne & MacKinnon, 2006). In her analysis of utilising mental health services to address overrepresentation of First Nations young people in the criminal justice system, Voronka (2013: p. 318) argues that the 'structural problems inherent in the criminal justice system' are individualised and become embedded in the 'core of their bodies: the structures of their biomedical souls', thus masking 'structural violence as personal pathology'. For Voronka, this interrelationship between criminal justice and mental health services 'shows us how systems use one another to offset and relocate the powers of governance' (ibid.: p. 321).

Joseph's exploration of the deportation of racialised criminalised disabled people in Canada:

> reveals the necessity of the mental health system, the criminal justice system, and the immigration system to present as independent, objective, and carrying out judicious institutional process while clandestinely acting in concert to resist appeals for adequate care, safety, or a consideration of external factors.
>
> (Joseph, 2015: p. 16; see also Joseph, 2019)

Writing in the context of the Global South, Mills (2014: p. 79) refers to the imposition of western mental health diagnostic frameworks and mental health treatments as a form of colonial violence. Mills argues that mental health is a colonial discourse (ibid.: p. 8) and traces continuities between contemporary rationales of protection through mental health treatment and detention and historical practices of colonisation that were rationalised on the basis of the 'uncivilised' native in need of protection (ibid.: pp. 89, 97).

Through court diversion, law renders 'non-colonial' the control of and violence against disabled people who are also Indigenous and First Nations or racialised. Law does so by reason of court diversion's purportedly therapeutic focus, coupled with it being underpinned by the aim of reducing overrepresentation in the criminal justice system. Court diversion simply moves these people to other sites and modes of control and effaces acknowledgement of the structural injustice and violence to Indigenous and First Nations people and racialised people from the criminal justice system. It thus prevents us from tracing *continuing* injustices across historical and foundation colonial acts of denial of sovereignty, land dispossession and genocide and contemporary incarceration both in prison *and* through mental health and disability systems. The non-colonial nature of court diversion reflects the broader phenomenon noted by Bond (2017) in the Australian context of purportedly beneficial strategies aimed at addressing Australian Aboriginal and Torres Strait Islander disadvantage (vis-à-vis white Australians) which only serve to reify settler colonial dynamics:

> Clearly, what is actually targeted here are Black lives and the unsafe Black body—which, we are told, are incapable of working or attending school. We see the gaze transfixed not on the systems that create disadvantage, but on remedying the behaviours of Black people through compliance to systems that have always failed us—and, let's be honest, have deliberately excluded us.
>
> Focusing on Black lives in this instance both lays blame on, and makes claims of, Black deviance from White norms, values, standards and expectations. The deviation from Black lives to White lives sanctions a 'new' targeting of Black lives by the state, and necessitates the continuation of White control over us and our lands. …
>
> Black deviance supports claims of White benevolence, in which White people are simultaneously positioned as our aspirational goal and saviours. It suggests to us that Black lives matter to them. Yet in emphasising our deviance, the sins of a system that White people uphold and benefit from remain unnamed and unnoticed.

It is vital that we foreground contemporary manifestations of colonialism, racism and white privilege in framing and contesting injustices related to disability and the criminal legal system.

Criminal legality and psychological individualism

Court diversion is positioned as non-discriminatory and just because of the role of dis/ability and in/capacity in structuring differential coercive interventions in ways that appear natural. In turning to the question I posed at the beginning of this section—how do we reconcile coercive intervention of criminalised disabled people *outside* of the very liberal legal limits that typically legitimate coercive intervention by criminal law—I suggest that this is on the basis that the relationship between court diversion and criminal legal intervention can be understood in terms of a 'psychological logic' that operates across these two forms of intervention. The notion of 'logic' directs us to understanding the ways in which different forms of intervention relate to each other to render coherent (and hence authorise) intervention of people in seemingly differential, unequal, inconsistent and even contradictory ways.

Individuals are legitimately treated by criminal law differently (and, I will also argue, at another level equally) along the lines of being either psychologically 'normal' or 'abnormal'. Norrie (2001: pp. 222–231) argues that since the modernisation of criminal law in the late nineteenth century, criminal legal intervention has been legitimised by appealing to what he refers to as universal legal individualism or 'juridical individualism'. Norrie proposes that criminal law operates through a 'logic of individual right' which 'sets up requirements of universality and equality in its application' that 'provides a rhetoric of individual liberty which transcends particular social interests' (ibid.: p. 23). By this is meant that every individual is equally subject to the possibility of having their liberty denied on the basis of being held to the same standards of behaviour. Norrie queries this logic, instead arguing that the logic 'obscures the social realities beneath the legal appearances' (ibid.: p. 23). For Norrie, criminal law holds itself up as providing *equal* protection of everyone's liberty while, through this insistence on equality of individuals, suppressing inequalities that manifest through criminal offending and the criminal justice system. He states: 'The "cunning" of the law lies in its ability to mask the onesidedness of its instrumental content through its formal character as a logic of universal individualism' (ibid.: p. 23).

Norrie argues that one aspect of this universal individualism is 'psychological individualism' (ibid.: pp. 28–29, pp. 223–224). All defendants are assumed to be guided by their individual, internal, psychological capacity and rationality. According to Norrie, two consequences flow from this. One is that individuals' behaviour is abstracted from social and historical contexts and, hence, that it is just, fair and humane to impose legal obligations and punishment on these defendants regardless of social inequalities (ibid.: pp. 21–23; see also Loughnan, 2012). A second consequence is that it helps to 'portray criminal law as existing within a consensual world in which all individuals qua individuals come together under law' and psychological individualism helps to remove social and political conflicts from the courtroom in advance by positing all legal subjects as always and already abstracted from such conflicts (ibid.: p. 223). Norrie concludes that 'the psychological individual at the heart of the criminal law is a political and ideological construction which operates to seal off the question of individual culpability from issues concerning the relationship between individual agency and social context' (ibid.: p. 223; see also Naffine, 2009: pp. 59–79). In this respect, it is important to reiterate that a majority of criminalised disabled individuals are dealt with through criminal legal intervention and, hence, through a psychologically able legal subjectivity. I will now go on to explain how court diversion is one way in which psychological individualism is sustained and, in turn, how court diversion and criminal legal intervention fit within a psychological logic through which they are both legitimated.

Norrie notes that:

> [t]he abstract form of the law is used to police the borders of the conviction process (that is, the law) against contextual raiding parties. There is a constant

> political task of maintaining the abstract psychological boundaries of doctrine against corruptive invasion from the socially, morally and politically constituted 'other'.
>
> (Norrie, 2001: p. 224)

In Foucauldian terms—boundaries necessarily produce outsides and excesses (Foucault, 2008a: p. 53). So, one consequence of bounding criminal legal intervention by psychological capacity and rationality is that some individuals who are considered psychologically incapable or irrational will then exceed the boundaries of this regulation, and it is inappropriate to view them as psychologically capable and rational (Eastman, 1992: p. 162). While in some instances this might be because they are unfit or not guilty by reason of mental illness, for others (particularly in lower courts) it will be because they do not reflect the rehabilitatable subject of criminal legal intervention. In occupying the margins of what is legally possible or effective and appropriate pursuant to criminal legal intervention, these criminalised disabled individuals risk being beyond control through criminal law.

However, such individuals can be recuperated back into lawful control through framing them as disabled legal subjects by reference to diagnosed disability. This framing becomes a basis on which to position as psychologically abnormal criminalised disabled people who might not be able to be controlled effectively, or at all, through criminal legal intervention and, hence, as necessarily other to the psychologically able criminal legal subject. They can be understood as a different *kind* of legal person on the basis that the mind, as the 'locus of humanness', is what defines the self (as compared to a physical difference in the body) (Delaney, 2003: p. 369; see also Loughnan, 2012: pp. 16–38). This is not a *political* distinction directed towards enabling discriminatory treatment, because it is couched in scientific and medical understandings of disability and, hence, viewed as a natural distinction. This tracks onto broader cultural understandings of disabled people as naturally of a different kind of human (Carlson, 2010: pp. 10, 12) or, arguably, less than fully human.

In this context of the ways in which law is structured by reference to dis/ability and in/capacity, court diversion has broader effects in constituting the 'normal' criminal legal subject and, in this respect, court diversion is actually at the core of constituting the authority of criminal legal intervention and the criminal legal domain as a whole. Court diversion legitimates criminal legal intervention and also helps to shore up the liberal criminal legal subject and, indeed, our social understandings of the 'human'. We need to be mindful of how disability (and Indigenous and First Nations disability) presents a 'particular threat to the social order' in terms of necessarily being 'evict[ed] … from the category of human' (Razack, 2015: p. 147). Indeed, recalling my discussion in the last section, it is important to inflect Norrie's ideas with how the operations of colonialism through criminal law become invisibilised through psychological individualism.

Being understood as a different *kind* of legal subject then opens up different forms of intervention linked to the kind of person criminalised disabled people are. They can no longer be held legally responsible for a criminal offence and punished for that criminal offence. Instead, they are to be subjected to coercive intervention on the basis of their disability. This is not unique to court diversion—elsewhere I have argued that the construction of disabled people as abnormal legal subjects justifies as natural their differential exposure to control and violence through other areas of law (Steele, 2016; 2017d; 2018c; 2018d). In this respect, court diversion exemplifies a broader phenomenon of law's role in sustaining violence, control and debilitation of disabled people.

Yet, on a more general level, disabled and non-disabled criminalised people are still *all* psychological beings. In this way a psychological logic, rather than a dichotomy, emerges. This logic, first, constitutes the completeness of the law's authority through a notion that everyone by mere fact of their personhood is a psychological being (as compared to the possible differentials that might emerge if individuals were instead framed in terms of social, gender, racial or economic dimensions) and, thus, all criminalised disabled people can be controlled by law. Secondly, this logic treats individuals in differential and unequal ways in relation to the target and method of this intervention, with this differential treatment being on the basis of a division of psychological personhood into psychological 'normality' and psychological 'abnormality' which is natural and, hence, apolitical. Psychological 'abnormality' is kept distinct from (and hence incomparable to or unable to be judged by the same standards as) psychological 'normality' by the construction of psychological 'abnormality' as an internal, individual condition, and, hence, as biologically different (rather than socially distinct)—most notably through reliance on diagnostic meanings of disability. There is a natural(ised) and absolute boundary between the psychologically 'normal' and 'abnormal' (even though, as I discuss in Chapters 5 and 7, specific individuals do cross this boundary). Therefore, court diversion is not viewed as discriminatory because of the psychological logic that individuals are fundamentally and naturally different kinds of legal subjects and, hence, beyond comparison for the purposes of comprehending unequal treatment as discrimination (Steele, 2016). And, in this logic, the circulation of settler colonialism is rendered invisible.

Court diversion and the completeness of law

Court diversion is central not only to maintaining the control of recalcitrant criminalised disabled people, but maintaining the completeness of criminal law as an exhaustive mode of control. Understanding the differential nature of coercive intervention of criminalised disabled people in terms of the psychological logic outlined above demonstrates that, far from undermining the authority of the criminal legal domain, court diversion supports the completeness of that domain. Yet, this also indicates the contingency of criminal law's exhaustive scope on the disciplinary categories through which it operates. In this way, criminal law's quest for certainty and fixity in its form, and 'completeness' or universality in its scope (that no one is beyond the law), is always in tension with the specificity of the disciplinary categories bounding laws and the capacity of these categories to include all individuals with their diverse characteristics (Golder & Fitzpatrick, 2009: pp. 83–84). Golder and Fitzpatrick capture this quality of law when they describe two different dimensions apparent in Foucault's account of law: 'law as a determinate and contained entity, and law as thoroughly illimitable and as responsive to what lies outside or beyond its position for the time being' (ibid.: pp. 2–3). Golder and Fitzpatrick argue that '[i]t is in the movement between these two apparently opposed dimensions that Foucault's law is revealed as a law of possibility, contingency and lability: that is, as a law always open to the possibility of being otherwise' (ibid.). Criminal law possesses an unstable, contingent and open dimension which is in tension with its desire to gain authority from the purported stability, separateness and closed nature of its purportedly universal scope. As Golder and Fitzpatrick (ibid.: p. 71) state, law generally:

> extends itself illimitably in its attempt to encompass and respond to what lies outside its definite content. This is a law of mutability, a law which is constantly in excess of its determinate self and which is uncontainable in and by its present instantiations. Law in this responsive dimension forms itself through an encounter with its outside, with what lies beyond itself. Law thence becomes self-resistant, disrupting itself through becoming receptive of resistances that constantly challenge its position, its content, its being.

As Golder and Fitzpatrick note, 'the condition of law is that of a perpetual hyphenation, reliant in some measure upon', inter alia, scientific knowledge (ibid.: p. 60). Law relies upon the disciplines, including psy disciplines, to shore up its completeness.

Applying this to an analysis of court diversion and its relationship to criminal law shifts attention away from criminal law as always and already having a complete, universal scope, purportedly applying to all individuals, to instead see criminal law as being in a constant process of change and court diversion as one way in which criminal law is responding to what is beyond its scope. Moreover, the externality of criminalised disabled people to criminal legal intervention, on the basis that it is not appropriate for them by reason of their disability (which could show the incompleteness of law's authority), becomes the basis for expanding law's authority over disabled people through court diversion. There is a productive subversion of excess by regulating criminalised disabled people through court diversion on the very basis of the ineffectiveness of criminal legal intervention: their disability.

Disability, legality and temporality

I argue that criminalised disabled people's debilitation through court diversion is *illegible*, indeed, *incomprehensible* as injustice because debilitation of criminalised disabled people is embedded in the very fabric of law itself. This embedding is by reason of a particular relationship between disability, legality and temporality. In this final section, I shift from seeking to understand how debilitation occurs through law to exploring why it is not seen as unjust when it does happen.

Critical legal scholars such as Mawani and Veitch argue that the representation in law of time obscures our ability to see injustice, notably law's complicity in institutional injustices (Mawani, 2014; 2015; Veitch, 2007). In law, time is not a pre-existing, objective, unitary chronological phenomenon. Instead, law produces time in specific contexts in ways that align with the state's objectives and legitimacy. For example, Mawani (2014: p. 69) has argued that while legal scholarship frequently takes law's time as self-evident, 'juridical concepts, legal discourses, and legal authority are underwritten by and draw their meanings from the production, specification, and arrangement of time' (ibid.: p. 71). Mawani urges 'a critical engagement with law's role in the production and organization of time as past, present, and future' (ibid.: p. 69). Critical legal scholarship on law and time orients us towards questioning how law *organises* time through separate legal processes for criminal legal intervention and disability-specific coercive intervention through court diversion, and how this orders how we see (or, more precisely, don't see) injustice.

Conventionally, the temporality of criminal legal intervention is mediated by the criminal offence. Criminal legal intervention, in the form of sentencing, has a retrospective temporal reference to a past offence, and the nature and period of intervention is determined by reference to that offence. In relation to criminal legal intervention in the form of bail or remand, it has a prospective reference point, anticipating the future trial in relation to the offence. Indeed, that is one reason why preventive detention and indefinite detention (in non-disability contexts) raise such civil rights concerns. However, in relation to *disabled people* in court diversion there are different temporal dynamics, because the focus is no longer on the past offence but the disability itself and its ongoing need for management. Drawing on Kafer's (2013) and Kim's (2016) work on disability and temporality, discussed in Chapter 3, it is arguable that disability itself is locked in a permanent temporal dislocation of requiring ongoing intervention and, thus, that disability makes possible a different legal threshold of permissible control and violence that *enables slow death* through law. Being mindful of Puar's invitation to think about the 'unevenness of how populations live and get to live time' (Puar, 2009: p. 166; see Soldatic, 2011: p. 11), court diversion highlights the *differential* temporal limits in law on the basis of dis/ability and the permissible violence against and kinds of lives for disabled people made possible by these differential temporal limits.

Turning from the individual to the population, and again to the problem of overrepresentation that provides impetus for court diversion, I suggested in Section 4.2 that this problem in terms of 'population' allows disability-specific intervention under the guise of trying to reduce overall numbers. Here I add to this by suggesting that the *legality* of these interventions is related not only to disability but to a particular relationship between disability, temporality and legality. Given that, thirty years on, court diversion is *still* being justified on the same basis of overrepresentation, either something is not working or, as I argue, it is working too well. Overrepresentation helps situate criminalised disabled people in an ongoing emergency—not so much an aberration of normal circumstances for this group but this group itself as an aberration of the normal, such that they become the emergency and will always require exceptional coercive intervention that sits outside of conventional liberal legality bounded by conviction and sentence. Criminalised disabled people *as emergency* makes possible and legitimates ongoing coercive intervention and a reduced interest in and scrutiny of the political implications of this intervention due to the urgency of acting (Steele, 2017d: p. 395). This entanglement of disability, temporality and legality not only enables intervention at the individual level but also becomes a biopolitical logic, through which disabled people en masse can be organised (see a similar observation in the context of migrant 'illegality' in Boon-Kuo, 2018: pp. 3–4).

This is particularly concerning for the increasing recognition of the specific issue of the overrepresentation of Indigenous and First Nations disabled people. Here I draw on Razack's observations in the context of coronial inquests and inquiries of Indigenous and First Nations people who died in Canadian police custody. Explicit recognition in law of disability might further pathologise and individualise the ongoing effects of colonialism, and, in particular, set up a relation of violent dependency: 'Perpetually needing assistance into modernity from an enlightened and compassionate European race' (Razack, 2015: p. 5). Razack suggests that this dependency legitimates violence against Indigenous and First Nations peoples and 'is also productive for settler subjectivities' because 'settlers are able to feel Indigenous disappearance and to imagine their own superiority' (ibid.) and in turn secure their entitlement to land which has been illegally and unjustly taken from Indigenous peoples (ibid.: p. 6). Court diversion might reflect what Razack refers to as 'a legal performance of Indigenous people as a dying race who are simply pathologically unable to cope with the demands of modern life' (ibid.; see further p. 7). This is because court diversion, as a solution to Indigenous and First Nations disabled overrepresentation, is premised not on facilitating self-determination but, rather, on the presumed fundamental need of Indigenous and First Nations criminalised disabled people for treatment and support by the (white colonial) disability and mental health systems via (white sovereign) law. In this respect, binding up Indigeneity with disability, carcerality and a temporality of ongoing overrepresentation has particularly unique impacts on Indigenous and First Nations criminalised disabled people. These impacts are that it sustains not only their debilitation, but through its 'staging of Indigenous pathology and dysfunction' and the state as 'benevolent' (ibid.: p. 9), settler colonial rule. As such, court diversion becomes a legitimate (even hyper-legitimate) mode of intervention to address health inequities in Indigenous and First Nations people while never confronting how criminal law and the criminal justice system is instrumental in sustaining colonial rule (ibid.: pp. 30–31). Court diversion, through its more recent positioning as a solution to the overrepresentation of Indigenous and First Nations criminalised disabled people, can transform 'the colonial condition into a medical one' (ibid.: p. 135) and, indeed, can make it more difficult to identify and contest settler colonialism, because such a response is counterintuitive to the purported progressive sentiments underpinning medicalisation—'that Indigenous people are ill and should be treated more humanely' (ibid.: p. 140). Court diversion can reflect a performance of moral *and legal* authority to rule over Indigenous and First Nations populations. It becomes a way through which sovereignty can be enacted over and, indeed, *through* Indigenous and First Nations criminalised disabled bodies without being explicitly about Indigeneity (ibid.: p. 81; see discussion in context of indefinite detention in Steele, 2018d). It could also be considered whether overrepresentation presents a 'crisis' to criminal law's authority, such that court diversion is a suspension of norms of criminal law with the ultimate goal of preserving criminal law's authority (and white sovereign law more broadly) and restoring 'normal' law for all (see, for example, McLoughlin, 2009; 2012).

In this and the preceding chapter, I have developed and utilised an interdisciplinary analytical frame for reconsidering court diversion. Contrary to the idea that court diversion shifts already disabled individuals *outside* the criminal justice system and into disability and mental health services for treatment and support which is in the interests of their wellbeing and empowerment, I have illustrated the ways in which law through court diversion sustains criminalised disabled people's debilitation. This is represented in law as necessary, non-violent, non-colonial and just. Court diversion both continues the ongoing carceral control specifically of criminalised disabled people through criminal legal intervention and strengthens, rather than dismantles, prison systems and the institutional archipelago more broadly.

Chapter 5

The finer details of debilitation through law

Introduction to an Australian diversion scheme

5.1 Introduction

This chapter provides broader legislative and lived contexts to the book's examination of diversion into community disability and mental health services, using case studies from the New South Wales diversion legislation. The key legislative provision is section 32 of the *Mental Health (Forensic Provisions) Act 1990* (NSW) ('NSW *Mental Health FP Act*'). This is the first of three chapters focused on an analysis of section 32. In diverting individuals into *community* disability and mental health services (as opposed to detention in a mental health facility, dealt with in a separate provision (s 33) of the Act), section 32 might be considered one of the more 'progressive' court diversion schemes across Anglo jurisdictions. The analysis of section 32 over the course of the next three chapters involves a close and careful reading of the legal framework of the scheme, with a particular focus on the decision-making process for diversion. The analysis underscores the importance of theorising court diversion by in-depth examination of legal dynamics, and provides broader theoretical and methodological insights to bring to analysis of other court diversion schemes and, indeed, to other modes of carceral control of criminalised disabled people.

The chapter begins with a brief introduction to the legislative framework and history of section 32. It then shifts to present institutional narratives of criminal justice pathways of two hypothetical individuals diverted pursuant to section 32 at some point in their life, focusing on the early and repeated nature of their criminal justice contact and the role of child welfare and disability and mental health services in criminalisation. I also explore the multiple dimensions of this criminal justice contact, as offender, victim and through civil mental health legislation. The picture drawn here of those who are diverted exposes a gap between the way in which disability and criminal law are presented in the diversion legislation itself (discussed in Chapters 6 and 7) and the material conditions of the criminalised disabled people who are diverted, which are characterised by violence, precarity, debility and state irresponsibility under conditions of settler colonialism. This gap provides an important starting point for consideration in Chapters 6 and 7 of how court diversion transforms individuals from criminal legal subjects to disabled legal subjects, and also makes individuals knowable by reference to a medicalised 'pure' disability that renders invisible in law present circumstances and life histories of debilitation in which criminal law and criminal justice systems are complicit.

5.2 Section 32

Section 32(1) of the NSW *Mental Health FP Act* provides for a court diversion scheme in the Local Court of New South Wales[1] (the court of summary jurisdiction dealing with less serious criminal offences). Section 32 applies to individuals appearing before the Local Court on criminal charges who are 'cognitively impaired', 'suffering from a mental illness' or 'suffering from a mental condition for which treatment is available in a mental health facility' (s 32(1)). Such individuals can have their charges dismissed and be discharged either unconditionally or subject to conditions lasting six months (s 32(3)). If conditional, the individual can be discharged 'into the care of a responsible person, unconditionally or subject to conditions' or 'on the condition that the defendant attend on a person or at a place specified by the magistrate' either 'for assessment or treatment (or both) of the defendant's mental condition or cognitive impairment' or 'to enable the provision of support in relation to the defendant's cognitive impairment' (s32(3)(a), (b)). Magistrates can also make an interlocutory order, which involves adjourning the proceedings for a period of time, effectively putting the determination of the criminal charges on hold (rather than dismissing the charges) (s32(2)). There is no time limit for how long such an order can be, and a period longer than six months might be stipulated if the charges are more serious, the individual's engagement with services needs to be trialled or the individual's behaviour is seen as particularly risky or challenging (*Mantell v Molyneux*). However, it is important to note that this form of diversion does not fit within the scope of my approach to court diversion (as discussed in Chapter 1) and hence is not the focus of the analysis that follows.

A section 32 order can be made at any time during the Local Court proceedings. An order is typically made following an oral application by the defence supported by an individual's carers, advocates and service providers. An application is typically accompanied by two documents: (i) a psychological, psychiatric or neuropsychological report detailing the defendant's diagnosis; and (ii) a 'treatment plan' (also referred to as a support plan or case plan) by a worker of a disability or mental health service outlining the treatment and services the defendant could access under a conditional section 32 order (Intellectual Disability Rights Service, 2011: pp. 22–32).

1 Section 32 also applies in the NSW Children's Court, but this book focuses on its operation in the adult jurisdiction.

A magistrate's decision to make a section 32 order is guided by a three-stage inquiry, articulated by Justice McColl in the New South Wales Court of Appeal decision of *DPP (NSW) v El Mawas* (2006) (the '*El Mawas* inquiry'):

1 '[I]t appears to the Magistrate' that the defendant is 'cognitively impaired', 'suffering from a mental illness' or 'suffering from a mental condition for which treatment is available in a mental health facility' (s 32(1)(a)).
2 It 'appears to the Magistrate' that it is 'more appropriate' for the defendant to be dealt with by section 32 than 'otherwise than in accordance with law' (s 32 (1)(b)).
3 An appropriate section 32 order can be made.

(*El Mawas* inquiry, 109–110 [75]–[80])

The *El Mawas* inquiry structures my analysis in Chapters Six and Seven and I return there to explore the jurisprudence in further detail.

During the period 2008–2018, the proportion of Local Court criminal charges finalised through section 32 (including interlocutory orders) has remained fairly consistent, at 1–2% (NSW Bureau of Crime Statistics and Research, 2019a). While there are no current statistics on the number of Local Court defendants who are disabled, a 2007 survey found that 55% of surveyed defendants had one or more psychiatric disorders (New South Wales Law Reform Commission, 2012b: p. 65) and a 2007 survey found that 3.5% of surveyed defendants had an intellectual disability (ibid.: p. 64). These figures suggest that only a minority of criminalised disabled people appearing in the Local Court receive section 32 orders.

If the defendant does not comply with the conditions in the six-month period following the making of the order, 'the Magistrate may deal with the charge as if the defendant had not been discharged' (s 32(3D)). A treatment provider under a section 32 order 'may report a failure to comply with a condition of the order by the other person' to the Community Offender Services of the Probation and Parole Service or Department of Justice (s 32A(1)). Treatment providers are given broad range in their reporting, insofar as they can make such reports '[d]espite any law' (s 32) and, in their report, can include 'any information that the treatment provider considers is relevant to the making of a decision in relation to the failure to comply concerned' (s 32A(2)). The number of orders pursuant to section 32A varies across the years of available data (2008–2016), ranging from zero in 2015 and 2016 to a peak of 158 in 2010 (NSW Bureau of Crime Statistics and Research, 2019b).

There are mental health court liaison services located at many larger NSW Local Courts that can assist with diagnosis and service brokerage for criminalised disabled people requiring mental health services and provide recommendations to magistrates concerning diversion into treatment (Justice Health and Forensic Mental Health Network, n.d.; see also Sharples et al., 2003). Historically, there have not been similar court-based services related to cognitive impairments, so generally lawyers, advocates and carers/family members have been responsible for identifying cognitive impairment services for treatment plans (Intellectual Disability Rights Service, 2011; Intellectual Disability Rights Service et al., 2008). However, as discussed below, the NSW government is currently trialling such a program at two local courts.

Critical concerns with section 32

Section 32 reflects many of the concerns with court diversion that were raised in Chapter 2. Section 32 can apply to individuals who have not been sentenced, convicted or even tried for a criminal offence, because a section 32 application can be made 'at the commencement or at any time during the course of the hearing of proceedings before a Magistrate' (s 32(1)). Furthermore, while a successful section 32 application results in dismissal of the charges (s 32(3)), '[a] decision under this section to dismiss charges against a defendant does not constitute a finding that the charges against the defendant are proven or otherwise' (s 32(4)).

Coercive intervention through section 32 surpasses the limits of sentencing law. Nor is a section 32 order limited by the principles of sentencing—that is, it is not determined by the defendant's liability for the criminal offence that brings them before the court, nor by sentencing principles such as proportionality, deterrence and rehabilitation (*Crimes (Sentencing Procedure) Act 1999* (NSW) s 3A). The six-month compliance period for a section 32 conditional order is arbitrary and cannot be altered by a magistrate—thus, the period of compliance is not calculated by reference to the particular offence with which they are charged. The coercive intervention through section 32 can therefore be disproportionate to the alleged offence, including in relation to minor offences that might have been disposed of by dismissal without proceeding to conviction, conviction with no other penalty, or a minor fine (see the sentencing options in *Crimes (Sentencing Procedure) Act 1999* (NSW) pt 2 divs 2–4). The administration of section 32 orders is not restricted to corrective services, as is largely the case with criminal legal coercive intervention (*Crimes (Administration of Sentences) Act 1999* (NSW)).

Section 32 may also apply to defendants who are unfit to be tried (NSWLRC, 2013: p. 344), this seeming to be contrary to common law rules that criminal proceedings should be stayed when an individual is found to be unfit. In the absence of a legislative scheme to enable their subsequent regulation, people found unfit in the NSW Local Court must otherwise be discharged or have their proceedings stayed (New South Wales Law Reform Commission, 2013: pp. 344–345). The New South Wales Law Reform Commission (NSWLRC) has noted that 'the current situation in the Local Court is anomalous and unsatisfactory. Defendants charged with minor offences may be diverted, whereas those charged with more serious offences may have to be discharged without supervision or treatment' (NSWLRC, 2013: p. 346, [12.20]). I will return to this tension in Chapter 7.

The diversionary purpose of section 32 was acknowledged by Justice Hume in the recent NSW Supreme Court decision in *DPP (NSW) v Saunders* (2017) at

[38]: 'It is clearly discernible from the terms of s 32 that its purpose is to allow, in appropriate cases, for accused persons with a developmental disability, a mental illness, or a mental condition for which treatment is available in a mental health facility, to be diverted from the criminal justice system'. Justice Hume also noted that Part 3 of the NSW *Mental Health FP Act*, which includes section 32, as well as diversion to inpatient mental health facilities (NSW *Mental Health FP Act*, s 33) is 'primarily concerned with diversion of eligible persons in appropriate cases from the criminal justice system, and thereby from the potential for criminal sanction' ([42]). However, in the leading (and reported) decision on section 32, *DPP (NSW) v El Mawas* (2006), McColl JA proposed that section 32 is both diversionary *and* punitive:

> adopting the *diversionary* route *does not mean that a defendant is not exposed to punishment*. While an order under s 32(3) is not custodial in the strict sense, it may involve the imposition of conditions restricting a discharged defendant's freedom of movement and actions. Compliance with those conditions is ensured by the Magistrate retaining a supervisory jurisdiction for 6 months.
>
> (108–109 [73] (McColl JA), emphasis added)

McColl JA also referred to the purpose of Part 3 of the NSW *Mental Health FP Act* as being focused on protecting the public from criminalised disabled people:

> Part 3 of the Act requires a Magistrate to balance the public interest in those charged with a criminal offence facing the full weight of the law against the public interest in treating, or regulating to the greatest extent practical, the conduct of individuals suffering from any of the mental conditions referred to in s 32(1) or mental illness (s 33) with the object of ensuring that the community is protected from the conduct of such persons.
>
> (*El Mawas* at 108 [71] (McColl JA))

This comment by McColl JA captures the tensions drawn out in Chapter 2, between access to liberty and resources on the one hand and coercion and control on the other. It also highlights the association between disability and danger and a link drawn between disability, treatment and coercion, compounded with the focus on treatment in the 'public interest' rather than in the interests of the individual. As I suggested in Chapter 4, and will go on to further develop in Chapters 6 and 7, these are productive tensions which sit at the very core of court diversion. This can be drawn out by reference to section 32's history, to which I now turn.

5.3 Enduring tensions in section 32

A brief examination of the historical development of court diversion in New South Wales illuminates well-embedded tensions of freedom and control. In this part I will trace a gradual move in New South Wales towards a more coercive and punitive court diversion regime, coupled with the regime's enduring reputation throughout its development as humane and therapeutic. In particular, I track the emergence and consolidation of the enforcement aspects of section 32.

Section 32 has its legislative origins in s 428W of the *Crimes Act 1900* (NSW). Section 428W formed part of the *Crimes (Mental Disorder) Amendment Act 1983* which inserted a new Part XIA, 'Unfitness to be Tried for an Offence', into the *Crimes Act 1900* (NSW) in 1983; this provision came into force in 1986. The inception of s 428W coincided with a period of emerging interest in provision of services to people with 'mental retardation' or 'intellectual handicap' and mental illness in the criminal justice system (see, Hayes & Hayes, 1982; 1984). This period also saw broader critical reflection on and evaluation of the success of deinstitutionalisation, particularly questioning the services available for individuals in the community and the similarities between these services and disability institutions (in the New South Wales context, see Hayes, 1984). The Richmond Report (Richmond, 1983), released in the months preceding the debate on the Bill containing s 428W, documented the failure of deinstitutionalisation to provide adequate support in the community.

The Bill containing s 428W was part of a package of mental health legislation focused on reforming the civil and forensic mental health systems. The legislation was lauded by both the government and the opposition as marking a humane and enlightened turn in the treatment of persons with mental illness. In introducing the cognate Bills, the Minister for Health referred to them as 'one of the most significant social reforms to be considered by this Parliament in recent decades' and 'signifying a major advance in the way our society regards and deals with victims of mental illness' (New South Wales, *Parliamentary Debates*, Legislative Assembly, 22 November 1983, 3087 [Laurie Brereton, Minister for Health]). Significantly, s 428W did not provide for enforcement of conditional orders. This is indicative of the way in which the coercive effects of section 32 have grown over the past 30 years and become increasingly normalised. I further explore this below.

In September 1990, part XIA of the *Crimes Act 1900* (NSW), including s 428W, was repealed and the forensic mental health laws were moved into their own Act: the *Mental Health (Criminal Procedure) Act 1990* (NSW), the name of which was changed in 2007 to the *Mental Health Legislation Amendment (Forensic Provisions) Act 2008* (NSW). At this point, s 428W became section 32.

In 1991, the NSWLRC was given the task of inquiring into 'the law and practice relating to the treatment of the intellectually disabled in the criminal justice system', including the extent to which diversion should be used (NSWLRC, 1996: p. xiii). This project 'arose from concern that people with an intellectual disability were over-represented as offenders and victims in, and/or were being treated inappropriately by, the criminal justice system' (ibid.: [1.3]). In the course of its consultation phase, the NSWLRC identified a number of disadvantages with section 32, including the unenforceability of conditional orders (ibid.: [5.69]).

Despite these leanings towards greater coercion, some submissions to the review criticised the NSWLRC's suggestion of introducing enforcement provisions. For example, Magistrate Beveridge stated: 'The problem—legal and philosophical—of a criminal court imposing sanctions upon a person against whom no criminal offence has been proved is really quite simple' (Beveridge, 1994). In a similar vein, Magistrate Cleary stated that any order 'for the compulsory care and treatment of any person against whom a charge has been dismissed' should be made through 'civil law not criminal' (Cleary, 1995; see also Ierace, 1992).

The NSWLRC did not ultimately recommend the introduction of enforcement provisions, stating that such a proposal, and the logistics of supervising compliance, were 'impractical' and that '[i]f some form of supervision is considered necessary, then the matter would be better dealt with according to law and the person could be placed on a supervised bond' (NSWLRC, 1996, 207 [5.92]). The NSWLRC stated that 'it appears to the Commission to be wrong in principle to have conditions (which are, in any event, unenforceable) imposed where there has been no hearing or finding of guilt' (ibid.: p. 207 [5.82]).

The period following the NSWLRC review marked a shift to greater concern with the efficient and effective administration of section 32. In 2002, section 32 was amended to insert sub-sections (3A)–(3D) into section 32. The effect of these amendments was to 'enable a person who breaches a condition of a discharge by a Magistrate under section 32 of the Act to be brought back before the Magistrate' (Explanatory Notes, Crimes Legislation Amendment Bill 2002 (NSW): p. 3). There was no debate in the Parliament concerning the introduction of the enforcement provisions. However, Spiers explains that this reform was recommended by the Interdepartmental Committee on the *Mental Health (Criminal Procedure) Act 1990* following argument by magistrates and legal practitioners that lack of enforcement mechanisms meant individuals were not complying with their orders, resulting in more severe criminal penalties for these individuals on subsequent occasions and lost opportunities to achieve therapeutic interventions (Spiers, 2004: p. 9).

It was not until twenty years after s 428W originally came into force that the enforcement provisions of section 32 were introduced. In 2005, a new s 32A was inserted into the *Mental Health (Criminal Procedure) Act 1990* (NSW), pursuant to which treatment providers involved could report breaches of section 32 orders, regardless of any other laws (for example, any duty of confidentiality) (Explanatory Notes, Mental Health (Criminal Procedure) Amendment Bill 2005 (NSW)). In the second reading speech for the Bill, the Parliamentary Secretary explained that section 32A 'is designed to facilitate the reporting of failures to comply with conditions, and to ameliorate concerns of service providers in relation to client confidentiality issues' which 'will strengthen the integrity of the operation of orders' (New South Wales, *Parliamentary Debates*, Legislative Assembly, 8 November 2005, 19214 (Alison Megarrity, Parliamentary Secretary)). In the course of the second reading of the Bill, she further stated:

> The foregoing amendments are expected to provide a safer and more efficient regime ... They provide greater opportunity for diversion from the criminal justice system for those who should *properly* be dealt with in an appropriate treatment and rehabilitative context *enforced* by the court.
>
> (New South Wales, *Parliamentary Debates*, Legislative Assembly, 8 November 2005, 19214 (emphasis added))

The Parliamentary Secretary's comments reflect a momentum towards consolidating the coercive aspects of section 32.

The twenty-first century has marked an increased focus in New South Wales on disabled people as a specific criminal justice population, and support for court diversion as a key way to reduce overrepresentation of this group. The key example here was the NSWLRC's project on people with cognitive impairment and mental health impairments in the criminal justice system (NSWLRC, 2010; 2012a; 2012b; 2013). In its disability criminal justice review, the NSWLRC devoted an entire consultation paper and final report to the issue of court diversion. These documents included detailed and extensive discussion of section 32 and also considered whether the NSWLRC should recommend introduction of mental health courts (NSWLRC, 2010; 2012b). The NSWLRC's focus in relation to section 32 was on 'identify[ing] the problems that have arisen in relation to [section 32] and mak[ing] recommendations to improve the operation of s 32' (NSWLRC, 2012b: p. 246). The NSWLRC does acknowledge submissions that 'there may be drawbacks to diversion in some circumstances', with such drawbacks including 'net-widening and sentence escalation', 'coerc[ing] accused people into participating', or 'participation [placing] onerous obligations on an accused person, particularly where there has been no finding of guilt' (ibid.: pp. 41–44). Yet, ultimately the NSWLRC concluded that 'diversion can be an effective means of reducing reoffending and producing better outcomes for people with cognitive and mental health impairments' (ibid.: p. 45).

Interestingly, the NSWLRC's review coincided with the coming into force of the CRPD. Citing Articles 5 (equality and non-discrimination), 13 (access to justice) and 14 (liberty and security of person), the NSWLRC stated that court diversion was one way to realise the human rights of criminalised disabled people (NSWLRC, 2012b: p. 33). However, the NSWLRC did not engage with interpretations of those Articles that focus on the discriminatory nature of disability-specific coercive interventions, nor with submissions suggesting that the CRPD required abolition of the forensic mental health system (Steele, 2011; see analysis of this omission by O'Mahony, 2013: pp. 481–482).

The NSWLRC made a number of recommendations relating to supervision and enforcement of section 32 orders. It recommended replacing the requirement for a 'treatment plan' with one for a 'diversion plan' (NSWLRC, 2012b: pp. 266–268). The 'diversion plan' would nominate a responsible person who will report to the court about the defendant's progress and outcomes (ibid.: pp. 266–270). The NSWLRC recommended that the possible length of the compliance period for a conditional order be extended to 12 months (ibid.: pp. 273–274). The NSWLRC also recommended that magistrates have enhanced power to 'monitor the progress of the defendant undertaking a diversion plan' (ibid.: p. 263). Moreover, the NSWLRC recommended that section 32 be the first legal consideration when unfitness is raised in the Local Court, but if the section 32 application is unsuccessful then the fitness provisions in the higher courts should apply as this would enable 'consistency across the courts in NSW' (ibid.: p. 351). All of these recommendations demonstrate a desire to retain, improve and expand section 32 alongside further consolidating its coercive dimensions and bringing the use of disability and mental health services further within criminal justice administration through supervision and reporting.

The reforms to section 32 recommended by the NSWLRC have not come to fruition in the legislation itself (aside from minor changes to disability terminology). Instead, the government has responded to some of the recommendations through service-based reforms related to the Australian National Disability Insurance Scheme (NDIS). The NDIS provides a new legal, financial and service framework for the funding and delivery of disability services (*National Disability Insurance Scheme Act 2013* (Cth)). The NDIS was introduced in a trial capacity in 2013, and was rolled out nationally from 2016 (Buckmaster & Clark, 2018: pp. 15, 19). The NDIS was widely hailed as a positive development in the status of disabled people in Australia, particularly through its central focus on 'choice and control'. However, since its roll-out, academics and disability rights advocates have queried the extent to which the NDIS can support disabled people on the 'margins', including those in the criminal justice system (Churchill, Sotiri & Rowe, 2017; Independent Advisory Council of the National Disability Insurance Scheme 2016; Rowe et al., 2017; Simpson, 2013; Soldatic et al., 2014). In its inquiry into the provision of services under the NDIS for people with psychosocial disabilities related to a mental health condition, the Joint Standing Committee on the National Disability Insurance Scheme (2017: p. xv) recommended the establishing of a 'NDIA unit specialising in the interaction of the Scheme with the criminal justice system' and 'the NDIA develops a specific strategy to deliver culturally appropriate services for Aboriginal and Torres Strait Islander people with disabilities who are in the criminal justice system' (ibid.: p. xvi).

The NDIS has impacted on disability criminal justice service provision in NSW in seemingly contradictory (but not surprising) ways that mark a culmination and consolidation of the balancing of the therapeutic and coercive in court diversion in a neoliberal context. By way of background, during the early 2000s much work was done within the NSW government's disability department to improve community based forensic disability services, particularly at the interface with section 32 (such as processes for development of treatment plans and provision of specialist group homes and case management) (Intellectual Disability Rights Service et al., 2008: pp. 45–54). In the late 2010s, the NSW government 'transferred the majority of its disability services to the non-government sector to support the Australia-wide delivery of the NDIS to enable greater choice for people with disability' (Ageing, Disability and Home Care, Department of Family and Community Services NSW, n.d.). This was identified as potentially having a negative impact on criminalised disabled people who had benefited from specialised support developed within the government department.

In December 2017 the NSW Department of Justice launched the 'Cognitive Impairment Diversion Program'. The program, part of the NSW government's response to the NSWLRC's 2012 report on diversion (NSW Government, 2017), is being trialled in two NSW Local Courts and applies to individuals aged 18 years or over who have cognitive impairment and voluntarily agree to participate (Department of Justice (NSW), n.d., p. 1). The program's objective 'is to increase the diversion of people with a cognitive impairment charged with low level offences away from the criminal justice system under section 32' (ibid.). In particular the program 'maximises opportunities created by the National Disability Insurance Scheme' (ibid., p. 1). Yet, while the NDIS is framed in terms of 'choice and control' there is a fundamental contradiction in embedding the NDIS in the section 32 legal framework (where individuals are coerced into engagement). Indeed, it is concerning that the program not only creates better pathways between section 32 and services but, simultaneously, increases the role of corrective services in supervision of those who are diverted. This is reflected in the three elements of the program: better identification of candidates for court diversion, better linking to disability services *and* (disturbingly) better community corrections monitoring of those who are diverted. The Department of Justice has explicitly stated that this third element would be a way to facilitate the use of enforcement provisions (ibid.).

Each participant in the program who is diverted pursuant to section 32 is assigned a Community Corrections Officer 'to monitor their compliance with the diversion orders' (ibid.: p. 2). This most recent reform seems to bring about a convergence of the disability and criminal justice systems in a way not previously formally coordinated (although already quite formalised in the context of mental health services in light of the longer history of mental health court liaison services located at many local courts). I suggest that this latest development reflects the neoliberal bifurcation of service users as deserving and undeserving, responsible and irresponsible.

This potted history demonstrates the gradual movement of section 32 towards greater coerciveness and integration with criminal justice administration. While its initial introduction was framed in terms of emancipating disabled people from the 'dark past' (Altermark, 2018: p. 2) of institutions, its subsequent thirty years reflects Altermark's (2017; 2018) observations of how juxtaposing the present to this dark past can easily hide new calibrations of control *within* the community. This tension is magnified in the contemporary context of the NDIS pilot scheme, where access to support in a frame of 'choice and control' sits comfortably unnoticed within a legal framework fundamentally premised on the negation of choice and control, reflecting how the institutional archipelago re-forms and endures across political shifts (Chapman, 2014b; Chapman, Carey & Ben-Moshe, 2014).

I now turn to situate New South Wales court diversion in the criminal justice and institutional lives of individuals who are diverted.

5.4 Who is diverted?

The application of court diversion laws in New South Wales to criminalised disabled people on the basis of diagnosed disability might lead us to think of those who are diverted purely in terms of diagnosed disability, and in terms of the specific charges bringing them before the court. Indeed, as I argue in Chapters 6 and 7, this understanding of those who are diverted sustains the legitimacy of law's debilitation of criminalised disabled people and negates the complicity of criminal law and criminal justice systems in the broader oppression of those who are diverted. As such, this section offers some reflections on the institutional and criminal justice encounters and life courses of two hypothetical individuals—Molly and James—who have both received diagnoses of cognitive impairment and mental illness at different times in their lives and have been diverted pursuant to section 32.

The narratives on these two individuals is informed by data on four individuals drawn from the 'People with Mental Health Disorders and Cognitive Disabilities in the Criminal Justice System in New South Wales' data set ('MHDCD data set'), a cohort of 2731 men and women who have been in prison in New South Wales, most of whom have been designated as having cognitive impairment and/or mental illness diagnosis.[2] The MHDCD data set contains linked data on the lifelong human services and criminal justice involvement of each individual and was constructed by merging extant administrative records from criminal justice and human service agencies such as the Attorney General's Department, Corrective Services, police, health and community services. Data indicate demographics, criminal justice contacts, social and health factors, and disability service usage. The majority of the data sources are quantitative, detailing episodes of service use. However, the data also include the police events narrative, which is the qualitative written running record of specific instances of an individual's contact with police over their life—as an alleged offender ('person of interest' or 'POI'), victim and/or a 'mentally ill person' under civil mental health legislation. The availability of data (in terms of particular government sources and time period) varies between individuals in the dataset. The data is historical in nature, ending (at the most recent) in 2009 when the data was linked; for some sources and individuals, the data ends earlier than 2009.

Data was drawn on four individuals who had been diverted at some point in their lives. The four individuals were selected to include both male and female subjects, and some who were Indigenous Australian. The institutional narratives

2 Ethics approval for this empirical research was granted by the University of Sydney Human Research Ethics Committee: Protocol no. 14568. This ethics approval was ratified by the University of New South Wales Human Research Ethics Committee: HREC ref no. HC12071. An associated larger project utilising data on Indigenous Australians in the MHDCD cohort, 'Indigenous Australians with Mental Health Disorders and Cognitive Disabilities in the Criminal Justice System' (IAMHDCD), was granted ethics approval by the University of New South Wales HREC, the Aboriginal Health and Medical Research Council of NSW (AH&MRC) and individual Aboriginal organisations with which the team worked (Baldry et al., 2015: p. 27).

presented in this chapter of the hypothetical Molly and James reflect composites of different aspects of the institutional stories told of the four actual individuals in the MHDCD dataset. This was done in order to protect the anonymity of the four individuals in the data set. This chapter provides a general discussion of key themes arising from the life circumstances and criminal justice experiences depicted through the institutional narratives of Molly and James. On one level, key themes arising from their institutional and criminal justice life courses are very particular to these individuals and do not reflect the circumstances of all criminalised disabled people who are diverted. However, on another level I make more general observations about carceral control, 'corrosive social disadvantage' (Dowse, 2018) and violence experienced by criminalised disabled people, including those who are diverted. That such general observations are possible is confirmed by earlier research by my colleagues and myself reporting on quantitative analysis of data related to all 149 (at that time) individuals in the MHDCD data set who had received section 32 orders (Steele, Dowse & Trofimovs, 2016). In this earlier quantitative research we found that many of those who had been diverted had multiple police contacts as persons of interest (as well as victims of crime and under civil mental health legislation) and multiple periods of incarceration over their lives. Many also experienced significant social disadvantage as adults—such as homelessness and limited access to disability services—and experienced early childhood disadvantage through high rates of out-of-home care (OOHC) and contact with juvenile justice. The Indigenous Australians in the sample had higher incidence of out-of-home care, lower access to disability support services, earlier police contact and higher rates of juvenile justice incarceration than the non-Indigenous sample members. Thus, my discussion in this section illuminates the kinds of dynamics shaping the institutional and criminal justice life courses of many criminalised disabled people who encounter court diversion in New South Wales.

It is important to note that the data informing James' and Molly's institutional narratives are not composed from direct accounts by the four actual individuals in the MHDCD dataset themselves. They are composed from the stories told in institutional records of those four individuals, the content of these stories was beyond the control and knowledge of the individuals themselves. The MHDCD data do not tell *their* story, but rather a story pieced together from various institutional encounters with them from the perspectives of those legally empowered to arrest, incarcerate, control, medically treat, educate and care for them. The story the data tell has been mediated through the institutions that these individuals encountered and filtered through the lens of institutional record keeping such that the data are objectifying and automatically imbued with the power dynamics of those specific institutional encounters, the epistemologies of each particular institution, and the broader settler colonial contexts in which they are situated. The institutional data illuminates epistemic and slow violence discussed in Chapter 3, in negating the experiences of the four individuals themselves and in erasing or subverting any of their acts of resistance against institutional authority (indeed making resistance difficult or even impossible to see in the data). This means that the institutional narratives I present of Molly and James are not providing a comprehensive account of how they experience the world but rather are giving us fragmented insights into how their lives are perceived and necessarily represented by the very systems that have such profound impacts in shaping the possibilities of their lives and legitimating the violence, harm and injustice of these systems (see similarly Pilling et al., 2018).

Some of the material I discuss in this chapter might be confronting, distressing or triggering. However, I believe it is important to set it out here because it tells stories that are rarely included in disability legal scholarship and often absent or disconnected from the work of legal decision makers and law reformers focused on technical legal tasks in more abstracted and disembodied contexts. I hope that reading this material might encourage us not only to reconsider what *court diversion* is doing, but also to avoid assuming court diversion is operating automatically and devoid of any human intervention, and thus ask broader ethical questions about the impacts on criminalised disabled people of the *work of lawyers, judges and law reformers* through court diversion (in the social work context, see Chapman, 2014a; Chapman & Withers, 2019).

Introduction to James and Molly

Molly

Molly is an Indigenous Australian in her mid-forties. She has moderate intellectual disability and is identified in hospital health records as having a variety of mental health disorders, such as mood affective disorders, schizophrenia, psychosis and mental and behavioural disorders related to substance use. Molly receives mental health services throughout her teens and twenties, and begins receiving disability services in her mid-thirties.

Molly has around 265 contacts with police. Molly's first recorded police contact occurs when she is eight years old, as a missing person while in OOHC; her first police contact as a person of interest ('POI') for having committed a criminal offence is at 11 years of age and occurs in the OOHC setting where she lives. Her subsequent alleged offending relates principally to property and minor drug possession offences, with over 175 charges in the space of 13 years. Molly has 19 periods of incarceration in juvenile justice and 13 periods of adult custody (including both remand and on sentence). She is noted as self-harming and being a suicide risk and offending while in prison.

Molly receives around 15 section 32 orders during her thirties and early forties. However, when she receives these Molly is usually appearing before the Local Court on multiple charges. Many of the section 32 orders apply to only some of her criminal charges before the court while she is convicted and at times sentenced to prison in relation to other charges (meaning she is incarcerated irrespective of some of the section 32 orders).

James

James is a non-Indigenous Australian in his late 30s. He has mild intellectual disability and is identified in hospital health records as having 'brain damage' and a variety of mental health disorders, including schizophrenia, bipolar affective disorder and mental and behavioural disorders due to substance use. James sporadically receives community and inpatient mental health services across his adult life. He spends many of his adult years homeless.

During his late twenties and thirties James receives two section 32 orders. There is no indication that he ever receives community disability services and so these orders must relate instead to community mental health treatment. His first recorded police contact as a POI is in his mid-teens for shoplifting. He has close to 200 contacts with police. However, the majority of his adult contact with police is not initially nor directly related to alleged offending; rather, it relates to mental health incidents such as self-harm and attempted suicide. At times these mental health incidents result in charges of property damage, assault, false calls to emergency services, breach of bail and breach of an apprehended violence order or 'AVO' (i.e., a restraining order). He is charged with nearly 50 offences but only ultimately convicted of around twenty of these. Police deal with James primarily through the mental health system (for example, use of civil mental health powers to transport him to a local hospital for assessment and possible treatment). He has 17 adult custodial episodes, the majority on remand. He is noted as engaging in offending and self-harm while in custody.

Discussion

As a preliminary point it is important to observe the relatively modest number of section 32 orders for Molly and James as compared to contact with police as a POI, police charges and time spent in custody. This suggests that for some criminalised disabled people who are diverted, these orders form a very small part of their overall criminal justice contact and they continue to be dealt with through criminal legal coercive intervention regardless of previous instances of court diversion. This observation is significant to the analysis in Chapters 6 and 7 of court diversion as shoring up the limits of criminal legal coercive intervention that apply to all criminalised disabled people (including those who are diverted), rather than moving them out of the criminal justice system or, indeed, dismantling the prison.

Lifelong social disadvantage

Molly's and James' life circumstances each suggest that criminalised disabled people who are diverted pursuant to section 32 experience 'corrosive social disadvantage' (Dowse, 2018), beginning in early childhood and enduring into adulthood.

Molly

Molly spends the majority of her childhood in OOHC as a state ward with numerous foster care placements and periods spent in children's homes. She experienced abuse prior to removal from her family. She has a family history of mental and behavioural disturbances and has family members who have died in police custody and prison.

Molly's time in OOHC, as described in police events narrative, is in an unhappy and unsafe living environment. For example, on one occasion police attend Molly's residence in relation to an incident of alleged property damage, assault and offensive behaviour by Molly and some co-residents. Police describe the children as being very wild and emotionally disturbed, all having histories of physical and psychological abuse and being incapable of normal social interactions. The police observe that the care workers take a hands off approach to the children and the children are not subject to usual family discipline.

Molly does not complete primary schooling. Her schooling includes time at mainstream schools, special schools and at a school for children with behavioural problems. The cessation of her schooling coincides with heightened police contact as a POI and some reported sexual assaults in her care residence.

Molly's contact with the criminal justice system does not cease when she receives disability services as an adult. Some of her contact with police at this point is related to assault and property damage linked to Molly's frustration with the levels of control in the space and the use of male caseworkers.

Molly has a number of justiciable matters beyond her numerous criminal matters—she receives Legal Aid assistance in relation to removal of her children from her care and complaints against government departments.

James

James lives with his mum and younger sister as a child. He attends a special school, but in his teens he is regularly noted as coming into contact with police for truancy and causing trouble at the local shopping malls (e.g. offensive language, shoplifting, smoking, graffiti). When he is nineteen, James is also coming into contact with police in relation to domestic disputes at his family home. James is noted by police as behaving in an aggressive manner towards his mum and sister, all three of whom are considered by police to be under the influence of alcohol. Police end up applying for an AVO on behalf of his mum and sister, with conditions that prevent James from continuing to live at the family home. After this time, when James has contact with police they note him as having no fixed address and as sleeping rough or in precarious hostel or boarding house accommodation.

Soon after James moves out of the family home, police note that he attends the office of his former special school in a heightened emotional state. Police are called and James is taken to the local hospital for mental health assessment. Police note that James says he was sexually and physically abused at the school when he was a student, but police dismiss this as irrational and as vague because he provides inconsistent dates and details.

Discussion

Both Molly and James have difficult childhood circumstances that likely contribute to the direction of their life courses. Molly has been removed from her family at a very young age. This signals the significance of OOHC to the institutional archipelago of carceral control for some criminalised disabled people. In recording their contact with Molly at her OOHC residence, police depict her childhood and living arrangements as chaotic, disrupted and unsafe, far removed from the perceived stability and security of the nuclear family (Goldson, 2009: p. 92). Yet surprisingly (and disturbingly), in recording these observations the police give a sense that there is something very mundanely unremarkable and nearly routine and expected about what they are observing, not least because of the references to the children being emotionally disturbed and exhibiting abnormal behaviour; this situates the 'problem' with their circumstances in the children's minds rather than in a fundamentally flawed child welfare system. Police never question why, for example, Molly's home workers are laissez faire, or why Molly is threatening suicide. There is no indication that Molly is considered to be living in an at-risk environment (noting they have been placed here after having been removed from purportedly at-risk family environments). Indeed, there is no indication in the police events narrative of any scrutiny by police of the OOHC organisations as somehow responsible for the state of affairs the police encounter—rather, police focus on the individual children as *the* problem for staff to manage, thus contributing to a dynamic of criminalising children who are in non-normative circumstances and legitimating the violence and harm they might be experiencing (Chapman, 2014a; Dowse, 2017). It is important to pause here to note that the circumstances of Molly in OOHC are dictated by the law and by legal actors—thus, law and the decisions and choices made by legal actors in interpreting and applying legislation permeate her life. Indeed, their impact is so pervasive as to be incapable of isolation and disentanglement and easily becomes invisible if we concentrate too much on the actions of those 'on the ground', such as out-of-home care workers and police. We need to reckon with this complicity of law *and* legal actors when reflecting on the courses criminalised disabled people's lives take, and in drawing out the slow violence of justice and social services.

James' homelessness, alcohol use and estrangement from his family reflect the lifelong socioeconomic impacts of child abuse (Hunter, 2014; Royal Commission into Institutional Responses to Child Sexual Abuse 2017b), and the difficulties experienced by adult survivors in being believed by police, notably when they manifest behaviour related to trauma (Royal Commission into Institutional Responses to Child Sexual Abuse 2017c). Both Molly's and James' circumstances also illustrate how criminalised disabled people's segregation can begin in childhood through child welfare and education systems.

The circumstances discussed here constitute what Dowse has described in relation to other individuals in the MHDCD data set as 'corrosive social disadvantage' (Dowse, 2018). Building on that observation, it is additionally vital to situate this social disadvantage in a settler colonial context. The social disadvantage experienced by Molly, notably state removal from her family and her placement in OOHC from an early age, can be considered in the context of settler colonial practices of child removal of Indigenous Australians (Human Rights and Equal Opportunities Commission (HREOC), 1997). Her involvement in OOHC as both a child *and* a parent suggests the structural, intergenerational and cyclical nature of OOHC and its broader effects on social disadvantage, trauma and criminalisation (Cunneen & Libesman, 2000: pp. 102–103; 2002: pp. 7–8; in a Canadian context, see Manitoba Advocate for Child and Youth, 2019). The criminalisation of Molly in OOHC and her subsequent positioning by the state as both criminal and disabled/mentally ill (arguably both possible in part by reason of the material effects of being in OOHC) individualises the historical and structural injustices of intergenerational and cyclical child removal and broader settler colonial dispossession, concealing these historic and ongoing injustices in the deviancy and pathology of the body (Steele, 2018d). Similar issues of intergenerational dynamics of Indigenous child removal were explored in the recent report into the life and death of 15-year-old First Nations Tina Fontaine in Manitoba (Manitoba Advocate for Child and Youth, 2019).

Ultimately, the discussion here of social disadvantage suggests that the circumstances of criminalised disabled people cannot be articulated through a prism of 'pure' disability and diagnostic frameworks at the heart of court diversion, and that to do so might actually negate structural and settler colonial conditions.

Criminalisation

Molly and James experience early and ongoing contact with police.

Molly

Molly's first recorded police contact is under the age of ten, when she is reported as a missing person having run away from her OOHC residence. She is noted as a missing person nearly 20 times prior to her first criminal charge (noting that in NSW the minimum age of criminal responsibility is ten years). The use of police to retrieve Molly gives no indication as to why such a young child is running away from her residence or whether the issues giving rise to this are being addressed, but it is certainly suggestive of the damaging and unhappy nature of her living environments.

When Molly is 11 years old, her contact with police morphs from 'absconding' from her residence into offences of property damage and assault against care workers and care residence property—a pattern that continues for the next few years. During her early period of alleged offending, Molly experiences her first custodial episode. She is remanded to juvenile justice custody overnight on the basis that police assess bail as being inappropriate, with the reason for remand recorded by the Department of Juvenile Justice as being lack of community ties. It is striking that Molly's first time in prison at such a young age is due to an absence of community ties when she is in fact in the care of an *entire government department* and bureaucracy purportedly tasked with ensuring her welfare.

Over the next year, Molly's care-related offending escalates with police being called to the residences where she lives 20 times for incidents generally involving property damage and assault. At times the care provider requests only police intervention with no charges, but on other occasions she is charged with a number of offences relating to assault, property damage and breaching bail. Over this period, bail breaches begin to become a pattern in Molly's criminal justice pathway; the care provider agrees to Molly living with them as part of her bail, and Molly's reoffending (generally against the care provider) or absconding from the residence constitute breaches of her bail—the effect of which is that Molly begins to spend longer periods on remand in juvenile justice custody. The use by OOHC staff of police as a discipline strategy, and the frequency with which police are made aware of Molly's bail breaches, is arguably particular to the institutional 'home'/caring relations. It is very unlikely that a parent in a biological/nuclear family would seek police intervention as a means of discipline, particularly to the extent as used in OOHC for Molly.

In her early thirties, Molly begins to live in various disability accommodation settings, beginning with hospital-based large-scale accommodation and then community disability-supported accommodation. At various times Molly is required to reside in the disability accommodation by reason of legal orders, such as those related to past criminal offences (bail, good behaviour bonds and section 32 orders) and guardianship orders. This shift to disability accommodation does not result in the complete cessation of Molly's contact with police. Molly has contact with police in relation to offending *within* the accommodation (rather than in public). This offending includes property damage and assault against disability support service property and staff, seemingly because she is frustrated with the control dynamics in the accommodation, such as not being able to access food in the locked fridge. Molly also has contact with police related to self-harming in the accommodation setting. Sometimes this self-harm occurs after an altercation with staff, and at times it is dismissed by police as attention-seeking. Some of Molly's contact with police is linked to her breaching orders requiring her to reside at disability accommodation and/or follow the directions of her case manager and staff of the accommodation.

Molly does spend periods of time in prison during the time she has accessed disability accommodation. In one hospital-based accommodation setting, Molly 'absconds' regularly and on a couple of occasions, nurses contact the police to request Molly be removed for breaching her bail conditions or to be assessed under civil mental health laws. Police dismiss these requests, noting that the hospital-based accommodation is the appropriate place for Molly and that even if she was charged or assessed she would end up there again anyway. There are noticeable shifts in the police dynamics when Molly moves into community-based disability supported accommodation with instances of the workers notifying police only for formal recording of an incident and at other times actively advocating for Molly to avoid charges or be granted bail.

James

Following James being excluded from his family home, his contact with police as a POI generally involves some kind of acute mental health crisis. James begins calling emergency services either threatening to commit suicide or making hoax bomb threats at his former school. He also calls the Office of Protective Commissioner or 'OPC' (the substituted decision makers appointed by the NSW Guardianship Tribunal pursuant to a financial management order to manage his money) and makes violent threats if they do not release extra money to him. Police are regularly responding to these incidents by transporting him to the local hospital for mental health assessment. Throughout the police events narrative, police explain these incidents as being motivated by attention-seeking and loneliness, observe the high number and frequency of his call-outs, express frustration with James being a drain on police time and resources and quantify the length of time spent transporting him to hospital and waiting with him at emergency. Police observe on a number of occasions the ineffectiveness of criminal justice interventions in altering James' behaviour. Police warn James that he will be charged with public mischief for wasting police resources. Police threats to charge James appear to have little deterrent effect, because James continues to engage in this behaviour. At times, bail conditions are used by police in an *attempt* to prevent James from calling emergency services and the OPC, although police are called to a number of incidents in breach of these conditions.

James has sporadic contact with police as POI in relation to visits to his family home after he has been refused admission to the mental health facility following being transported there by police. These incidents result in charges of breach of AVOs. James also has contact with police in relation to (sometimes physically violent) altercations at the various boarding houses and hostels where he sometimes has temporary accommodation. For a number of these incidents James is charged and remanded in custody, having been refused bail because he has no fixed address at which he can reside.

Discussion

Molly's experience in OOHC underscores the significance of the child welfare system to early police contact of some criminalised disabled people who are diverted, reflecting a broader issue of OOHC as a catalyst for criminalisation of some disabled people (see, e.g., Dowse, 2017; Gerard, McGrath, Colvin, & McFarlane, 2019; Greig, McGrath & McFarlane, 2019; on the child welfare/crime nexus more broadly, in Australia see McFarlane, 2010; in England see Pidd & Wolfe Robinson, 2019). The quick escalation of Molly's police contact and the increasing use of remand reflects how criminalisation can occur at a point of precarity for this group—being in OOHC and having possibly also come from family situations of violence and neglect—confirming Goldson's point that children in the criminal justice system who have highly disadvantaged and abusive backgrounds are reconstructed from 'children with problems' to 'children as problems' (Goldson, 2009: p. 96). Baldry and Dowse similarly discuss the rapid transformation of 'high needs' to 'high risk', then the transformation of 'high risk' into 'dangerous', and the transformation of 'dangerous' into 'needing to be dealt with by the criminal justice system' (Baldry & Dowse, 2013: p. 224; see also p. 231). This is particularly disturbing given the recognition of the impact of child sexual abuse in institutional settings (including OOHC) on incarceration as an adult (Royal Commission into Institutional Responses to Child Sexual Abuse, 2017b: pp. 143–146).

Moreover, this relationship between OOHC and criminalisation needs to be situated in a settler colonial context and, hence, as part of systematic violence through child welfare and criminal justice systems (Cunneen & Libesman, 2000). A recent independent review of Aboriginal and Torres Strait Islander young people in NSW OOHC, chaired by law academic and Davis (an Aboriginal (Cobble Cobble) woman), has confirmed 'care criminalisation' continues to be a significant issue specifically for Aboriginal and Torres Strait Islander young people in OOHC (Davis, 2019: pp. 235–245; on the concept of 'matriculation' in relation to Aboriginal and Torres Strait Islander people, see Avery, 2018). As Chapman and Withers note:

> The race, class, and disability statistics on child welfare and criminal justice involvement are much too skewed to support a liberalist belief that everyone has an equal opportunity in life and that these systems do what they are said to do—that is, serve and protect the innocent and deter, punish, help, or rehabilitate only those who transgress consensual norms of acceptable behaviour.
>
> (Chapman & Withers, 2019: p. 347)

Molly's contact with police in the disability service context troubles the conventional assumption that—post-deinstitutionalisation—criminalisation of disabled people is associated with a lack of support and over presence in the public space, and that disability-supported accommodation will address criminalisation that comes from 'public' space by providing a 'private' space for these individuals to live and spend their time. Molly's contact with police illustrates the significance of disability services to her criminalisation. The point here is not that disability support accommodation per se results in criminalisation but, rather, that this space, and the relations and laws that structure this space, provide new possibilities for police contact. In particular, laws that are supposed to be progressive in keeping disabled people in the community and connecting them with support (such as section 32 orders and guardianship orders) provide new possibilities for police contact. There are many significant parallels between the nature of the alleged offending and the responses of staff in relation to OOHC and disability-supported accommodation, such as the significance of offences against staff and property and the role of police in responding to challenging behaviour or absconding. Indeed, the use of the word 'abscond' across both of these systems to describe when residents leave and fail to return by a designated time to these spaces signals the carceral assumptions that underpin these spaces. These parallels suggest commonalities in how 'islands' of 'care' in the institutional archipelago are generative of further carceral control through criminal justice 'islands'—the interlocking and kinetic qualities of the archipelago.

James' contact with police and subsequent criminal charges relating to breaching AVOs (civil legal orders) illustrates the significance of the civil law to criminalisation and incarceration of criminalised disabled people (see, e.g., NSWLRC, 2012a). His response to the OPC's management of his finances highlights the criminalisation of what might be read as resistance to coercion, control and denial of legal capacity and autonomy. James' contact with police also highlights the criminalisation of distress. The framing of his behaviour as attention-seeking and as a drain on police resources suggests a collective and structural absence of meaningful ways to support and engage with people at moments of distress and how this can have a particularly acute impact on individuals who are already known to police or who are socially isolated and without formal or informal supports. Criminalising distress is specifically problematic where this distress is connected to past experiences of violence (be it interpersonal, institutional, settler colonial etc.), and this is an issue that has not been thoroughly considered in government reviews on institutional violence, most recently the Australian Royal Commission into Institutional Responses to Child Sexual Abuse (Steele, 2017c). More broadly, there are many examples of criminalised disabled people dying in police or prison custody because their requests for help are dismissed as attention-seeking, as exemplified by the death of Ashley Smith (Perkel, 2013).

My discussion here of criminalisation has shown that while there are very specific and unique sets of circumstances that precede individuals' contact with police and criminal charges, for criminalised disabled people who are diverted pursuant to section 32, factors of social deprivation and precarity (such as social isolation, homelessness, lack of disability support and being in OOHC) may be contributing factors, as can interactions with OOHC and disability support services. The focus in court diversion on provision of disability and mental health services will simply sustain rather than end disability oppression if it cannot acknowledge and address these systemic dynamics.

James' and Molly's non-compliance with AVO and bail conditions demonstrates that while the institutional archipelago is complex and multifaceted, and surpasses the options available to control non-disabled criminalised people, it can ultimately *still* be incomplete, and that criminalised disabled people can present a threat to completeness of criminal law. This suggests that law and the disciplines are constantly seeking to recuperate these individuals within coercive intervention, as much as it also suggests the disruptive possibilities these individuals present to the exhaustiveness of this control. It is important to consider whether court diversion is such a vehicle for recuperation of criminalised disabled people into the institutional archipelago, or whether this provision itself signals the fragility and incompleteness of criminal law. Situating a discussion of the limits of criminal law in a settler colonial context (noting the central role of criminal law and the criminal justice system in sustaining dispossession), we might also ask whether court diversion provides any entry points into destabilising settler colonial rule and white sovereign law, or whether it only reiterates the colonial legal subjectivities that underpin this.

Incarceration

Molly and James each have multiple custodial episodes and in some of these they are detained in prison mental health units. Their time in custody demonstrates the significance of incarceration (even at points in time later than section 32 orders) and the violent and harmful effects of incarceration.

James

The majority of James' 17 custody episodes in adult prisons are instances on remand for periods ranging from one day to seven-and-a-half months. The reasons for these periods on remand include breaches of bail and having no fixed address. James also has multiple police custody episodes (twice as many as in prison), generally while waiting to be charged or interviewed, and including for breaches of bail.

James is noted as being a management problem in custody and as having a history of aggression and harm to others. He spends a number of periods in protective custody, as well as periods in segregation for disciplinary reasons. He is noted as having over 40 offences while in custody—including not complying with prison officer orders, abusive language, assault and intimidation. He has around 30 alerts for self-harm.

Molly

As a young person Molly has 19 episodes of juvenile custody over a period of seven years. These range in length from one day to five months, with the majority being periods on remand rather than sentences. As discussed earlier, OOHC is a significant dynamic in her custody—in terms of the focus of the incidents giving rise to the charges, the involvement of police in the incidents, and the inability to be granted bail.

As an adult in her late teens and early twenties, Molly is cycling in and out of prison and police custody. She has 13 periods of custody in adult prisons. Custody periods range from a few days through to one-and-a-half years and the majority are for sentences, with only one period (of one month) on remand. In her adult years prior to being in disability supported accommodation, Molly is frequently in police custody for short periods—in the space of eight years she has 60 police custody episodes.

Self-harm figures heavily in Molly's incarceration; with over 20 self-harm alerts in juvenile justice custody and a further 33 self-harm alerts in adult custody for acts such as tying clothing around her neck, cutting her wrists and swallowing metal objects. Molly's first incidence of attempting to self-harm and suicide occurs at age 11 when she is remanded in custody for around 4 weeks following an OOHC-related incident.

Discussion

James' and Molly's time in custody demonstrates the cyclical nature of incarceration irrespective of the availability of court diversion (noting that Molly's section 32 orders do not even always enable her to avoid incarceration because of concurrent sentences). This demonstrates that court diversion does not necessarily prevent criminalisation *or* incarceration (let alone the harmful effects of incarceration). Prison is a dangerous, harmful, distressing and violent environment, both generally (Scraton & McCulloch, 2009) and specifically to disabled people (Ribet, 2010). However, the self-harm is particularly pronounced in relation to Molly. Molly's self-harm and her incarceration more broadly reflect the vulnerability in incarceration of Aboriginal and Torres Strait Islander Australians, such as deaths in custody and distress (see, for example, Royal Commission into Aboriginal Deaths in Custody, 1991). It also reflects the ongoing links between Aboriginal and Torres Strait Islander incarceration, settler colonial violence and persistent denial of Aboriginal and Torres Strait Islander sovereignty and self-determination (see Cunneen, 2009: pp. 210–211, 222). Molly's experience of incarceration highlights how criminalised disabled people, particularly those whose criminalisation begins in childhood, are situated in a slow death—an ongoing state of precarity and deprivation—central to which is the slow violence of prison management (Kilty & Lehalle, 2019). In a context of both Gilmore's theoretical observations about racism as 'production and exploitation of group-differentiated vulnerability to premature death' (Gilmore, 2007: p. 28) and empirical research variously establishing premature death of people with intellectual or learning disabilities (O'Leary et al., 2018), people with mental illness (Lawrence et al., 2013; Saxena, 2018), prisoners (Massoglia & Pridemore, 2015), and Indigenous and First Nations people (Bramley et al., 2004; Ring, 2003), we might critically reflect on the specific exposure of *criminalised disabled people* to premature death and the extent to which court diversion disrupts or contributes to this phenomenon and to structural dynamics of slow death and slow violence.

Here I want to pause and momentarily shift from my hypothetical institutional narrative to the data informing these narratives and the state's data collection itself. The data used in this chapter have not ended up in state records through an automated system; rather, health service and criminal justice workers have entered this information into systems as or soon after the events reported. Children may be incarcerated and subjected to self-harm and violence which can be neatly summarised in data entry without triggering their release or any legal redress (or even systemic improvements to these spaces). This highlights how pervasively normalised and taken for granted are systems of carceral control and collective tolerance for the structural harm of certain groups of people, particularly Aboriginal and Torres Strait Islander criminalised disabled people. Being at risk of self-harm or death in custody, having multiple family members die in custody, or having experienced sexual abuse in institutional settings are rendered mundane pieces of institutional information. The lack of empathy and concern in the data reflects the observations made by Porter (2016)—a descendant of the Brinja clan of the Yuin nation—in the context of the death in police custody from septicaemia and pneumonia of Ms Dhu (an Aboriginal Australian women of the Yamatji-Nanda Nation and the Banjima People): 'Such details are haunting not only because of the stark nature of their content, but for what they represent: a complete denial of human compassion and dignity, and a national failure'. Thus, record-keeping practices might be understood as the 'violence of neglect' (Cunneen, 2009; see also Kilty & Lehalle, 2019: pp. 317–321). We might go so far as to suggest that inaction via record-keeping constitutes the kind of racist violence Foucault referred to, a slow violence.

The contradictions between data collection and what that data discloses reflect Razack's observations in the context of First Nations people who have died in police custody. She notes a tension whereby these individuals are known for their risk of harm and yet not responded to through care, prompting her to observe: 'While Indigenous people are literally the business of the state in certain locations, *they are not its concern*' (Razack, 2015: pp. 52–53, emphasis added; see also Bond, 2017). Razack powerfully captures the disturbing contradiction in the context of Molly's incarceration and, indeed, that pervades this institutional data more broadly. This contradiction is that the state is author and custodian of such a wealth of information about the harm and violence these individuals are subjected to and yet has not prevented this from occurring, nor transformed the structural conditions that allow it to continue (which are in the power of the state alone to transform). The state has invested such time and labour in monitoring and collecting the data and yet this process has simply fed the routinised operation of carceral control—business as usual—rather than prompted fundamental questions about the ethics and necessity of these carceral practices. Reading the data now it is strikingly obvious that something simply is not right with a system that leaves people in slow death. Drawing on Razack to understand this contradiction, she suggests that this dynamic of the state 'engaging' with Indigenous people but not 'attending to [their] needs' is one way that state actors can confirm the individual's 'alterity and simultaneously their own legitimacy' in a context where '[s] ettler entitlement rests on a conviction of one's capacity to be a modern subject and the corresponding incapacity of an Indigenous person to enter modern life' (Razack, 2015: p. 53). The 'indifference to Indigenous life demonstrated in the everyday routines of health care and policing' can be understood as ways through which colonial subjectivities are sustained and dispossession continues (ibid.: p. 104; see also Bond, 2017). It is striking that despite the resonances of their circumstances with broader structural conditions of Aboriginal and Torres Strait Islander Australians, the problems encountered by Molly are never framed in structural terms of Indigenous/settler relations. It is thus important to consider whether court diversion is capable of confronting and disrupting this settler colonial violence or whether it simply reiterates this violence.

James' and Molly's incarceration illustrates the textured nature of carceral control in the institutional archipelago, for example, the impact of remand and breaches of justice orders on incarceration, thus reflecting the significance to incarceration of the framework of community-based criminal legal orders which one might instead assume would place individuals in the community. James' disciplinary offences during incarceration – which could additionally be acts of distress or resistance – expose the way in which the legal regime of control and management in prison can itself generate further criminalisation and further punishment.

While the harmful effects of prison discussed here might be conventionally positioned as a persuasive reason for the greater use of court diversion, the data also reveals that individuals continue to be incarcerated following diversion (and, indeed, this is anticipated by the breach provisions in section 32). As such, we need to carefully consider how court diversion makes possible and legitimates the violence and harm of incarceration and state irresponsibility for its injustices.

Policing through civil mental health legislation

As well as having multiple contacts with police as POIs, Molly and James also have other forms of contact with police, both as victims of crime and under civil mental health legislation. In this section I focus on James' mental health contact with police before discussing Molly's and James' victim contact in the following section.

Police have powers under civil mental health legislation to take an individual to a hospital for assessment by a medical practitioner with the view of possibly 'scheduling' the individual to a mental health facility for involuntary containment and treatment. Apprehension under these circumstances indicates that police believe the person is experiencing a mental health issue at the time of contact (not necessarily that the individual will subsequently receive a mental health-related diagnosis and receive treatment).

James

Civil mental health legislation is a key feature of James' contact with police. James has around 60 recorded contacts with police which police categorise as being on the basis of mental health. Moreover of his contacts as a POI many occur in the context of acute periods of distress but are read by police as offending (for example, self-harm or suicide threats read as public nuisance). Police frequently respond to James' self-harm and threats of self-harm and suicide by taking him to the local public hospital for assessment and possible admission. At times he is medicated, kept for observation or scheduled as an involuntary patient; on a number of other occasions he is placed back in the hands of the police because hospital staff refuse to admit him (for example on the basis he is exhibiting challenging behaviour rather than mental illness, or engaging in attention-seeking, as opposed to genuine self-harm attempts).

Discussion

James' contact with police clearly demonstrates the way in which civil mental health legislation provides additional opportunities for police contact and for criminalisation. Civil mental health legislation is used by police to deal with (or perhaps to avoid dealing with) James' behaviour, which could otherwise be treated as criminal behaviour. This suggests civil mental health-related police contact and POI police contact are intimately linked rather than being concerned with different categories of individuals or separate kinds of behaviour. Together, they form a network of institutional responses to criminalised disabled people. In a context where James is recognised by police as creating public nuisance, mental health facilities provide an option for keeping James confined and away from the community. Medication enables James to be confined from *within* his body *without* the need to be physically confined within a facility (Fabris, 2011).

However, James' contact with police suggests that carceral control through a civil mental health system is not just about intervention and coercion *within* the mental health system, but is also about being *moved between* the criminal justice and mental health systems. Like James, some criminalised disabled people do not have a fixed place in either the criminal justice system or the mental health system (nor, indeed, any fixed place of residence either) but, instead, are in a constant process of *circulation between* institutions and as a result have rather fluid and unstable institutional identities. Menzies and Chunn (1998: p. 275; see generally pp. 273–278) make a similar observation in a historical context, noting how some women indefinitely detained in British Columbia's psychiatric system circulated through the psychiatric and criminal justice systems with neither wishing to have them as their responsibility, rendering them 'polydeviant women who circulated between institutional and civil settings as a kind of drifting diaspora'. They observe:

> When faced with such marginal women, the main motivation of forensic authorities was to contend with whatever immediate crises they might engender, then to circulate them out of the hospital at the earliest opportunity. ... Wherever they did come to reside, these women were generally seen to fit nowhere in particular, and they constituted irritations and classification problems for everyone upon whom they were imposed.
>
> (Menzies and Chunn, 1998: p. 275)

Finally, James' contact with police illustrates the institutional contingency to some of James' diagnoses. When James is taken to the hospital by police pursuant to their civil mental health powers for assessment and possible admission and treatment, the hospital *diagnoses* him. This diagnosis, which originates in criminal justice contact, then forms part of his *health* record of diagnoses. Whether he is diagnosed, and the specific diagnosis he receives, appears contingent on the institutional self-identity and the resources available in the public health system. The criminal justice system and the police have a fundamental role in shaping the kind of diagnosed individual that he is, rather than the police acting upon a pre-existing diagnosed individual.

Ultimately, this discussion highlights the centrality of civil mental health law to the carceral control of criminalised disabled people who are diverted, rather than mental health services being an antidote to criminalisation and incarceration.

Police contact as a victim of crime

James and Molly also have contact with police as victims of crime. The violence itself and the police responses are in different ways linked to their precarity and their contact with police as POI. The police data from which these hypothetical institutional narratives are drawn do not provide any definitive information on the final outcomes of these victim contacts including if perpetrators are charged.

James

James has around 25 recorded contacts with police as a victim. Approximately half of these relate to physical violence in the context of physical altercations with other residents in his precarious housing arrangements in hostels and boarding houses (including when he is living in a tent in the backyard of a boarding house). In many of these contacts police also note him as perpetrator of violence and also identify the impact of alcohol and other drugs on all involved in the altercations. The other half relate to his attempts to report his experiences of child sexual abuse at his special school. On the first instance of such reporting, police note that they spent two hours speaking with James but were are unable to ascertain sufficient details from him and that he was exhibiting odd physical and emotional behaviour which suggested the unreliable nature of the information being provided. On later instances, police begin to refer to earlier contact with police as POI to suggest he is making up the abuse to avoid charges related to his contact with emergency services and at other times describe him as delusional and transport him to a hospital for mental health assessment. Indeed, as time goes on many of his police contacts where he discloses the sexual abuse are simply categorised as 'mental health' contacts, rather than victim contacts.

Molly

Molly has around 50 recorded contacts with police as a victim. Around 30 of these are specifically identified as reports of sexual violence and approximately half of these occur in institutional settings of OOHC and disability accommodation. The police have a variety of responses to Molly's victim reports.

On one occasion police transport Molly to the local public hospital for admission under mental health powers after police are called to her care residence in relation to Molly locking herself in the bathroom and threatening to kill herself. Police do not take seriously Molly's reports of having been sexually assaulted by care workers, emphasising that she makes these allegations in the course of contact with police for property damage at the care home.

Generally when police make note in the police events narrative of sexual assault allegations made by Molly in adulthood, they identify a variety of reasons for doubting the truth of Molly's reports. Police refer to there being no signs of struggle or injury, that Molly does not appear emotionally affected, inconsistencies in her versions of event and that her reports are uncorroborated. On other occasions, police question the reliability of the reports because Molly makes these reports against her carers when she is already known to police as someone who has exhibited challenging and offending behaviour in those institutional settings.

On one occasion Molly reports to police incidents of violence by other inmates during one of her periods of incarceration. The police events narrative states she discloses these incidents during a court appearance but refuses to make a formal report because she is too distressed. Police dismiss Molly's report as a fictional report which was made in order to evoke pity in the judge for a lighter sentence.

Discussion

These two institutional narratives demonstrate that there is not necessarily an absolute dichotomy between criminalisation and victimisation for those who are diverted. While statistics suggest high incidence of sexual assault in the prison population irrespective of disability (notably women in prison; see Stathopoulos, 2012), there are very particular ways in which disability is harnessed to further exclude criminalised disabled people from legitimate victim status (Steele, 2017c). This is particularly concerning given there are many ways in which law limits access to justice for criminalised people, including access to justice for earlier instances of institutional sexual violence in settings beyond prison.[3] The responses of police to Molly's and James' reports of childhood sexual abuse in OOHC and school settings are particularly disturbing given the details of widespread institutional child abuse, notably in out-of-home care, that have emerged

3 For example, the exclusion of prisons and juvenile detention centres so as to prevent apprehended domestic violence orders in prison (see, e.g., *Crimes (Domestic and Personal) Violence Act 2007* (NSW), s 5(1)(e)), prisoners incarcerated for serious offences must seek leave of court to commence civil proceedings while in prison (*Felons (Civil Proceedings) Act 1981* (NSW)), there are limits to civil liability damages that can be obtained while in prison (*Civil Liability Act 2002* (NSW), Pt 2A) and people who have been sentenced to a period of five years or more in prison cannot automatically apply to the national redress scheme set up in the aftermath of the Royal Commission into Institutional Responses to Child Sexual Abuse (*National Redress Scheme for Institutional Child Sexual Abuse Act* (Cth), Pt 3–2, Div 2).

from the Australian Royal Commission into Institutional Responses to Child Sexual Abuse (2017a).

In the context of Molly, police draw on gendered and abled assumptions about 'ideal victims' of rape in dismissing the reliability of her reports (Steele, 2017c). Yet, there is also a more pervasive dynamic in police contact as victims by Molly and to some extent James—the way in which gender, disability and criminality coalesce to form a basis on which to question the reliability of the reports and to become naturally positioned as undeserving of victim status.

I suggest (counter-intuitively) that these dynamics of disability, incarceration and violence illuminate how justice system responses to victimisation might themselves become part of carceral control (Steele, 2017c). Hence, we need to consider the interrelationships in the institutional archipelago between court diversion, other modes of punishment or care, and justice system responses to victimisation. We must also think about whether court diversion provides possibilities to acknowledge and redress the violence in which the criminal justice and disability and mental health systems are complicit.

My discussion of the case studies in this section has highlighted that while James and Molly were each diverted at some point in their lives, provision of disability and mental health services cannot serve to capacitate them fully, if at all, but instead simply folds back into debilitating carceral control and slow death. For similar reasons, these case studies highlight the limitations of the CRPD in providing a framework to respond to the circumstances these individuals face. For example, we can ask what the CRPD's focus on abolishing disability-specific criminal laws and enhancing accommodations within the criminal justice system would offer to Molly. Many of Molly's disability-specific section 32 orders ran parallel to periods of incarceration, and it is unclear how any disability accommodations aimed at making individuals more equally treated within prison does anything to disrupt the settler colonial context of the criminal justice system.

Yet, the analysis here goes beyond anticipating the limitations and failures of court diversion. The analysis of institutional data also underscores the complicity of legal and helping professions working in these institutional contexts in debilitation, and presents us with what Chapman and Withers powerfully state in their consideration of the structural inequalities and violence in the child welfare and criminal justice systems:

> We invite readers to make a choice: Are we going to believe that some people are inherently more inferior to others, inherently less responsible for their actions, and inherently more violent? Are we going to seriously engage with the clear and evident forces of ongoing structural violence? If the major determining factor in who ends up involved with criminal justice or child protective services is systemic oppression, which it is, then this oppression

> demands a fundamental reconsideration of everyday social services and other social relations within our society.
>
> (Chapman & Withers, 2019: p. 348)

To their observations I would add the need to reconsider everyday legal and justice services and legal relations. I invite readers to contemplate this as we turn to analyse court diversion in greater detail, because I return to these questions of professional accountability and responsibility in Chapter 8.

Chapter 6

Jurisdiction, disability and lawful relations

6.1 Making diversion possible and lawful

In this chapter I continue the analysis of court diversion by reference to a case study from New South Wales, Australia. The chapter focuses on the first step in the judicial decision to divert a criminalised disabled person under section 32 of the *Mental Health (Forensic Provisions) Act 1990* (NSW) ('section 32')—whether the court has jurisdiction to order diversion of an individual appearing before the court on criminal charges. This question of jurisdiction is answered by the individual having a diagnosed disability. While this step might seem self-evident and benign, I argue that it deserves critical attention because this step transforms the basis of lawful relations in court diversion to a concern with ongoing behaviour associated with internal, medical disability in contrast to a concern with past behaviour pertinent to conviction for a criminal offence. The core point I make in this chapter is that the court's reliance on psy professions and the process of diagnosis in determining jurisdiction to order court diversion turns judicial focus away from the criminal offence and inward to the body and thus opens up the possibility of ongoing, carceral control and violence of a nature and extent not possible through criminal law. In turn this first step in judicial decision-making limits the potential for law through court diversion to capacitate rather than debilitate individuals who are diverted.

The finding that a criminalised disabled individual comes within the court's jurisdiction to order court diversion is related to the court's 'authority to decide' (Leeming, 2012: p. 1). In legal terms, this is referred to as the judge being satisfied of the 'jurisdictional fact' of diagnosed disability (which I also refer to as judicial finding of a diagnosed disability). In the course of outlining a three-stage inquiry for the determination of section 32 applications, Justice McColl in the New South Wales Court of Appeal decision of *DPP (NSW) v El Mawas* (2006) (the '*El Mawas* inquiry') identified that the first stage is 'to determine, in accordance with s 32(1)(a), whether the defendant is eligible to be dealt with under that section. That question clearly involves a finding of fact and is properly described as the jurisdictional question' (*DPP (NSW) v El Mawas* (2006) 109 [75]). The 'jurisdictional fact' in section 32 is that 'it appears to the Magistrate' that the defendant is 'cognitively impaired' (or, as it was at the time of court data collection, 'developmentally disabled'), 'suffering from a mental illness' or 'suffering from a mental condition for which treatment is available in a mental health facility' (s 32(1)(a)). Judicial finding of a diagnosed disability is informed by a report by a 'psy' professional (that is, psychologists, psychiatrists and neuropsychologists) (Intellectual Disability Rights Service, 2011: pp. 22–32).

Satisfaction of the jurisdictional fact of court diversion adds another legal domain (i.e. a basis on which judges have lawful authority to make decisions in relation to individuals appearing before the court). Criminalised disabled people by definition must already be within the Local Court's criminal legal domain (ss 31(1), 32(1)) and able to be dealt with through trial/plea, conviction/acquittal and sentence like all other criminalised people. Judicial finding of a diagnosed disability simply opens up an additional and alternative *disability* legal domain through which magistrates can choose to deal with an individual's charges.

Leeming (2012: p. 2) reminds us that jurisdiction is not to be taken for granted or simply implied. It is 'not a status, like adulthood or bankrupt or national or resident, which can be attained or lost', but a conferral of power and 'hence the conditions of that conferral cannot be breached' (ibid.: p. 3). So judicial finding of a diagnosed disability lies at the heart of the lawfulness, justice and legitimacy of carceral control through court diversion.

In the following sections of this chapter I move beyond Leeming's characterisation of jurisdiction and draw on critical approaches to jurisdiction which illuminate the role of jurisdiction in not merely activating judicial authority over preformed legal subjects but in actually making individuals and entire populations into the 'natural' and legitimate subjects of judicial authority to order carceral control and violence. In turn, a critique of the jurisdictional fact is central to understanding the 'injustice' of court diversion, because it is a key way through which criminalised disabled people come to be justly known and acted on as a separate category of legal subjects both situated outside criminal legal liberal citizenship and exposed to greater legal options for coercive intervention. This critique is part of this book's broader grappling with why court diversion sits so comfortably in law rather than prompting mass political outrage: how it is accommodated in law and politically tolerated in society.

Section 6.2 connects critical approaches to jurisdiction and disability to show how the first stage of the *El Mawas* inquiry deploys Foucauldian classification to situate criminalised disabled individuals in a separate disability legal domain that enables disability-specific coercive intervention. In Section 6.3, the chapter focuses on how the jurisdictional fact of diagnosed disability has a particularly significant impact in rendering as apolitical and noncolonial the expanded scope for coercive intervention of criminalised disabled people, notably Indigenous and First Nations criminalised disabled people. It does so by making it difficult for us to see the broader structural and settler colonial contexts in which court diversion is situated. Chapter 7 then turns to analyse the second and third stages of the *El Mawas* inquiry.

Section 32 Court Data

In making my argument over the next two chapters, I draw on a sample of section 32 court appearances. This is a small sample of 14 section 32 applications made in the New South Wales Local Court ('the Section 32 Court Data').[1] The data collected consist of court transcripts of the section 32 hearing, field notes of court observations and court files. Generally, each court file consisted of a report by a psy professional, letters by treating health professionals, a treatment plan by a disability service, documentation relating to mental health casework services or Community Treatment Orders (for those with mental illness), New South Wales Police Facts Sheet and Court Attendance Notices in relation to each charge, New South Wales Police convictions record, court documents relating to bail, the section 32 order (or other order for those for whom section 32 application was unsuccessful), and court registry administrative documents (for example, noting appearances at each court date). The project was designed to gather a snapshot of section 32 cases appearing before NSW Local Courts over a 13-month time frame (July 2010–August 2011). All data collected were de-identified and all sample members were given pseudonyms.

There are 14 individuals in the sample, five females and nine males. They included four Indigenous Australian individuals (three female, one male) and ten who were not Indigenous Australian (two female, eight male). None of the non-Indigenous sample members have Anglo-Celtic surnames, and two migrated as children with their families to Australia from countries involved in armed conflict. Of the 15 section 32 applications made in relation to the 14 individuals (one individual made two section 32 applications on separate occasions), 11 were granted, two refused and two granted only in relation to some of the charges.

Of the 13 section 32 orders made, 11 were conditional and two were unconditional. A majority were making a section 32 application in relation to multiple charges—between two and nine charges (only two had a single charge; one of these individuals had a small number of penalty notice offences and the other had no criminal history). Of the 12 applications involving multiple charges, the majority occurred across multiple (between two and four) separate incidents and only three cases had all of their charges in a single incident.

6.2 Making court diversion a lawful option: alternative legal subjectivity

In essence, judicial finding of a diagnosed disability can be viewed as a technique through which a magistrate actively brings individuals within lawful authority—determination of the jurisdictional fact makes possible a disabled legal subjectivity and, hence, crafts lawful relations between that legal subject and the court

1 Institutional research ethics approval for this empirical research was granted by the University of Sydney Australia Human Research Ethics Committee: Protocol No 12513.

characterised by disability. This confirms a magistrate's authority to know and act on them in a way so different to what is possible in the criminal legal domain, thus rendering this subjectification non-discriminatory and just. Recalling the earlier discussion of 'disability' (rather than the offence) threading together the legal process and ultimate outcome of court diversion, this chapter shows how this threading is initiated by a rather routine and mundane judicial practice.

Therefore, classification in a context of coercive intervention done pursuant to law is not only about making control *possible* (per Foucault and, indeed, the disability carceral scholarship). It is also about making this control *lawful and just* (Godden, 2007: p. 181). Law and legal process is central to the carceral control and violence done to criminalised disabled people *through law*, and jurisdiction has a foundational role.

Critical approaches to jurisdiction

Critical approaches to jurisdiction help us see how legal recognition of disability through provision of court diversion does not achieve positive 'inclusion' in a broader sense of inclusion into political community and full humanness. Instead, inclusion enables the forging of 'lawful' relations between criminalised disabled individuals and magistrates that makes possible carceral control that is otherwise legally impossible.

Traditionally and as discussed in Section 6.1 above, questions of jurisdiction have been approached as technical legal matters. In contrast, scholarship utilising critical approaches to jurisdiction illuminates, as Valverde (2015: p. 82) notes, 'struggles that ... are waged in a quiet and legalistic manner as fights about jurisdiction actually involve—and end up deciding—much larger, extralegal issues of power and authority'. In a strict legal sense, jurisdiction is typically understood in terms of static 'spheres' of territorial and subject matter jurisdiction within which an individual's legal matter must fit in order to make possible the judge's authority to decide (Leeming, 2012). Yet, in the critical legal scholarship, jurisdiction is not merely the static space within which judicial decision-making takes place, but rather is approached as dynamic. Dorsett and McVeigh approach jurisdiction as an active process undertaken by judges, through which individuals are brought within the lawful authority of judicial decision-making; and the specific basis on which they are brought within this authority then shapes the legality—and, hence, the justice and legitimacy—of subsequent material interventions they order (see generally Dorsett & McVeigh, 2012; 2014; McVeigh, 2007; see also Pasternak, 2014). The discretion available to courts in deciding whether to proceed through criminal law or apply section 32 exemplifies this dynamism.

At an individual level, jurisdiction is the avenue by which individuals come to be included as legal subjects within law and legal authority (Dorsett & McVeigh, 2012: p. 4). For example, Godden (2007: p. 181) states that 'law, through an assertion of jurisdiction, acts on or through bodies to "identify" and ascribe legal status to the subject/individual' and that:

> jurisdiction is not simply the assertion of bare control over bodies in a territorial compass but also comprehends the manner and form by which law insinuates itself as the indispensable means of control by establishing a necessary nexus between body and 'law'.
>
> (ibid.: pp. 181–182)

Pursuant to critical approaches to jurisdiction, the transformation of individuals into legal subjects is not an abstract discursive process, but actually involves material, embodied actions by judges.

According to Dorsett and McVeigh (2012: p. 58), 'legal categorisation is a technology which names and orders legal knowledge' and 'creates and crafts the forms of lawful relations' (ibid.: p. 71). It involves the distinctions drawn between different kinds of legal matters and locating them in different 'domains' (ibid., 2012: pp. 71–75). Thus, an analysis of the jurisdictional dynamics of court diversion helps in understanding how particular criminalised disabled individuals become legal subjects of disability-specific coercive intervention (at a point in time when they are not legally capable of being subjected to criminal legal coercive intervention because they have not been convicted or sentenced), and an appreciation of the nuances of law's (and the judiciary's) complicity in the enactment and legitimacy of this control. I suggest that this indicates that legal recognition of disability through court diversion enables inclusion in a legal domain of carceral control, rather than achieving broader inclusion into political community and full humanness.

As well as operating at an individual level, jurisdiction also has effects at a systemic and population level. Valverde (2015: p. 83) notes that dynamics of jurisdiction not only 'certify exercises of authority' but also 'work … as a sorting process that acts to conceal from view the qualitative differences in governance'. In this exercise, dispersing and allocating authority to govern particular populations to different decision makers (e.g. different government departments, different legal domains or different levels in state/federal governments) then render self-evident different ways of governing those populations: 'by deciding the "who governs" question, the game of jurisdiction simultaneously but implicitly determines *how* something is to be governed' (ibid.: p. 84). This dispersal and ordering renders jurisdiction an 'anti-politics machine' in giving jurisdiction 'this quite magical power to depoliticize governance' (ibid.).

In connecting Valverde's ideas on jurisdiction to the Foucauldian concept of subjectification, the centrality of diagnosis in determining jurisdiction to order court diversion turns judicial focus away from the criminal offence and inward to the body and thus opens up the possibility of ongoing, carceral control and violence of a nature and extent not possible through criminal law. I argue that this turn towards the body does not register as politically contentious because jurisdiction sorts individuals appearing before the court on criminal charges into legal domains (criminal legal or disability legal) that can make possible and legitimate seemingly contradictory or unequal ways of dealing with them (coercive intervention relative to the specific convicted criminal offence/s as compared to coercive intervention relative to one's disability) because each legal domain makes individuals into different kinds of legal subjects. This sorting makes it more difficult to compare—and, hence, to see the unequal treatment as discriminatory, including inequalities between criminal legal intervention and court diversion's disability-specific coercive intervention. Moreover, it is possible for the one embodied individual to be dealt with through different legal domains, by being transformed into different legal subjectivities (see the example in Chapter 5 of Molly receiving a section 32 order and criminal legal interventions in the one lot of charges, or Molly and James having section 32 orders and criminal legal interventions across different sets of charges). Thus, bringing an individual into a specific legal domain makes it possible to know and act on that individual in a very particular way and to make it impossible to compare that to how individuals are treated in other domains. At a systemic level, judicial finding of a diagnosed disability has the biopolitical effect of dividing and ordering criminalised people into different legal domains (distinct areas of judicial authority). It also has the biopolitical effect of ordering disabled people for the purposes of access to liberty and resources, on the basis of whether they have criminal charges (if they do then their 'access' occurs through this disability legal domain and is ultimately tied up with carceral control); hence, judicial finding of a diagnosed disability bifurcates disabled people along lines of criminality and is complicit in debilitation specifically of criminalised disabled people.

I now turn to look more closely at the diagnosed disability character of the jurisdictional fact.

Diagnosed disability and lawful authority

In determining the jurisdictional fact of section 32, the individual's disability must 'appear to the Magistrate'. Reliance upon diagnostic terminology in relation to what should 'appear' to the magistrate imports with it medicalised understandings of disability and the related epistemic authority of psy professionals (Withers, 2012a: pp. 35–36), which suggests the self-evident and scientifically objective nature of what will either exist or not for the magistrate to perceive. Moreover, while generally, magistrates can inform themselves however they think fit (s 36), in practice magistrates inform themselves by way of a diagnosis contained in a report by a psy professional (Intellectual Disability Rights Service, 2011: pp. 22–32). In essence, through judicial consideration of the jurisdictional fact, a criminalised disabled individual is in practice transformed into a disabled legal subject who is *diagnosed* with a developmental disability, mental illness or mental condition.

Drawing on the discussion in Chapter 3 of the disciplinary nature of the medical model of disability—disability as an individual pathology that must be eliminated or contained through therapeutic intervention—we can now appreciate how this jurisdictional fact makes possible an approach to criminalised disabled people that focuses on their disability as a basis for coercive intervention. This is so even in the face of the conventional focus on the criminal offence and the strict limits this focus gives to the scope of coercive intervention in the criminal legal domain.

This disciplinary nature of disability in the jurisdictional fact is aided by its reliance on diagnosis. Diagnosis is typically seen as the process of discovering a pre-existing natural condition within the individual (Gillman et al., 2000: p. 397). The classificatory systems through which diagnostic definitions can be applied to individuals are also not simply objective, neutral processes of discovery of pre-existing conditions. Rather, they are processes that *produce* disability or, as Linton (1998: p. 6) states, brings 'impairment' itself into existence. Gillman, Heyman and Swain (2000: p. 401) describe diagnosis as a 'discursive practice'. These authors state that 'the outcomes of assessment and diagnosis are not representations of objective truth or reality about an individual' (ibid.: p. 402). Rather, as they write, '[d]iagnostic labels, whether they apply to mental, physical, or intellectual impairment, are not only descriptive, but also constitutive of people's lives, that is, they "bring forth" pathology, create problem saturated identities, and construct careers as patients and cases' (ibid.: p. 403). Thus, diagnosis not only produces disability but also generates the need for intervention, because the process of diagnosis itself is always geared towards the ultimate management or treatment of an individual rather than simply identifying a particular condition as an end in itself (see, for example, Hammell, 2004: p. 408).

Reliance on diagnosis opens up a different basis for lawful relations between the individual and the magistrate, one that is focused on the individual in terms of the ongoing behaviour associated with their internal, medical disability as opposed to their past behaviour pertaining to specific criminal offences. This particular approach to disability in the jurisdictional fact is in contrast to, for example, an approach to disability as a politicised identity characterised by ableist oppression and shaped by settler colonialism. As such, this 'fact' of diagnosed disability marks a temporal and somatic shift in the site of carceral intervention to the disabled body and its ongoing behaviour, rather than to discrete instances of past behaviour mediated by the particular elements of a criminal offence, and in so doing expands the scope of legality vis-à-vis coercive intervention of individuals designated as disabled.

Drawing on Valverde's idea of the 'who' determining the 'how' of governance, the proliferation of forms of lawful relations through court diversion and dispersal of lawful authority between two legal domains within the NSW Local Court—the criminal legal domain and disability legal domain—means that at this very preliminary stage of the *El Mawas* inquiry criminalised disabled people who meet the jurisdictional fact become capable of possibly being known and acted on as two very different distinct kinds of legal subjects, *and* that non-disabled criminalised people continue to be capable of being controlled only through the singular criminal legal domain. Also, criminalised disabled people are subject to greater legal options for carceral control (as compared to non-disabled criminalised people *and* non-criminalised disabled people), and this inequality is embedded in the very jurisdictional ordering of the NSW Local Court. At the same time, this ordering of individuals in different legal domains as different kinds of legal subjects depoliticises the differential legal thresholds for ordering coercive intervention: the very different kinds of coercive intervention *and*, ultimately, the differential access of criminalised disabled people to criminal legal liberal citizenship. Moreover, insofar as '[s]tate claims to jurisdiction seek to naturalize its spatial differentiation, representing scale as impartial rankings whose inauguration is safely located outside the frame' (Pasternak, 2014: p. 153), ordering the *legality* of coercive intervention according to the offence and disability naturalises the different thresholds and scope of legality of coercive intervention that can apply to criminalised disabled people (Steele, 2017d; 2018c; 2018d, see also Boon-Kuo, 2018: pp. 184–185).

Organising people by reference to disability hides the fact that this disability legal domain continues settler colonialism in expanding the range of lawful modes of coercive intervention of Aboriginal and Torres Strait Islanders in the criminal justice system, a point I elaborate on in Section 6.3. Furthermore, judicial finding of a diagnosed disability sustains rather than disrupts the psychological logic running across the two legal domains such that criminalised people can be legitimately and 'equally' subjected to coercive intervention through the criminal legal domain or disability legal domain (I return to this in Chapter 7). Court diversion not only segregates criminalised disabled people within law but, more precisely and significantly, analysis of judicial finding of a diagnosed disability in section 32 shows the biopolitical significance of court diversion in carving out an additional legal domain for criminalised disabled people as distinct from both criminalised non-disabled people and non-criminalised disabled people and, hence, the particular nature of their debilitation along lines of disability and criminality.

Yet, contesting these political effects quickly encounters the very real problem of judicial finding of a diagnosed disability being so routine and procedural as to be profoundly self-evident and unremarkable (Valverde, 2015: p. 85). The self-evidence of the jurisdictional fact is reflected in the Section 32 Court Data. Each of the individuals in the sample of 14 provided a psy professional report (or a document by a social worker or disability support worker referencing such reports or medical records) in support of the jurisdictional question. The prosecution did not dispute the jurisdictional fact in relation to any of the 15 section 32 applications made in relation to the 14 sample members. The magistrate in each matter in the sample found that the first stage of the *El Mawas* inquiry had been satisfied (in those matters where section 32 orders were ultimately not made, this was due to the second and third stages of the *El Mawas* inquiry). Yet, only in some cases did the magistrate formally observe in their decision the 'fact' of diagnosed disability contained in the reports. In some cases this was done without specifying which of the three impairment categories the individuals' diagnosed disability would place them within in order to satisfy the first stage. For example, in the case of Rebecca, an Indigenous Australian woman, the magistrate did not make explicit reference to one of the three categories listed in section 32, but instead specified her diagnosed disability as self-evidently placing her within the scope of one of these categories:

> It is clear to me from the comprehensive report before me prepared by [...] that Rebecca suffers from an intellectual disability to a moderate level. She's also over the years been medicated for depression and has a history of self-harm and with severe challenging behaviours. She has previously been diagnosed as having a borderline personality disorder. But in any event, the intellectual disability alone would bring her within the purview of the section.

In other cases, there was no specification of the diagnosed disability or how the diagnosed disability fit within the particular categories in s 32(1). For example, in Dmitri's matter, the magistrate states, 'I note also that I am satisfied that the first limb has been covered'. The magistrate in Michael's matter makes no reference at all to the first stage of section 32.

There were other instances in the Section 32 Court Data, notably in relation to defendants with a diagnosis of acquired brain injury (which at the time of the data collection arguably did not technically fit within section 32), where the magistrate did not identify the specific impairment category listed in section 32(1) within which the defendant fell; instead, the magistrate found that the defendant simply met the first stage of the inquiry. This signals a disjuncture between who *can* fall within this category pursuant to a strict legal reading of section 32(1)(a) and who magistrates consider *should* fall within this category, perhaps ultimately directed towards whether they would be more effectively controlled through disability and mental health services (which is supposed to be considered only once the jurisdictional fact is satisfied).

Considered together, the reported decisions and the Section 32 Court Data show that while judicial finding of a diagnosed disability—as it is specifically expressed in the text of section 32 and as it is described in the case law on the jurisdictional fact more broadly—is portrayed as a careful check on the scope of state (legal and judicial) authority, it is in fact being determined with minimal judicial scrutiny because of deference to psy knowledge. Disability simply 'is', and classifying criminalised people as disabled when there is a psy report is unproblematic and inevitable. While this might not matter if we approach court diversion as a *beneficial* provision, we might be very concerned if we instead approach court diversion as a troubling expansion of the lawful modes of carceral control and debilitation of criminalised disabled people.

6.3 Apolitical and non-colonial lawful relations

Critical legal scholars have argued that appreciating the full scope of injustice requires questioning law's complicity in harms—not only materially, through what law permits to be enacted on bodies, but also through the law's cultural or representational dominance in the meaning given to these material practices and the bodies on which they are enacted (e.g. Cover, 1986; Veitch, 2007). Legal authority and action can be understood as being not open-ended but, rather, 'defined by limitations that it *defines for itself* and its representations of its own legal and material boundaries circumvents claims made to its legitimacy (Douglas, Sarat & Umphrey, 2005: p. 9, emphasis in original). As such, it is important to see the jurisdictional fact of court diversion as a way through which law represents itself as just, non-violent and non-colonial.

The association with 'scientific rigour and formal knowledge' means diagnosis becomes the *truth* of an individual's situation (Gillman et al., 2000: pp. 397, 399; see also Jarman, 2011: pp. 24–25). The published decisions illustrate how a magistrate's judicial finding of a diagnosed disability is unquestionably associated with scientific truth and, hence, as apolitical. The relative insignificance of the first stage of the section 32 inquiry has been observed in the published decisions on section 32. For example, in *DPP (NSW) v Lopez-Aguilar* [2013] NSWSC 1019 (5 August 2013) Harrison J considered a DPP (Director of Public Prosecutions) appeal from a Local Court decision to dismiss Lopez-Aguilar's charges pursuant to section 32. One of the grounds of appeal was that the magistrate 'failed to make any finding as to whether or why Ms Lopez-Aguilar was eligible to be dealt with under s 32 of the Act' (that is, the first stage of the *El Mawas* inquiry) (ibid.: [3]). The DPP submitted that even if the first stage was not an issue in the proceedings, the magistrate was still required to record the fact that they were satisfied that jurisdiction was made out, even if briefly. On appeal, Harrison J held that even if this error of law was made out, it would not justify the intervention of the Court. This was on the basis that 'his Honour was entitled to rely upon the prosecutor's appropriate concession about the matter, if he agreed with it, and to proceed, in what I take to be a very busy list, to attend to the matters that were seriously in contest'. Justice Harrison went on to note: 'Any other approach fails unfairly to take practical account of the relentless and pressing realities of the administration of criminal justice in the Local Court on a daily basis in New South Wales' (ibid.: [19]).

Similarly, Button J commented in *DPP (NSW) v Soliman* (2013) at [56] that:

> the requirements of a judgment in an application under [section 32] will very much depend upon the circumstances, and therefore one should be careful not to be overly prescriptive. ... If the evidence is overwhelming with regard to the jurisdictional question, then a magistrate may need to take very little time with it.

In these published decisions the jurisdictional fact is presented by judges as no more than a formal and procedural observation of a 'fact', and is, indeed, even a trivial and mundane judicial act of no great significance to the ultimate justice of a specific order. Yet, as noted earlier, this conceals the significant subject-producing and authority-legitimating work that magistrates are engaged in through the jurisdictional fact. While this might be a commonplace feature of judicial decision-making, in the specific context of court diversion the routine judicial finding of a diagnosed disability highlights the particular way in which, from the very first step in the making of section 32 orders, legal recognition of disability cannot capacitate because it is actually what makes possible disability-specific carceral control through court diversion.

Grounding the Local Court's lawful authority to order court diversion in terms of diagnosed disability, criminalised disabled people can become legal subjects defined purely by reference to their disability as an individual who *is* 'cognitively *impaired*' (or, as it was at the time of the court data collection, 'developmentally *disabled*'), '*suffering* from mental illness' or '*suffering* from a mental condition' (s 32(1)(a), emphasis added). Defining legal subjects by pure reference to medicalised disability means that other aspects of individuals' circumstances become unknown, in the sense of being legally irrelevant. More specifically, because court diversion, to borrow from Withers (2012a: p. 54), 'individualizes disability, roots it in the body and seeks to cure or reduce it' through the jurisdictional fact, the individual, pathological disabled body becomes the only source of suffering for criminalised disabled people. Judicial finding of a diagnosed disability is central to transforming structural dynamics and forces of oppression into individual pathology and in rendering coercive intervention as apolitical. This is problematic not only because it negates many aspects of individuals' experiences, but also because it then inhibits our ability to see subsequent coercive intervention as itself a source of suffering and thus restricts the possible range of options for responding to those that will act on individuals' disabilities through coercive intervention (Steele et al., 2016). The solution necessarily becomes individualised therapeutic responses rather than systemic responses that can dismantle and transform structural and settler colonial control and violence (Voronka, 2013).

Moreover, because diagnosed disability is the jurisdictional fact that *authorises* magistrates to order court diversion, disability becomes intimately bound up with what makes court diversion a just and legitimate exercise of state authority per se (which, of course, is then compounded by the humane connotations of the therapeutic nature of the section 32 order); and thus disability becomes further removed from injustice, discrimination and debility. For example, thinking back to James' and Molly's circumstances in the previous chapter, we can ask how diagnosed disability can possibly represent even a small part of the complex structural conditions that shape their lives; whether these diagnoses can possibly recognise the complicity in their circumstances of law and child welfare, disability, mental health and criminal justice systems; and how their diagnosis can even be separated from these systems and their associated violence, irresponsibility and unaccountability. The jurisdictional character of court diversion makes such questions incomprehensible and, thus, circumvents engagement with messy entanglements of disability, violence and law.

It is significant here to note that judicial finding of a diagnosed disability in section 32 might have particularly pernicious effects on Aboriginal and Torres Strait Islander Australian criminalised disabled people, because expanding the lawful authority of the Local Court to order their coercive intervention through disability renders this carceral control 'non-colonial' (Chapman, 2014b; see generally discussion in Chapter 4). Noting that 'jurisdiction has much to contribute to discussions of law and colonialism and the ways in which the state's legal authority is ordered' (Pasternak, 2014: p. 147), here the jurisdiction directly over—or even within—the Indigenous and First Nation *body* as a *disabled* body both extends and deepens settler colonial rule and masks its continuities of control between disability-specific coercive interventions and Indigenous-specific and mainstream criminal justice carceral control through the apolitical and pathological prism of disability.

The non-colonial character of carceral control in court diversion by reason of the jurisdictional fact is supported by the psy professional reports that document the diagnosed disability. These construct the individual by principal reference to their disability and exclude impacts of dynamics and forces of oppression. For example, Davis suggests that disability is typically viewed as an 'absolute' category—it has no origins, but instead just always *is*. Even when it is acquired, its origins are in the body (Davis, 1995: p. 7). Gillman, Heyman and Swain state that diagnosis does not simply represent a 'reality' based on a neutral diagnostic framework but rather the diagnostic framework itself 'is founded on theoretical and ideological assumptions that organise what can be seen and conversely, *what should be ignored*' (Gillman et al., 2000: p. 399, emphasis added).

While the diagnostic process is focused on compiling a history of the individual, it still ultimately negates any history of the impairment and of the individual's life beyond narrow, medical causation. By way of example, some individuals in the Section 32 Court Data were Indigenous, others had migrated from non-Anglo countries and others were from culturally and linguistically diverse backgrounds. In the psy professional reports on the individuals in the Section 32 Court Data there are cursory references to childhood sexual and physical abuse, childhood and adult trauma, childhood neglect, adult sexual assault, exposure to armed conflict, placement in out-of-home care (and abuse in out-of-home care), poor educational experiences, receipt of welfare payments, residing in public housing or boarding houses, and periods of sleeping rough. Yet, the reports in the Section 32 Court Data are structured around the diagnosis. Discussion of these other factors does not appear in itself to be considered relevant but, rather, derives its significance from the diagnosis: either explaining the aetiology of disability in narrow, individualised, medical causal terms or being seen as a result or context of the psychosocial and behavioural effects of the diagnosis. Their disability and, hence, their *bodies* are the problem and the site of legitimate intervention. A similar point has been made in relation to the disability-specific phenomena of 'challenging behaviour' as legitimating restraint (Dowse, 2017).

The origins of disability are rarely discussed, except in relation to brain injury where it is noted in immediate, individualised causal terms (for example, a car accident, a household fire) rather than in historical, social and political contexts. There are no attempts in the psy professional reports to link disability to interlocking dynamics and forces of oppression. In relation to Indigenous Australian individuals in the sample, there is no consideration of the impact of settler colonial relations, including the historical, intergenerational and ongoing effects of dispossession, extreme deprivation, forced removal of children or incarceration. Nor is there consideration of the ways in which geopolitical issues around histories of imperialism, state violence and armed conflict impacted on the two individuals who migrated from countries in armed conflict. Moreover, there is no consideration given to the ongoing impacts of policing, incarceration and institutional irresponsibility and there are no arguments made about the need to address the systemic issues that frame the individual's disability and presence before the court. The same is largely true of the 'criminal domain'; there is little or no scope for these issues to be taken into account in sentencing. Yet what is important here is that court diversion is framed as being a positive improvement on criminal law because it is more attentive to an individual's subjective (disability) circumstances. In this context, it is arguable that the very institutional act of law attributing legal status to diagnosed disability does not merely negate structural and settler colonialism and violence but is itself a further act of symbolic violence (see similarly Joseph, 2014: p. 288; Beaupert 2018a; 2018b) insofar as it renders that individual knowable and legible in law by singular reference to diagnosis. As Chapman and Withers (2019: p. 221) note: 'Casting a person or an imagined type of person as thoroughly knowable is always violent. It involves subtracting purpose, responsibility, agency, or animacy from framings of how that person or "those people" function.' In the course of judicial finding of a diagnosed disability, magistrates necessarily reduce criminalised disabled people to one feature—their disability—and to one epistemic framework for knowing this—psy knowledge—that erases the complexity and richness of who they are and also invalidates their perspectives on who they are (which might very well include not being disabled).

The depoliticising effects of court diversion have implications for criminalised disabled people beyond symbolic violence. The jurisdictional fact of diagnosed disability limits the potential for legal recognition of disability in court diversion to be capacitating, because it situates individuals in a legal domain of coercive intervention that makes possible material violence through disability and mental health services and fails to address injustices within the criminal justice system (such as exposure to police violence, racism, ableism etc.) and the inherent injustices and violence of non-consensual disability and mental health services.

In this chapter I have shown that judicial finding of a diagnosed disability makes possible and legitimate the lawful authority of magistrates to order disability-specific coercive intervention of criminalised disabled people when they have not been sentenced or possibly even convicted. This occurs by forging lawful relations between individuals and the magistrate by principal reference to disability rather than by reference to the criminal offence. The jurisdictional fact of court diversion can be understood as one specific legal dynamic through which law is debilitating because it shapes and restricts the terms on which criminalised disabled people can be legitimately subjected to coercive intervention *and* the much-restricted terms of 'access' to liberty, resources and inclusion.

This analysis brings legal nuance to Foucault's work on classification and carceral control and the disciplining effects of diagnosed disability, in showing the importance of jurisdiction in rendering differential carceral control lawful and, hence, just and non-violent. We can also appreciate the until-now underdeveloped legal dynamics of Puar's and others' scholarship on debility (discussed in Chapter 3), because we can understand the complicity of legal doctrine, legal process and the judiciary in debilitation and how mundane and unremarkable procedural dimensions of law can make possible and mask debilitation (see also Spade (2015) on 'administrative violence'). While court diversion might prima facie be considered to capacitate individuals because it recognises their disability as a basis on which to give them access to disability and mental health services and freedom from prison, the jurisdictional fact shows how disability in court diversion holds people in a certain restricted set of entitlements that never go beyond their individualised, medicalised body. In framing lawful authority by reference to disability, individuals are cast outside of criminal legal liberal citizenship (and, in turn, political community and full humanness) through the unremarkable and mundane jurisdictional fact.

My analysis highlights courts as a key institutional site in the 'institutional archipelago' of disabled carceral practices, in its own right and in its role in facilitating connections and movements between other sites. Moreover, following from Ben-Moshe's (2014: p. 269) point that 'resisting incarceration is not as much about abolishing carceral spaces, as it is about demolishing the ideology that necessitates the processes of incarceration and segregation', this chapter confirms the necessity to address underlying medico-legal ontologies of disability and their circulation in law. The analysis highlights the importance of diagnosis and psy knowledge in grounding lawful authority and crafting lawful relations.

As noted by Pasternak (2014: p. 152), '[j]urisdiction is both a spatial and a legal concept: it is a claim to governance that refers to the legal relationship between a politically organized community and the space it inhabits'. The analysis of the jurisdictional dynamics of section 32 provides a legal context to the criticisms of 'inclusion' made by disability carceral scholars that 'inclusion' either rhetorical or material can in fact be mobilised for punitive ends (see similarly Abbas & Voronka, 2014; Chapman et al., 2014; Spivakovsky, 2017; Voronka, 2016). This is because my analysis highlights the importance of paying close attention to the particular *kind* of legal person who is 'included' in law. It might be useful to think of jurisdictional inclusion by reference to Mitchell and Snyder's (2014) notion of 'inclusionism' (discussed in Chapter 3), given that 'inclusion' in the disability legal domain of court diversion bifurcates disabled people and enables both coercive intervention of non-convicted disabled people and the complete negation of systemic issues of inequality, inequity and violence. It is perhaps an extreme example of the observations made by Spade (2015) in the context of legal inclusion of trans people through discrimination laws: the push for formal legal recognition of and inclusion in law ultimately results in the recuperation of 'outsiders' into unequal, unjust and violent systems of rule.

We need to politicise jurisdiction and question (rather than take as self-evident) the way in which the state, through jurisdiction, arranges disabled populations to both enable coercive interventions *and* render these necessary and just. This applies to court diversion schemes and to the broad array of other disability-specific legal regimes for coercive intervention. In particular, and in light of Mills' (2014) argument of mental health as colonising, there is a need to think about the *contemporary* institutional arrangements of settler colonialism specifically in the jurisdictional dynamics of lawful authority as they relate to disability-specific coercive intervention of Aboriginal and Torres Strait Islander Australians. The need to think about contemporary arrangements is particularly pressing by reason of identification in government inquiries of court diversion and disability/health interventions as solutions to Indigenous and First Nations overrepresentation in prison, as discussed in the Introduction and Chapter 1.

Thus, judicial finding of a diagnosed disability provides both the *possibility* and *legality* of the Local Court's authority to make a section 32 order and, as such, has a significant and foundational (but easily overlooked) role in rendering lawful, non-violent and just the disability-specific coercive intervention. However, it is important to note that not every individual who meets the first stage of the *El Mawas* inquiry will ultimately receive a section 32 order. Through their determination of the 'jurisdictional fact' of section 32, criminalised disabled people are no longer embedded in the criminal legal domain but, instead, for the remainder of the *El Mawas* inquiry, hover across two legal domains in relation to which their coercive intervention is now possible and lawful; and, if they are diverted pursuant to section 32, their disability-specific coercive intervention is just and legitimate. Thus, it is through their consideration of the second and third stages of the *El Mawas* inquiry that magistrates choose within which of these legal domains an individual's charges will be dealt with and, ultimately, whether court diversion will be ordered. Continuing with my analysis of court diversion through the New South Wales case study, I consider these two stages in Chapter 7.

Chapter 7

Choosing carceral control

7.1 Deciding to divert

The expanded carceral control—and, in turn, debilitation of criminalised disabled individuals—through court diversion is situated in a wider context of diversion's structural role in shoring up the regulative gaps and legal legitimacy of criminal law. This is exemplified by analysis in this chapter of the case study from New South Wales, Australia of court diversion pursuant to section 32 of the *Mental Health (Forensic Provisions) Act 1990* (NSW) ('section 32'). This chapter focuses on the second and third stages of the three-stage inquiry guiding judicial decision-making on section 32 which was articulated by Justice McColl in the New South Wales Court of Appeal decision of *DPP (NSW) v El Mawas* (2016) (the '*El Mawas* inquiry'). Recalling from Chapter 6, the first stage of the *El Mawas* inquiry—that it appears to the Magistrate that the defendant has a diagnosed disability—was shown to carve out a disability legal domain which grounds judicial authority to order court diversion in diagnosed disability rather than being grounded in a criminal offence as per the criminal legal domain. As such, this first stage was shown to turn judicial focus inward to the body and open up the possibility of ongoing, carceral control and violence of a nature and extent not possible through criminal law. Once the Magistrate is satisfied of the first step, the Magistrate then turns to the second step which concerns the appropriateness for the individual of court diversion as compared to criminal legal intervention and the third step is the availability of mental health and disability services to effectively control the individual.

This chapter approaches an analysis of the second and third steps of the New South Wales court diversion judicial decision-making process by bringing Foucauldian and critical disability scholarship on carceral control to an exploration of legal dynamics structuring the relationship between criminal law and court diversion. Ultimately, while a diverted individual avoids criminal legal intervention, the services that they must instead engage with set up ongoing dynamics of control. Ideals of independence, autonomy, empowerment and inclusion which are associated with these services and can be collectively understood as self-realisation of the liberal citizen are subtly operationalised towards ends of control, rather than giving individuals meaningful opportunities for consenting (or not consenting) to boundaries or constraints they might find useful. Moreover, the differential nature of coercive intervention across the criminal legal and disability legal domains, far from undermining the authority of the criminal legal domain, is an integral part of the overall psychological ordering of coercive interventions on criminalised people, and supports the completeness of lawful authority rather than pointing to the fragility of its scope. The judicial decision-making process of court diversion is central to court diversion undercutting the possibility of radical transformation of criminal justice systems—because it supplements rather than disrupts the criminal legal domain—and bifurcates disabled populations along lines of both criminality and disability.

This chapter begins with an overview of the second stage of the *El Mawas* inquiry. In Section 7.3 I draw on Foucault's ideas of 'doubling' and 'isotopic' regulation (discussed in Chapter 4) to conceptualise the contingency of appropriateness of court diversion to the limits of criminal legal coercive intervention. In Sections 7.4 and 7.5, I explore how magistrates determine appropriateness through an analysis of the Section 32 Court Data. In Section 7.6 the third stage of the *El Mawas* inquiry is introduced and in Section 7.7 I explore how disability and mental health services control through ideals of self-realisation. Finally, in Section 7.8 I briefly discuss the political implications of the conditionality of section 32 orders.

7.2 Appropriateness of court diversion

Court diversion simultaneously expands the legal options for coercive intervention of criminalised disabled people and legitimates conventional criminal legal intervention. This expansion is demonstrated by the case study of court diversion in New South Wales. After being satisfied at the first stage of the inquiry of the jurisdictional fact of diagnosed disability, the magistrate must at the second stage of the *El Mawas* inquiry be of the view that it is more appropriate that the individual have their charges dealt with through court diversion rather than the principles and processes of the criminal legal domain.

While the first stage of the *El Mawas* inquiry is the observation of a 'fact', the second stage is a discretionary judgement involving consideration of a number of factors and in relation to which, as McColl JA in *El Mawas* (109 [76]) states, 'the Magistrate is permitted latitude as to the decision which might be made, a latitude confined only by the subject matter and object of the Act'. The published cases have identified a number of considerations relevant to the second stage of the *El Mawas* inquiry. These include: (i) the facts and circumstances of the offence (ibid.: 109 [77], 110 [84] (McColl JA)); (ii) the seriousness of the alleged offences (ibid.: 95 [6] (Spigelman CJ), 109–110 [77]–[79] (McColl JA));[1] (iii) whether there is a causal link between the diagnosed disability and the offence (ibid.: 95

1 See also *Mantell v Molyneux* (2006) 68 NSWLR 46, 57 [40]; *Police v Goodworth* [2007] NSWLC 2 (28 March 2007); *Police v Winter* [2008] NSWLC 15 (22 August 2008).

[6]–[8] (Spigelman CJ)), 110 [84] (McColl JA);[2] (iv) the existence and content of a treatment plan (ibid.: 95 [10] (Spigelman CJ), 110 [84] (McColl JA)); (v) the sentencing options realistically available and appropriate in the event the offence were proved (*Mantell* (2006) 68 NSWLR 46, 57 [40], 59 [48]); (vi) the individual's criminal history (ibid.: 57–58 [41]); and (vii) the whole of the legislative scheme, including the limited six-month period in which an individual can be supervised by a section 32(3) order (ibid., 59 [47]). It is clear from these discretionary factors that at the second stage of the *El Mawas* inquiry the focus shifts from the individual's diagnosed disability itself to criminal justice considerations of optimal carceral control in the context of diagnosed disability.

This question of appropriateness as positing two options is significant for three reasons. First, the second stage of the *El Mawas* inquiry assumes that the individual will ultimately be convicted and sentenced if they are not diverted and, thus, sidesteps the issue that at this point the individual cannot be subject to criminal legal intervention as they have not been sentenced or even convicted. This implicitly removes from consideration the option that the individual might be acquitted and not be subject to any carceral control. The presumption of innocence, the central protection against arbitrary exercise of state power in the criminal justice system in a positivist view of criminal law, is not even recognised as a possibility in choosing between modes of coercive intervention. The second stage inquiry is a further way (additional to the jurisdictional fact) criminalised disabled people are cast outside criminal legal liberal citizenship and sustains the association between carcerality, legality and disability that positions criminalised disabled people as always in need of control.

Second, because the question of appropriateness posits a choice between only two domains of coercive intervention, there is no consideration of what—out of an almost infinite range of legal *and non-legal* options—would be the most appropriate way to deal with an individual. Other than an unconditional court diversion order pursuant to section 32(3), the question of appropriateness does not provide an option for an individual not to be subjected to any form of coercive intervention. For criminalised disabled people court diversion and criminal legal intervention form a loop that excludes options other than lawful coercive intervention. This loop takes for granted the necessity of coercive intervention per se and directs attention instead to which legal domain and mode of coercive intervention should apply. This reflects Foucault's (2009: p. 13) observation that:

> [t]he question of an alternative to prison … is a false or at least a loaded question since it in effect asks people to take for granted the existence of a penal regime that grants to particular individuals the right to punish people for particular things, and to consequently think about which system of punishment should operate: imprisonment or some other form of punishment.

2 See also *Broome v Liristis* [2011] NSWDC 40 (15 June 2011) [40]–[42]; compare *Police v Deng* [2008] NSWLC 2 (30 January 2008).

Thus, this stage of the inquiry has an important role in affirming the legality and necessity per se of conventional criminal legal intervention even though it is viewed as less appropriate for a select minority (that is, it is not undermined in total). This is because court diversion only temporarily suspends the operation of the criminal legal domain in relation to specific individuals on the basis of diagnosed disability. The criminal legal domain and criminal justice system at large remain unaffected, and individuals who are diverted on one occasion are not permanently beyond the criminal legal domain either in relation to current or future charges. Far from addressing overrepresentation in the criminal justice system, court diversion intensifies and expands the institutional archipelago of carceral control. It assumes the legitimacy and necessity of carceral control and obscures larger political questions about the existence of prison and, indeed, the institutional archipelago more broadly. This is a very real problem—as I mentioned in the Introduction, law reform and government inquiries on disability criminal justice typically acknowledge problems with prison (such as violence and discrimination against disabled people), only to suggest court diversion or other modes of 'community-based' or 'therapeutic' control rather than dismantling the prison itself.

The third reason the question of appropriateness is significant is that reference to dealing with the individual 'otherwise in accordance with law' gives the false sense that court diversion is somehow moving individuals beyond the coercive force of law into a space of liberty. This is not the case, not only by reason of the court orders made, but also because of the important liminal attachment criminalised disabled people continue to have to the criminal legal domain through conditional section 32 orders, which I discuss in Section 7.8.

7.3 The isotopic and legitimating relationship between legal domains

There is an *isotopic* relationship between the disability legal domain of court diversion and the criminal legal domain. This relationship is demonstrated by the second stage of the *El Mawas* inquiry. The focus at the second stage on the relative appropriateness of two legal domains of coercive intervention means that court diversion is always relative to an assessment of the effectiveness of coercive intervention through the criminal legal domain. As discussed in Chapter 4, isotopy is a Foucauldian concept that refers to a number of supplementary disciplinary systems characterised by the limits of other disciplinary categories, which are capable of 'retrieving' residual individuals in order to make their disciplinary regulation possible. The second stage of the *El Mawas* inquiry allows the magistrate to subvert the ineffectiveness of criminal legal intervention in relation to criminalised disabled people (for example, where an individual does not possess the mens rea, is unfit to be tried, or will not be rehabilitated or deterred through sentencing) into a basis for expanded control through disability and mental health services (rather than signalling the ineffectiveness of the criminal legal domain by reason of its incomplete scope). The 'relative inappropriateness' of criminal legal intervention does not signal its demise—on the contrary, court diversion shores up its legitimacy. Understanding this relational dynamic requires taking a step back to consider the boundaries of the criminal legal domain.

For an individual to be found criminally responsible they need to have the mental capacity to possess the subjective intention or knowledge (mens rea) to choose to commit a particular offence (*He Kaw Teh v The Queen* (1985) 157 CLR 523) and the mental and physical capacity to voluntarily control the physical movements that form the basis of the physical action (actus reus) constituting the criminal offence (*Ryan v The Queen* (1967) 121 CLR 205). Moreover, an individual needs to possess sufficient mental capacity to be fit to plead and be tried (*Presser v R* [1958] VR 45). If an individual is convicted, then sentencing principles of specific deterrence and rehabilitation are implicitly premised on the assumption that the sentence will impact on the individual's future capacitous and rational choices not to offend.

These dynamics of psychological capacity and rationality reflect Norrie's (2001) argument about the 'psychological individualism' that bounds and legitimates coercive intervention through the criminal legal domain. Recalling from Chapter 6 that boundaries are constitutive of the legal domains they border, I propose that the psychological rationality and capacity that bound the criminal legal domain can be understood more specifically as psychological *normality*. Conversely, criminalised disabled people who are viewed as exceeding control through the criminal legal domain can be viewed as psychologically *abnormal* and, as such, in a liminal but constitutive relation to the criminal legal domain. The figure of the psychologically abnormal criminalised disabled legal subject unable to be effectively controlled in the criminal legal domain constitutes the able, rational, freely choosing, legal subject that is legitimately situated in the criminal legal domain (which, of course, is not the reality of the embodied individuals who are overwhelmingly subjects of criminal law) (Dilts, 2012). This psychological-based legal subjectivity erases inequalities arising from other social, political, historical and material factors that are experienced by the embodied individuals in the criminal justice system, and masks the significant structural and settler colonial dynamics that shape unequal power relations between the state and the largely disadvantaged individuals who find themselves in the criminal legal domain (Norrie, 2001: pp. 15–31). Diagnosed disability, as psychological abnormality, shores up the legitimacy of criminal legal intervention because excluding individuals from this domain on the basis of their diagnosed disability is what renders coercive intervention in the psychologically normal non-violent and just. In turn, it becomes difficult to see the *injustice* of court diversion for unsentenced and unconvicted criminalised disabled individuals because court diversion is so implicated in achieving *justice* for those who would otherwise be incarcerated in prison (Steele, 2018c).

Thus, the second stage of the *El Mawas* inquiry enables carceral control and also has an important discursive role in representing the limits of the criminal legal domain as attributable to individual pathology. This reflects Voronka's argument (see Chapter 4) that the 'structural problems inherent in the criminal justice system' are individualised and become embedded in individuals' bodies, thus masking 'structural violence as personal pathology' (Voronka, 2013: p. 318). In positing a choice between two legal domains based on appropriateness, the focus at this stage of court diversion judicial decision-making narrows to a very instrumental consideration of the interface of diagnosed disability and carceral control and excludes from discussion structural issues such as poverty, precarity, child welfare, sexual and physical violence, drug addiction, trauma and the iterative impacts of the criminal justice system itself. This 'illimitability' of law is but one dimension of law which sits beside its 'determinate' and 'fixed' dimension, and 'its cohering force subsists precisely in an antinomic imperative, in this incessant movement between the two dimensions' (Golder & Fitzpatrick, 2010: p. xxi). It is necessary that there is this outside to the criminal legal domain, because the externality of some individuals with diagnosed disability and the possibility of difference in cognitive and mental functioning constructs as humane and non-arbitrary criminal law's coercive effects. At the same time, the reliance upon psychological legal concepts and their conflation with diagnosed disability (as individualised, asocial and apolitical conditions) makes everyone equal across the criminal legal domain and disability legal domain on the basis of a shared psychological personhood (with differentiation only on the basis of the level of psychological functioning).

This constitutive effect of the liminality of criminalised disabled people, as exemplified in the second stage of the *El Mawas* inquiry, signals the profound political problems in aspiring to the inclusion of criminalised disabled people by legislatively inscribing disability in criminal law through court diversion. Such a strategy does not transform the political conditions for criminalised disabled people—either the minority who become subject to disability-specific provisions or the majority who are subject to criminal legal intervention. It is important to note that, as per Foucault and the broader criminological literature, arguably all criminalised people are known to some extent in psychological terms and in terms of degeneracy as compared to non-criminalised people. My argument here is that because of the jurisdictional character of court diversion discussed in Chapter 6, this knowing of criminalised disabled people as psychologically abnormal has very specific impacts on *legality* of carceral control—both what is possible through the disability legal domain of court diversion specifically on the basis of disability and irrespective of criminal responsibility, and also what is possible in relation to psychologically normal criminal legal subjects by reason of their criminal responsibility. In essence, knowing criminalised disabled people as psychologically abnormal enables an expansion of carceral control beyond what is possible for non-disabled criminalised people *and* affirms the carceral control that is possible for non-disabled criminalised people.

I now turn to explore the ways in which magistrates navigate making the choice of the most appropriate carceral control at the second stage of the *El Mawas* inquiry.

7.4 Alternative ways of knowing criminalised disabled individuals

Psy knowledge is central to knowing criminalised disabled individuals other than as criminal legal subjects, as demonstrated by an exploration of the second stage of the *El Mawas* inquiry. At this stage, the choice between which legal domain of coercive intervention is most appropriate for a criminalised disabled individual is made by drawing on alternative legal subjectivities opened up through consideration of the jurisdictional fact. This is reflected in McColl JA's guidance in *DPP v El Mawas* on the magistrate's task in determining a section 32 application:

> Part 3 of the Act requires a Magistrate to balance the public interest in those charged with a criminal offence facing the full weight of the law against the public interest in treating, or regulating to the greatest extent practical, the conduct of individuals suffering from any of the mental conditions referred to in s 32(1) or mental illness (s 33) with the object of ensuring that the community is protected from the conduct of such persons.
>
> (*El Mawas* (108 [71]))

McColl JA's statement indicates that the question of which mode of control is most appropriate is determined by reference to the particular legal subjectivity the individual is known through. The first legal subjectivity is that which is most familiar—criminal legal subjectivity based on a criminal offence. Here, coercive intervention is premised on the individual meeting the elements of criminal responsibility for a criminal offence by having the requisite psychological capacity and rationality to choose to commit the physical act (actus reus) and form the mental intention to commit the act (mens rea). This is an individual whom it would *not* be more appropriate to divert.

The second way of viewing the individual apparent in McColl JA's statement is by reference to disabled legal subjectivity. Here, the legality of coercive intervention does not hinge on a criminal offence but, rather, on ongoing disability-related conduct which requires future management. When an individual is viewed in this way, the task of convicting and sentencing in relation to a specific criminal offence becomes a mere drop in the ocean of the larger problem of their ongoing deviant conduct by reason of their diagnosed disability. The reference to 'conduct' marks a shift from a discrete and time-isolated set of actions constituting the actus reus of an alleged offence to ongoing behaviour that exceeds the temporal boundaries of a particular moment or event and is inherent in the individual's self with no clear beginning or end. Further, the reference by McColl JA to 'regulating' the 'conduct' of disabled individuals marks a shift from punishment for a specific criminal offence to the individual being subjected to a more general and prospective practice of risk management. At this second stage of the *El Mawas* inquiry, magistrates have a choice between two legal domains by reason of the two different legal subjectivities through which to know the association between the individual and their criminal charges: the offence and the diagnosed disability.

In choosing between these legal domains, the magistrate is guided by two sets of documents: the police documents and the psy professional documents. The psy professional reports provide a detailed examination of the individual through the lens of their diagnosed disability and assume an ongoing pattern of behaviour inherent to the individual by reason of their disability which cannot be confined to the specific elements of a past criminal offence. In this respect, the psy professional reports play an important 'doubling' role (as discussed in Chapter 4).

The following section draws on the Section 32 Court Data to illustrate this doubling by comparing police documents with reports by psy professionals, after which I turn to how magistrates navigate these legal subjectivities in choosing the mode and domain of carceral control.

Police documents and the criminal legal subject of the criminal legal domain

The police facts sheets submitted by the prosecution contain the police's account of the facts of the alleged offence largely in relation to the actus reus and mens rea of each particular offence. They provide a way of knowing the individual as a criminal legal subject. This is reflected in descriptions of Section 32 Court Data sample members in the police facts sheets. For example, in the antecedents of one of Shane's facts sheets relating to possessing prohibited drugs, the police state:

> The accused has 61 prior charges, predominantly relating to property and drug-related offences.

In two of Rebecca's facts sheets relating to charges of making false call to emergency service number and offensive behaviour, the police emphasise Rebecca's recidivism:

> The accused is a recidivist offender when it comes to making false calls to emergency services. She shows no remorse and despite numerous warnings is uncooperative with police. She shows total disregard for the consequences of her action and will not stop until arrested.

In one of Souriya's facts sheet relating to an offence of entering enclosed lands, the antecedents state:

> The accused has 65 prior charges many of which involve stealing and break, enter and steal offences. Even taking into account her intellectual impairment, police believe the accused is a recidivist offender and must be put before the court accordingly.

In each of these excerpts, the individuals are portrayed as habitual or nuisance offenders, that is, as individuals who engage in multiple discrete offences rather than individuals who are engaging in ongoing disability-related conduct. (In the psy professional reports, as will be discussed in the next part, recidivism might be read through disability as a pathological and ongoing lack of impulse control or lack of insight into actions.) The reference by police in Souriya's antecedents to her 'intellectual impairment' does not displace the choice she exercises in engaging in these discrete offences.

The conviction records detailing past convictions and sentences enable a view of an individual as being held criminally responsible on a number of previous occasions and, hence, as a long-term subject of coercive interventions through the criminal legal domain. Some of the individuals in the Section 32 Court Data have conviction records that go for tens of pages (for example, Souriya's is 31 pages).

Psy professional reports and the doubling of the criminal legal subject

In contrast, the psy professional reports provide a detailed examination of the individual through the lens of their diagnosed disability. These reports provide an alternative way of knowing the individual as a disabled legal subject whose deviant behaviour is of an ongoing nature and cannot be confined to the specific elements of a criminal offence.

Viewing individuals through their diagnosed disability in the psy professional reports doubles (per Foucault) the author of the offence (that is, an individual who engages in a specific criminal offence) with a general delinquent character who engages in deviant conduct on an ongoing basis. This is apparent in the references in the reports to diagnoses framed in terms of deviations from norms of behaviour and cognition, which form the foundation for two other doublings.

The second of the three forms of doubling is that viewing individuals through their diagnosed disability in the psy professional reports doubles the offence itself with an ongoing form of conduct. This occurs in a number of ways that build upon the diagnosis of the individual as deviating from norms of behaviour. One way is the reference in reports to para-criminal behavioural concepts, such as 'maladaptive' behaviour and 'challenging' behaviour. This disability-specific kind of behaviour is framed in clinical discourse as conduct that obstructs effective provision of treatment and services or the ability to function within the community more broadly. While these forms of behaviour do not involve actual breaches of criminal law, they parallel criminal legal conduct by referring to deviance against social norms or defiance of authority that is not temporally discrete and which attaches to the individual's psychological and biomedical makeup. For example, Joshua is described as having 'challenging behaviour' and 'oppositional defiant disorder' since childhood. Rebecca's report diagnoses her with 'moderate intellectual disability with severely challenging behaviour'. Samantha's reports, written when she was a teenager, use the concept of 'maladaptive behaviour' including 'temper tantrums', 'defiance', 'inappropriate sexual behaviour', as well as 'over dependence', 'biting fingernails' and 'being generally unhappy'. Both Rebecca and Samantha are Indigenous Australian. One of Samantha's reports refers to her attending a special school and being in the care of her grandparents as a child due to domestic violence. One of Rebecca's reports refers to her being in the care of various extended family members, having finished schooling by early high school and having been the victim of a severe sexual assault when she was a child. Yet these childhoods are read through a lens of diagnosed disability rather than in terms of interrelations between ableism and gendered and racialised settler colonial relations.

Some critical disability scholars have problematised the concept of 'challenging behaviour' on the basis that it pathologises individuals' resistance to authority and abuse and shifts attention away from systemic consideration of the problems, illegitimacy, violence, failures and, indeed, existence of institutions (see Beaupert, 2018a; 2018b; Dowse, 2017; Goodley, & Runswick-Cole, 2011; Nunkoosing & Haydon-Laurelut, 2012; O'Connell, 2017; Spivakovsky, 2017; Steele, 2018b). Moreover, Beaupert (2018a; 2018b) has shown the racialisation of challenging behaviour, which is but one example of a long history of resistance to settler colonial and racial violence being subverted into pathology. In contrast to these critical approaches, in the context of section 32 through the prism of challenging behaviour, it is not merely the individual's behaviour that needs to be addressed but, rather, the entire individual. As Nunkoosing and Haydon-Laurelut (2012: p. 198) state: 'The person with intellectual disability and challenging behaviour does not just have troubles; he or she is seen as trouble.' Challenging behaviour is generative of far-reaching control.

The third doubling that occurs through the psy professional reports is the doubling of the psy professional as a judge. This is because the psy professionals express views as to the individuals' conduct being a basis for intervention and management. Rebecca's report states that she 'needs ongoing intervention and a behavioural plan for her extremely challenging behaviour'. In Samantha's case, the report states that her maladaptive behaviour 'indicates that intervention is required'.

Thus, by viewing the individual through their diagnosed disability the psy professional reports double the offender with a delinquent character whose deviancy is central to their existence rather than relative to a specific offence; double the offence with a pattern of conduct that exceeds a specific offence; and double the psy professional as a judge so that decisions as to intervention are premised on the diagnosed disability rather than the criminal offence. Through these doublings the alternative association between the criminalised disabled individual and their charges, evident in McColl JA's statement above, is now accorded a scientific necessity and legitimacy (rather than a politically dubious casting of individuals outside of criminal legal liberal citizenship) and denies individuals their epistemic authority (Liegghio, 2013: p. 124).

Competing ways of knowing

In this section I draw on the Section 32 Court Data to illustrate ways in which the prosecution and defence use police and psy documentation to present the individual in terms of criminal legal or disabled legal subjectivity and, hence, support their particular position on court diversion.

Fadi's matter was an alleged shoplifting offence, where a female accomplice was waiting outside the shop to receive the goods taken by Fadi. The defence submitted:

> My client was encouraged into this behaviour by someone with whom he had a temporary affiliation. I would suggest borne entirely out of his loneliness and boredom at the relentless monotony of his life … My understanding is that one of those family members would almost inevitably accompany my client when he left the house not least because my client was unable to find his way home. On these occasions it seems that for whatever reason my client left the house unaccompanied. He fell into the company by default, I would suggest, of these people who immediately perceived him to be, and quite rightly so as it transpires, someone who was entirely gullible and who would perform their bidding aware or not of whether it was right or wrong … I would suggest that the nexus in that regard is that my client's intellectual disability is at the axis of that gullibility. That it is that very factor which made him gullible and made him vulnerable to these people and to the suggestion that he shoplift with those people. That combined with the lack of services that he's had access to, the monotony of his life, the fact that he's had no-one assisting him with his condition …

Here, the defence frames Fadi's alleged criminal conduct in terms of vulnerability and social isolation deriving from his disability and the lack of disability services. In comparison, a specific basis on which the prosecution opposed diversion was that, despite his diagnosed disability, Fadi's conduct could still fit within the model of the choosing criminal legal subject. This is demonstrated by the following excerpt:

PROSECUTOR: The concern is that, I haven't read it all in detail but what has triggered this spate of offending, and there does seem to be some indication that there's some planning and calculation in relation to it so there is—

HER HONOUR: Yes.

PROSECUTOR: Although he does, there are reports from the various people saying he does have certain mental health issues, which I can't quibble with, there does seem to be some understanding of what he has done, some understanding of the criminality of his actions.

Here, the Prosecutor focuses on the 'planning and calculation' and 'understanding' as suggesting Fadi can be known as a criminal legal subject.

Joshua's matter involved a number of charges, including peep and pry and larceny (in relation to his neighbour) and intimidation (in relation to his former counsellor after he was banned from the service). In relation to the stalking, the defence submitted:

> They are offences which do speak of a pattern of behaviour that's quite concerning. The development of, of obsessions with particular people, in one case

his former counsellor ... Whilst on the one hand he really obviously cries out for attention and help, and certainly he was very aggrieved at being banned from [service] and not being able to see his former counsellor ...

What's really lacking here, and Joshua has expressed this to me ... is, because we were asking him what will it take to stop you engaging in this, in this sort of behaviour and he said if I had something to do. ... When he was able to go to [service] before he was banned as a result of his unhealthy attachment to [counsellor], he had activities. ... He was able to go there to spend time there during the day, be engaged in activities which were appropriate to his age and his intellectual capacity. He now has very little to do on a day to day basis. He has very limited social networks, and that is, that is something which to date has been really lacking from his support plan. That's perhaps to some extent not surprising that he has been going, hanging around the hospital, making a nuisance.

Here, the defence describes Joshua's stalking behaviour in terms of a general pattern of conduct associated with his absence of structured day activities and support, the necessity of which is linked to his diagnosed disability. In comparison, the prosecution in Joshua's matter submits:

Your Honour, we say that the offences involving the intimidation, the peep and pry, ... the contravene [of an apprehended violence order] involving antecedents, they are all serious offences, Your Honour. They are disturbing in nature. It seems that the offending by Joshua has been escalating and the type of offences that he's committing are not victimless crimes, and we say that there is a community interest in having him dealt with according to law.

Here, the prosecution focuses on the serious, disturbing and escalating nature of Joshua's offences as necessitating he be dealt with in the criminal legal domain.

A further example is provided by Souriya's second section 32 application, concerning a charge of entering enclosed lands after having left her locked disability-supported accommodation premises. The defence states:

She's very high needs and the behaviour intervention and support plan outlines that her behaviour is quite impulsive and emotionally reactive and to get away from her feelings and poor self-esteem she absconds. Your Honour, she places herself at great risk when she does and so it's very much a work in progress.

The defence frames Souriya's offending in terms of her diagnosed disability and as a risk to herself rather than to others. In comparison, the prosecution is of the view that Souriya can be viewed as a criminal legal subject because she chose to engage in a discrete criminal act:

Just in relation to the facts, when the accused was confronted it just appears that she understands what she's doing is wrong and she continues to do it.

Here the prosecution depicts her behaviour as rational ('understands') although the prosecution does ultimately concede later on in the matter that there is no legal option other than to make a section 32 application in light of her disability-related unfitness.

This part has illustrated the ways in which the documentation submitted to the magistrate in the course of determining an application for diversion provides two ways of knowing an individual and their criminal charges: one *because* of the diagnosed disability, the other *despite* the diagnosed disability. Discussion now turns to a consideration of the ways in which magistrates then use these competing ways of knowing the individual in order to choose which legal domain of coercive intervention is most appropriate.

7.5 Choosing the legal domain of carceral control

Presented with alternative legal subjectivities by the defence and prosecution, magistrates choose between them by reference to whether the individual can be controlled through the criminal legal domain. It is only when they cannot be effectively controlled in this domain that diversion is considered more appropriate. This choice is made by reference to three sets of legal limits on coercive intervention in the criminal legal domain: (a) criminal responsibility and conviction, (b) deterrence, rehabilitation and sentence, and (c) fitness and trial.

Disability and the absence of criminal responsibility

For some criminalised disabled people, magistrates consider it more appropriate they be diverted because they are viewed as unsuitable candidates for criminal responsibility and conviction.

In Shane's section 32 application in relation to charges of possessing prohibited drug (cannabis), goods in personal custody suspected being stolen, and unlawful entry on inclosed lands, the magistrate states:

> Quite clearly, apart from the conditions that I have already mentioned, he is also HIV positive, he also uses illicit substances as part of and clearly related to his condition. In other words, there is a very close connection between the offending conduct and the nature of his condition. His impulsivity, his lack of judgement, all of those are apparent in these offences, but they are also the direct result of the conditions and the intellectual disability from which he suffers.

Here, the magistrate views the relationship between Shane and criminal law as grounded in his diagnosed disability, as demonstrated by the references to him acting 'impulsively' and with 'lack of judgement'.

In Mahmud's matter, which relates to assault occasioning actual bodily harm of the owners of the boarding house where he lives following an altercation over the number of visitors he had to his room and assault of police officer in execution of duty, the magistrate states:

> Mahmud has not had many opportunities. I have to say that from reading that report—he's had limited opportunities in his life. He suffered greatly when he was much younger and he's now there is somebody who's looking at the brain injuries in relation to him … I have to weigh up when I look at these matters whether it's appropriate in all the facts before me, the reports, the facts and everything else, and his record, he hasn't got a long record (as some of those have got), he has he's been dealt with by section 32 before. That doesn't mean he can't be dealt with again, but I have to say I then have to look at whether it's been in anyway a help to him, but this is a different matter. He's now coming to a brain injury group who are willing to assist him and he's willing to go there.

Here, the magistrate indicates that Mahmud should not be viewed as criminally responsible because his behaviour is the result of a historical lack of services coupled with his diagnosed disability. Yet, a further reading could be to consider the precarious and exploitative housing situation, especially the lack of privacy and the level of control the boarding house operator has over his social relationships—noting that boarding houses are a particular structural issue post-deinstitutionalisation (Drake, 2014). The magistrate also observes that diversion might not be appropriate if previous such orders have been ineffective, thus highlighting the subsidiary relationship of court diversion to criminal law. The magistrate is ultimately of the view that the assault occasioning actual bodily harm charges can be dismissed through court diversion. Yet, the magistrate does not dismiss Mahmud's assault officer and resist arrest charges and he is convicted of these and punished with a fine. Similar to the situation of Molly discussed in Chapter 5, Mahmud is simultaneously dealt with as a criminal legal subject and disabled legal subject, which enables control through both domains (and shows the fluidity and instrumentality of legal subjectivity vis-à-vis carceral control of criminalised disabled people).

Some individuals in the Section 32 Court Data are viewed by magistrates as incapable of being held criminally responsible because they were faced with extraordinary circumstances with which they could not cope because of their diagnosed disability. For example, in relation to Megan's diversion application made in relation to a charge of assault occasioning actual bodily harm (domestic violence related), one charge of breach bail, one charge of contravene prohibition/restriction in AVO and two charges of intentionally/recklessly destroy or damage property, relating to a series of alleged confrontations with her ex-boyfriend and his parents (who have custody of their child), the magistrate states:

> I am advised that there has been no further offending since these offences in June 2010 and that Megan's stability has improved markedly to the point where she is showing the ability to deal with situations a lot better than she has in the past.

> I note the criminal history before the Court indicates that the matters at the District Court [concerning an unrelated assault of a police officer in a public place] and the matters before this Court are her only prior criminal history. Clearly it was a point in her life where stability had not been able to be maintained.

Megan's charges were seen by the magistrate as occurring in an acutely stressful time in her life (childbirth, possible postnatal depression, separation from the baby's father and baby being informally cared for by the father's parents). Yet, arguably the interrelations between her diagnosed disability and broader gendered and settler colonial dynamics are negated in relation to Megan. She is an Indigenous Australian who was herself in foster care from early school age, prior to which, it is suggested, she was the victim of physical and sexual abuse. Megan was subsequently physically abused in foster care. She ended up homeless and living between youth refuges and mental health facilities (including because of self-harm), during which time she was sexually assaulted.

In the examples above, the magistrates do express some genuine sympathy for the individuals appearing before them and it might be that their view as to appropriateness is driven in part by humanitarian concerns. However, as I have argued more broadly, these humanitarian concerns are still channelled into a carceral response; moreover, judges do not engage with structural issues such as housing precarity, child removal or colonialism but, instead, read the circumstances through disability. Further, framing these circumstances as 'unusual' negates the mundane regularity and systemic way in which criminalised disabled people experience distressing, challenging and oppressive circumstances.

The views of the magistrates in relation to these individuals discussed above can be compared to Eleni's case, where the magistrate is of the view that Eleni's substance use is a fundamental barrier to seeing her as a disabled legal subject:

DEFENCE: Your Honour I would submit that that's perhaps, that your Honour could find that she does suffer from a mental illness.

The report that I handed up under Dr ... says that she certainly suffers from a borderline personality disorder. She has other medical difficulties, including epilepsy and has had problems in the past, particularly in relation to self harm and suicide attempts. So I certainly would submit that it's open to you—

HER HONOUR: You've left out drug addiction.

DEFENCE: Certainly would submit—

HER HONOUR: You've left out drug abuse.

DEFENCE: Yes your Honour, but I would certainly submit that she satisfies the first thing, that she suffers from some kind of mental illness. Her drug abuse, which certainly don't wish to shy away from, I would submit has been a form of self-medication.

The magistrate concedes that the first stage of the section 32 inquiry is satisfied, but emphasises the problem of the substance use in relation to the second stage of the inquiry:

> I have a number of reports before me that are not entirely conclusive with regards to the mental health of Eleni with regards to her falling within the provisions of Section 32, but I think one needs to look at it fairly liberally. There is a borderline personality disorder, but it is no doubt exacerbated by her constant and continued drug abuse problem. There is that factor and of course her mental health has not been assisted by her use of drugs.
>
> So I will accept for the purpose of looking at whether section 32 is applicable in these circumstances to find that she does fall within the first limb of Section 32, but in terms of the second limb of Section 32 I decline to deal with her under the provisions of Mental Health …

In her decision refusing the application, the magistrate states:

> She is someone who continues to commit these types of offences and when you look at the facts and the very calculated and deceitful way that she goes about it, squatting down, concealing the items the way that she—when she was going through the boot of someone else's car to steal, when she was approached by the custodian of the vehicle, how she was manipulative and to try and get herself out from underneath the detection. She is very calculating in what she does. She is very controlled and for that reason I decline to deal with the matters under section 32 … The only option is to deal with them according to law because she continues to commit offences.

The magistrate then goes on to sentence her to a series of suspended sentences, warning her that if she commits another offence, 'I will be sending you to gaol'. In Eleni's case, the apparent choice underpinning her substance use and the calculated nature of her offending to support her addiction coincide (Spivakovsky & Seear, 2017). In contrast to the earlier three examples, the magistrate here seems less willing to extend sympathy to Eleni by reason of her drug addiction (even though she is also noted as experiencing trauma from witnessing a friend commit suicide). These contrasting approaches to criminalised disabled individuals track onto dichotomies of the deserving and undeserving disabled along the lines of neoliberal values—those who should be entitled to government support in order to be recuperated into (an approximation to) the normal, responsible citizen; and those who are not entitled because they constitute failures of self-governance.

Disability and ineffective sentencing

An individual might also be considered by the magistrate to be more appropriately dealt with through diversion because their diagnosed disability means that sentencing would be ineffective in altering their behaviour. This is demonstrated by Shane's case. The magistrate states:

> This is a case where, in my view, the balance is well and truly on dealing with it under the provisions in mental health rather than at law. I mean, after all, a bond, at best, a s 9 bond would simply bring in yet another agency, Probation and Parole, and in my view and my experience has been that Probation and Parole's ability to deal with somebody as high maintenance as this defendant, they are not equipped to do that … Imagine, at the end of the day, if he was on a s 9 bond and it was breached. The Court would be faced with the inevitable consequence of needing to consider imprisonment, and that would be entirely inappropriate for Shane.

The magistrate was of the view that Shane exceeds the limits of what is possible through sentencing, particularly because of the limits to supervision through corrective services. Such coercive intervention would be unlikely to rehabilitate him or deter him from future criminal offending, because his criminal charges were part of an ongoing disability-related conduct and probation and parole services could not deal with such 'high maintenance' defendants. This characterisation is significant given that Shane is an Indigenous Australian disabled person who is well-embedded in the criminal justice system, has drug addiction, HIV and Hepatitis C, completed only a few years of high schooling, had early childhood contact with drugs, and experienced periods of homelessness, incarceration in prison and detention in mental health facilities. Recalling Voronka's discussion of the pathologisation of recidivism, attributing this criminal justice involvement to his disability seems to elide the significant structural and settler colonial dynamics that might shape his circumstances.

In Samantha's matter, the magistrate states:

> On balance, it is more appropriate that she be compelled to comply with the directions of her case manager than be dealt with in any manner under criminal law … I am satisfied that the treatment orders that I have just made have the best chance of ensuring compliance with future court orders and no further breaches of the AVO.

Here, the magistrate is of the view that Samantha is incapable of complying with legal conditions through the force of the 'law' itself and requires case management to ensure compliance. The magistrate concludes that case management through diversion provides the best chance of ensuring compliance with future court orders, including the AVO.

In relation to Souriya's first section 32 application concerning two charges in a disability support service context—a charge of common assault (against a disability support worker at her accommodation) and a charge of goods in personal custody suspected of being stolen—the magistrate is reluctantly of the view that her diagnosed disability places her beyond the limits of what is possible through sentencing in the criminal legal domain:

HER HONOUR: It would seem to me that this person is under guardianship, with limited ability. They have a shocking record, absolutely shocking record but they are under guardianship because they are incapable. I mean what do you do with these people? They're out there in the wilderness, they're going around bashing up people and doing all sorts of things, everybody says they're mental. It doesn't help the people that they've committed the crimes upon. But that's not the test.

DEFENCE: No.

HER HONOUR: The test is, is it in the public interest.

DEFENCE: Yes.

HER HONOUR: That she be dealt with other than in accordance with law, that is under the mental health legislation.

The magistrate concedes that there is no other option for Souriya other than diversion. The vivid description of Souriya 'in the wilderness' creates the idea of the feral child who is 'marked as perpetually available for all kinds of intrusions, public and private. … Their savagery justified their incarceration, disciplinary regulation, subjection to experiment, and, ultimately, abandonment by the professions presumably devoted to their salvage' (Mitchell & Snyder, 2005: p. 628). Noting that Souriya is described as being of Middle Eastern and Muslim background, the animalistic description evokes notions of a disabled *and* racialised degenerate threat to the fitness of the overall population. Indeed, noting that court diversion is not simply control but a form of racist violence (in Foucauldian terms) we might here think of Razack's argument under settler-colonialism, animalisation renders individuals more easily marked for violence and death (Razack, 2015: pp. 168–169; see also Patel, 2014). Moreover, the magistrate's references to 'they' and 'these people' have the discursive effect of moving beyond the construction of Souriya as an individual subject of section 32 to an ontological construction of all those diverted under section 32 as uncontrollable through the criminal legal domain and inherently outside of civilised humanity. Through Souriya, all criminalised disabled people are 'represented in terms of lack, who is not "one of us" or deserving of our support or care' (Joseph, 2015: p. 16).

Similarly, in relation to her second section 32 application concerning a charge of entering inclosed land (Souriya allegedly entered a residential house and, when detected by a resident of the house, claimed she was looking for a bathroom), the magistrate states:

HER HONOUR: She's not helping herself, I mean in the end regardless of anything she is certainly capable of stealing things, isn't she?

DEFENCE: Yes. Her bail report is very lengthy but she has not had a single conviction despite the number of times she's been charged because of her level of functioning. She's always found unfit or dealt with under s 32 I'm afraid and it's difficult to see what else can be done. She's just childlike basically.

…

HER HONOUR: … I think the word is wilful, it's wilful behaviour. In the end she might end up in gaol if she keeps going unfortunately.

In her decision on this application the magistrate then states:

> As I understand from the documents before me she is a person who appears sometimes to understand what she is doing in a wilful sort of a way, I call it that but I am not a psychologist, but she keeps performing in this way because of her mental disabilities she is the age of a six year old.
>
> These are difficult matters because persons cannot keep offending in the law. However, is it in the best interests—reading the facts and everything before me what to do in this matter, is it in the community's best interests that she be dealt with. I understand that she is abiding by her home care plan of which I have a copy here and that she does appear now to be less involved in behaviour that is antisocial in relation to the criminal law.

The repeated references to Souriya's behaviour as wilful, compounded with the Magistrate noting she is the 'age of a six year old', invokes images of a misbehaving child rather than an adult engaging in specific criminal offences. This tracks onto a long tradition of justifying violence and control of disabled people through infantilisation (Kafer, 2013). Souriya's infantilisation renders her more appropriately dealt with by disability services than criminal legal intervention.

The magistrate in Joshua's matter (relating to the stalking and intimidation and peep and pry charges) states:

> Now it's not because there are so many matters that I hesitate, but I comment on that because it is a fact here and some of these charges that he's been charged with and I have the facts of them are, as the Sergeant has said, quite serious. They're not the most serious offences, but they are serious because they involve persons who are in the public who are trying to assist people—in crisis centres, at [public hospital], acute crisis centres, [public hospital], nurses, and, and people who Joshua has developed an attachment to which is unhealthy ... When I look at these matters, there does seem to be some escalation in relation to it, not the most serious escalation, but certainly an escalation in relation to what he is doing.

Thus, the magistrate's decision on the second stage of the *El Mawas* inquiry in Joshua's matter demonstrates that in some instances the seriousness of the offences overrides the possibility that control through diversion might otherwise be more effective. Joshua's matter demonstrates the significance of criminal justice considerations (rather than purely disability considerations) at the second stage of the inquiry.

Disability and the inability to be tried

The inability to be tried (and to be dealt with through the legislative scheme for detention following a finding of unfitness which is available in the higher courts) is the third basis on which an individual's diagnosed disability may render diversion more appropriate than criminal legal intervention. While the effect of the common law rules of fitness is that an individual is beyond trial if they are unfit, there is no legislative framework specifically in the Local Court for subsequently detaining in the forensic mental health system individuals who are found unfit. Thus, there is a gap in the regulation of unfit individuals in the Local Court. In this respect, section 32 has been used to deal with these compounded limits of trial and of the gaps in the forensic mental health system (even though the legality of this is questionable).

In Souriya's first section 32 matter, as a basis for diversion the defence argued that Souriya was unfit. Around four months later, Souriya was again before the same magistrate in relation to fresh charges. The magistrate was keen to deal with the matter by way of court diversion, even in Souriya's absence, because the alternative option was a permanent stay. In Souriya's matter, the defence uses the Local Court gap in the forensic mental health system strategically to achieve court diversion because this plays on fears of the potential for unfit individuals to be completely beyond any coercive intervention.

The magistrate's approach in Souriya's matter can be contrasted with the approach in Joshua's matter (over which the same magistrate presided). The defence's attempt to play on the limits of the forensic mental health system was less successful. Joshua's matter was heard approximately six months prior to Souriya's and seemingly when the magistrate held a different view as to the legal situation in relation to unfitness in the Local Court. When the defence tried to raise the absence of fitness or the absence of specific intent mens rea, the magistrate was of the view that if a section 32 application was refused and then unfitness or absence of mens rea was raised then she would have no jurisdiction to consider these issues *because* there were no legislative mechanisms in the Local Court to enable the subsequent control of such individuals through the forensic mental health system. This, of course, seems to collapse the important distinction between the common law rules excluding an individual from trial or criminal responsibility and the forensic mental health legislative provisions including that individual in an alternative legal domain—the availability of the first not necessarily dependent upon the presence of the latter. The discussion on this point between the magistrate and the defence went around in circles for quite some time and became increasingly heated. The defence in Joshua's matter ultimately made a section 32 application which was refused, with guilty pleas entered on a later date.

This part has demonstrated that the question of appropriateness is specifically concerned with criminal justice considerations of the extent to which an individual's diagnosed disability means that they should be controlled through court diversion because they are at the limits of effective control through the criminal legal domain. If the legal framework of court diversion simultaneously expands the legal options for coercive intervention of criminalised disabled people and legitimates conventional criminal legal intervention, then it can never provide the tools for dismantling the institutional archipelago and interlocking dynamics and forces of oppression that sustain the carceral control and debilitation of criminalised disabled people—it is, instead, part of the problem. Court diversion orders might very well provide some improvements to an individual's material circumstances, and might be motivated by lawyers' and magistrates' genuine desire to bring about positive changes in these individuals' lives. Yet, ultimately, improving life circumstances via coerced engagement with services arguably can only ever address the underlying causes of the circumstances that elicited the magistrate's sympathy or concern to a very limited, individualised and short-term extent. There is no guarantee that their social or legal circumstances will be any better in the long term, including if they happen to be charged again (as suggested by the hypothetical institutional narratives discussed in Chapter 5).

This chapter now turns to the final stage of the *El Mawas* inquiry: the practicality and efficacy of court diversion.

7.6 Practicality and efficacy of court diversion

Court diversion ultimately sustains carceral control of criminalised disabled people, because of the non-consensual dynamics that shape engagement with disability and mental health services, rather than giving individuals meaningful opportunities for consenting (or not consenting) to boundaries or constraints they might find useful. This is illuminated by consideration of the final stage of New South Wales court diversion judicial decision-making. Once the magistrate has formed the view that an individual has a diagnosed disability and has concluded that it is more appropriate by reason of that diagnosed disability for the individual to be dealt with through diversion, the magistrate turns to consider the final stage of the *El Mawas* inquiry: the practicality and efficacy of the specific section 32 order. At this stage the magistrate considers whether specific services are available and suitable. Even if a section 32 order is lawfully possible and more appropriate, a magistrate will not make such an order if there are no services available to actually administer the order.

Section 32(2) and (3) provide the specific form that the orders can take. The magistrate may make an interim order, such as adjourning the proceedings or granting bail (s 32(2)). The magistrate may make a final order. This final order may be unconditional, such that the individual's charges are dismissed outright with no requirement to engage with disability and mental health services (s 32(3)(c)). A final order can be subject to conditions lasting six months (s 32(3)). If conditional, the individual can be discharged 'into the care of a responsible person, unconditionally or subject to conditions' or 'on the condition that the defendant attend on a person or at a place specified by the magistrate' either 'for assessment or treatment (or both) of the defendant's mental condition or cognitive impairment' or 'to enable the provision of support in relation to the defendant's cognitive impairment' (s32(3)(a), (b)). Thus, at a basic level, the magistrate must determine three things: whether the order will be an interlocutory order (s 32(2)) or final order (s 32(3)); if the order is to be a final order, whether that order will be conditional (s 32(3)(a), (b)) or unconditional (s 32(3)(c)); and what particular conditions to set if the order is to be conditional.

In essence, the third stage of the *El Mawas* inquiry demonstrates that court diversion more broadly is directed towards the use of disability and mental health services, and perhaps counter-intuitively their promises of fostering the self-realised liberal citizen to enable effective carceral control of disabled people. McColl JA in *El Mawas* (110 [80]) likens the choice as to conditionality of the diversion order to 'discretion exercised by a sentencing judge' and thus acknowledges the controlling nature of court diversion but simultaneously negates how this control is situated *outside* the legal limits imposed by sentencing law.

In relation to the issue of whether the final order will be conditional or unconditional, the reported cases, anecdotal evidence and the Section 32 Court Data all indicate that, in practice, there are few unconditional orders made, particularly in relation to criminalised disabled people who are well-embedded in the criminal justice system. Unconditional orders are more likely for individuals who have no offending history, who have a mental health diagnosis and who are leading high-functioning lives. Or, unconditional orders might be made if the individual is already well controlled through disability and mental health services.

In the Section 32 Court Data, Shane is the only individual in the sample who receives an unconditional order. Shane receives an unconditional order on the basis that the services provided in his treatment plan were so thorough and were already in operation, such that any coercive order compelling Shane to engage with them would be superfluous, a point discussed earlier in this chapter. In Shane's matter the magistrate stated:

> They are doing an incredibly good job, I do not see how they can do more. I do not see that any conditions on a treatment plan would make any difference to the way he is being dealt with which, in my view, is entirely satisfactorily.

Importantly, even though Shane was not legally coerced through a conditional order to engage with disability services, the assumption was that he would be engaging in these services to such an extent that the coercive effect of the section 32 order would be 'superfluous': it was assumed he was being subjected to a high level of control, one that exceeded the possibilities of criminal law. Moreover, Shane's disability service provision was structured by adult guardianship and financial management orders—such that his control still had a legal dimension, and one that would endure beyond the six month period of court diversion. The magistrate's reasons for Shane's unconditional diversion illuminate how court diversion is situated within an institutional archipelago of diverse sites, modes and legal forms of carceral control where the criminal legal domain is not the hierarchically optimum and exclusive legal domain of control.

A conditional section 32 order pursuant to section 32(3) involves dismissal of an individual's charges and discharge from the court process, coupled with the individual either being placed in the care of a responsible person or being required to be assessed or treated. In relation to individuals who are primarily receiving mental health services, this typically involves being discharged conditional to attending appointments for assessment and treatment. For individuals who are primarily receiving disability services, this generally involves being discharged into the care of a case manager specified in a treatment plan submitted by the defence and having to comply with all reasonable directions made by the case manager (presumably the expectation being that the individual will comply with the treatment plan to be administered by the case manager).

Court diversion still puts the expectation on the individual to change (through involvement with disability and mental health services) rather than focusing on changing society, notably through the fact that diversion orders cannot bind anyone or any service other than the diverted individual him or herself (*Minister for Corrective Services v Harris* (Unreported), Supreme Court of New South Wales, Brownie J, 10 July 1987). In essence, this shows the very profound ways in which disability-specific criminal laws can never 'capacitate' (in the Puar sense) criminalised disabled people into full citizenship, because the individual is responsibilised to the point of being punished for the services and support disabled people have missed out on in the aftermath of deinstitutionalisation. In a neoliberal context of self-directed funding and consumer choice, court diversion bifurcates disabled populations along lines of criminality, and in doing so removes the opportunity for self-direction and choice from criminalised disabled people by coupling their access with carceral control while at the same time masking this control in terms of self-realisation. As well as its impact on the individuals who are diverted, service access via carceral control has biopolitical effects at a population level, in stratifying disabled populations in a post-deinstitutionalisation era to sustain the ongoing inequality and relative deprivation and precarity of those who are criminalised even in the face of disability rights.

7.7 Empowering, humane and therapeutic control

In general, a magistrate is constrained to making orders related to an individual's diagnosed disability, more specifically to the management or remediation of the individual's diagnosed disability through care, assessment or treatment. In a contemporary context, disability and mental health services—community mental health treatment, disability group homes, case management, life skills training, community access and counselling—are framed as humane and beneficial and are widely assumed to be the key means through which disabled individuals and populations can not only have their disability needs addressed but achieve ideals of independence, autonomy, empowerment, and inclusion and ultimately become self-realised liberal citizens.

However, by drawing on Foucauldian theory and critical disability studies as discussed in Chapter 3, we can articulate a very different perspective, a counter-narrative that suggests the control and violence of these services occurs *through* their humane and therapeutic characteristics. Even though individuals are not repressively detained and isolated from the community (as they were in an earlier era of institutionalisation), instead being supported to live freely and inclusively within the community (including when they might be detained in a group home, as I will show by reference to Souriya), they are still subject to non-consensual restraints and regulated through the highly structured and supervised nature of their living environments, service relationships, daily routines and lifestyles, which contour their available choices, relationships and spatial location. Nevertheless, the discursive framing of these services in terms of self-realisation, coupled with their juxtaposition to the 'dark past' of institutionalisation (Altermark, 2018), means that disability and mental health services are widely viewed as humane and therapeutic, masking their controlling and violent nature. Altermark (2018: p. 89) describes this tension between freedom and control (the 'dual logics of manufacturing and restricting citizenship') as not simply accidental or incidental but at the very heart of contemporary disability services.

Here, I suggest that the magistrate's consideration of the third stage of the *El Mawas* inquiry straddles and ultimately reiterates this tension inherent in disability and mental health services. The magistrate's consideration of the practicality and efficacy of services demonstrates a dual concern with humaneness (albeit limited to assistance with disability-related needs narrowly construed) and control (which as per Chapter 5 runs throughout the legislative development of section 32) which is then instantiated through ordering the use of these services through diversion.

The key reference point for the magistrate's determination of the third stage of the *El Mawas* inquiry is the treatment plan handed up by the defence. This document is developed by a disability or mental health service provider or by a psy professional who is involved with the individual (see generally Intellectual Disability Rights Service, 2011: pp. 20–32). In this section I focus on disability service treatment plans related to individuals who are receiving case management and disability-supported accommodation services. While not all individuals who are diverted will receive these services, careful attention is given to them here because these services are seen as the ideal form of service provision and are becoming more widely employed in relation to criminalised disabled people in the criminal justice system. They exemplify the contradictory nature of disability and mental health services in court diversion as enacting control and violence that is concealed as empowering, humane and therapeutic.

The treatment plans in the Section 32 Court Data for individuals receiving case management and disability-supported accommodation services reflect on an individual level many of the aspects of disciplinary regulation identified by Foucault, as discussed in Chapter 3. At a population level, they demonstrate how disability and mental health services order criminalised disabled populations into a spatial buffer between the prison and the 'community'. Moreover, they also reflect the way in which court diversion builds connections between legal domains, material sites and institutional contexts of coercive intervention—section 32 not only governs individual instances of control but sits at the border of different systems of control, thus facilitating seamless movement of individuals and populations between institutions and forms of control (Steele, 2017a).

Restricting choices

As Altermark notes in his analysis of Swedish group homes, disability services are directed towards the development of disabled people as self-realised liberal subjects in very particular ways. They do not simply create opportunities for disabled people to do whatever they please, but instead help to make disabled people into citizens who can make the 'right' choices (Altermark, 2018: pp. 97–102) and be 'able to make choices, to move around society, and to reflect on the consequences of one's actions' (ibid.: p. 93). Yet there is an inherent contradiction in this process—because disabled individuals are presently considered incapable of making good choices they are subject to a higher standard of normality, in the sense of a more restricted range of permissible choices than non-disabled people, because they cannot make *informed bad* choices (ibid.: p. 102). Disability services have an integral role in shaping the decision-making of disabled people—both 'making and restricting intellectually disabled citizens-subjects' and, ultimately, controlling them (ibid.: p. 104). Altermark explains that this occurs through monitoring behaviour, a hierarchy of support workers and service users, a constant regime of control that is sufficiently flexible to be motivating/persuasive or coercive, and individualised control that is responsive to the particular circumstances of each individual (ibid.: pp. 104–105). Thus, self-realisation is about an ongoing process of helping individuals become very particular kinds of citizens who, in future, will make good choices; this is necessarily premised on present control because, contradictorily, their current inability to make good choices requires discipline and coercion—individuals are simultaneously acted on to achieve inclusion and exclusion (ibid.: p. 103).

This tension between self-realisation and control is evident in the treatment plans for individuals receiving case management and disability-supported accommodation services. One respect in which this guidance of behaviour is apparent in the Section 32 Court Data is through the focus on interventions aimed at the general behaviour and lifestyle of the individuals—such as teaching 'life skills' (for example, cooking, hygiene and laundry), improving social skills (for example, through structured day programs) and teaching appropriate behaviour in the community (for example, through supervised community access). The focus is on encouraging and supporting an individual to choose to engage with these services and choose to develop their behaviour and skills, rather than coercing them or forcing them to do so. Skills development is framed by a pervasive discourse of empowerment and self-realisation—that is, the individual is not being forced to manage their disability but, instead, is being given skills to live a fuller life despite their disability.

Yet, as Barbara Cruikshank (1999) has argued, such discourses mask the ways in which individuals' behaviour is actually constrained through their self-realisation. Control to make 'good' choices is evident in the treatment plans through such aspects as rewards systems, positive reinforcement, use of persuasion in decision-making as opposed to dictating choices, and inclusion of individuals in service planning (see also Altermark, 2018: pp. 96–97). For example, Shane's treatment plan includes a timetable that has a place to put a positive acknowledgement when tasks are completed and he is given a physical reward to prevent him from stealing. Moreover, for some, self-realisation is located in a broader context of risk management, as illustrated by risk management documents that accompany some of the individuals' treatment plans. The defence in Shane's case handed up a report that uses a risk assessment tool to determine levels of risk in relation to various aspects of Shane's daily life. The document then represents the assessment in tabular form using colour-coding—red, amber and green—to indicate levels of risk. In this document, Shane's life is divided into components: accidental movement, behaviours, unsafe action, hazard exposure, recurrent medical conditions, resistance to support during activities of daily living and manual handling, infectious diseases, environmental and social components, and 'other'. Within each of these components of Shane's life, there are around five or so issues identified and risk-assessed. For example, 'unsafe action' includes the following issues: gambling, drugs, medication, unsafe sex, alcohol, smoking, criminal activity and wander/abscond, in relation to which Shane is classified variously as red and amber. The risk assessment table is then followed by a client risk management plan, which addresses each risk area in the red and amber risk categories and details conditions, means of prevention, response, and management support plans. For example, in relation to criminal activity (which is specified as shoplifting and stealing items from the public), the plan notes that there is no known trigger for his behaviour but that it might occur when he is out in the community. The plan therefore recommends staff interaction with Shane when he is engaged in shopping and banking, implementation of a regular reward system, and daily and weekly routines. This sets up an anticipatory and preventive dynamic that frames control as necessary to preserve the opportunity for gradual self-realisation as an individual who makes good choices—risk management is framed in terms of support, needs and goals rather than being represented as punitive or restrictive (see similarly discussion of 'Paul' in Levinson, 2010: pp. 213–241). Even the choice of language—'client' and 'management support plans'—creates a sense both that this is beneficial to the individual and that the individual is an agent in these processes. Moreover, the focus on 'risk' in shaping court diversion treatment and support is particularly problematic in relation to criminalised disabled people who are Indigenous and First Nations or of a racialised minority because '[r]isk assessment is one way in which White cultural norms are silently embedded within the structures of policy and practice' (Cunneen, 2019b: p. 13).

This productive tension between self-realisation and control can also accommodate the kinds of physical restrictions we might more readily associate with the 'dark past' of institutionalisation *because* these restrictions are framed in terms of the (possibly eternal) journey towards the future, sensible and responsible citizen. For example, Souriya has maximum restrictions in place through guardianship legislation, referred to in the documentation as a '100% containment model'. She is living in a facility with locked doors and windows, she has staff support in the community (including accompanying her into public toilets) and any unsupervised departures can result in use of the retrieval order attached to her guardianship order, through which police can be contacted by the service to bring Souriya coercively back to her residence. Souriya also has restricted access to potentially dangerous items (such as knives), alcohol and drugs, money and the phone. Staff also control her self-purchasing of treat foods and her consumption of meals she brings home from her parents (who are from a Middle Eastern cultural background), and also regulate the amount of food she eats between mealtimes. She is also subject to room searches and bag and personal searches (with metal detector) after independent access to the community. The behaviour intervention report notes that Souriya engages in highly impulsive and emotionally reactive behaviours such as absconding, stealing and sex work, as well as junk food over-eating, excessive smoking and impulsive spending. It is significant to observe that these restrictions on Souriya to protect her against at-risk behaviours are situated in a life punctuated by control, violence and resistance. Souriya experienced childhood circumstances of violence and precarity. Following harsh family disciplinary techniques she was running away from home from her early teens and living on the street, engaging in drug use and sex work. Souriya was also made a state ward in her early teens. As an adult she has been admitted to mental health facilities and treated with antipsychotics while in custody.

Despite these extreme restrictions on Souriya's liberty and choices, the documents frame this approach in terms of support, with the focus being on the ways in which restrictions can be a conduit for self-realisation and that over time they will be minimised with the ultimate aim of giving her more independence and autonomy. A letter from the clinical consultant who advises the disability support service notes that staff members have increased the provision of 'meaningful activities' to Souriya. These are available to her in the house to minimise the time she spends 'ruminating over her desire to live independently in the community', which the letter's author states is often Souriya's expressed rationale for absconding from her accommodation. Following Nunkoosing and Haydon-Laurelut (2011), Souriya's 'ruminating' could be viewed as legitimate protest or resistance to the power and control exercised over her life by the service; instead, it is seen purely in terms of a barrier to be managed through distraction in order to enhance the service intervention.

Distribution in space

The disability and mental health services at the core of section 32 treatment plans control through the 'distribution' of individuals in space (Foucault, 1979: pp. 141–145). By this I mean that, generally, services do not fix individuals within an enclosed space (as in a prison cell) but are instead monitored and regulated in their movement through space (ibid.: p. 143). In the words of Altermark (2018: p. 90), '[t]his is not power that restrains freedom but that incites people to be free in a particular way'. The presumed independence associated with living in the community which is valorised in post-deinstitutionalisation becomes a malleable and invisible mode of control through court diversion.

Altermark (ibid.) argues that the 'regime of government' that balances freedom and control is a decentralised system that 'operates in and through relationships formed at the lowest levels of policy implementation, between support workers and people with intellectual disabilities living in group homes'. The treatment plans in the Section 32 Court Data indicate that when individuals are in disability-supported accommodation they have relative freedom of movement in the community and (for the most part) are not locked in their accommodation. However, they may still be subject to ongoing supervision, which facilitates the disability support workers' awareness of the prospective movements, and retrospectively records the actual movements, of the individual. Moreover, while these individuals *do* have freedom to leave their accommodation, their movements in the community can also be monitored. In this approach, moving within the community is given the labels of 'community access' and 'free time', which is suggestive of discrete, time-limited activities that reduce the opportunity for unplanned community access. For example, Megan's treatment plan states that the disability service will 'support' her when 'accessing the community'. Shane's treatment plan specifically identifies 'community access'. The plan states that Shane can access the community without support, but there is guidance for staff around the ways in which to positively guide Shane in accessing the community, notably by identifying specific activities to ensure meaningful use of time and ensuring Shane takes prescribed medications and meets all health specialist appointments. Some individuals in the Section 32 Court Data also had guardianship orders that gave their guardian some scope to use police to retrieve them if they had not returned to their accommodation within a certain timeframe. While non-criminalised disabled individuals might have similar supports in place, supervision and community chaperoning are problematic in a court diversion context because any resistance to or non-compliance with these practices on the part of the individual can be deemed a breach of their order and result in them being channelled back into the criminal legal system.

For individuals whose diversion involves a mental health community treatment order or receiving regular medication or counselling, individuals are controlled in space because their mobility is restricted by the regularity of attending appointments at a specified place or through the confining effects of medication (Fabris, 2011).

While a key feature of disability support and mental health services is that they promote individuals' independence and freedom of movement in the 'community', and this is true to the extent that the individuals are not locked up in large scale institutions, the operationalisation of the concept of 'community access' in a criminal justice context runs counter to the fostering of independence and autonomy. Disciplinary regulation 'diffus[es] outside of prisons the functions of surveillance that will henceforth be exercised not on the individual confined to his cell but dispersed across his apparent life of freedom' (Foucault, 2009: p. 17). The community is a distinct place which diverted individuals are outside of and have to 'access' (with the support/supervision of disability support workers) and individuals' movements and time in the community are controlled. Biopolitically, court diversion bifurcates disabled populations so as to unequally organise disabled people's material and political proximity to the community ***through*** the rhetoric of self-realisation along lines of criminality. Bifurcation manifests in the development more recently of specialised forensic community disability services and group homes that provide bespoke support in separate physical spaces than those for non-criminalised disabled people. This point is supported by Levinson's ethnography of a group home in New York City, which draws on Foucauldian theory of governmentality. Discussing in general terms the government of disability in the era of group homes and post-deinstitutionalisation, Levinson (2010: p. 46) observes a fundamental tension inherent in the historical and political context of the group home between supervision and freedom: 'As a technical solution to the appalling violations of institutional life, what a community residence must do is translate the ideals of rights and integration into actual services that both supervise individuals and promote their independence' (see also Spivakovsky, 2017). One of the key benefits of court diversion—that it enables individuals in a material sense to remain in the community and receive the support they need to live in the community—is itself one of the ways in which individuals are controlled through court diversion. I am not here proposing that absolute freedom is ever possible for disabled people or anyone else for that matter because choices are always structured by personal circumstances and dynamics and forces of oppression such as white supremacy, heteropatriarchy, colonialism and capitalism etc. What I am arguing is that court diversion structures and constrains individuals' choices specifically at the intersection of disability and criminality. Contrary to its framing in terms of aspirations of self-realisation, court diversion arbitrarily restricts the access that criminalised disabled people have to a range of options as to how and where they live their lives in the community, including by denying these individuals meaningful opportunities for consenting (or not consenting) to boundaries or constraints they might find useful.

Even in relation to those individuals who have significant restrictions on their liberty or privileges, a pervasive framing of disability support services as ultimately empowering these individuals persists. There is a shift in emphasis from the imposed nature of the restrictions themselves to an emphasis on working with the individual to gradually remove the necessity for these restrictions (Foucault, 1979: pp. 177–181). This is demonstrated by Souriya's treatment plan documentation. An important temporality is at play here, where the present violence of being subjected to these restrictions is transformed into a necessary sacrifice in the ongoing task of realising her future freedom from them.

Structuring time and activity

Through court diversion, disability and mental health services control individuals by structuring their time and activity. In part this reflects the disciplinary technique of 'control of activity' (Foucault, 1979: pp. 149–156). Control of activity involves creating the conditions for individuals to use their time and activity in the most efficient way. This disciplinary technique is focused, at a micro level, on guiding individuals to manage their own conduct (see generally Levinson, 2010), operating in an overarching macro context of space and relationships that structures and restricts the general scope of choices the individual can make and how they can spend their time. In a context where '[d]einstitutionalisation was supposed to represent a liberating practice where staff no longer have the traditional control over the living conditions of the patients, who become users and citizens' (Larsen & Topor, 2017, p. 149), individuals instead become more indirectly managed by staff through the control over *time* in the name of support. The way in which criminalised disabled people's time needs to be accounted for might also speak to a longer historical concern with 'idleness' (ibid.: p. 149). On this basis it might be suggested that scheduling activities (even if just 'free time') is a way to recuperate criminalised disabled people into being busy neoliberal citizens—in order to be entitled to enjoy independence and autonomy, contradictorily criminalised disabled people need to be accountable for how they spend their time.

In the context of court diversion, on a general level the control of activity is apparent from the Intellectual Disability Rights Service's (2011: p. 31) description of treatment plans in its court diversion guide for legal practitioners as 'cover[ing] all areas of a person's life'—reflecting group homes exacting 'total life management' (Drinkwater, 2005: p. 232). This micro-analytics of disciplinary power is specifically reflected in the format of treatment plans in the Section 32 Court Data, which are presented in tabular form, broken down into various 'domains' of daily living. The table is a visual representation of the micro-operations and bodily functions of the individual. For example, Megan's treatment plan is in a tabular format with various domains of living: accommodation, behaviour support, case management, additional support, financial, vocational/day programs, staff protocols, community access, family/important relationships, health and external liaison. In relation to each of these domains of living there is a discussion of the service provision, actions to be taken and persons responsible for these actions. These 'domains of living' quite comprehensively cover many aspects of Megan's life, ranging over where she lives, whom she has social contact with, what she does during the day, when she can go into the community and her health, as well as the more 'therapeutic' aspects of case management and behaviour support. The planning that occurs through case management is a fluid process, with plans constantly revised and changed in response to the individuals' behaviour and circumstances, and, in this respect, provides a responsive mode of control. This is evident in the defence's explanation of Rebecca's disability support services which notes monthly review of her behaviour support plan.

The disciplinary strategy of control of activity is also apparent in the layered nature of regulation apparent in the treatment plans, where individuals are acted on through a variety of ways of shaping conduct; these can be located on a spectrum from the macro level, affecting the general scope of choices available to the individual, to the micro level, which structures specific choices in relation to daily conduct. This is well illustrated by Shane's case. Shane lives in a 24-hour supervised accommodation facility for clients with challenging behaviour and complex needs. Shane has restrictive practices in place, including restricted access to knives (due to threatening staff when agitated), laundry (due to irresponsible washing habits), food (due to drinking excessive amounts of milk, cordial and coffee) and tobacco products (he is on an hourly smoking plan). Shane is under guardianship and financial management orders, which govern on a macro level the choices that he (and others) can make about services, accommodation and finances—the big-picture decisions which, in turn, structure and limit the scope of more specific decisions made on a daily basis. The guardianship order also regulates use of restrictive practices. The central feature of Shane's disability support service is the supervised accommodation (which he lives in pursuant to the guardianship order). Living in this space in turn enables case management, skills development, monitored community access and supervision. These general areas then involve more specific interventions at a micro level. For example, Shane's case management involves support with 'daily living and personal care' that includes assistance with 'shopping, banking, budgeting, hygiene skills, cleaning, medication, cooking and general household skills'—areas that would encapsulate many of the micro level tasks that individuals engage in on a daily basis, thus illustrating the depth of control of activity which can be realised through disability support services. Staff support Shane, who is Aboriginal, to have regular contact with Aboriginal elders at a local Aboriginal men's group and contact with his family, noting that this provides him a sense of belonging and stability.

The daily schedule is another specific way in which the disciplinary technique of 'control of activity' is evident in the treatment plans for individuals receiving case management and supported accommodation disability services. Reminiscent of Foucault's (1979: p. 154) prison timetable, characterised by the exhaustive use of free time, some of these individuals had a schedule that provided details of daily routines. For example, Shane has a 'Daily Planner' that identifies activities/tasks to occupy him 24 hours of each day. Even 'free time' is a scheduled and time-limited activity. Similarly, Rebecca's timetable details activities for three hour time slots 7am–10pm. Souriya has a 'routine' in place in order to enable her to have appropriate control over her daily life in the broader context of a 100% containment model of restrictions. Individuals' activity is thus highly controlled; they are to be in certain spaces and doing certain activities at particular times, to an exhaustive degree. The disciplining effects of time might also manifest in a different way for individuals whose diversion focuses on attending appointments for treatment or case management, where there is structuring of time through regular appointments and medication (Soldatic, 2011).

Disability and mental health services are not an alternative to control per se, or a humane and empowering alternative to the oppressive and disempowering prison. Rather, to draw on Foucault who is writing in the context of alternatives to prison, they are 'not so much alternatives as quite simply attempts to ensure through different kinds of mechanisms and set-ups the functions that up to then have been those of prisons themselves' (Foucault, 2009: p. 15). We might thus argue that court diversion facilitates that continuity of coercive intervention and sustains the rhetorical hierarchies such as institution versus community, prison versus group home, freedom versus restraint that mask the pervasiveness of carceral control *across* legal domains, material sites and institutional contexts.

7.8 Criminal legal domain as residual domain of carceral control: conditionality

While I have shown in the earlier sections how court diversion facilitates more effective circulation of criminalised disabled individuals through the institutional archipelago by moving individuals (who might otherwise fall between the service 'gaps') into disability and mental health services, here I suggest that the conditionality of section 32 orders means that court diversion keeps criminalised individuals in a dormant and residual relation to the criminal legal domain.

Conditional section 32 orders are supported by a legislative framework for a 'treatment provider' to report any breaches by the individual of the order during the six months following the making of the order (s32A). An individual who breaches a section 32 order might ultimately have the order revoked and have their charges heard (ss 32(3A)–32(3D)). Thus, a 'conditional' section 32 order involves compelling an individual to engage with disability and mental health services under the threat of having their charges brought back to court and dealt with through the criminal legal domain. The 'conditional' nature of section 32 orders, when coupled with the use of disability and mental health services in these orders, may have counterproductive effects on reducing overrepresentation. This is because, as the discussion of Molly's disability service use in Chapter 5 illustrated, there are ways in which disability and mental health services might contribute to the further criminalisation of their clients when the service provision is framed by criminal legal orders and supervision and reporting obligations (see also Steele, 2017a; on behaviour management as an aspect of organisational management see Dowse, 2017; Spivakovsky, 2017).

Through court diversion criminal legal intervention is suspended (rather than completely removed) in relation to these individuals. Ironically, if the section 32 order is breached, the reversion back to the 'law' (that is, the criminal legal domain) means, first, that the criminal legal domain is retained as an appropriate domain for coercive intervention in relation to the individual (who was initially diverted from that domain on the basis of the lesser appropriateness of that domain), and, second, that the individual ultimately remains liminally connected to the criminal legal domain. The conditionality of section 32 orders reflects a continuation rather than negation of the prison because, to borrow from the words of Foucault (2009: p. 17), in the context of the carceral continuum they 'are simply a way of delaying or deferring imprisonment, or a way of diluting the time of imprisonment over a whole period of one's life' rather than abolishing incarceration. Individuals who are diverted maintain a formal legal connection to the criminal legal domain. This is further enhanced on a material level by the role of disability services in reporting breaches and the role of police in enforcing guardianship and civil mental health orders (McCausland & Baldry, 2017; Steele, 2018d). This interrelationship between criminal justice and disability and mental health services 'shows us how systems use one another to offset and relocate the powers of governance' (Voronka, 2013: p. 321; see similarly in the HIV context Carter, 2016) in two directions—from the criminal justice to disability and mental health systems, and (upon breach) from the disability and mental health system back to the criminal justice system.

In this chapter, I have shown that a judge's decision to divert an individual hinges on making a choice between two legal domains and modes of carceral control. This choice brings criminal legal domains and disabled legal domains into a constitutive relation, enables criminalised disabled people to be subjected to carceral control—irrespective of the fact they have not been sentenced or even convicted—*and* legitimates the carceral control of others on the basis of the justness of their conviction and sentencing. When we shift from viewing court diversion in isolation and, instead, appreciate court diversion's relationship to criminal legal intervention, it becomes evident that it is impossible for *all* criminalised disabled people to access court diversion, because court diversion functions as a constitutive exception to criminal legal intervention. When we view court diversion as part of the broader institutional archipelago, we can understand how it functions to more effectively regulate the flow of criminalised disabled populations between modes of carceral control, rather than undermining carceral control itself. The control that is conventionally assumed to reside exclusively in prison is diffused in the community through disability and mental health services (see also in the disability context Baldry, Dowse & Clarence, 2011: pp. 9, 15; Baldry, 2010: pp. 260–261). The fact that court diversion is conventionally juxtaposed with disability institutions of confinement (e.g. mental asylums, disability hospitals) *and* the prison as offering 'freedom', 'inclusion' and 'support' shows that carceral control manifests in different rhetorical, material and institutional forms and is situated in different policy and ideological rationalities *but remains* consistent and pervasive in the lives of criminalised disabled people (see also Steele 2017a; 2018c). As such, changing the political, social and legal circumstances of criminalised disabled people will do little to disrupt the processes of control while the underlying relations between disability, legality and carcerality, with their peculiar temporal dynamics, endure in law. This is particularly concerning in relation to Aboriginal and Torres Strait Islander Australians, as it suggests court diversion and disability and mental health services are implicated in settler colonial carceral control *outside* of prison.

The very close analysis of the New South Wales court diversion case study over the past three chapters provides scholars and activists who are theoretically and politically engaged with disability criminal justice issues with a basis on which to seriously question court diversion and its typical positioning as a humane alternative to criminal legal intervention and prison. The analysis has shown that it is vital to attend to the specific legal dimensions and dynamics of particular court diversion schemes and, indeed, other disability-specific legal schemes of coercive intervention, both to understand the very specific ways disabled bodies are made up as lawful and legitimate subjects of control and violence, and to identify strategies for contesting the endurance through law of disabled carceral control. This book now turns to exploring practical and conceptual strategies for moving beyond carceral control.

Chapter 8

Disability, criminal justice and law

Beyond court diversion

8.1 What are the alternatives to court diversion?

This chapter shifts the discussion beyond court diversion to consider options for contesting criminalised disabled people's carceral control and debilitation through law. The preceding chapters challenged the conventional approach to court diversion as a beneficial solution to the overrepresentation of criminalised disabled people, offering instead an understanding of court diversion as expanding legal options for carceral control specifically of criminalised disabled people. This book has focused on drawing attention to the injustices of the control that occurs through court diversion. Yet, it is important to note that this book has not sought to make any universal claims about law's role per se in control and regulation. Rather, I have made a very particular argument specifically about the nature of and justifications for the control of criminalised disabled people. This control, which is of a carceral, psychiatric and medical nature, is underpinned by assumptions about the inherent need for intervention in criminalised disabled people's bodies and lives and the assumed benefits of this intervention to these individuals and to society more broadly. As such, the control that occurs through court diversion is violent, discriminatory and debilitating. In short, this book has shown that rather than a valorised solution, court diversion is actually part of a much larger problem (extending beyond mere overrepresentation in the criminal justice system) that must be fought against: criminalised disabled people's debilitation through law.

Seeking to address this problem requires a focus on transformative strategies directed towards dismantling the institutional archipelago (including prison) and supporting criminalised disabled people's individual and collective self-determination and flourishing, rather than channelling energy into tinkering, expanding and fine-tuning court diversion schemes. We should be directed towards anti-carceral alternatives to both the prison *and* the full range of sites, modes and legal domains (including across the criminal justice and disability and mental health systems) through which criminalised disabled people are subject to prison-like control, even when this control occurs through medical treatment, psychiatric care or disability support. Conversely, we should give individuals meaningful opportunities for accessing a range of resources, networks and services that might assist them to live their lives in the way they wish and provide opportunities for them to consent (or not consent) to boundaries or constraints they might find useful. We must shift from strategies that aim only to reform the criminal justice system to those that transform legal, criminal justice and disability and mental health systems (Ben-Moshe, 2014: p. 255). It is vital to challenge associations in law between disability, carcerality and legality, and resist medicalised or politicised, articulations of 'pure' disability that enable bifurcation and differential oppression of disabled populations. Transformative strategies must contest, rather than reify, interlocking dynamics and forces of oppression and could build alliances with other anti-oppression movements to jointly counter the conditions in which criminalised disabled people are situated. Beyond this, we must unpick the entanglements of law, disability and the human in order to contest the self-evident and mundane positioning in law of disabled people as beyond equality and justice and, ultimately, beyond full political community and humanity.

Spade, writing in the context of trans politics, argues that a transformative approach 'is rooted in a shared imagination of a world without imprisonment, colonialism, immigration enforcement, sexual violence, or wealth disparity. It is sustained by social movement infrastructure that is democratic, non-hierarchical, and centred in healing' (Spade, 2015: p. xvi). Such an approach has been championed by the queer abolitionist movement (see Bassichis, Lee & Spade, 2011; Lamble, 2011; Mogul, Ritchie & Whitlock, 2011). This approach also resonates with the North American Disability Justice movement. For Disability Justice activists, the task is not merely to bring about 'the end of oppressive systems' but, additionally, to work towards a positive alternative grounded in 'the creation and the sustaining of just, equitable and life-giving, loving societies and worlds' (Berne & Sins Invalid, 2016; see also Parker, 2017).

The options discussed in this chapter cut across practice and scholarship and are directed towards this much more ambitious transformative framework, but with a particular focus on the place of law. I do not offer a meta-level, grand framework that exhaustively outlines the end of the carceral state. Instead, I foreground the diverse initiatives already underway, which are led by disabled people, Indigenous and First Nations people and their allies. These initiatives, many of which run on few resources and little state support, demonstrate different ways in which communities can resist and subvert the institutional archipelago. Through these initiatives, communities have developed alternatives to state-led criminal justice interventions that support, safety, accountability and redress in ways that do not feed into or rely upon carceral control and that contribute to reframing our cultural understandings of disability, human and justice. Together, these initiatives suggest transformative approaches that reflect 'slow justice'—the gradual and diffused wearing down of the carceral state, rather than a momentous and centralised moment of transformation (on 'slow justice' see Van Veen, Teghtsoonian & Morrow, 2019). Section 8.2 discusses community-led support and accountability systems underpinned by self-determination and flourishing at the individual and collective levels. In Section 8.3, I argue the need to recognise violence and harm experienced by criminalised disabled people, particularly that in which the criminal justice system, disability and mental health systems and law are complicit, and redress it at the individual and collective level. Mindful of the role of the legal profession (lawyers and judges) in court diversion, in Section 8.4 I suggest the development of critical disability approaches to legal pedagogy. Then, in Section 8.5, I propose a more creative engagement with law reform that engages cultural ideas about disability. Section 8.6 suggests strategic engagement with the CRPD only if it can be used to contest (rather than reify) the bifurcation of disabled populations that enables oppression specifically of criminalised disabled people. Last, in Section 8.7, I propose the need for richer and more nuanced critical jurisprudences of disability.

Richardson and McSherry (2010: p. 253) stated ten years ago that '[t]he political reality is that problem-solving courts such as mental health courts and similar diversion programs are here to stay'. A decade on this statement still holds true, as court diversion consolidates its place in Anglo jurisdictions and is identified (along with a disability framework more broadly) as relevant to an ever-increasing range of criminal justice populations and 'problems'. Thus, in contesting criminalised disabled people's oppression we cannot, in the short term, wholly turn our back on court diversion. Instead, we must balance our transformative strategies against the need to attend to the immediate circumstances of criminalised disabled people. This balance must be achieved by seeking criminal legal outcomes that support criminalised disabled people's 'daily well-being, healing, leadership, and survival' (Bassichis, Lee & Spade, 2011: p. 19). We should also work more 'up stream' (Wildeman, 2018b) or at the 'top of the cliff' (Baldry, 2018) to prevent individuals becoming criminalised, so as to reduce the use of court diversion and other forms of carceral control in the criminal justice system. We should work to enhance access to existing disability and mental health and social service systems *outside* of civil and criminal justice coercive frameworks, and expand the range of resources, networks and supports that are available. As my discussion in Section 8.2 will show, this work is already taking place through initiatives led by disabled people, Indigenous and First Nations peoples and their allies. We should also ensure that any use of court diversion is undertaken in full recognition that it is a form of carceral control, and advocate for court diversion to be subjected to the same legal and civil rights scrutiny as criminal legal interventions. We can also enhance scrutiny of criminal legal, criminal justice and disability and mental health systems and utilise existing options of litigation and protest to ensure accountability for any abuse of power and harm (Wildeman, 2018b), including lending support to action led by criminalised disabled people and activist organisations.

By focusing on grounded examples of the initiatives currently led by disabled people and Indigenous and First Nations peoples and their allies—as compared to presenting an abstract theoretical blueprint for change—I ultimately show that developing transformative alternatives to court diversion and the institutional archipelago is not a utopian or aspirational project. Indeed, there is already significant work being undertaken in this regard and the examples I discuss here model what is possible.

8.2 Community-led support, safety and accountability

Community-led processes for support and accountability should be at the core of a transformative approach that is directed towards individual and collective self-determination and flourishing. At a very broad level, scholars and advocates can support and amplify the work of consumer/user/survivor-led movements, including self-advocacy or people first advocacy. In this part, I develop this point by presenting diverse examples of the considerable work already being done by disabled people, Indigenous and First Nations peoples and their allies.

In her discussion of alternatives to the institutional archipelago, Ben-Moshe identifies a range of possibilities extending from 'techniques of relaxation and contemplation' through to 'Soteria' houses consisting of small 'homelike environment[s]' (where a group of individuals live together contributing to the running of the house and participating in an array of activities), through to peer-led counselling, resource centres and support services (Ben-Moshe, 2014: pp. 260–263; see also Rossiter & Rinaldi, 2018: pp. 94–102). One example of alternatives to coercive intervention identified by Ben-Moshe (Ben-Moshe, 2014: p. 262) is the Icarus Project. The Icarus Project describes itself as

> a support network and education project by and for people who experience the world in ways that are often diagnosed as mental illness. We advance social justice by fostering mutual aid practices that reconnect healing and collective liberation. We transform ourselves through transforming the world around us.
> (The Icarus Project, n.d.)

The Icarus Project operates in an anti-oppression framework. It provides services that are driven by values of self-determination, respect and responsibility. These services include publications, workshops and training for individuals to develop skills in self-care and to assist peers and service providers in their support of people in emotional distress.

Tam (2013: p. 283) raises some concerns about the Icarus Project, in the context of a broader argument that 'decolonization [should be] understood as necessarily a part of addressing madness as a systemic oppression'. By reference to a close analysis of one of its publications (ibid.: pp. 287–292), Tam argues that the Icarus Project fails to engage with 'broader political and economic conditions of marginalization', 'the politics of [settler colonial] nation-building', and transnational and colonial contexts of capitalism (ibid.: p. 287). Tam's critique of the Icarus Project signals the complexity and necessity of developing community-led processes for self-determination of disabled people that are situated in a wider project of contesting interlocking dynamics and forces of oppression. In a similar vein, Wildeman (2016: p. 179) suggests that contesting coercive mental health laws could be approached by doing away with political categories defined by reference to mental health—'*disengag[ing]* the work of social justice from the constructs of mental health'—because these categories prevent us from seeing structural inequalities in the operation of mental health laws across the population. Wildeman urges 'more intensive engagement with socioeconomic inequality', such as issues relating to poverty and environmental degradation, as well as the interactions of multiple forms of oppression, for example by reason of gender, race etc. (ibid.).

Alternatives to court diversion for Indigenous and First Nations peoples need to be understood in the broader context of Indigenous and First Nations self-determination and nation-building.[1] In the Australian context, Avery and the First People's Disability Network argue that enhancing self-determination of Aboriginal and Torres Strait Islander disabled peoples, including their access to culture and Country, should be central to strategies, support mechanisms and policy (Avery, 2018). Avery details experiences of discrimination experienced by disabled First Peoples in the non-Indigenous Australian community and contrasts this with the positive, strengths-based and humane reception of disability in Aboriginal and Torres Strait Islander culture and the importance of culture to improving well-being. Indeed, Aboriginal and Torres Strait Islander disabled people enjoy similar levels of access to culture as non-disabled Indigenous Australians (Avery, 2018: p. 183). On this basis Avery proposes 'an Indigenous cultural model of inclusion' that 'seeks to improve the human condition through positive affirmation, as distinct to merely negating the adverse impact of difference' by 'fostering social inclusion, through the active participation in community and cultural activities' (ibid.: p. 191). Avery notes, however, that 'the status of the research is not sufficiently advanced to be prescriptive on how this translates into policy and practice' and that the 'model of cultural inclusion is presented as a vision and direction for a future Aboriginal and Torres Strait Islander disability research agenda' that, in time, can inform policy and practice (ibid.). This approach aligns with earlier research by Aboriginal psychologist Dudgeon (descended from the Beniol Bardi people) and others, discussed in the Introduction.

There are innumerable examples in the Australian context of community-led support for Aboriginal and Torres Strait Islander Australian criminalised disabled people that are premised on self-determination at a collective level, use community knowledge to develop local strategies, and are situated in a broader holistic context of community, culture and Country. These initiatives include night patrols, police custody visiting and support, elders groups, healing services, suicide prevention, legal assistance and family violence prevention (for a range of examples see Behrendt, Porter & Vivian, forthcoming; Cunneen, Porter & Behrendt, forthcoming: ch 4). The Custody Notification Service (CNS), which operates in New South Wales and the Australian Capital Territory (see Aboriginal Legal

1 For a recent overview of examples in a variety of Anglo jurisdictions, see Behrendt, Porter & Vivian, forthcoming; for projects focused on self-determination, see Harvard Project on American Indian Economic Development (n.d.) and Jumbunna Institute for Indigenous Education and Research (n.d.); for scholarly interventions, see Coulthard (2014), Harjo (2019), Million (2013a) and Simpson (2014); for reflections on the limitations of criminology thinking in this area, see Porter (2019).

Service NSW/ACT, n.d.) and the Cell Visitor service operated by Murri Watch in Queensland (Murri Watch, n.d.) are examples of Indigenous and First Nations-led interventions for cultural safety in the context of Aboriginal and Torres Islander people apprehended by police. The CNS '[d]ecreases preventable injuries or deaths in police cell custody' and '[i]ncreases legal and health protections for a person in police cell custody' (Aboriginal Legal Service NSW/ACT, n.d.). Another example is the Aboriginal Community Controlled Organisation, Djirra. Djirra provides holistic responses to family violence for Aboriginal and Torres Strait Islander people, including through legal representation, community-based early intervention programs and policy and law reform advocacy (Djirra, n.d.).

Aboriginal communities of Broome, Derby and Fitzroy in the West Kimberley region (Western Australia) have led the development of a 'decolonising model' diversionary scheme for Aboriginal people. Working with academics Blagg and Tulich, this diversionary scheme moves people back on Country and into community-owned processes 'led and managed by Indigenous communities' (Blagg & Tulich, 2018: p. 7). Blagg and Tulich explain that:

> Developing strategies to end the cycle of Indigenous incarceration necessitates decolonising the justice system, not simply reforming it. This means engaging with the question of Indigenous sovereignty, particularly in the form of demands for the return of land, and the devolution of the care and control of young people to community owned and place-based Indigenous organisations. This decolonising model moves 'place', or 'country', from the periphery to the centre of intervention.
>
> (ibid.; see also Chisholm, Tulich & Blagg, 2017: pp. 103–106)

For Indigenous and First Nations criminalised disabled people, 'self-determination', as a counter to coercive intervention in the institutional archipelago, needs to be interpreted beyond individualised autonomy over one's body to a broader notion of collective autonomy over land, culture and community (Chisholm, Tulich & Blagg, 2017: pp. 103–106).

Another example is the work being led by the Dharriwaa Elders Group in the remote Aboriginal community of Walgett (New South Wales) in partnership with McCausland, MacGillivray, legal academics and environmental scientists from the University of New South Wales. They are working on the project 'Yuwaya Ngarra-li' (which means 'Vision' in the Yuwaalaraay/Gamilaraay languages). The Elder Group's vision is 'that Aboriginal children and young people in Walgett can learn, work, be safe, supported and thrive within a robust sense of belonging to their families, community, culture and country' (Dharriwaa Elders Group, 2018). As such, this project is directed towards 'improv[ing] the wellbeing, social, built and physical environment and life pathways of Aboriginal people in Walgett through collaborating on evidence-based programs, research projects and capacity building' (McCausland, 2018). This community-led research project emerged out of the MHDCD research (from which the hypothetical institutional narratives discussed in Chapter 5 were drawn). The MHDCD report on Indigenous Australians with disability in the criminal justice system (Baldry et al., 2015) found that 'due to systemic disadvantage and discrimination, many Aboriginal people become "managed" by police, courts and prisons' (McCausland, 2018). The research 'highlighted the dire lack of appropriate community-based services and support' and recommended 'community-led knowledge, solutions and services should be properly supported and resourced' (ibid.). The Yuwaya Ngarra-li project addresses issues of criminalisation and incarceration of Aboriginal and Torres Strait Islander people and policing, as well as making broader connections to child welfare, health, housing and employment within an overarching framework of developing the strength and capacity of the community. As MacGillivray and McCausland note,

> we have been informed by community voices to come to the position that while shifting police policies and practices is important, the solutions to the systemic criminalisation of Aboriginal peoples with mental and cognitive disability do not lie with friendlier policing or ascribing a therapeutic role to the criminal justice system. What is required is a genuine shift in power focused on self-determination and community-led responses to the systemic discrimination and disadvantage experienced by Aboriginal and Torres Strait Islander peoples so that police are no longer the frontline (mis)managers of thousands of people with unmet health and disability needs.
>
> (MacGillivray & McCausland, 2019: pp. 1–2)

Each of these examples emerged from the specific needs of a particular community rather than being part of a formal state program of services rolled out in a top-down and blanket manner. This underscores the importance of locally specific and collective self-determination, and of having approaches that focus not only on individual flourishing but also on developing sustainable communities and contesting (rather than reifying) interlocking forces and dynamics of oppression.

As well as community-led alternatives to coercive intervention, we might also consider alternatives to accountability for criminalised disabled people who do engage in harmful behaviour. Alternative processes for accountability can ensure that individuals have opportunities to change their future behaviour in a broader framework of strengthening and enriching interpersonal relationships and communities and contesting oppressive structural conditions. One such framework, which has emerged out of a number of marginalised communities such as queer and trans, racialised, Indigenous/First Nations, and disabled communities in North America, is 'transformative justice'. Disability Justice activist Mingus describes transformative justice as 'a political framework and approach for responding to violence, harm and abuse. At its most basic, it seeks to respond to violence without creating more violence and/or engaging in harm reduction to lessen the violence. [Transformative justice] can be thought of as a way of "making things right," getting in "right relation," or creating justice together' (Mingus, 2019).

The key features of transformative justice approaches are summarised by Lamble as: 'Keeping a community focus on survivor support', '[r]efusing to resort to, or rely on, threats of punishment, isolation or exclusion', '[b]uilding community capacity/fostering skills for everyday intervention and prevention of violence' and '[d]eveloping a more holistic analysis' (Lamble, 2014).

Transformative justice is different to 'restorative justice'. Restorative justice aims to: 'restore intimate relationships and community bonds that have been damaged by interpersonal violence, through practices of community dialog and appeals to collective values' (Kershnar et al., 2007: p. 20). Members of the transformative justice collective, Generation Five, acknowledge that many restorative justice models 'do expand the possibilities of accountability and transformation through engaging and educating members of the intimate and/or community networks in which the abuse occurs' (Kershnar et al., 2007: p. 21). However, they argue that these benefits can be undercut by the fact that many restorative justice models have been co-opted by the state such as through use of state coercion in the models themselves or the timing of the models to apply to individuals after they have been through conventional punishment (e.g. restorative justice processes post-release from prison). Members of Generation Five argue that 'such models have been appropriated by the criminal legal system as a way to involve the community in punishing the person that has been violent and then "restoring" the conditions that already existed when the abuse originally took place' (Kershnar et al., 2007: p. 21). Generation Five conclude that, unlike transformative justice, restorative justice models 'often focus on the restoration of the *status quo* and ignore the challenge of transforming the conditions of social, economic and political injustice that are the context for, and cause of, violence' (Kershnar et al., 2007: p. 21; see similarly Harris, 2008: pp. 556–559; Zehr, 2011).

In contrast to restorative justice, transformative justice approaches are 'community-based alternatives' to the criminal legal system in 'recognition of the role played by the criminal legal system in perpetrating and failing to protect people from violence' (Mogul, Ritchie & Whitlock, 2011: p. 149). Approaches grounded in transformative justice 'strive to address interpersonal violence outside of the state-sanctioned violence and oppression of criminal justice and child protective systems—without replicating the violence of these systems in the alternatives practised' (Chapman & Withers, 2019: p. 357). These approaches 'actively cultivate the things we know prevent violence such as healing, accountability, resilience, and safety for all involved' (Mingus, 2019). Chapman and Withers (2019: p. 357) explain that '[t]ransformative justice approaches work with the tension between careful reflection and concrete action, and also between immediate responses and long-term political change'. In transformative justice, violence is a 'collective responsibility' (Mingus, 2019) and '[t]he end goal is not only to restore relationships but to transform society in the process' such that '[t]he focus is not (only) on the specific harm done but on structures that create oppression and inequality in the first place' (Ben-Moshe, 2014: p. 260; see also Spade, 2015: pp. 122–127). Mingus (2019) explains that transformative justice 'recognizes that we must transform the conditions which help to create acts of violence or make them possible. Often this includes transforming harmful oppressive dynamics, our relationships to each other, and our communities at large.' Transformative justice focuses on harms arising from interpersonal violence such as intimate partner violence and child abuse (Spade, 2015: p. 122).

Transformative justice initiatives might provide possibilities for addressing interpersonal violence perpetrated by criminalised disabled people in ways that avoid the criminal legal domain and which subsequently *challenge* rather than fold back into carceral control and reification of interlocking forces and dynamics of oppression. This is particularly so because these approaches do not exceptionalise disability but, instead, apply to all individuals within a community. However, more exploration is needed. It is unclear whether this framework can provide a holistic alternative to the full scope of offending through which disabled people are criminalised, such as drug offending, public order offending and property offences. Moreover, the focus on ending interpersonal violence leaves open questions about how appropriate the framework is to addressing offending by criminalised disabled people that occurs in the context of relations of institutional control (e.g. child welfare or disability support) and responding to institutional violence against criminalised disabled people which is so central to disabled people's oppression (an issue raised in Section 8.6, below). Transformative justice is premised on offending that occurs within a 'community' and that can then be responded to within that community; it is unclear how this will relate to criminalised disabled people who might be isolated (not least if they are homeless or cycling in and out of prison and mental health facilities). Last, it is also unclear to what extent transformative justice can apply in other contexts, particularly noting the earlier discussion of place-based initiatives on Country. However, it is an area that deserves greater consideration for the possibilities it provides for responding to individual instances of criminal offending in ways that transform the structural conditions of communities.

8.3 Redressing violence and harm

Meaningfully contesting criminalised disabled people's oppression must be directed towards not only ending carceral control, but also redressing violence and other harms experienced by criminalised disabled people. In Chapter 5 I highlighted the pervasive nature of violence against and harm of criminalised disabled people and the entanglement of criminalisation, medicalisation, incarceration and victimisation. I also noted that the actions of lawyers, judges and law reformers are pervasive throughout this violence (much of which is legal violence or takes place in institutional settings where individuals have ended up by legal decisions). Yet, in Chapters 3, 4, 6 and 7, I argued that not only does court diversion itself perpetrate violence (in multiple different and broadly construed ways) but it also fails to provide any means for recognising and redressing past harms experienced by criminalised disabled people, notably those in which criminal legal, criminal justice system or disability and mental health systems are complicit.

It is vital that criminalised disabled people be at the centre of responses to violence. For example, the Psychiatric Disabilities Anti-violence Coalition (2015: p. 6) argues that responses to violence must 'position the voices of psychiatric survivors who have experienced violence at the centre of this discussion'. The Coalition explains that:

> Because their expertise is not recognized as such, their meaningful participation in system planning, responses to crises, and accountability has been only marginal. More often than not, psychiatric survivor voices are relegated to 'participatory' models that are tokenistic at best; for example, when people are invited to participate in ways that assume their 'disability identity' will suffice to do political and social change work.
>
> (ibid.: p. 25)

The Coalition recommends 'use of a psychiatric survivor anti-violence Framework' (ibid.). This framework involves examining, analysing and responding in a way that situates an incident in a systemic context and is informed by psychiatric survivors' research and experiences (ibid.: pp. 26–27). A related aspect of redress could be diverting resources away from forced treatment and specifically towards 'survivor research that asks the questions that matter' (Brosnan, 2018).

Court diversion is part of a bigger problem (noted in Chapter 2) of law preventing translation of harms against disabled people into injustices to be remedied and, thus, enabling state and institutional irresponsibility. Within law, disability is more familiar as an *injury* to be remedied, rather than disabled people being recognised as agential subjects of injustice not necessarily related to their medicalised disability. For example, Rossiter and Rinaldi (2018: p. 66) have argued in the context of the Huronia Regional Center in Ontario (Canada) that a settlement redress scheme for disabled individuals 're-inscribes systemic forms of injustice'. The challenges of recognising and redressing injustice are particularly acute in relation to criminalised disabled people, where disability as a barrier to recognition of injustice is compounded with laws that limit recognition of injustices and access to redress on the basis of criminality or incarceration. For example, in some jurisdictions domestic violence is not legally recognised in prison, prisoners cannot commence civil legal action as of right, and prisoners may also be limited in access to statutory victim redress schemes.

Legal dynamics that prevent recognition of injustice at a more individualised level are situated in a broader settler colonial context that fails to recognise the ongoing illegitimacy and illegality of dispossession of land and genocide of Indigenous and First Nations people, as well as the harms and injustices this has wrought (Razack, 2015). Court diversion sustains these legal dynamics by positioning the state—through criminal legal, criminal justice and disability and mental health systems—as therapeutic healer and rescuer.

Therefore, I propose that in thinking about options for contesting criminalised disabled people's carceral control and debilitation through law, we should develop strategies for recognising violence and harm experienced by criminalised disabled people as injustices and redress these accordingly. While it is absolutely important individuals have access to remedies for specific harms, it is also vital to resist exclusively individualised remedial approaches that cannot comprehend structural, historical and intergenerational harms—particularly those associated with settler colonialism—that exceed a singular victim and perpetrator. Balint, Evans, McMillan and others propose the concept of 'structural justice' as a framework that can address the intergenerational, historical, and structural injustices in settler colonial contexts (Balint, Evans and McMillan, 2014; Balint et al., 2017; Balint et al., 2018). They document how artistic practice (notably theatre performance) can be one way through which to 'do' structural justice.

Further, in the disability context, with its temporalities of dark pasts and enlightened futures (Altermark, 2018), there is a real risk that injustices are understood only in the past tense and as having been 'fixed' by 'progressive' reforms (Abbas & Voronka, 2014). It is important that redressing injustices experienced by criminalised disabled people resists these temporalities, by framing justice as an ongoing obligation of the state rather than a one-off event. As Kim notes in the context of occupational illness, debilitation and deaths caused by the manufacturing process of electronics in South Korea, while injustice is material and embodied and lives on through disabled people's lives and survival,

> justice—in demands for reparations and apologies for harms inflicted—is often cast as a universal and final outcome that cannot be revisited. Justice is described as 'not done yet' or 'done', as if justice were something to be completed at a certain time by a set of actions upon which affected people and society in general agree. Furthermore, justice is conceived as an object of doing; yet the passive voice indicates that it is not always clear who and what does justice. The legal recognition of injustice, apology, and monetary compensation conditioned by irreversibility and followed by the demand to heal almost always do not do justice to those who were harmed or to the systems of violence that continue to do harm.
>
> (Kim, 2019: p. 3)

Justice must always be in motion and in relation—it is an ongoing commitment to conduct rather than an isolated act of finality. Drawing on the work of Dean (2015) in the context of remembering disappeared Indigenous women in Vancouver, we might think of the ongoing relevance of historical injustices in terms of 'inheritance'. This concept has connotations of past injustices living on and inhabiting our present legal systems and of contemporary legal actors receiving these past injustices and holding them in their collective possession. This notion of 'inheritance' is particularly potent in forging connections between disability injustice across time, people and place. The concept might provide opportunities for current legal actors engaged in disability and mental health law to assume a shared ethical responsibility to both work in current legal systems and shape future legal systems in ways that are attentive to redressing (and not repeating) what 'lives on' from the enduring injustices experienced by criminalised disabled people.

Following on from the concept of 'inheritance', the Sites of Conscience movement might provide one such approach to a more ongoing, collective process of redressing injustice specifically in relation to institutional violence experienced by criminalised disabled people. Sites of Conscience are 'public memorials that make a specific commitment to democratic engagement through programs that stimulate dialogue on pressing social issues today and that provide opportunities for public involvement in those issues' (Brett et al., 2007: p. 1). They provide the opportunity to 'remember the past to build a better present and future' (ibid.: p. 7). The Sites of Conscience approach could be drawn upon to connect past injustices arising from institutional violence experienced by criminalised disabled people to future disability and mental health law reform and judicial decision-making that is situated in a purportedly enlightened, deinstitutionalised context. This approach has the potential to foreground the memories and perspectives of people who have been institutionalised, avoid the erasure of past injustices that might occur through the redevelopment of former institutional sites, provide a space for acknowledging resistance of people who have been institutionalised, and help ensure the injustices of institutionalisation live on in our collective legal memory to shape future law reform and legal decision-making (Steele et al., 2020). Moreover, as I and my co-authors recently noted in the context of one such Site of Conscience in Australia, Sites of Conscience can enhance attentiveness to:

> settler colonial dynamics, including to Indigenous histories and significance of … places where institutions of confinement are now situated, the particular impacts of institutionalisation on Indigenous Australians, and the role in Indigenous healing, self-determination and nation building of reclamation of … sites of institutions of confinement.
>
> (Steele et al., 2020 (forthcoming); see also Guenther, 2018)

I return to consider memorialisation in my discussion of legal pedagogy. In a similar vein, artistic and curatorial practices, such as film, performance, fine arts and comedy (see, for example, Sins Invalid, n.d.) as well as museum exhibitions (see, for example, Sandell, Dodd & Garland-Thomson, 2013) might also be methods for speaking back and providing counter-narratives to challenge dominant, medicalised understandings of disability and the necessity of therapeutic intervention and carceral control.

8.4 Critical disability legal pedagogy

Legal pedagogy should be an integral aspect of contesting criminalised disabled people's carceral control and debilitation. I suggest this by reason of the role of the legal profession (lawyers and judges) in court diversion and the broader institutional archipelago (as illustrated by the empirical analysis in Chapters 6 and 7).

On a deeper level, I make this suggestion due to a recurring question I have asked myself while writing this book: What should our ethical responsibilities be to those whose injustices we bear witness to, as lawyers, activists and legal scholars; and how can we begin to develop in law students the critical awareness and skills through which to meet these responsibilities? I propose the development of critical disability approaches to legal pedagogy through which students critically reflect on the impact of law (legislation, legal decision-making, law reform) and legal actors on criminalised disabled people *as well as* the abstract role of disability in ordering and legitimating carceral control and debilitation on marginalised populations more generally. Such an approach should draw on anti-colonial pedagogies that 'invite students to examine their complicity in an ongoing colonialism' (Razack, 2015: p. 208) and anti-oppression pedagogies. Ultimately, students should develop an awareness of the complicity of legal practitioners through their (often desk-based) conduct in material harms done to criminalised disabled people by law, and develop knowledge and practical skills to enable them to engage in ethical decision-making and support the kinds of initiatives and movements discussed in Sections 8.2 and 8.3 above. Indeed, the development of critical pedagogies must foreground contributions by the organisations and individuals involved in these initiatives and movements.

Developing critical disability legal pedagogies is challenging, not least because medicalised and negative ontologies of disability are deeply embedded throughout law (Campbell, 2009). As discussed in Chapters 3, 4 and 6, these ontologies underpin core legal concepts such as capacity, rationality and reasonableness, and they order legal domains, all of which makes possible and natural differential access to liberal legal citizenship and full humanness. Readers who have studied or taught law might know that these legal ontologies are largely unremarkable and self-evident. There is minimal critical discussion of the impact of law on *disabled people* in the teaching of core law subjects. This is so even in those subjects about areas of law where disabled people (including criminalised disabled people) might be particularly affected, such as criminal law (as offenders and victims), administrative law (review of decisions concerning service provision and funding) and tort law (lack of access to civil remedies for assault and false imprisonment related to coercive intervention). It is even so when cases featuring lawful violence to disabled people are used in the service of teaching general legal principles (for example, doctrine of necessity and third-party consent to medical treatment being taught by reference to cases on sterilisation), let alone deeper consideration of how disability in a more disembodied and abstract sense structures and legitimates white state sovereignty, legal authority and legal violence more broadly (such as through legal capacity). Chapman and Withers (2019: pp. 348–356; see also Chapman 2014a) have done such work in the context of social work professional practice, so the same can and should be done in law.

Legal teachers need to be aware that because they are, in effect, teaching violence when they teach law without critical reflection on disability in the various ways identified above, they are representing violence—both against disabled people and through legal ontologies of disability—as rightly lawful and just, and this sustains other dynamics and forces of oppression. Law students need to be able to confront the violence and harm done by law and navigate the ethical possibilities, tensions and contradictions arising from various roles within the legal profession (Steele, 2017b). Such exploration will be uncomfortable and challenging (for an example in the social work context, see Chapman, 2014b), but this approach can be directed towards constructing new ethical frameworks and encouraging students to think creatively about how they can support criminalised disabled people's individual and collective self-determination and flourishing through (or even outside of or against) white sovereign law. Noting the observation made in Chapter 7 about the possibility that magistrates and defence lawyers might be grappling with how to support criminalised disabled people within the criminal legal domain, I suggest that such critical pedagogy is much-needed in legal education. Indeed, it is needed in relation to all disciplines implicated in the institutional archipelago, including social work, medicine, nursing, psychology and counselling.

I am mindful that this silence and depoliticisation of disability in legal education is occurring at the same time that there is increased awareness of mental illness in law students and legal professionals (see, Kelk, Medlow & Hickie, 2010; 2011). This phenomenon has been problematised in terms of (a respectable) notion of 'wellness'—as evidenced by the Australian Wellness Network for Law (n.d.)—solutions which focus on voluntary strategies that circumvent the politics of coercive intervention and the settler colonial, class, racial and other dynamics that can shape the circumstances of disabled people on the 'other side' of the law as legal subjects of disability-specific coercive intervention (on the politics of disability support in university contexts see Gorman, 2013). There is a strikingly odd and unsettling contradiction at play, which I can only reconcile in terms of bifurcation (discussed in Chapter 3): through the legal academy's recognition of mental illness, law students are capacitated, while the teaching of law simultaneously debilitates criminalised disabled people. I propose that, in order for law students to fully understand the complicity of lawyers in disability oppression, a critical disability pedagogical approach must encourage students to explore connections, contradictions and tensions between, on the one hand, mental health in law students and the legal profession (how it is problematised and responded to) and, on the other, the legal status of criminalised disabled people as well as disability as an abstract structuring and legitimating concept in law. The legal academy and legal profession as a whole should be involved in advocating for abolition of disability-specific coercive intervention and other oppressive dimensions of law.

Drawing on aspects of 'place conscious' pedagogy might be one way in which to engage law students more directly with lawyers' complicity in criminalised disabled injustice. Conventional legal education typically takes place in a classroom on the university campus or online from home and is reliant upon books and lectures that provide indirect textual representations of law and in/justice. Legal education is abstracted from the people and places that laws impact. It replicates the desk-based actions of lawyers, judges and legislators that were intimated by Cover (1986) in his seminal piece on legal violence—disembodied, detached from the lived and material consequences of these actions. In contrast, place-conscious pedagogy locates education at the point of students' material and physical circumstances, encouraging them to understand where they are situated in the world and, thus, to be more aware of their actions and accountability to others (see Kennedy, Mundy & Nielsen, 2016).

Sites of Conscience (discussed in Section 8.3 above) might be one powerful vehicle for place-conscious legal pedagogy. Sites of conscience not only mark a shift in *where* teaching occurs but also in *how* teaching occurs and in *who* is teaching. They can provide law students with direct contact with material places where injustice has occurred through law, and thus through the actions of lawyers. They can provide students with an opportunity to listen to and face survivors of injustice and harm which has been done by law. Students have an opportunity to make connections between desk-based legislation and court/administrative orders and material harm to specific individuals, and connections between historical injustice and current laws—redress, continuation of past injustice, intergenerational impacts. Indeed, in a recent excursion I ran to Australia's first Site of Conscience, the Parramatta Female Factory Precinct (Hibberd & Djuric, 2013; Hibberd with Djuric, 2019), students noted the lack of legal accountability for institutional injustices, ongoing and intergenerational trauma resulting from institutionalisation and institutional abuse, failure of contemporary justice processes to respond to historical injustice, and the importance of reclaiming history even if the past cannot be changed or corrected (Steele, 2018a; Steele et al., 2020). Sites of Conscience, and place-conscious pedagogy more broadly, hold significant potential in relation to critical disability legal pedagogy, providing a tangible and direct example of the impact of law and policy and the failures and limitations of contemporary justice processes vis-à-vis criminalised disabled people and, in turn, engaging students' critical thinking and self-awareness about law, lawyering and legal ethics (Steele et al., 2020). As Chapman and Withers (2019: p. 358) note in the context of social work professional practice:

> Rejecting a narrative of one's own innocence calls on each of us to consider our implications in both interpersonal harm and systemic interlocking oppressions. It means understanding that, even with 'good' intentions, even if we see ourselves as 'good' people, we can nevertheless cause harm and participate in structural violence, and we must strive to be accountable if and when we do so.

Additional to critical disability legal pedagogy, the legal profession should reflect on its complicity in criminalised disabled people's oppression. Consideration should be given to the collective ethical and legal obligations and accountability arising from this complicity, including apologies by law societies and structural justice initiatives (see, for example, the apology to Aboriginal and Torres Strait Islanders by the Australian Psychological Society: Carey et al., 2017).

8.5 Creative engagement with law reform

As I noted in the Introduction, the past decade has seen increased attention to court diversion in law reform and government reports across a number of Anglo jurisdictions. In Chapters 2 and 4, I raised concern about law reform processes taking an unreflective approach to court diversion—both to court diversion as a 'solution' to overrepresentation and to the construction of the 'problem' of overrepresentation itself—which suggests the complicity of these processes in disabled oppression. Here, I suggest that a more creative and critical engagement with law reform might provide some possibility for contesting disabled oppression.

Such an approach to engagement with law reform draws on Golder's argument (in the context of law reform related to the 'homosexual advance' defence) of a different 'method' for law reform. Golder (2004) proposes a 'poetics of law reform', attentive to the cultural dynamics of law such as how legal subjectivity is constructed and the binaries that order law. In the context of court diversion, a poetics of law reform could involve critiquing the binaries of dis/ability and in/capacity that order legal domains (see Clough, 2018), the association between medicalised disability and coercive intervention that grounds disabled legal subjectivity (see Steele, 2017d; 2018b), and the relationships between disability, carcerality, legality and temporality that enable different legal thresholds of coercive intervention in relation to criminalised disabled people and casts them outside liberal legal citizenship and full humanity. This poetics should not only occur through conventional scholarship but also through artistic and curatorial practices (see, for example, the work of the Parramatta Female Factory Precinct Association: Hibberd with Djuric, 2019).

Mindful of Spivakovsky and Seear's arguments about the constructed nature of law reform 'problems' (discussed in Chapter 1 and Chapter 4), I suggest that a poetics of law reform should extend to taking a critical approach to the 'problem' that drives disability criminal law reform—including critiquing the terms of reference or scope of a particular review or inquiry. This speaks to the observations in Chapter 4 concerning the problematising of disabled incarceration in terms of overrepresentation as a form of massification that works to legitimate incarceration per se, structural inequalities that make certain groups of people more likely to be incarcerated and, ultimately, the ongoing incarceration of criminalised disabled people. Rather than take for granted the starting point of overrepresentation, engagement with law reform can provide a counter-narrative of the 'problem' that is instead focused on deep structural issues of carceral control of criminalised disabled people within a context of enduring settler colonial rule and interlocking systems of oppression (Wildeman, 2018b).

A poetics of law reform should be directed towards opening up the possibility for the kinds of alternatives proposed in Sections 8.2 to 8.4 above. Writing in the context of trans people, Spade argues that '[u]sing legal reform requires a careful, reflective analysis in each instance of the potential impact on the survival of trans populations', asking such questions as 'Is this change merely symbolic, or will it prevent trans poverty, criminalization, deportation, and death? Will this reform strengthen key systems of control or dismantle them?' (Spade, 2015: p. 88). Spade states that instrumental engagement with law must always be directed towards dismantling, rather than furthering, carceral control: 'we must ensure that legal work is always aimed at dismantling the prison industrial complex and supporting people entangled in it, knowing the system is likely to try to co-opt our critiques to produce opportunities for expansion' (ibid.: p. 89). As such, 'poetic' engagement with the cultural dynamics of disability that underpin laws pertaining to carceral control should ultimately be directed toward addressing material social and economic inequalities experienced by criminalised disabled people (Wildeman, 2018b; Withers, 2012a: p. 48).

Last, any engagement with law reform by scholars and activists as a means of contesting criminalised disabled people's carceral control and debilitation should question law reform's formal and procedural dynamics, alert to the possibility that these dynamics might restrict law reform to a process that authorises and protects law's authority rather than a process that opens law up to significant disruption (Balint, Evans & McMillan, 2016). Activists and scholars might look to other methodologies of doing law reform, such as Sites of Conscience, because a transformative approach to reform of disability criminal justice might ultimately require transforming law reform processes themselves.

8.6 Strategic engagement with human rights

In Chapter 2 I expressed concern with limitations of engaging with the CRPD in the context of criminalised disabled people, suggesting the CRPD is anti-disability-specific but not anti-carceral. My subsequent analysis of court diversion in Chapters 3 to 7 has confirmed my suspicions about the ambivalence of the CRPD towards criminal legal intervention (notably incarceration in prison). This is for two reasons. One is its primary focus on disability-specific coercive intervention. The other reason is the CRPD's silence on abjected or degenerate disabled populations, associated with its attachment to a rather 'pure' disability that largely overlooks eugenics logics, settler colonialism and other interlocking forces and dynamics of oppression that can result in bifurcation of disabled populations (all of which was illustrated strikingly in the UN Disability Committee's decision in *Noble*). This leads me to conclude that, while it might seem counter-intuitive in the current context where the CRPD has become the routine 'go to' political frame in relation to disabled injustice, scholars and activists need to be very careful and strategic in their engagement with the CRPD. An unreflective, instrumental and technical use of the CRPD risks further legitimating and embedding carceral control and debilitation of criminalised disabled people—despite, and indeed through, abolition of disability-specific coercive intervention (including court diversion) and aspiring towards disability equality in access to criminal legal and criminal justice systems.

I recognise that this position places me at odds with the majority of legal scholarship on the CRPD, which has been attentive to questions of interpretation and application; a minority view in line with that captured by Bartlett:

> The party celebrating the passage and ratification of the CRPD is now over, however, and on the morning after, as we look out (perhaps slightly hung over) on this brave new world that has been created, we need to figure out how to live in it, how to make the CRPD actually work in practice.
>
> (Bartlett, 2012, p. 777)

Yet, I would go further and suggest that a focus on how we can 'live in it' and make the CRPD work in practice needs to be tempered with activists' and scholars' critical reflection on the CRPD's limitations, contradictions and tensions. This critical reflection should involve engagement with the kinds of longstanding debates which have engaged critical human rights scholarship more broadly. These debates include those around state sovereignty, the meaning of humanity and the human, the colonial and imperial dimensions of human rights, and human rights' relationship to capital and neoliberalism. Such critical reflection is beginning to emerge in the CRPD-related scholarship.[2] Moreover, North American Disability Justice activists have raised concerns relevant to the CRPD in the broader context of disability rights movements. A.J. Withers notes:

> Rights movements are, at their core, about accessing the privileges that a person would otherwise be able to access if they were not a member of an oppressed group. Rights models are reformist; power is to be accessed, not unravelled.
>
> (Withers, 2012a: p. 85)

Patty Berne (2016) has argued that '[r]ights-based strategies often address the symptoms of inequity but not the root', such as ableism, and that in the US the Disability Rights Movement has 'invisibilized the lives of peoples who lived at intersecting junctures of oppression', including 'disabled people of color', 'queers with disabilities', 'people with disabilities who are houseless', 'people with disabilities who are incarcerated' and 'people with disabilities who have had their ancestral lands stolen'.

Golder (2015: p. 155) suggests a strategic engagement with human rights, observing that, for Foucault, human rights simultaneously present possibilities for disrupting and redefining power relations and subjectivity at the same time that they can reinscribe or re-form the biopolitical dimensions of these. Yet, Golder argues that for Foucault this 'ambivalence' is productive—it is

2 See, for example, Baldry (2018), Beaupert (2018a), Chisholm, Tulich & Blagg (2017), Jaffee (2016), Meekosha & Soldatic (2011), Puar (2017), Ribet (2011), Steele (2017d), Wildeman (2016) and Wildeman (2018b).

something to 'negotiate' and 'work with' (ibid.: p. 91). Golder interprets Foucault's engagement with human rights as 'critical counter-conduct': the tactical use of human rights in a particular 'game' (political context) in a way that does not affirm the 'rules' of the game (the broader power relations or subjectivities that shape the political context) but instead subverts or challenges the rules. To make this argument, Golder contrasts two differing approaches by Foucault to the use of human rights. As mentioned earlier (Chapter 4), Foucault did not engage with human rights in his opposition to the death penalty. Golder suggests this is because the right to life would not have contested the carceral lives to which prisoners remain subject. In contrast, Foucault did draw on human rights in his support for euthanasia in seeking to resist this area being dominated by the medical profession and reduced to medical epistemologies of worthy life and death. Foucault's engagement with human rights signals the importance of critical disability scholars being attendant not only to whether the construction of 'human' in human rights extends to disabled people, but also to 'life' or forms of 'life' that people or 'humans' with disability are allowed to inhabit through human rights. As such, in contesting criminalised disabled people's debilitation through law, it is not politically necessary or desirable to absolutely reject human rights; instead, it is vital to see human rights as but one of many political tools, to be deployed where their use can disrupt rather than fold back into biopolitical control (ibid.). Strategic engagement with human rights is particularly important in relation to Indigenous and First Nations criminalised disabled people, by reason of the contradictions in accessing justice via a system fundamentally premised on the primacy of white sovereignty and the dehumanisation of Indigenous and First Nations people (see Behrendt, 2003; Behrendt, Cunneen & Libesman, 2009: pp. 296–314; Bond, 2017; Gilbert, 1993; Watson, 2015).

Drawing on these ideas, I propose that any strategic engagement with the CRPD should include offering creative interpretations of its articles to make them applicable to the particular circumstances of criminalised disabled people. For example, in the context of Indigenous and First Nations criminalised people, Article 12 on equality before the law could be proposed as a basis on which they should be given collective self-determination, while Article 16 on freedom from violence might be a basis for advocating for structural redress of genocide. In relation to criminalised disabled people generally, Article 19 on community living could be interpreted as requiring prison abolition alongside further abolition of disability-specific institutions. It is equally important to be alert to the use of the CRPD by governments to rationalise the bifurcation of disabled populations (such as the overwhelming focus in CRPD-engaged law reform on civil mental health and guardianship laws as compared to forensic mental health and criminal laws) and, in turn, exclude criminalised disabled people from more capacitating reforms. In these contexts, it might be necessary to call out the biopolitical effects of the CRPD and resist their application.

8.7 Critical jurisprudence of disability: law's role in the endurance of degeneracy and the institution

My final suggestion for meaningfully contesting criminalised disabled people's debilitation is a critical jurisprudence of disability. Of course, there is a growing body of sociolegal and critical legal scholarship on disability, much of which I have drawn upon in this book. However, what I am proposing here is jurisprudence that speaks directly to the specific legal contradictions and tensions experienced by *criminalised* disabled people that have emerged in my analysis of court diversion. I propose this jurisprudence could trace the endurance of two phenomena in law—degeneracy and the disability institution—and, in order to understand how bifurcation might occur through law, track the endurance of these against the emergence and development of more 'positive' domestic legal developments for disabled people, such as laws on anti-discrimination and equality, community living and self-directed funding. We might gain new insights into how these seemingly contrary legal developments—greater equality and autonomy in law for some disabled people on the one hand and continued debilitation in law of criminalised disabled people on the other hand—are not contradictory or unintended but actually in productive tension as part of coherent biopolitical dynamics of bifurcation, capacitation and debilitation contingent to fitness of the neoliberal white settler nation-state.

Both degeneracy and the disability institution are typically viewed as historical in nature—degeneracy is associated with eugenics and the institution is associated with the asylum. It might seem counterintuitive to turn to two concepts conventionally understood as part of a bygone era that contemporary disability law and policy has purportedly moved beyond. Yet, as Altermark (2017: p. 3) notes in the context of the figure of the asylum in contemporary intellectual disability politics, 'the perceived break between the oppression of the past and the emancipatory ambitions of present policies operates as an unacknowledged presumption for how the contemporary government of intellectual disability is interpreted'. Thus, my proposed jurisprudence is focused on tracing the endurance and responsiveness of degeneracy and the disability institution, to draw out how these phenomena continue to inform how laws are ordered and operate and to whom they apply, while at the same time they might serve a rhetorical function of being the point of juxtaposition to give meaning to current 'positive' laws, such as anti-discrimination and equality law and laws on community living and self-directed funding—and, in so doing, affirm the legitimacy and naturalness of bifurcation in law. Questions driving this jurisprudence include: what remains of disability institutionalisation in law when material sites of disability institutionalisation disappear and laws support community living, and how do ideas of degeneracy endure in law and continue to shape the lives of criminalised disabled people despite the emergence of disability discrimination law?

As well as tracking these as separate phenomena, it would also be useful to trace the interrelationship of degeneracy and the disability institution in law. By commencing at the starting point of the institutionalisation of an undifferentiated degenerate population (rather than disabled, racialised, poor populations) it might be possible to glean new insights about carceral control that speak more directly to neoliberal and settler colonial biopolitics of fitness and understand how institutions variously order individuals between and within spaces as separate or conglomerate populations, while at the same time interrogating why disability has endured as a key basis for separation (as suggested by Chapman, 2014b). There is already an emerging scholarship outside of the legal discipline on which to draw, including Joseph's work on eugenics and contemporary forensic mental health and immigration law (Joseph, 2015), Voronka's work on degeneracy, mental asylums and gentrification (Voronka, 2003), Schweik's scholarship on eugenics and ugly laws (Schweik, 2009), McWhorter's genealogy of abnormality and eugenics in the context of race and sexuality (McWhorter, 2009; see also Lowik, 2018), Altermark's work on post-institutionalisation and citizenship (Altermark, 2018), the scholarship on the institutional archipelago (for example, Chapman, Carey & Ben-Moshe, 2014; Carey, Ben-Moshe & Chapman, 2014) and the work of scholars critiquing the repurposing of institutions (for example, Moon, Kearns & Joseph, 2015; Punzi, 2019). I propose bringing to this emerging scholarship a focus on legal dynamics that has to date been underdeveloped. Such a project could trace legal developments within specific jurisdictions, as well as the transnational dynamics of the development of mental health laws both in colonial legal systems and more recently with CRPD-related international law and development work in the Global South.

A critical jurisprudence of disability by reference to the endurance of degeneracy and the disability institution comes up against the preliminary challenge that neither of these phenomena are explicitly present in law. While law is central to purposing sites as institutions and authorising institutionalisation of individuals, law fragments this into separate legislation and different legal categories and legal processes (mental health facility and mental health law, prison and criminal law, group home and guardianship law). Similarly, the legal ordering of identity categories such as disability, race, sexuality and class as siloed and distinct—for example, in anti-discrimination and equality law—prevents us from seeing the messy coalescence of the abjected undersides of these categories in a singular group of degeneracy. Thus, part of the task of this jurisprudence is to interrogate how and why these phenomena remain largely illegible in law, while continuing to have an impact in shaping law's differential impact on disabled populations.

These scholarly projects in jurisprudence are not mere intellectual exercises (although they would be welcome additions to sociolegal scholarship). I suggest they can have very real implications in guiding how activists, advocates and lawyers understand law's relationship to criminalised disabled people and, in turn, how they form coalitions with other anti-oppression movements and can engage with law to avoid reifying carceral control and debilitation. For example, this jurisprudence can give activists, advocates and lawyers a deeper understanding of the limits of turning to disabled legal subjectivity in criminal law (as I have already illustrated through my analysis of court diversion), as well as in more positive areas of law such as anti-discrimination law, to the extent that disabled legal subjectivity (which is seemingly homogeneous and pitted against an abled population) might instead accommodate bifurcation and, hence, inequality between disabled people depending on the extent to which disabled individuals can be recuperated into respectability and normality. If different identity groups are all pitted against the one fit, white settler subject then it makes sense—as the Disability Justice activism and queer abolitionists among others already do—to form coalitions and alliances across identity groups to contest this concentration of privilege, authority and violence. Indeed, McWhorter (2009: p. 326) suggests in her genealogy of racism and sexual oppression the importance of resisting normality: 'The first step toward dismantling biopolitical—that is, racist—networks of power … is to refuse to do their work for them, to refuse to do the work of self- (and other-) policing in the name of the normal'. This critical jurisprudence of disability could raise new questions about what it might mean for disability activists, advocates and scholars to have degeneracy and fitness as key reference points, as opposed to a specific, homogeneous, siloed 'pure' disability identity category.

Ultimately, we need to develop strategies that can work against and outside of the logics and the material and institutional spaces of criminal law, criminal justice systems and medical and care systems, and look to nurturing other sociopolitical sites of resistance and support. In engaging with interlocking dynamics and forces of oppression as they manifest in and through law and criminal justice systems, the challenge is to avoid expanding the disciplinary and biopolitical possibilities of disability and, instead, to disrupt the framework that makes this regulation such a permissible, natural, enduring and overlooked part of law. This challenge provides fertile ground for original and exciting theoretical and political engagement by disability, sociolegal and critical humanities scholars, as well as disability activists, advocates and lawyers, with court diversion and novel re-engagement by activists, advocates and lawyers with oppression that is embedded in the very foundations, subjectivities and structure of the law.

Conclusion

In *Disability, Criminal Justice and Law* I have provided scholars, activists, lawyers and policy-makers an opportunity to question the conventional approach to court diversion as a humane and beneficial 'solution' to the 'problem' of over-representation of disabled people in the criminal justice system, and to challenge underpinning assumptions about the relationships between disability, criminal justice and law. I have shown that court diversion is part of a deeply entrenched, larger *problem*: criminalised disabled people's carceral control, violence and, ultimately, debilitation and the rendering of this as lawful and just. By drawing on theoretical ideas related to disability, carcerality and legality, I argue that, through legal recognition of their disability, court diversion enables criminalised disabled people who are not sentenced and might not even be convicted, to nevertheless be subjected to coercive intervention through disability and mental health services. Rather than making universal claims about law's role in coercion and regulation, I have made a very particular argument specifically about the nature of and justifications for the carceral, psychiatric and medical control of criminalised disabled people and drawn attention to the discriminatory, violent and unjust effects of this control.

In a context where coercive interventions are central to historical and contemporary disability oppression, court diversion folds back into these patterns and can forestall more radical, collective and transformative alternatives for realising disability justice. Court diversion has no positive structural implications for addressing and redressing settler colonialism, imperialism and systems of ableism, classism, racism and sexism that shape the social and political contexts of disabled people's access to resources, support and inclusion, and their broader possibilities for self-determination and flourishing. I have urged that we shift our energies away from tinkering, expanding and fine-tuning court process and towards strategies that can radically transform legal, criminal justice and mental health and disability systems and, indeed, our broader society and communities. The argument I have developed in this book might be challenging, unsettling and confronting for some readers, notably those who, out of a commitment to disability rights, have advocated for, supported, developed or operationalised court diversion. My intention is not to undermine the energy and goodwill that has underpinned this work but instead to propose these folk consider engaging with strategies that are oriented away from inadvertently or advertently sustaining coercive intervention and towards broader visions of social justice.

In *Disability, Criminal Justice and Law* I have demonstrated that it is misplaced to base activism or critique on an assumed hierarchy of coercive intervention that places prison at its peak (and assumes disability and mental health systems are benevolent and benign in comparison). In drawing on disability carceral scholarship, I have shown—in Chapters 3, 4, 6 and 7—that prison is but one option alongside numerous disability-specific coercive interventions that jointly make possible carceral control of criminalised disabled people. Court diversion provides a legal process to channel disabled people more seamlessly between the many 'islands' of coercive intervention in the long-established 'institutional archipelago'. Ultimately, my analysis of court diversion resonates with Spade's suggestion that decarceration generally should focus on the prison and extend to 'demedicalisation' (Spade, 2015: p. 93), in a context where medical, health and disability-focused responses are often positioned as solutions. Moreover, I have shown that privileging the prison as the exclusive or primary mode of carceral control enables other more 'humane' forms of carceral control—notably court diversion—to flourish in its shadow and mask the complicity of legal, criminal justice and disability and mental health systems in disability oppression. As such, I have brought to the disability carceral scholarship sociolegal attention to the finer jurisdictional and legal dynamics of disabled carceral control (see also Steele, 2017a; 2018c) and, in turn, illustrated the possibilities *and risks* of using law (particularly disability legal categories and disability-specific coercive interventions) to contest disability oppression.

While increased access to mental health and disability services through court diversion might be positioned as a more *progressive* alternative to prison, my analysis has shown that these health-based 'solutions' are actually part of what sustains (and negates) oppression. This conclusion is important for disability scholars and activists, as well as scholars and activists focused on the intersections of anti-oppression politics and criminal justice system. Law's channelling of criminalised individuals belonging to other oppressed groups—such as Indigenous and First Nations people, racialised minorities and women who have experienced violence—into diagnostic and medical categories and into medicalised systems of control simultaneously extends their subjection to carceral control and negates the politics and even visibility of this control. My analysis of court diversion provides a compelling basis for critical reflection and reassessment for those supporting health-based criminal justice options for other oppressed groups. We should be directed towards anti-carceral alternatives to the prison *and* to the full range of sites, modes and legal domains (including across the criminal justice and disability and mental health systems) through which criminalised people, disabled and otherwise, are subject to control.

Because court diversion is in a subsidiary relationship to criminal legal intervention (as discussed in Chapters 4 and 7), it gets in the way of a more structural and transformative critique of prisons and criminal legal domain. Moreover, rather than the challenges of effectively controlling criminalised disabled people through the criminal legal domain signalling the failure or incompleteness of criminal law, court diversion subverts these challenges into a basis for expanded control of these individuals through disability and mental health services—as illustrated through analysis of the second stage of the *El Mawas* inquiry in Chapter 7. My analysis raises significant concerns about how criminal justice systems and criminal legal domains can be transformed through court diversion from sources of oppression, harm and white sovereign rule to being remedial of problems that are represented as external to them and, instead, as deeply embedded within individuals. Disability becomes central to the legitimation of criminal justice systems and criminal legal domains; thus, the push to single out disability in criminal law simply further reifies the legitimacy and justice of the oppression of criminalised disabled people. Indeed, in the context of Indigenous and First Nations disabled people, court diversion becomes a way through which criminal justice systems and criminal legal domains become positioned as benevolent rescuer of Indigenous and First Nations disabled people while simultaneously undercutting Indigenous and First Nations self-determination and nation-building, and recognition and redress for genocide and land dispossession (particularly given that sovereignty was never ceded). We should reflect on what the implications are of Million's concerns about the biopolitical nature of Western, medicalised approaches to Indigenous 'trauma' and 'healing' with respect to legal solutions to Indigenous overrepresentation in the criminal justice system that are disability-specific (including those framed by the CRPD).

I have shown the contradictions and complexities of relying on law, and specifically criminal law, to address oppression of criminalised disabled people. This book has highlighted the tension between the legal recognition of disability as a dimension of identity, and the disciplinary and biopolitical ends to which disability can be put by law. Court diversion's jurisdictional and legal dynamics mean that individuals who are diverted have their identity, behaviour and life circumstances read through individualised, medicalised and pathologised understandings of disability. This ultimately positions criminalised disabled people as problems to be fixed rather than acknowledging the structural conditions shaping individuals' and whole populations' identities, behaviour, life circumstances and relative opportunities for flourishing.

The freedom from prison and access to disability and mental health services at the heart of conventional support for court diversion (as discussed in Chapter 1) are undercut by the coercive framework in which this freedom and access are situated. This resonates with the critiques that have complicated the notion of 'freedom', as it applies to disabled people in contemporary post-deinstitutionalisation societies (Levinson, 2010; Spivakovsky, 2017; Stanev & Wildeman, 2018), in showing specifically law's complicity in both constructing and regulating 'freedom' outside of prison (Steele, 2018d). It also confirms the ableism embedded in liberal ideas of freedom, which presume that people are generally otherwise at liberty and in control of their bodies outside of prison, and thus reifies the numerous forms of coercion specifically of disabled people outside of prison (Steele, 2018d). This also negates settler colonial structural conditions that position Indigenous and First Nations peoples and racialised populations as being legitimately deprived of their liberty (Amir & Kotef, 2018; Blagg & Anthony, 2018; Kotef, 2015; Roberts, 2017). I have also shown how court diversion's provision of 'coercive' access to disability and mental health services might sit within broader neoliberal contradictions explored in the theoretical work across disability and queer studies about bifurcation of entitlement in neoliberalism (Haritaworn, 2015). Criminalised disabled people enjoy access to resources only through being subjected to coercion and violence, arguably because they are incapable of recuperation into the economy, reflecting Fritsch's argument that '[n]on-normative ways of being disabled, forms of disability that do not fit into the neat packages of a highly mobile, young, wheelchair user working to be independently productive, are easily dismissed as not truly deserving of benefits or accommodations' (Fritsch, 2015: p. 33). These conclusions invite greater attention being given to the particular ways in which court diversion makes criminalised disabled bodies profitable by generating demand for specialised (and coercive) services, treatment and accommodation, in lieu of them being considered capable of productive labour (Ben-Moshe & Stewart, 2017; McRuer, 2014).

Those who are diverted are cast outside of criminal legal liberal citizenship and, ultimately, full humanity. Court diversion might be one way in which law is complicit in the positioning of criminalised disabled people (many of whom are also Indigenous, racialised or poor) as other than human (Wynter, 1994) and, hence, as violable and lethal. Thus, while court diversion sustains violence against criminalised disabled people in a number of ways—the material violence of coercive intervention and the epistemic violence of judicial decision-making processes—one of its most profound injustices is in affirming the ontological violence that permeates the legal system, and society more broadly, of viewing disabled people (particularly *criminalised* disabled people) and other populations positioned as 'degenerate'—such as Indigenous and First Nations people, poor people and racialised populations—as less than fully human.

Despite its violent effects, court diversion resists recognition as unjust. Court diversion occupies a point of convergence of injustices of criminalised disabled people that has the productive effect of transforming these into justice. Court diversion simultaneously erases the injustice of prison by removing from this space the most vulnerable disabled people at risk of harm, and obscures the injustice of disability-specific coercive interventions insofar as they are seen as an option of safety and self-actualisation in their juxtaposition with prison. Building on my discussion of the work of Razack, Chapman and Voronka in Chapters 3 and 4, court diversion also sustains structural violence through legitimating the prison and settler colonial legal relations that position Indigenous and First Nations peoples as pathological and in need of rescue, and in failing to address interlocking forces and dynamics of oppression to support struggles for social emancipation and Indigenous and First Nations self-determination..

Through displacing the criminal offence as the site of intervention, and instead foregrounding disability, court diversion sustains an association between legality, disability and carcerality. This association legitimates as necessary and beneficial ongoing coercive intervention in criminalised disabled individuals' bodies and lives that would be considered unjust in relation to non-disabled people. This association is deeply troubling, because it maintains ways of knowing and being in law that seem to keep criminalised disabled people in a perpetual state of control. It is also troubling because the increasing mainstreaming of disability (and court diversion) in criminal law generally suggests that disability can become a way through which control and violence against other marginalised populations are not merely possible but lawful and, in turn, just.

I have shown in *Disability, Criminal Justice and Law* the importance of moving beyond disability as a homogeneous political category and, instead, being alert to how the biopolitical construction of the human in terms of fitness and degeneracy results in bifurcation of disabled populations. Through my analysis of court diversion I have shown that this bifurcation has very real impacts on the extent to which certain disabled populations can access citizenship, liberty and resources through law. Through court diversion law sustains debilitation of particularly oppressed sub-populations of disabled people who are the 'underside' of the valorised rights-bearing disabled citizen deserving of liberty and voluntary access to disability and mental health services (Puar, 2017: p. xvii). Thus, while in some contexts legal recognition of disability might make possible individual rights to equality and access to resources, in a criminal justice context legal recognition of disability and the coercive use of disability and mental health services can have the contrary effect. As I suggested in Chapter 8, it is vital to further interrogate law's complicity in debilitation of criminalised disabled people, including by examining the parallel development of positive disability laws alongside the endurance and recalibration, post-deinstitutionalisation, of disability criminal justice laws and, more broadly, eugenic logics.

Recalling Chapman's argument of the 'non-colonial' effect of disability-based interventions in Indigenous and First Nations communities (Chapman, 2014b), my analysis of court diversion has highlighted the need for sociolegal analysis of how disability and mental health law is implicated in ongoing settler colonialism. The hypothetical institutional narrative of Molly, in particular, is a timely reminder that court diversion is hopelessly inadequate at challenging structural conditions experienced by Indigenous and First Nations criminalised disabled people under settler colonial rule and white sovereign law. This book is an invitation to all disability law scholars to reckon with the ongoing absolution of responsibility and accountability for colonisation *through* disability and mental health law. Noting the discussion in Chapter 8 on critical legal pedagogy and legal professional ethical accountability, I encourage disability law scholars to unearth dynamics of colonialism in disability and mental health laws—including those embedded within legal epistemologies and ontologies of disability. I encourage them to foreground in their scholarship an interrogation of colonialism and engagement with questions of legal systems' and the legal profession's complicity in and hence need for accountability for colonialism. I also encourage them to consider whether and how disability law can be used in supporting Indigenous and First Nations initiatives for self-determination and nation-building and initiatives for justice led by racial minorities (including those led by diasporas formed from generations of slavery and indentured labour).

On a related note, *Disability, Criminal Justice and Law* underscores the importance of sociolegal scholars and disability rights activists questioning the limitations and contradictions of the CRPD in relation to criminalised disabled people (and other populations of disabled people marked as 'degenerate', such as disabled people who use drugs, are homeless, engage in sex work or have been in the child welfare system). While the CRPD might provide the political tools to argue for the abolition of disability-specific coercive interventions, the best it has to offer in relation to criminal legal intervention is to make access to and treatment in the criminal justice system more equitable and fair, rather than giving the tools to radically transform this system, including abolishing prison. Furthermore, while the understanding of disability in the CRPD is 'progressive' as compared to a medical model, we may ask whether this definition can contend with degeneracy that arises from biopolitical conceptions of the human (rather than specific stigma or stereotypes about disability) and the resulting bifurcation of disabled populations in ways that variously capacitate and debilitate. My analysis opens up the CRPD scholarship to the broader critical and political concerns of anti-colonial and anti-oppression scholarship and activism.

I have shown that court diversion has broader effects in legitimating criminal legal intervention and constituting the 'normal' criminal legal subject. In this respect, a powerful insight to emerge from this book's analysis of court diversion is that disability, by its limiting and constituting function, can be understood as being at the core of the legality and, hence, justice of criminal legal intervention (notably incarceration in prison) and, indeed, of criminal law more broadly. While this book has focused closely on one legal mechanism in domestic law, its ramifications are far-reaching and indicate that more scholarly and activist attention must be paid to the relationship between disability, legality, oppression and privilege at a more general level, given the foundational role of psychologically 'normal' concepts such as capacity, rationality, ordinariness, consent and reasonableness. My analysis of court diversion provides openings to sociolegal scholars to analyse legal concepts at the core of jurisdiction, legal personhood and sovereignty, and to do so in ways that illuminate law's complicity across diverse but interlocking systems of oppression. Such analysis is relevant to all legal subjects, given that psychological individualism provides a legitimate basis for coercive intervention regardless of an individual's material social and political circumstances (Naffine, 2009: p. 79).

While some might argue that court diversion is 'the best option we have', I urge scholars, activists and policy-makers to grasp the structural dynamics of court diversion and criminal law that mean court diversion can only ever apply to a minority of criminalised disabled people and that sustain the existence and legitimacy of prison and criminal legal domains and criminal justice systems. In providing a procedure for moving a *minority* of disabled individuals in the criminal justice system off the trajectory towards prison, court diversion has no structural implications for the ongoing existence and operation of prison in relation to the *majority* of criminalised disabled people. Court diversion can never radically transform the material, institutional and legal structural conditions for criminalised disabled people—it can only ever further legitimate them. This tension between very limited individual 'entitlement' through court diversion and mass continued oppression through the continued existence of the prison resonates with Miriam Ticktin's similar conclusion in the context of medical humanitarian visas in France, saying that 'responding to the suffering individual can work to preclude responses to and by the suffering (and often angry) masses' (Ticktin, 2011: p. 222). Ticktin argues that solutions must avoid focusing on 'saving … individuals deemed "exceptional" and hence morally legitimate' and '*not* making exceptions when it comes to questions of inequality, suffering, and violence or when it comes to the possibility of human flourishing' (ibid.: p. 223, emphasis in original).

Disability has a role in ordering and legitimating criminal law, yet it also has an unnerving disordering effect insofar as it suggests the incompleteness and fragility of criminal law and of legal authority more broadly. This was evident in the discussion in Chapter 5 on the ways in which James' and Molly's institutional narratives presented limits to the scope of criminal law in relation to the ineffectiveness of policing, bailand criminal legal orders to alter their behaviour, and in the challenge that Souriya presented to the magistrate as recounted in Chapter 7. Shildrick (2009: p. 7) states in relation to disability subjectivity more broadly, '[i]f the subject is no longer the stable and grounding category that it was once assumed to be, if it too is a discursive construction, then all sorts of epistemic and ontological claims must be rethought'. Building on Shildrick, my analysis says as much about the possibilities for dis-ordering law as it does about the current place of disability in ordering criminal law. Critiquing disability in court diversion provides openings into possibilities of disrupting the taken-for-granted foundations of criminal law and criminal legal epistemology and ontology and, ultimately, transforming criminal law itself.

Ultimately, it is essential that we adopt anti-carceral strategies that do not expand—indeed, that dismantle—the prison and entire institutional archipelago. Yet, beyond this, recalling my discussion in the Introduction of court diversion as but one example of the myriad ways in which law accommodates a lower threshold of violence and injustice for disabled people, it is vital that we unpick the entanglements of law, disability and the human in order to contest the self-evident and mundane positioning in law of disabled people as beyond equality and justice and, ultimately, beyond full political community and humanity. Similar to the argument made in the context of trans/queer prison abolition about the need to challenge the relationship between carceral logics and gender and sexuality (see Bassichis, Lee & Spade, 2011; Lamble, 2011; Spade, 2011), I argue that challenging the relationship between *disability* and *carceral logics* is central to contesting disability coercive intervention in all of its various legal, institutional and material architectural forms. As Ben-Moshe states,

> resisting incarceration is not as much about abolishing carceral spaces, as it is about demolishing the ideology that necessitates the processes of incarceration and segregation. … The aspiration is to fundamentally change the way we respond to difference or harm, the way normalcy is defined, the ways resources are distributed and accessed, and the ways we respond to each other.
>
> (Ben-Moshe, 2014: p. 269)

Challenging the carcerality of disability not only requires careful interrogation of the relationships between disability and criminality, punishment, risk, therapy and danger, but also interrogation of concepts too often assumed as the end-point of disability rights, such as inclusion, community, support, and legal capacity. In the course of this interrogation, it is vital to foreground broader biopolitical links between disability and such dynamics as humanitarianism, settler colonialism and neoliberalism; and to questions of state sovereignty and state violence.

In their introduction to *Disability Incarcerated*, Chapman and colleagues foreground the multiple temporal scales of injustice inherent in disabled carceral practices—historical injustices dating back centuries, as well as injustices associated with the 'future yet to come' of individuals who will be subjected to disabled carceral practices in the coming years and decades (Chapman, Carey & Ben-Moshe, 2014: p. 18). They observe that this future 'is a looming presence that has to be lived with, that has to be contended with today'. Sharing their concern, through reconsidering court diversion I have shown that in order to actively work towards a wider re-imagining of a more progressive and just socio-legal order it is crucial we develop more complex and nuanced understandings of 'justice' that fully reckon with law's complicity in debilitation of criminalised disabled people. Until we do so, we must all struggle with being accountable for the *ongoing* injustices wrought by the incarceration, violence and, at times, death of criminalised disabled people and both work within legal, health and welfare systems and live within communities that allow this to happen. In the words of anti-psychiatry activists Hazen and Minkowitz (2012: p. 7): 'The scope of the task should not overwhelm us, but inspire us to begin'.

Bibliography

Abbas, J & Voronka, V 2014, 'Remembering institutional erasures: the meaning of histories of disability incarceration in Ontario', in L Ben-Moshe, C Chapman & AC Carey (eds), *Disability incarcerated: imprisonment and disability in the United States and Canada*, Palgrave Macmillan, New York, pp. 121–138.

Adams, DL & Erevelles N 2017, 'Unexpected spaces of confinement: aversive technologies, intellectual disability, and "bare life"', *Punishment & Society*, vol. 19, no. 3, pp. 348–365, DOI: doi:10.1177/1462474517705147.

Allen, B 2005, 'Foucault's nominalisation', in S Tremain (ed), *Foucault and the government of disability*, University of Michigan Press, Ann Arbor, pp. 93–107.

Altermark, N 2017. 'The post-institutional era: visions of history in research on intellectual disability', *Disability & Society*, vol. 32, no. 9, pp. 1–18, DOI: doi:10.1080/09687599.2017.1322497.

Altermark, N 2018, *Citizenship, inclusion and intellectual disability*, Routledge, London and New York.

Amir, M & Kotef, H 2018, 'In-secure identities: on securitization of abnormality', *Environment and Planning D: Society and Space*, vol. 36, no. 2, pp. 236–254, DOI: doi:10.1177/0263775817744780.

Arstein-Kerslake, A, Gooding, P, Andrews, L & McSherry, B 2017, 'Human rights and unfitness to plead: the demands of the Convention on the Rights of Persons with Disabilities', *Human Rights Law Review*, vol. 17, pp. 399–419, DOI: doi:10.1093/hrlr/ngx025.

Ashworth, A & Zedner, L 2015, *Preventive justice*, Oxford University Press, Oxford.

Australian Human Rights Commission2014, *Equal before the law: towards disability justice strategies*, February 2014, online: www.humanrights.gov.au/sites/default/files/document/publication/2014_Equal_Before_the_Law.pdf.

Australian Institute of Health and Welfare2015, *The health of Australia's prisoners 2015*, Cat. no. PHE 207. AIHW, Canberra, online: www.aihw.gov.au/getmedia/9c42d6f3-2631-4452-b0df-9067fd71e33a/aihw-phe-207.pdf.aspx?inline=true.

Australian Law Reform Commission2014, *Equality, capacity and disability in Commonwealth laws*, ALRC Report No 24, 24 November 2014, online: https://www.alrc.gov.au/sites/default/files/pdfs/publications/alrc_124_whole_pdf_file.pdf.

Avery, S 2018, *Culture is inclusion: A narrative of Aboriginal and Torres Strait Islander people with disability*, First People's Disability Network (Australia), Sydney.

Baba, S 2018, 'Canadian developments in alternative sentencing: mental health courts (part 2)', *McGill Journal of Law and Health*, 6 February 2018, online: https://mjlh.mcgill.ca/2018/02/06/canadian-developments-in-alternative-sentencing-mental-health-courts-part-2/.

Baldry, E 2010, 'Women in transition: from prison to …', *Current Issues in Criminal Justice*, vol. 22, no. 2, pp. 253–267, DOI: doi:10.1080/10345329.2010.12035885.

Baldry E 2018, 'Rights of persons with disabilities not to be criminalised', in E Stanley (ed), *Human rights and incarceration: Critical explorations*, Palgrave Macmillan, Cham, pp. 53–77.

Baldry, E, Carlton, B & Cunneen C 2015, 'Abolitionism and the paradox of penal reform in Australia: colonialism, context, cultures and cooption', *Social Justice: A Journal of Crime, Conflict and World Order*, vol. 41, pp. 168–189, DOI: doi:10.2139/ssrn.2200781.

Baldry, E & Cunneen, C 2014, 'Imprisoned Indigenous women and the shadow of colonial patriarchy', *Australian & New Zealand Journal of Criminology*, vol. 47, no. 2, pp. 276–298, DOI: doi:10.1177/0004865813503351.

Baldry, E & Dowse, L 2013, 'Compounding mental and cognitive disability and disadvantage: police as care managers', in D Chappell (ed), *Policing and the mentally ill: international perspectives*, CRC Press, Cham, pp. 219–234.

Baldry, E, Dowse, L & Clarence, M 2011, 'People with mental and cognitive disabilities: pathways into prison', Background Paper, Australian Correctional Leadership Program, October 2011.

Baldry, E, McCausland, R, Dowse, L & McIntyre, E 2015, *A predictable and preventable path: IAMHDCD Report*, University of New South Wales, Sydney.

Balint, J, Evans, J & McMillan, N 2014, 'Rethinking transitional justice, redressing Indigenous harm: a new conceptual approach', *The International Journal of Transitional Justice*, vol. 8, pp. 194–216, DOI: https://doi.org/10.1093/ijtj/iju004.

Balint, J, Evans, J & McMillan, N 2016, 'Justice claims in colonial contexts: commissions of inquiry in historical perspective', *Australian Feminist Law Journal*, vol. 42, no. 1, pp. 75–96, DOI: doi:10.1080/13200968.2016.1175335.

Balint, J, Evans, J, McMillan, M & McMillan, N 2017, 'Introduction: "moving on"? Official responses to mass harm and the question of justice', *Oñati Socio-legal Series*, vol. 7, no. 2, 254–260, online: http://opo.iisj.net/index.php/osls/article/viewFile/897/987.

Balint, J, Brown, L, Dullard, C, Evans, J, McMillan, N & McMillan, M 2018, 'The minutes of evidence project: "doing structural justice"', *State Crime Journal*, vol. 7, no. 2, pp. 389–409, DOI: doi:10.13169/statecrime.7.2.0389.

Bartlett, P 2012, 'The United Nations Convention on the Rights of Persons with Disabilities and mental health law', *Modern Law Review*, vol. 75, no. 5, pp. 752–778, DOI: doi:10.1111/j.1468–2230.2012.00923.x.

Bartlett P & Sandland R 2014, *Mental health law: policy and practice*, 4th ed, Oxford University Press, Oxford.

Bassichis, M 2007, *"It's war in here": A report on the treatment of transgender and intersex people in New York State Men's Prisons*, Spade, D (ed), The Sylvia Rivera Law Project, New York, online: https://incarceratedworkers.org/sites/default/files/resource_file/study-on-trans-people-in-prison.pdf.

Bassichis, M, Lee, A & Spade, D 2011, 'Building an abolitionist trans & queer movement with everything we've got', in EA Stanley & N Smith (eds), *Captive genders: trans embodiment and the prison industrial complex*, AK Press, Oakland, pp. 15–40.

Bazelon Center for Mental Health Lawn.d., *The role of mental health courts in system reform*, online: www.bazelon.org/wp-content/uploads/2018/03/Role-of-Mental-Health-Courts.pdf.

Beaudette, JN, Power, J, & Stewart, LA 2015, *National prevalence of mental disorders among incoming federally-sentenced men offenders* (Research Report, R-357), Correctional Service Canada, Ottawa.

Beaupert, F 2018a, 'Freedom of opinion and expression: from the perspective of psychosocial disability and madness', *Laws*, vol. 7, no. 3, DOI: doi:10.3390/laws7010003.

Beaupert, F 2018b, 'Silencing prote(x)t: disrupting the scripts of mental health law', *UNSW Law Journal*, vol. 41, no. 3, pp. 746–782, online: www.unswlawjournal.unsw.edu.au/wp-content/uploads/2018/09/Beaupert.pdf.

Behrendt, L 2003, *Achieving social justice: Indigenous rights and Australia's future*, The Federation Press, Sydney.

Behrendt, L, Cunneen, C & Libesman, T 2009, *Indigenous legal relations in Australia*, Oxford University Press, South Melbourne.

Behrendt, L, Porter, A & Vivian, Aforthcoming, *Aboriginal self-determination in the Victorian justice context: Towards an Aboriginal Community Controlled justice system*, Jumbunna Institute for Indigenous Education and Research, University of Technology, Sydney.

Ben-Moshe, L 2011, 'Disabling incarceration: connecting disability to divergent confinements in the USA', *Critical Sociology*, vol. 39, no. 3, pp. 385–403, DOI: doi:10.1177/0896920511430864.

Ben-Moshe, L 2014, 'Alternatives to (disability) incarceration', in L Ben-Moshe, C Chapman, & AC Carey (eds), *Disability incarcerated: imprisonment and disability in the United States and Canada*, Palgrave Macmillan, New York, pp. 255–272.

Ben-Moshe, L 2017, 'Why prisons are not "the new asylums"', *Punishment & Society*, vol. 19, no. 3, pp. 272–289, DOI: doi:10.1177/1462474517704852.

Ben-Moshe, L, Chapman, C & Carey, AC (eds) 2014, *Disability incarcerated: imprisonment and disability in the United States and Canada*, Palgrave Macmillan, New York.

Ben-Moshe, L & Meiners, E 2014, 'Beyond prisons, mental health clinics: when austerity opens cages, where do the services go?', *Public Eye*, Fall 2014, online: www.politicalresearch.org/2014/10/09/beyond-prisons-mental-health-clinics-when-austerity-opens-cages-where-do-the-services-go/#sthash.2wGZhneO.dpbs.

Ben-Moshe, L & Stewart J 2017, 'Disablement, prison and historical segregation: 15 years later', in R Malhotra (ed), *Disability politics in a global economy: essays in honour of Marta Russell*, Routledge, Abingdon & New York, pp. 87–104.

Berlant, L 2007, 'Slow death (sovereignty, obesity, lateral agency)', *Critical Inquiry*, vol. 33, no. 4, pp. 754–780, DOI: doi:10.1086/521568.

Berne, P 2016, 'Disability justice – a working draft', in Sins Invalid (ed), *Skin, tooth and bone: the basis of movement is our people: a disability justice primer*, Sins Invalid, pp. 9–15, online: www.yumpu.com/en/document/read/56942783/skin-tooth-and-bone/10.

Berne, P & Sins Invalid2016, '10 principles of disability justice', in Sins Invalid (ed), *Skin, tooth and bone: the basis of movement is our people: a disability justice primer*, Sins Invalid, pp. 16–22, online: www.yumpu.com/en/document/read/56942783/skin-tooth-and-bone/10.

Bielefeld, S & Beaupert, F 2019, 'Income management and intersectionality: analysing compulsory income management through the lenses of critical race theory and disability studies ('discrit')', *Sydney Law Review*, vol. 41, no. 3, online: http://classic.austlii.edu.au/au/journals/SydLawRw/2019/14.html.

Blagg, H & Anthony, T 2018, '"Stone walls do not a prison make": bare life and the carceral archipelago in colonial and postcolonial societies', in E Stanley (ed), *Human rights and incarceration: critical explorations*, Palgrave Macmillan, Cham, pp. 257–283.

Blagg, H & Tulich, T 2018, 'Diversionary pathways for Aboriginal youth with fetal alcohol spectrum disorder', *Trends & Issues in Crime and Criminal Justice*, No 557August 2018, online: https://aic.gov.au/publications/tandi/tandi557.

Blagg, H, Tulich, T & Bush, Z 2017, 'Indefinite detention meets colonial dispossession: Indigenous youths with foetal alcohol spectrum disorders in a white settler justice system', *Social & Legal Studies*, vol. 26, no. 3, pp. 333–358, DOI: doi:10.1177/0964663916676650.

Boon-Kuo, L 2018, *Policing undocumented migrants: law, violence and responsibility*, Routledge, Abingdon.

Bozza, J 2011, 'Seeing the forest through the trees: thinking critically about mental health courts', *Chapman Journal of Criminal Justice*, vol. 2, pp. 165–190, online: http://works.bepress.com/john_bozza/4/.

Bradley, K 2009, *The Bradley report: Lord Bradley's review of people with mental health problems or learning disabilities in the criminal justice system*, Department of Health (UK), London, online: https://webarchive.nationalarchives.gov.uk/20130105193845/http://www.dh.gov.uk/prod_consum_dh/groups/dh_digitalassets/documents/digitalasset/dh_098698.pdf.

Bramley, D, Herbert, P, Jackson, HP, & Chassin, M 2004, 'Indigenous disparities in disease-specific mortality, a cross-country comparison: New Zealand, Australia, Canada, and the United States', *New Zealand Medical Journal*, vol. 117, no. 1207, pp. 1–13, Online: http://www.nzma.org.nz/journal/117-1207/1215.

Brett, S, Bickford, L, Ševcenko, L & Rios, M 2007, *Memorialization and democracy: state policy and civic action*, FLASCO Chile, International Coalition of Historic Site Museums of Conscience & International Center for Transitional Justice, online: www.ictj.org/sites/default/files/ICTJ-Global-Memorialization-Democracy-2007-English_0.pdf.

Bromwich, R J 2015, *Looking for Ashley: re-reading what the Smith case reveals about the governance of girls, mothers and families in Canada*, Demeter Press, Brantford.

Brookbanks, W 2013, 'Managing the challenges and protecting the rights of intellectually disabled offenders', in B McSherry & I Freckelton (eds), *Coercive care: rights, law and policy*, Routledge, London and New York, pp. 218–240. Brosnan, L 2018, 'Who's talking about us without us? A survivor research interjection into an academic psychiatry debate on compulsory community treatment orders in Ireland', *Laws*, vol. 7, pp. 1–15, DOI: doi:10.3390/laws7040033.

Brown, G, Barker, J, McMillan, K, Norman, R, Derkzen, D, & Stewart, L 2018, *National prevalence of mental disorders among federally sentenced women offenders: in custody sample* (Research Report, R-406), Correctional Service of Canada, Ottawa.

Buckmaster, L & Clark, S 2018, *The National Disability Insurance Scheme: a chronology*, Research paper series, 2018–2019, 13 July 2018, online: https://parlinfo.aph.gov.au/parlInfo/download/library/prspub/6083264/upload_binary/6083264.pdf.

Cadwallader, JR, Spivakovsky, C, Steele, L & Wadiwel, D 2018, 'Institutional violence against people with disability: recent legal and political developments', *Current Issues in Criminal Justice*, vol. 29, no. 3, pp. 259–272, online: www.austlii.edu.au/au/journals/CICrimJust/2018/5.html.

Campbell, FK 2009, *Contours of ableism: the production of disability and abledness*, Palgrave Macmillan, New York.

Carey, AC, Ben-Moshe, L & Chapman, C 2014, 'Preface: an overview of *Disability incarcerated*', in L Ben-Moshe, C Chapman & AC Carey (eds), *Disability incarcerated: imprisonment and disability in the United States and Canada*, Palgrave Macmillan, New York, pp. ix–xiv.

Carey, TA, Dudgeon, P, Hammond, SW, Hirvonen, T, Kyrios, M, Roufeil, L & Smith, P 2017, 'The Australian Psychological Society's apology to Aboriginal and Torres Strait Islander People', *Australian Psychologist*, vol. 52, no. 4, pp. 261–267, DOI: doi:10.1111/ap.12300.

Carlson, L 2010, *The faces of intellectual disability: philosophical reflections*, Indiana University Press, Bloomington.

Carlton, B & Russell, EK 2018, *Resisting carceral violence: women's imprisonment and the politics of abolition*, Palgrave Macmillan, Cham.

Carney, T 2017, 'Prioritising supported decision-making: running on empty or a basis for glacial-to-steady progress?', *Laws*, vol. 6, no. 4, pp. 1–14, DOI: doi:10.3390/laws6040018.

Carter, D 2016, 'HIV transmission, public health detention and the recalcitrant subject of discipline: Kuoth, Lam v R and the co-constitution of public health and criminal law', *Griffith Law Review*, vol. 25, no. 2, pp. 172–196, DOI: doi:10.1080/10383441.2016.1238563.

Carvalho, H 2017, *The preventive turn in criminal law*, Oxford University Press, Oxford.

Center for Addiction and Mental Health2013, *Mental health and criminal justice policy framework, October 2013*, Centre for Addiction and Mental Health, Toronto, online: www.camh.ca/-/media/files/pdfs—public-policy-submissions/mh_criminal_justice_policy_framework-pdf.pdf.

Chapman, C 2014a, 'Becoming perpetrator: how I came to accept restraining and confining disabled aboriginal children', in B Burstow, BA LeFrancois & S Diamond (eds), *Psychiatry disrupted: theorizing resistance and crafting the (r)evolution*, McGill-Queen's University Press, Montreal & Kingston, pp. 16–33.

Chapman, C 2014b, 'Five centuries' material reforms and ethical reformulations of social elimination', in L Ben-Moshe, C Chapman & AC Carey (eds), *Disability incarcerated: imprisonment and disability in the United States and Canada*, Palgrave Macmillan, New York, pp. 25–44.

Chapman, C, Carey AC & Ben-Moshe, L 2014, 'Reconsidering confinement: interlocking locations and logics of incarceration', in L Ben-Moshe, C Chapman & AC Carey (eds), *Disability incarcerated: imprisonment and disability in the United States and Canada*, Palgrave Macmillan, New York, pp. 3–24.

Chapman, C & Withers, AJ 2019, *A violent history of benevolence: interlocking oppression in the moral economies of social working*, University of Toronto Press, Toronto.

Chen, M 2012, *Animacies: biopolitics, racial mattering and queer affect*, Duke University Press, Durham & London.

Chisholm, R, Tulich, T & Blagg, H 2017, 'Indigenous young people with foetal alcohol spectrum disorders: The Convention on the Rights of Persons with Disabilities and reform to the law governing fitness to stand trial in Western Australia', *Law in Context*, vol. 35, no. 2, pp. 85–107.

Chrisjohn, R, McKay, S & Smith, A 2017, *Dying to please you: Indigenous suicide in contemporary Canada*, Theytus Books, Penicton.

Churchill, A, Sotiri, M & Rowe, S 2017, *Access to the NDIS for people with cognitive disability and complex needs who are in contact with the criminal justice system: key challenges*, Report for The Community Restorative Centre, Sydney, January 2017, online: www.crcnsw.org.au/wp-content/uploads/2017/01/CRC_NDIS_BriefingPaper_Jan2017.pdf.

Clare, E 2017, *Brilliant imperfection: grappling with cure*, Duke University Press, Durham.

Clough, B 2018, 'New legal landscapes: (re)constructing the boundaries of mental capacity law', *Medical Law Review*, vol. 26, no. 2, pp. 246–275, DOI: doi:10.1093/medlaw/fwy012.

Cohen, S 1985, *Visions of social control: crime, punishment and classification*, Polity Press, Glasgow.

Coleborne, C &MacKinnon, D 2006, 'Psychiatry and its institutions in Australia and New Zealand: an overview', *International Review of Psychiatry*, vol. 18, no. 4, pp. 371–380, DOI: doi:10.1080/09540260600813248.

Coles, D, Roberts, R & Cavcav, S 2018, 'Still dying on the inside: examining deaths in women's prisons', *Inquest*, May 2018, online: www.inquest.org.uk/Handlers/Download.ashx?IDMF=8d39dc1d-02f7-48eb-b9ac-2c063d01656a.

Corston, J 2007, *A review of women with particular vulnerabilities in the criminal justice system*, HMSO, London.

Coulthard, GS 2014, *Red skin, white masks: rejecting the colonial politics of recognition*, University of Minnesota Press, Minneapolis.

Council of State Governments2002, *Criminal Justice/Mental Health Consensus project*, Council of State Governments, New York, https://csgjusticecenter.org/mental-health-projects/report-of-the-consensus-project/.

Council of State Governments, 2005, *A guide to mental health court design and implementation*, Council of State Governments, New York, online: https://csgjusticecenter.org/wp-content/uploads/2012/12/Guide-MHC-Design.pdf.

Council of State Governments2008, *Mental health courts: a primer for policymakers and practitioners*, Council of State Governments, New York, online: https://csgjusticecenter.org/wp-content/uploads/2012/12/mhc-primer.pdf. Cover, R 1986, 'Violence and the word', *Yale Law Journal*, vol. 95, no. 8, pp. 1601–1629, DOI: doi:10.2307/796468.

Cruikshank, B 1999, *The will to empower: democratic citizens and other subjects*, Cornell University Press, Ithaca.

Cunneen, C 2009, 'Indigenous incarceration: the violence of colonial law and justice', in P Scraton & J McCulloch (eds), *The violence of incarceration*, Routledge, New York & Milton Park, pp. 209–224.

Cunneen, C 2019a, 'Institutional racism and (in)justice: Australia in the 21st century', *Decolonization of Criminology and Justice*, vol. 1, no. 1, pp. 29–51, DOI: https://doi.org/10.24135/dcj.v1i1.9.

Cunneen, C 2019b, 'Youth justice and racialization: comparative reflections', *Theoretical Criminology*, DOI: https://doi.org/10.1177/1362480619889039.

Cunneen, C, Baldry, E, Brown, D, Brown, M, Schwartz, M & Steel, A 2013, *Penal culture and hyperincarceration: the revival of the prison*, Routledge, Farnham.

Cunneen, C & Libesman, T 2000, 'Postcolonial trauma: the contemporary removal of Indigenous children and young people from their families in Australia', *Australian Journal of Social Issues*, vol. 35, no. 2, pp. 99–115, DOI: doi:10.1002/j.1839-4655.2000.tb01088.x.

Cunneen, C & Libesman, T 2002, 'Removed and discarded: the contemporary legacy of the stolen generations', *Australian Indigenous Law Reporter*, vol. 7, no. 1, pp. 1–20, online: http://hdl.handle.net/10453/5584.

Cunneen, C, Porter, A & Behrendt, Lforthcoming, Discussion paper: Aboriginal youth cautioning, Jumbunna Institute for Indigenous Education and Research, University of Technology, Sydney.

Cunneen, C & Tauri, J 2016, *Indigenous criminology*, Policy Press, Bristol.

Daley, A, Costa, L & Beresford, P (eds) 2019, *Madness, violence and power: a critical collection*, University of Toronto Press, Toronto.

Davidson, F 2015, *Mental health liaison and diversion: court liaison services and mental health court programs in Australia*, The Australian Centre for Research Excellence in Offender Health, online: https://offenderhealth.net.au/sites/default/files/Mental%20Health%20and%20Diversion%20National%20Report.pdf.

Davis, A 2005, *Abolition democracy: beyond empire, prisons and torture*, Seven Stories Press, New York.

Davis, LJ 1995, *Enforcing normalcy: disability, deafness and the body*, Verso, London & New York.

Davis, M 2019, *Family is culture: independent review into Aboriginal OOHC in NSW*, Aboriginal Care Review Team, Ashfield, https://www.familyisculture.nsw.gov.au/_data/assets/pdf_file/0011/726329/Family-Is-Culture-Reviw-Report.pdf.

Daya, I 2019, 'Stop hurting … start helping', paper presented at Reawaken conference: connection, compassion, meaningful action, Adelaide, Australia, 8–12 April 2019.

Dayan, C 2007, *The story of cruel and unusual*, University of California Press, Berkeley.

Dayan, C 2011, *The law is a white dog: how legal rituals make and unmake persons*, Princeton University Press, Princeton.

Dayan, C 2014, 'With law at the edge of life', *The South Atlantic Quarterly*, vol. 113, n. 3, pp 629–639, DOI: doi:10.1215/00382876-2692218.

Dean, A 2015, *Remembering Vancouver's disappeared women: settler colonialism and the difficulty of inheritance*, University of Toronto Press, Toronto.

Delaney, D 2003, *Law and nature*, Cambridge University Press, Cambridge & New York.

Dias, S, Ware, RS, Kinner, SA & Lennox, NG 2013, 'Co-occurring mental disorder and intellectual disability in a large sample of Australian prisoners', *Australian & New Zealand Journal of Psychiatry*, vol. 47, no. 10, pp. 938–944, DOI: doi:10.1177/0004867413492220.

Dilts, A 2014, *Punishment and inclusion: race, membership, and the limits of American liberalism*, Fordham University Press, New York. Dolmage, JT 2018, *Disabled upon arrival: eugenics, immigration, and the construction of race and disability*, The Ohio State University Press, Columbus.

Dorsett, S & McVeigh, S 2012, *Jurisdiction*, Routledge-Cavendish, London.

Dorsett, S & McVeigh, S 2014, 'Jurisprudences of jurisdiction: matters of public authority', *Griffith Law Review*, vol. 23, no. 4, pp. 569–588, DOI: doi:10.1080/10383441.2014.1017036.

Douglas, L, Sarat, A & Umphrey, MM 2005, 'At the limits of law: an introduction', in L Douglas, A Sarat, & MM Umphrey (eds), *The limits of law*, Stanford University Press, Stanford, pp. 1–20.

Dowse, L 2017, 'Disruptive, dangerous and disturbing: the "challenge" of behaviour in the construction of normalcy and vulnerability', *Continuum*, vol. 31, no. 3, pp. 447–457, DOI: doi:10.1080/10304312.2016.1275148.

Dowse, L 2018, 'Reconciling cognitive disability and corrosive social disadvantage: barriers to intersectional research, policy and practice', paper presented at Disability and (virtual) institutions?: interventions, integration and inclusion, International Institute for the Sociology of Law, Onati, Spain, 21–22 June 2018.

Drake, G 2014, 'The transinstitutionalisation of people living in licensed boarding houses in Sydney', *Australian Social Work*, vol. 67, no. 2, pp. 240–255, DOI: doi:10.1080/0312407X.2013.843714.

Drinkwater, C 2005, 'Supported living and the production of individuals', in S Tremain (ed), *Foucault and the government of disability*, University of Michigan Press, Ann Arbor, pp. 229–244.

Dudgeon, P, Bray, A, D'Costa, B & Walker, R 2017, 'Decolonising psychology: validating social and emotional wellbeing', *Australian Psychologist*, vol. 52, pp. 316–325, DOI: doi:10.1111/ap.12294.

Eastman, N 1992, 'Psychiatric, psychological, and legal models of man', *International Journal of Law and Psychiatry*, vol. 15, pp. 157–169, DOI: doi:10.1016/0160-2527(92)90011-O.

Edgar, K & Rickford, D 2009, *Too little too late: an independent review of unmet mental health need in prison*, Prison Reform Trust, online: http://www.prisonreformtrust.org.uk/Portals/0/Documents/Too%20Little%20Too%20Late%20-%20a%20review%20of%20unmet%20mental%20health%20need%20in%20prison%20.pdf.

El-Enany, N & Bruce-Jones, E (eds), 2015, *Race and policing in England and Wales*, Runnymede Trust, London, online: www.runnymedetrust.org/uploads/Race%20and%20Policing%20v5.pdf.

Erevelles, N 2011, *Disability and difference in global contexts: enabling a transformative body politic*, Palgrave Macmillan, New York.

Fabris, E 2011, *Tranquil prisons: chemical incarceration under community treatment orders*, University of Toronto Press, Toronto.

Fabris, E & Aubrecht, K 2014, 'Chemical constraint: experiences of psychiatric coercion, restraint, and detention as carceratory techniques', in L Ben-Moshe, C Chapman & AC Carey (eds), *Disability incarcerated: imprisonment and disability in the United States and Canada*, Palgrave Macmillan, New York, pp. 185–199.

Faraci, SM 2004, 'Slip slidin' away: will our nation's mental health court experiment diminish the rights of the mentally ill', *Quinnipiac Law Review*, vol. 22, pp. 811–848.

Fazel, S, Xenitidis, K & Powell, J 2008, 'The prevalence of intellectual disabilities among 12000 prisoners—a systematic review', *International Journal of Law and Psychiatry*, vol. 31, pp. 369–373, DOI: doi:10.1016/j.ijlp.2008.06.001.

Fennell, P 1991, 'Diversion of mentally disordered offenders from custody', *Criminal Law Review*, pp. 333–348.

Fennell, P 2011, *Mental health: law and practice*, 2nd ed, Jordan Publishing, Bristol.

Ferrazzi, P, Krupa, T & Lysaght, R 2013, 'Mental health courts, court diversion, and Canada's obligations under the United Nations Convention on the Rights of Persons with Disabilities', *Canadian Journal of Community Mental Health*, vol. 32, no. 4, pp. 43–57, DOI: doi:10.7870/cjcmh-2013-2030.

First Peoples Disability Justice Consortium (ed) 2016, *Aboriginal and Torres Strait Islander perspectives on the recurrent and indefinite detention of people with cognitive and psychiatric impairment*, April 2016, online: http://fpdn.org.au/the-recurrent-and-indefinite-detention-of-people-with-cognitive-and-psychiatric-impairment/.

Foucault, M 1979, *Discipline and punish: the birth of the prison* (A Sheridan, trans), Penguin, London.

Foucault, M 1997a, 'Lecture 7 January 1976', in M Bertani & A Fontana (eds), *Society must be defended* (D Macey, trans), Penguin Books, London, pp. 1–21.

Foucault, M 1997b, 'Lecture 14 January 1976', in M Bertani & A Fontana (eds), *Society must be defended* (D Macey, trans), Penguin Books, London, pp. 23–41.

Foucault, M 1997c, 'Lecture 17 March 1976', in M Bertani & A Fontana (eds), *Society must be defended* (D Macey, trans), Penguin Books, London, pp. 239–264.

Foucault, M 2000, 'The subject and power', in JD Faubion (ed), *Power: essential works of Foucault 1954–1984*, volume 3, (trans. of "Le Sujet et le Pouvoir," in D. Defert, F. Ewald & J. Lagrange, eds., *Dits et écrits 1954–1888: vol IV 1980–1988*), Penguin Books, London & New York City, pp. 326–348.

Foucault, M 2003a, 'Lecture 8 January 1975', in V Marchetti & A Salomoni (eds), *Abnormal: lectures at the Collège de France, 1974–1975* (G Burchell, trans), Picador, New York, pp. 231-262.

Foucault, M 2003b, 'Lecture 8 January 1975', in V Marchetti & A Salomoni (eds), *Abnormal: lectures at the Collège de France, 1974–1975* (G Burchell, trans), Picador, New York, pp. 291-322.

Foucault, M 2004a, 'Lecture 19 March 1978', in M Senellart (ed), *Security, territory, population: lectures at the Collège de France, 1977–1978* (G Burchell, trans), Picador, New York, pp. 1–27.

Foucault, M 2004b, 'Lecture 18 January 1978', in M Senellart (ed), *Security, territory, population: lectures at the Collège de France, 1977–1978* (G Burchell, trans), Picador, New York, pp. 29–53.

Foucault, M 2004c, 'Lecture 25 January 1978', in M Senellart (ed), *Security, territory, population: lectures at the Collège de France, 1977–1978* (G Burchell, trans), Picador, New York, pp. 55–86.

Foucault, M 2004d, 'Lecture 1 February 1978', in M Senellart (ed), *Security, territory, population: lectures at the Collège de France, 1977–1978* (G Burchell, trans), Picador, New York, pp. 87–114.

Foucault, M 2004e, 'Lecture 8 February', in M Senellart (ed), *Security, territory, population: lectures at the Collège de France, 1977–1978* (G Burchell, trans), Picador, New York, pp. 115–134.

Foucault, M 2008a, 'Lecture 21 November 1973', in J Lagrange (ed), *Psychiatric power: lectures at the Collège de France 1973–1974* (G Burchell, trans), Palgrave Macmillan, Basingstoke & New York, pp. 39–61.

Foucault, M 2008b, *The history of sexuality: the will to knowledge*, volume 1 (R Hurley, trans), Penguin, London.

Foucault, M 2009, 'Alternatives to the prison: dissemination or decline of social control?' *Theory, Culture & Society*, vol. 26, no. 6, pp. 12–24, DOI: doi:10.1177/0263276409353775.

Fritsch, K 2015, 'Gradations of debility and capacity: biocapitalism and the neoliberalization of disability relations', *Canadian Journal of Disability Studies*, vol. 4, no. 2, pp. 13–48, DOI: doi:10.15353/cjds.v4i2.208.

Garda Síochána & Mental Health Commission2009, *Report of Joint Working Group on Mental Health Services and the Police 2009*, Mental Health Commission, Dublin, online: www.mhcirl.ie/File/Rpt_JWG_MHS_Police.pdf.

Gerard, A, McGrath, A, Colvin, E & McFarlane, K 2019, ' "I'm not getting out of bed!" the criminalisation of young people in residential care', *Australian and New Zealand Journal of Criminology*, vol. 52, no. 1, pp. 76–93, DOI: doi:10.1177/0004865818778739.

Gilbert, K 1993, *Aboriginal sovereignty: justice, the law and land*, Burrimbinga Books, Canberra.

Gillman, M, Heyman, B & Swain J 2000, 'What's in a name? The implications of diagnosis for people with learning difficulties and their family carers', *Disability & Society*, vol. 15, no. 3, pp. 389–409, DOI: doi:10.1080/713661959.

Gilmore, RW 2007, *Golden gulag: prisons, surplus, crisis, and opposition in globalizing California*, University of California Press, Berkeley, Los Angeles & London.

Godden, L 2007, 'A jurisdiction of body and desire: exploring the boundaries of bodily control in prostitution law', in S McVeigh (ed), *Jurisprudence of jurisdiction*, Routledge-Cavendish, London, pp. 181–201.

Goffman, E 2017, *Asylums: essays on the social situation of mental patients and other inmates*, Routledge, Abingdon. Golder, B 2004, '"It forced me to open more than I could bear": HAD, paedophilia, and the discursive limits of the male heterosexual body', in AT Kenyon & P Rush (eds), *An aesthetics of law and culture: texts, images, screens*, Elsevier, Amsterdam & London, pp. 53–72.

Golder, B 2015, *Foucault and the politics of rights*, Stanford University Press, Stanford.

Golder, B & Fitzpatrick P 2009, *Foucault's law*, Routledge-Cavendish, Abingdon.

Golder, B & Fitzpatrick P 2010, 'Introduction: the laws of Michel Foucault', in B Golder & P Fitzpatrick (eds), *Foucault and law*, Ashgate, Aldershot, pp. xi–xxvi.

Golder, B & McLoughlin, D 2018, 'An introduction to "The politics of legality in a neoliberal age"', in B Golder & D McLoughlin (eds), *The politics of legality in a neoliberal age*, Routledge, Abingdon & New York, pp. 1–16.

Goldson, B 2009, 'Child incarceration: institutional abuse, the violent state and the politics of impunity', in P Scraton & J McCulloch (eds), *The violence of incarceration*, Routledge, Farnham, pp. 86–106.

Gonzalez, JMR, Cannell, MB, Jetelina, KK, & Froehlich-Grobe, KF 2016, 'Disproportionate prevalence rate of prisoners with disabilities: Evidence from a nationally representative sample', *Journal of Disability Policy Studies*, vol. 27, no. 2, pp. 106–115, DOI: doi:10.1177/1044207315616809.

Gooding, P & O'Mahony, C 2016, 'Laws on unfitness to stand trial and the UN Convention on the Rights of Persons with Disabilities: Comparing reform in England, Wales, Northern Ireland and Australia', *International Journal of Law, Crime and Justice*, vol. 44, pp. 122–145, DOI: doi:10.1016/j.ijlcj.2015.07.002.

Goodley, Dan 2014, *Dis/ability studies: theorising disablism and ableism*, Routledge, Abingdon.

Goodley, D & Runswick-Cole K 2011, 'The violence of disablism', *Sociology of Health & Illness*, vol. 33, no. 4, pp. 602–617, DOI: doi:10.1111/j.1467–9566.2010.01302.x.

Goodley, D, Runswick-Cole, K & Liddiard, K 2016, 'The dishuman child', *Discourse: Studies in the Cultural Politics of Education*, vol. 37, no. 5, pp. 770–784, DOI: doi:10.1080/01596306.2015.1075731.

Gorman, R 2013, 'Thinking through race, class, and mad identity politics', in B Lefrancois, R Menzies & G Reaume (eds), *Mad matters: a critical reader in Canadian mad studies*, Canadian Scholars Press, Toronto, pp. 269–280.

Greig, H, McGrath, A & McFarlane, K 2019, '"Taking the wheels off": young people with cognitive impairment in out-of-home care', *Psychiatry, Psychology and Law*, online first, DOI: doi:10.1080/13218719.2019.1644249. Hammell, KW 2004, 'Deviating from the norm: A sceptical interrogation of the classificatory practices of the ICF', *British Journal of Occupational Therapy*, vol. 67, no. 9, pp. 408–411, DOI: doi:10.1177/030802260406700906.

Hannah-Moffat, K & Klassen, A 2015, 'Normalizing exceptions: solitary confinement and the micro-politics of risk/need in Canada', in K Reiter & A Koenig (eds), *Extreme punishment: comparative studies in detention, incarceration and solitary confinement*, Palgrave Macmillan, Basingstoke & New York: pp. 135–155.

Harcourt, BE 2006, 'From the asylum to the prison: rethinking the incarceration revolution', *Texas Law Review*, vol. 84, pp. 1751–1786, online: https://www.law.uchicago.edu/files/file/harcourt_institutionalization_final.pdf.

Haritaworn, J 2015, *Queer lovers and hateful others: regenerating violent times and places*, Pluto Press, London.

Harjo, L 2019, *Spiral to the stars: Mvskoke tools of futurity*, University of Arizona Press, Tucson.

Harris, MK 2008, 'Transformative justice: the transformation of restorative justice', in D Sullivan & L Tifft (eds), *Handbook of restorative justice: a global perspective*, Routledge, London, pp. 555–566.

Hatch, A 2019, *Silent cells: the secret drugging of captive America*, University of Minnesota Press, Minneapolis.

Hatch, AR, Xavier-Brier, M, Attell, B & Viscarra, E 2015, 'Soldier, elder, prisoner, ward: psychotropics in the era of transinstitutionalization', in BL Perry (ed), *50 years after deinstitutionalization: mental illness in contemporary communities*, Emerald Publishing, Bingley.

Hayes, SC & Hayes, R 1982, *Mental retardation: law, policy and administration*, Law Book Co, Sydney.

Hayes, SC & Hayes, R 1984, *Simply criminal*, Law Book Co, Sydney.

Hayes, S & McIlwain, D 2006, *The incidence of intellectual disability in the New South Wales prison population: an empirical study*, University of Sydney, Sydney, online: http://crg.aic.gov.au/reports/6-87.pdf.

Hayes, SC, Shackell, P, Mottram, P & Lancaster, R 2007, 'The prevalence of intellectual disability in a major UK prison', *British Journal of Learning Disabilities*, vol. 35, no. 3, pp. 162–167, DOI: doi:10.1111/j.1468-3156.2007.00461.x.

Hazen, D & Minkowitz, T 2012, 'A discussion paper on policy issues at the intersection of the mental health system and the prison system', Center for the Human Rights of Users and Survivors of Psychiatry, online: www.wnusp.net/documents/2012/WNUSP_Discussion_Paper_Prisons_MH.pdf.

Hibberd, L & Djuric, B 2013, 'Art after oblivion: the Parramatta Female Factory Precinct Memory Project', *Artlink*, vol. 33, no. 3, pp. 68–71.

Hibberd, L with Djuric, B 2019, *Parragirls: reimagining Parramatta Girls Home through art and memory*, NewSouth Press, Sydney.

Hickey, H 2014, 'Indigenous people with disabilities: the missing link', in M Sabatello & M Schulze (eds), *Human rights and disability advocacy*, University of Pennsylvania Press, Philadelphia, pp. 157–169.

Hiday, VA 2008, 'Mental health courts', in BL Culter (ed), *Encyclopedia of psychology and law*, SAGE Publications, Thousand Oaks, pp. 488–490.

Hollinsworth, D 2013, 'Decolonizing indigenous disability in Australia', *Disability & Society*, vol. 28, no. 5, pp. 601–615, DOI: doi:10.1080/09687599.2012.717879.

Hughes K, Bellis MA, Jones L, Wood S, Bates G, Eckley L, McCoy E, Mikton C, Shakespeare T & Officer A 2012, 'Prevalence and risk of violence against adults with disabilities: a systematic review and meta-analysis of observational studies', *Lancet*, vol. 379, no. 9826, pp. 1621–1629, DOI: doi:10.1016/S0410-6736(11)61851-61855.

Human Rights and Equal Opportunity Commission (HREOC) 1997, *Bringing them home: report of the National Inquiry into the Separation of Aboriginal and Torres Strait Islander Children from Their Families*, Human Rights and Equal Opportunity Commission, Sydney.

Independent Advisory Council of the National Disability Insurance Scheme 2016, *Equitable access to the NDIS by people with cognitive disability in touch with the criminal justice system*, NDIS-IAC, online: https://static1.squarespace.com/static/5898f042a5790ab2e0e2056c/t/5b19eba2758d468f46547d1f/1528425385964/May+2016+Equitable%2Baccess%2Bto%2Bthe%2BNDIS%2Bby%2Bpeople%2Bwith%2Bcognitive%2Bdisability%2Bin%2Btouch%2Bwith%2Bthe%2Bcriminal%2Bjustice%2Bsystem.pdf.

Indig D, Gear C, & Wilhelm K 2016, *Comorbid substance use disorders and mental health disorders among New Zealand prisoners*, New Zealand Department of Corrections, Wellington, online: www.corrections.govt.nz/__data/assets/pdf_file/0011/846362/Comorbid_substance_use_disorders_and_mental_health_disorders_among_NZ_prisoners_June_2016_final.pdf.

Intellectual Disability Rights Service 2011, *Step by step guide to making a section 32 application for a person with intellectual disability*, Intellectual Disability Rights Service Inc, Redfern, online: www.idrs.org.au/education/s32-guide/IDRS_Section_32_Guide_online.pdf.

Intellectual Disability Rights Service, Coalition on Intellectual Disability & Criminal Justice & NSW Council for Intellectual Disability 2008, *Enabling justice: a report on problems and solutions in relation to diversion of alleged offenders with intellectual disability from the New South Wales Local Courts system: with particular reference to the practical operation of s 32 of the Mental Health (Criminal Procedure Act 1990 (NSW))*, Intellectual Disability Rights Service, Redfern, online: www.idrs.org.au/pdf/historic/enabling_justice.pdf.

Interdepartmental Group (Republic of Ireland) to Examine Issues Relating to People With Mental Illness Who Come in Contact With the Criminal Justice System2016, *First interim report*, online: www.inis.gov.ie/en/JELR/interdepartmental-group-to-examine-issues-relating-to-people-with-mental-illness-who-come-in-contact-with-the-criminal-justice-system_first-interim-report.pdf/Files/interdepartmental-group-to-examine-issues-relating-to-people-with-mental-illness-who-come-in-contact-with-the-criminal-justice-system_first-interim-report.pdf.

Irish Penal Reform Trust 2001, *Community solutions to the criminalisation of the mentally ill in Ireland*, Irish Penal Reform Trust, Dublin, online: www.iprt.ie/files/out_of_mind_out_of_sight1.pdf.

Jaffee, LJ 2016, 'Disrupting global disability frameworks: settler colonialism and the geopolitics of disability in Palestine/Israel', *Disability & Society*, vol. 31, no. 1, pp. 116–130, DOI: doi:10.1080/09687599.2015.1119038.

James, DV 2006, 'Court diversion in perspective', *Australian and New Zealand Journal of Psychiatry*, vol. 40, no. 6–7, pp. 529–538, DOI: doi:10.1080/j.1440-1614.2006.01835.x.

James, DV 2010, 'Diversion of mentally disordered people from the criminal justice system in England and Wales: an overview', *International Journal of Law and Psychiatry*, vol. 33, no. 4, pp. 241–248, DOI: doi:10.1016/j.ijlp.2010.06.006.

Jarman, M 2011, 'Coming up from underground: uneasy dialogues at the intersections of race, mental illness, and disability studies', in CM Bell (ed), *Blackness and disability: critical examinations and cultural interventions*, Michigan State University Press, East Lansing, pp. 9 29.

John Howard Society of Ontario 2015, *Unlocking change: decriminalizing mental health issues in Ontario*, John Howard Society of Ontario, Toronto, online: www.johnhoward.on.ca/wp-content/uploads/2015/07/Unlocking-Change-Final-August-2015.pdf.

Johns, F 2015, *Non-legality in international law: unruly law*, Cambridge University Press, Cambridge.

Johnston, EL 2013, 'Theorizing mental health courts', *Washington University Law Review*, vol. 89, no. 3, pp. 519–579, online: https://openscholarship.wustl.edu/law_lawreview/vol89/iss3/2.

Joint Standing Committee on the National Disability Insurance Scheme 2017, *Provision of services under the NDIS for people with psychosocial disabilities related to a mental health condition*, online: www.aph.gov.au/Parliamentary_Business/Committees/Joint/National_Disability_Insurance_Scheme/MentalHealth.

Jones, J 2007, 'Persons with intellectual disabilities in the criminal justice system: review of issues', *International Journal of Offender Therapy and Comparative Criminology*, vol. 51, no. 6, pp. 723–733, DOI: doi:10.1177/0306624X07299343.

Joseph, AJ 2014, 'A prescription for violence: the legacy of colonization in contemporary forensic mental health and the production of difference', *Critical Criminology*, vol. 22, no. 2, pp. 273–292, DOI: doi:10.1007/s10612-10013-9208-9201.

Joseph, AJ 2015, *Deportation and the confluence of violence within forensic mental health and immigration systems*, Palgrave-Macmillan, Basingstoke & Hampshire.

Joseph, AJ 2019, 'Contemporary form of legislative imprisonment and colonial violence in forensic mental health', in A Daley, L Costa & P Beresford (eds), *Madness, violence and power: a critical collection*, University of Toronto Press, Toronto, pp. 169–183.

Kafer, A 2013, *Feminist, queer, crip*, Indiana University Press, Bloomington.

Kaiser, HA 2010, 'Too good to be true: second thoughts on the proliferation of mental health courts', *Canadian Journal of Community Mental Health*, vol. 29, no. 2, pp. 19–25, DOI: doi:10.7870/cjcmh-2010-0016.

Kelk, N, Medlow, S & Hickie, I 2010, 'Distress and depression among Australian law students: incidence, attitudes and the role of universities', *Sydney Law Review*, vol. 32, no. 1, pp. 113–122, online: www6.austlii.edu.au/cgi-bin/viewdoc/au/journals/SydLawRw/2010/5.html?context=1;query=hickie and medlow;mask_path=au/journals/SydLawRw.

Kelk, N, Medlow, S & Hickie, I 2011, 'Depression and the law: experiences of Australian barristers and solicitors', *Sydney Law Review*, vol. 33, no. 4, pp. 771–779, online: www6.austlii.edu.au/cgi-bin/viewdoc/au/journals/SydLawRw/2011/31.html?context=1;query=hickie and medlow;mask_path=au/journals/SydLawRw.

Kennedy, A, Mundy, T & Nielsen, J 2016, '"Bush law 101": realising place and conscious pedagogy in the Law Curriculum', *Journal of University Teaching and Learning Practice*, vol. 13, no. 1, pp. 1–20, online: https://ro.uow.edu.au/jutlp/vol13/iss1/6/.

Kershnar, S, Haines, S, Harkins, G, Greig, A, Wiesner, C, Levy, M, Shah, P, Kim, M & Carr, J 2007, *Toward transformative justice: a liberatory approach to child sexual abuse and other forms of intimate and community violence*, Generation Five, online: http://www.generationfive.org/wp-content/uploads/2013/07/G5_Toward_Transformative_Justice-Document.pdf.

Kilty, J & Lehalle S 2019, 'Mad, bad, and stuck in the hole: carceral segregation as slow violence', in A Daley, L Costa & P Beresford (eds), *Madness, violence and power: a critical collection*, University of Toronto Press, Toronto, pp. 310–329.

Kim, E 2016, *Curative violence: rehabilitating disability, gender, and sexuality in modern Korea*, Duke University Press, Durham & London.

Kim, E 2019, 'Continuing presence of discarded bodies: occupational harm, necro-activism, and living justice', *Catalyst: Feminism, Theory, Technoscience*, vol. 5, no. 1, pp. 1–31, DOI: doi:10.28968/cftt.v5i1.29616.

Kotef, H 2015, *Movement and the ordering of freedom: on liberal governances of mobility*, Duke University Press, Durham & London.

Laberge, D & Morin, D 1995, 'The overuse of criminal justice dispositions: failure of diversionary policies in the management of mental health problems', *International Journal of Law and Psychiatry*, vol. 18, no. 4, pp. 389–414, DOI: doi:10.1016/0160-2527(95)00019-E.

Laing, J 2000, *Care or custody? Mentally disordered offenders in the criminal justice system*, Oxford University Press, Oxford.

Lamble, S 2011, 'Transforming carceral logics: 10 reasons to dismantle the prison industrial complex using a queer/trans analysis', in EA Stanley & N Smith (eds), *Captive genders: trans embodiment and the prison industrial complex*, AK Press, Oakland, pp. 235–265.

Lamble S 2014, 'Transformative justice and community anti-violence initiatives', presentation to roundtable Violence against women and girls: from intervention to prevention, Centre for Crime and Justice Studies, 19 November 2014, online: www.crimeandjustice.org.uk/sites/crimeandjustice.org.uk/files/Lamble%20slides%20Nov%202014.pdf.

Lammy, D 2017, *The Lammy review: an independent review into the treatment of, and outcomes for, Black, Asian and Minority Ethnic individuals in the criminal justice system*, Lammy Review, London, online: https://assets.publishing.service.gov.uk/government/uploads/system/uploads/attachment_data/file/643001/lammy-review-final-report.pdf.

Larsen, IB & Topor, A 2017, 'A place for the heart: a journey in the post-asylum landscape. Metaphors and materiality', *Health & Place*, vol. 45, pp. 145–151, DOI: doi:10.1016/j.healthplace.2017.03.015.

Law Commission 2013, *Criminal liability: insanity and automatism: a discussion paper*, Law Commission, London, online: www.lawcom.gov.uk/app/uploads/2015/06/insanity_discussion.pdf.

Lawrence, D, Hancock, K & Kisely, S 2013, 'The gap in life expectancy from preventable physical illness in psychiatric patients in Western Australia: retrospective analysis of population based registers', *British Medical Journal*, vol. 346, pp. 1–14, DOI: doi:10.1136/bmj.f2539.

Lee, J 2013, 'Mad as hell: the objectifying experience of symbolic violence', in B Lefrancois, R Menzies & G Reaume (eds), *Mad matters: a critical reader in Canadian mad studies*, Canadian Scholars Press Inc, Toronto, pp. 105–119.

Leeming, M 2012, *Authority to decide: the law of jurisdiction in Australia*, The Federation Press, Annandale.

Levinson, J 2010, *Making life work: freedom and disability in a community group home*, University of Minnesota Press, Minneapolis.

Liegghio, M 2013, 'A denial of being: psychiatrization as epistemic violence', in B Lefrancois, R Menzies & G Reaume (eds), *Mad matters: a critical reader in Canadian mad studies*, Canadian Scholars Press Inc, Toronto, pp. 122–129.

Linton, S 1998, *Claiming disability: knowledge and identity*, New York University Press, New York.

Loughnan, A 2012, *Manifest madness: mental incapacity in criminal law*, Oxford University Press, Oxford.

Lowik, AJ 2018, 'Reproducing eugenics, reproducing while Trans: the state sterilization of Trans people', *Journal of GLBT Family Studies*, vol. 14, no. 5, pp. 425–445, DOI: doi:10.1080/1550428X.2017.1393361.

Luther, G 2016, 'Mental health, treatment and the criminal justice process', in JA Chandler & CM Flood (eds), *Law and mind: mental health law and policy in Canada*, LexisNexis, Toronto, pp. 283–301.

MacGillivray, P & McCausland, R 2019, 'A community-led response to the criminalisation of Aboriginal people: draft paper', paper presented at Critical Policing Research in Action workshop, 10–11 April 2019, hosted by UNSW Law and Centre for Crime, Law, Justice.

Manitoba Advocate for Child and Youth 2019, *A place where it feels like home: the story of Tina Fontaine. A special report published after an investigation in accordance with Part 4 and Part 5 of the Advocate for Children and Youth Act*, https://manitobaadvocate.ca/wp-content/uploads/MACY-Special-Report-March-2019-Tina-Fontaine-FINAL1.pdf.

Massoglia, M & Pridemore, WA 2015, 'Incarceration and health', *Annual Review of Sociology*, vol. 41, pp. 1–22, DOI: doi:10.1146/annurev-soc-073014–112326.

Mawani, R 2014, 'Law as temporality: colonial politics and Indian settlers', *UC Irvine Law Review*, vol. 4, pp. 65–96, online: https://scholarship.law.uci.edu/ucilr/vol4/iss1/5.

Mawani, R 2015, 'The times of law', *Law & Social Inquiry*, vol. 40, pp. 253–263, DOI: doi:10.1111/lsi.12117.

McCausland, R & Baldry E 2017, '"I feel like I failed him by ringing the police": criminalising disability in Australia', *Punishment & Society*, vol. 19, no. 3, pp. 290–309, DOI: doi:10.1177/1462474517696126.

McConnell, D & Llewellyn, G 2000, 'Disability and discrimination in statutory child protection proceedings', *Disability & Society*, vol. 15, no. 6, pp. 883–895, DOI: doi:10.1080/713662015.

McFarlane, K 2010, 'From care to custody: young women in out-of-home care in the criminal justice system', *Current Issues in Criminal Justice*, vol. 22, no. 2, pp. 345–353, online: www.austlii.edu.au/au/journals/CICrimJust/2010/36.pdf.

McGuire, A 2015, '"Life worth defending": biopolitical frames of terror in the war on autism', in S Tremain (ed), *Foucault and the government of disability*, revised and expanded edition, University of Michigan Press, Ann Arbor, pp. 350–371.

McLoughlin, D 2009, 'Crisis, modernity, authority: Carl Schmitt on order and the state', *Australian Feminist Law Journal*, vol. 31, no. 1, pp. 135–152, DOI: doi:10.1080/13200968.2009.10854431.

McLoughlin, D 2012, 'Giorgio Agamben on security, government and the crisis of law', *Griffith Law Review*, vol. 21, no. 3, pp. 680–707 DOI: doi:10.1080/10383441.2012.10854758.

McRuer, R 2014, 'Epilogue: Disability, Inc.', in L Ben-Moshe, C Chapman & AC Carey (eds), *Disability incarcerated: imprisonment and disability in the United States and Canada*, Palgrave Macmillan, New York, pp. 273–280.

McSherry, B, 2009, 'Hospital orders for offenders with mental illnesses: an appropriate diversionary option', *Journal of Law and Medicine*, vol. 16, pp. 568–573.

McVeigh, S (ed) 2007, *Jurisprudence of jurisdiction*, Routledge-Cavendish, New York.

McWhorter, L 2009, *Racism and sexual oppression in Anglo-America: a genealogy*, Indiana University Press, Bloomington and Indianapolis.

Meekosha, H & Soldatic K 2011, 'Human rights and the Global South: the case of disability', *Third World Quarterly*, vol. 32, no. 8, pp. 1383–1397, DOI: doi:10.1080/01436597.2011.614800.

Mental Health Commission of NSW2017, *Towards a just system: mental illness and cognitive impairment in the criminal justice system*, Mental Health Commission of NSW, Sydney, online: https://nswmentalhealthcommission.com.au/sites/default/files/documents/justice_paper_final_web.pdf.

Menzies, RJ & Chunn DE 1998, 'The gender politics of criminal insanity: "Order-in-Council" women in British Columbia, 1888–1950', *Social History*, vol. 31, no. 62, pp. 241–279, online: https://hssh.journals.yorku.ca/index.php/hssh/article/view/4667/.

Million, D 2000, 'Policing the Rez: keeping no peace in Indian country', *Social Justice*, vol. 27, no. 3, pp. 101–119.

Million D 2013a, *Therapeutic nations: healing in an age of Indigenous human rights*, University of Arizona Press, Tucson.

Million, D 2013b, 'Trauma, power, and the therapeutic: speaking psychotherapeutic narratives in an era of Indigenous human rights', in J Henderson & P Wakeham (eds), *Reconciling Canada: critical perspectives on the culture*, University of Toronto Press, Toronto, pp. 159–177.

Mills, C 2014, *Decolonizing global mental health: the psychiatrization of the majority world*, Routledge, London & New York.

Ministry of Justice (New Zealand) 2016, *Mental health courts: evidence brief*, online: www.justice.govt.nz/assets/Documents/Publications/Mental-Health-Courts.pdf.

Minkowitz, T 2007, 'The United Nations Convention on the Rights of Persons with Disabilities and the right to be free from nonconsensual psychiatric interventions', *Syracuse Journal of International Law and Commerce*, vol. 34, no. 2, pp. 405–428.

Minkowitz, T 2010, 'Abolishing mental health laws to comply with the Convention on the Rights of Persons with Disabilities', in B McSherry & P Weller (eds), *Rethinking rights-based mental health laws*, Hart Publishing, Oxford, pp. 151–177.

Minkowitz, T 2014, 'Rethinking criminal responsibility from a critical disability perspective: the abolition of insanity/incapacity acquittals and unfitness to plead, and beyond', *Griffith Law Review*, vol. 23, no. 3, pp. 434–466, DOI: doi:10.1080/10383441.2014.1013177.

Minkowitz, T 2017, 'CRPD and transformative equality', *The International Journal of Law in Context*, vol. 13, no. 2, pp. 77–86, DOI: doi:10.1017/S1744552316000483.

Mitchell, DT & Snyder SL 2005, 'Compulsory feral-ization: institutionalizing disability studies', *PMLA*, vol. 120, no. 2, pp. 627–634.

Mitchell, DT & Snyder SL 2014, *The biopolitics of disability: neoliberalism, ablenationalism, and peripheral embodiment*, University of Michigan Press, Ann Arbor.

Mogul, JL, Ritchie, AJ & Whitlock, K 2011, *Queer (in)justice: the criminalization of LGBT people in the United States*, Beacon Press, Boston.

Moon, G, Kearns, R & Joseph, A 2015, *The afterlives of the psychiatric asylum: recycling concepts, sites and memories*, Ashgate, Farnham.

Naffine, N 2009, *Law's meaning of life: philosophy, religion, Darwin and the legal person*, Hart Publishing, Oxford & Portland.

National Inquiry into Missing and Murdered Indigenous Women and Girls 2019a, Reclaiming power and place: the final report of the National Inquiry into Missing and Murdered Indigenous Women and Girls, Volume 1a, online: www.mmiwg-ffada.ca/wp-content/uploads/2019/06/Final_Report_Vol_1a.pdf.

National Inquiry into Missing and Murdered Indigenous Women and Girls 2019b, Reclaiming power and place: the final report of the National Inquiry into Missing and Murdered Indigenous Women and Girls, Volume 1b, online: www.mmiwg-ffada.ca/wp-content/uploads/2019/06/Final_Report_Vol_1b.pdf.

New South Wales Law Reform Commission (NSWLRC)1996, People with an intellectual disability in the criminal justice system, Report No 80, New South Wales Law Reform Commission, Sydney.

New South Wales Law Reform Commission (NSWLRC) 2010, People with cognitive and mental health impairments in the criminal justice system: diversion, NSWLRC Consultation Paper No 7, New South Wales Law Reform Commission, Sydney, online: www.lawreform.justice.nsw.gov.au/Documents/Publications/Consultation-Papers/CP07.pdf.

New South Wales Law Reform Commission (NSWLRC) 2012a, People with cognitive and mental health impairments in the criminal justice system: apprehended violence orders, NSWLRC Questions Paper No. 1, New South Wales Law Reform Commission, Sydney, online: https://www.lawreform.justice.nsw.gov.au/Documents/Completed-projects/2010-onwards/Mental-health/Question-Papers/QP1.pdf.

New South Wales Law Reform Commission (NSWLRC) 2012b, People with cognitive and mental health impairments in the criminal justice system: diversion, NSWLRC Report No. 135, New South Wales Law Reform Commission, Sydney, online: www.lawreform.justice.nsw.gov.au/Documents/Publications/Reports/Report-135.pdf.

New South Wales Law Reform Commission 2013, People with cognitive and mental health impairments in the criminal justice system: criminal responsibility and consequences, Report No 138, New South Wales Law Reform Commission, Sydney, online: www.lawreform.justice.nsw.gov.au/Documents/Publications/Reports/Report-138.pdf.

Nixon R 2013, *Slow violence and the environmentalism of the poor*, Harvard University Press, Cambridge.

Norrie, AW 2001, *Crime, reason and history: a critical introduction to criminal law*, Butterworths, London.

Northern Territory Law Reform Committee 2016, Report on the interaction between people with mental health issues and the criminal justice system, Report No 42, Northern Territory Law Reform Committee, Darwin, online: https://justice.nt.gov.au/__data/assets/pdf_file/0007/365146/Report-on-the-Interaction-between-people-with-Mental-Health-Issues-and-the-Criminal-Justice-System_Report-No.-42_FINAL.pdf.

Nunkoosing, K & Haydon-Laurelut M 2011, 'Intellectual disabilities, challenging behaviour and referral texts: a critical discourse analysis', *Disability & Society*, vol. 26, no. 4, pp. 405–417, DOI: doi:10.1080/09687599.2011.567791.

Nunkoosing, K & Haydon-Laurelut M 2012, 'Intellectual disability trouble: Foucault and Goffman on "challenging behaviour"', in D Goodley, B Hughes & L Davis (eds), *Disability and social theory: new developments and directions*, Palgrave Macmillan, New York, pp. 195–211.

O'Connell, K 2017, 'Should we take the "disability" out of discrimination laws? Students with challenging behaviour and the definition of disability', *Law in Context*, vol. 35, no. 2, pp. 108–128.

O'Leary, L, Cooper, SA & Hughes-McCormack, L 2018, 'Early death and causes of death of people with intellectual disabilities: a systematic review', *Journal of Applied Research in Intellectual Disabilities*, vol. 31, no. 3, pp. 325–342, DOI: doi:10.1111/jar.12417.

O'Mahony, C 2013, *Diversion: a comparative study of law and policy relating to defendants and offenders with mental health problems and intellectual disability*, PhD thesis submitted to National University of Ireland, Galway.

Parsonage, M 2009, *Diversion: a better way for criminal justice and mental health*, Sainsbury Centre for Mental Health, London, online: www.ohrn.nhs.uk/resource/policy/DiversionSCMH.pdf.

Pasternak, S 2014, 'Jurisdiction and settler colonization: where do laws meet', *Canadian Journal of Law & Society*, vol. 29, no. 2, pp. 145–161, DOI: doi:10.1017/cls.2014.5.

Patel, S 2014, 'Racing madness: the terrorizing madness of the post 9/11 terrorist body', in L Ben-Moshe, C Chapman & AC Carey (eds), *Disability incarcerated: imprisonment and disability in the United States and Canada*, Palgrave Macmillan, New York, pp. 201–216.

Peay, J 2011, *Mental health and crime*, Routledge, New York.

Perlin, M 2013, '"There are no trials inside the gates of Eden": mental health courts, the Convention on the Rights of Persons with Disabilities, dignity and the promise of therapeutic jurisprudence', in B McSherry & I Freckelton (eds), *Coercive care: rights, law and policy*, Routledge, London and New York, pp. 193–217.

Peters, Y 2003, *Federally sentenced women with mental disabilities: a dark corner in Canadian human rights*, DisAbled Women's Action Network (DAWN) Canada, online: www.caefs.ca/wp-content/uploads/2013/05/dawn1.pdf.

Pilling, MD, Daley, A, Gibson, MF, Ross, LE, & Zaheer, J 2018, 'Assessing "insight", determining agency and autonomy: implicating social identities', in J Kilty & E Dej (eds), *Containing madness: gender and 'psy' in institutional contexts*, Palgrave Macmillan, Cham.

Plumb, A 2015, 'UN Convention on the Rights of Persons with Disabilities: out of the frying pan into the fire? Mental health service users and survivors aligning with the disability movement', in H Spandler, J Anderson & B Sapey (eds), *Madness, distress and the politics of disablement*, Policy Press, Bristol, pp. 183–198.

Porter, A 2019, 'Aboriginal sovereignty, "crime" and criminology', *Current Issues in Criminal Justice*, vol. 31, no. 1, pp. 122–142, DOI: doi:10.1080/10345329.2018.1559747.

Pring, J 2017, 'Welfare reforms and the attack on disabled people', in V Cooper & D Whyte (eds), *The violence of austerity*, Pluto Press, London, pp. 51–58.

Prison Reform Trust 2017, *Counted out: black, asian and minority ethnic women in the criminal justice system*, online: www.prisonreformtrust.org.uk/Portals/0/Documents/Counted%20Out.pdf.

Psychiatric Disabilities Anti–violence Coalition2015, *Clearing a path: a psychiatric survivor anti-violence framework*, Psychiatric Disabilities Anti-violence Coalition, Toronto.

Puar, J 2017, *Right to maim: debility, capacity, disability*, Duke University Press, Durham & London.

Puar, JK 2009, 'Prognosis time: towards a geopolitics of affect, debility and capacity', *Women & Performance: A Journal of Feminist Theory*, vol. 19, no. 2, pp. 161–172, DOI: doi:10.1080/07407700903034147.

Punzi, E 2019, 'Ghost walks or thoughtful remembrance. How should the heritage of psychiatry be approached?', *Journal of Critical Psychology, Counselling and Psychotherapy*, vol. 19, no. 4, pp. 242–251.

Pyne, A 2016, '"Rolling the dice": barriers to effective summary diversion in the Northern Territory', *Psychiatry, Psychology and Law*, vol. 23, no. 1, pp. 37–46, DOI: doi:10.1080/13218719.2015.1030011.

Quirourette, M, Hannah-Moffat, K & Maurotto, P 2016, '"A precarious place": housing and clients of specialized courts', *British Journal of Criminology*, vol. 56, no. 2, pp. 370–388, DOI: doi:10.1093/bjc/azv050.

Raju, P & Penak, N 2019, 'Indigenizing the narrative: a conversation on disability assessments', in A Daley, L Costa & P Beresford (eds), *Madness, violence and power: a critical collection*, University of Toronto Press, Toronto, pp. 136–149.

Razack, S 1998, *Looking white people in the eye: gender, race, and culture in courtrooms and classrooms*, University of Toronto Press, Toronto.

Razack, S 2015, *Dying from improvement: inquests and inquiries into Indigenous deaths in custody*, University of Toronto Press, Toronto. Redlich, A 2005, 'Voluntary, but knowing and intelligent? Comprehension in mental health courts', *Psychology, Public Policy, and Law*, vol. 11, no. 4, pp. 605–619, DOI:. doi:10.1037/1076-8971.11.4.605.

Redlich, AD 2008, 'Sentencing diversion programs', in BL Culter (ed), *Encyclopedia of psychology and law*, SAGE Publications, Thousand Oaks, pp. 710–713.

Ribet, B 2010, 'Naming prison rape as disablement: a critical analysis of the Prison Litigation Reform Act, the Americans with Disabilities Act, and the imperatives of survivor-oriented advocacy', *Virginia Journal of Social Policy and the Law*, vol. 17, no. 2, pp. 281–317.

Ribet, B 2011, 'Emergent disability and the limits of equality: a critical reading of the UN Convention on the Rights of Persons with Disabilities', *Yale Human Rights and Development Law Journal*, vol. 14, no. 1, pp. 155–204, online: http://digitalcommons.law.yale.edu/yhrdlj/vol14/iss1/4.

Richards, K 2014, 'Blurred lines: reconsidering the concept of "diversion" in youth justice systems in Australia', *Youth Justice*, vol. 14, no. 2, pp. 122–139, DOI: doi:10.1177/1473225414526799.

Richardson, E 2016, *Envisioning Next Generation Mental Health Courts for Australia*, PhD thesis submitted to Monash University, Melbourne.

Richardson, E 2019, 'Mental health courts: providing access to justice for people with mental illness and cognitive impairments', *Alternative Law Journal*, vol. 44, no. 2, pp. 100–107, DOI: doi:10.1177/1037969X19845681.

Richardson, E & McSherry, B 2010, 'Diversion down under—programs for offenders with mental illnesses in Australia', *International Journal of Law and Psychiatry*, vol. 33, no. 4, pp. 249–257, DOI: doi:10.1016/j.ijlp.2010.06.007.

Richardson, E, Thom, K & McKenna, B 2013, 'The evolution of problem-solving courts in Australia and New Zealand: a Trans-Tasman comparative perspective', in RL Wiener & EM Brank (eds), *Problem Solving Courts*, Springer, New York, pp. 185–210.

Richmond, DT 1983, *Inquiry into health services for the psychiatrically ill and developmentally disabled*, various volumes, NSW Department of Health, online: https://nswmentalhealthcommission.com.au/sites/default/files/Inquriy%20into%20Health%20Services%20for%20the%20Psychiatrically%20Ill%20and%20Developmentally%20Disabled%20-%20Richmond%20Report%20-%201983.pdf.

Ring, I 2003, 'The health status of indigenous peoples and others', *British Medical Journal*, vol. 327, pp. 404–405, DOI: doi:10.1136/bmj.327.7412.404.

Roberts, D 2017, *Killing the black body: race, reproduction and the meaning of liberty*, Vintage Books, New York.

Roper, C 2018, 'Capacity does not reside in me', in C Spivakovsky, K Seear & A Carter (eds), *Critical perspectives on coercive interventions: law, medicine and society*, Routledge, Abingdon & New York, pp. 85–96.

Roper, C 2019, 'Ethical peril, violence, and "dirty hands": ethical consequences of mental health laws', *Journal of Ethics in Mental Health*, vol. 10, pp. 1–17, online: https://jemh.ca/issues/v9/documents/JEMH_Inc_vi.pdf.

Roper, C & Gooding, P 2018, 'This is not a story: from ethical loneliness to respect for diverse ways of knowing, thinking and being', in E Flynn, A Arstein-Kerslake, C de Bhalis & ML Serra (eds), *Global perspectives on legal capacity reform: our voices, our stories*, Routledge, Abingdon, pp. 154–164.

Rose, N 1996, *Inventing our selves: psychology, power, and personhood*, Cambridge University Press, Cambridge & New York.

Rose, N 1999, *Powers of freedom: reframing political thought*, Cambridge University Press, Cambridge & New York.

Rossiter, K & Rinaldi, J 2018, *Institutional violence and disability: punishing conditions*, Routledge, Abingdon.

Royal Commission and Board of Inquiry into the Protection and Detention of Children in the Northern Territory2017a, Final Report, November 2017, vol 2A, online: www.royalcommission.gov.au/royal-commission-detention-and-protection-children-northern-territory.

Royal Commission and Board of Inquiry into the Protection and Detention of Children in the Northern Territory2017b, Final Report, November 2017, vol 2B, online: www.royalcommission.gov.au/royal-commission-detention-and-protection-children-northern-territory.

Royal Commission into Aboriginal Deaths in Custody 1991, National report, various volumes, Australian Government Publishing Service, Canberra, online: www.austlii.edu.au/au/other/IndigLRes/rciadic/.

Royal Commission into Institutional Responses to Child Sexual Abuse 2017a, *Final report: volume 2, nature and cause*, Commonwealth of Australia, Canberra, online: www.childabuseroyalcommission.gov.au/sites/default/files/final_report_-_volume_2_nature_and_cause.pdf.

Royal Commission into Institutional Responses to Child Sexual Abuse 2017b, Final report: volume 3, impacts, Commonwealth of Australia, Canberra, online: www.childabuseroyalcommission.gov.au/sites/default/files/final_report_-_volume_3_impacts.pdf.

Royal Commission into Institutional Responses to Child Sexual Abuse 2017c, Criminal justice: executive summary and parts I-II, Commonwealth of Australia, Canberra, online: https://www.childabuseroyalcommission.gov.au/sites/default/files/file-list/final_report_-_criminal_justice_report_-_executive_summary_and_parts_i_to_ii.pdf.

Russell, M & Stewart, J 2001, 'Disablement, prison, and historical segregation', *Monthly Review*, vol. 53, no. 3, pp. 61–75, online: https://monthlyreview.org/2001/07/01/disablement-prison-and-historical-segregation/.

Rutherford, M 2010, *Blurring the boundaries: the convergence of mental health and criminal justice policy, legislation, and systems and practices*, Sainsbury Centre for Mental Health, London.

Ryan, S & Whelan, D 2012, 'Diversion of offenders with mental disorders: mental health courts', *Web Journal of Current Legal Issues*, vol. 1, online: http://webjcli.ncl.ac.uk/2012/issue1/ryan1.html.

Sandell, R, Dodd, J & Garland-Thomson, R (eds) 2013, *Re-presenting disability: activism and agency in the museum*, Routledge, London & New York.

Saxena, S 2018, 'Excess mortality among people with mental disorders: a public health priority', *The Lancet*, vol. 3, no. 6, pp. e264–e265, DOI: doi:10.1016/S2468-2667(18)30099-30099.

Schneider, RD 2010, 'Mental health courts and diversion programs: a global survey', *International Journal of Law and Psychiatry*, vol. 33, pp. 201–206, DOI: doi:10.1016/j.ijlp.2010.07.001.

Schneider, RD, Bloom, H & Heerema, M 2007, *Mental health courts: decriminalizing the mentally ill*, Irwin Law, Toronto.

Schneider, RD, Crocker, AG & Leclair, MC 2016, 'Mental health courts and diversion programs', in JA Chandler & CM Flood (eds), *Law and mind: mental health law and policy in Canada*, LexisNexis, Toronto, pp. 303–323.

Schweik, SM 2009, *Ugly laws: disability in public*, New York University Press, New York.

Scott, DA, McGilloway, S, Dempster, M, Browne, F, Donnelly, M 2013, 'Effectiveness of criminal justice liaison and diversion services for offenders with mental disorders: a review', *Psychiatric Services*, vol. 64, no. 9, pp. 843–849, DOI: doi:10.1176/appi.ps.201200144.

Scottish Association for Mental Healthn.d., *The right road: making diversion work for people with mental health problems*, Scottish Association for Mental Health, Glasgow, http://www.sccjr.ac.uk/wp-content/uploads/2014/09/TheRightRoadExecutiveSummary.pdf.

Scraton, P & McCulloch J (eds) 2009, *The violence of incarceration*, Routledge, New York & Milton Park.

Seltzer, T 2005, 'Mental health courts: a misguided attempt to address the criminal justice system's unfair treatment of people with mental illnesses', *Psychology, Public Policy, and Law*, vol. 11, no. 4, pp. 570–586, DOI: doi:10.1037/1076-8971.11.4.570.

Sharma, K 2018, *"I needed help, instead I was punished": abuse and neglect of prisoners with disabilities in Australia*, Human Rights Watch, online: www.hrw.org/sites/default/files/report_pdf/australia0218_web.pdf.

Sharples J, Lewin, TJ, Hinton, RJ, Sly, KA, Coles, GW, Johnston, PJ & Carr, VJ 2003, 'Offending behaviour and mental illness: characteristics of a mental health court liaison service', *Psychiatry, Psychology and Law*, vol. 10, no. 2, pp. 300–315, DOI: doi:10.1375/pplt.2003.10.2.300.

Sheldon, CT, Spector, KR & Birdsell, M 2019, 'Uncovering law's multiple violences at the inquest into the death of Ashley Smith', in A Daley, L Costa & P Beresford (eds), *Madness, violence and power: a critical collection*, University of Toronto Press, Toronto, pp. 196–220.

Shildrick, M 2009, *Dangerous discourses of disability, subjectivity and sexuality*, Palgrave Macmillan, Basingstoke.

Simpson, A 2014, *Mohawk interruptus: political life across the borders of settler states*, Duke University Press, Durham & London.

Simpson, J 2013, *Participants or just policed? Guide to the role of DisabilityCare Australia with people with intellectual disability who have contact with the criminal justice system*, Report for the New South Wales Council for Intellectual Disability, May 2013, Sydney, online: www.nswcid.org.au/images/pdf/participantsOrJustPolicedSummary.pdf.

Sins Invalid 2016, 'Sins Invalid statement on police violence', in Sins Invalid (ed), *Skin, tooth and bone: the basis of movement is our people: a disability justice primer*, Sins Invalid, pp. 35–37, online: www.yumpu.com/en/document/read/56942783/skin-tooth-and-bone/10.

Slinger, E & Roesch, R 2010, 'Problem-solving courts in Canada: a review and a call for empirically-based evaluation methods', *International Journal of Law and Psychiatry*, vol. 33, pp. 258–264, DOI: doi:10.1016/j.ijlp.2010.06.008.

Snedker, S 2018, *Therapeutic justice: crime, treatment courts and mental illness*, Palgrave Macmillan, Cham.

Soldatic, K 2011, 'Appointment time: disability and neoliberal workfare temporalities', *Critical Sociology*, vol. 39, no. 3, pp. 405–419, DOI: doi:10.1177/0896920511430168.

Soldatic, K 2015, 'Post colonial re productions: disability, indigeneity and the formation of the white masculine settler state of Australia', *Social Identities*, vol. 21, no. 1, pp. 53–68, DOI: doi:10.1080/13504630.2014.995352.

Soldatic, K & Fiske, L 2009, 'Bodies "locked up": intersections of disability and race in Australian immigration', *Disability & Society*, vol. 24, no. 3, pp. 289–301, DOI: doi:10.1080/09687590902789453.

Soldatic, K, van Toorn, G, Dowse L & Muir, K 2014, 'Intellectual disability and complex intersections: marginalisation under the National Disability Insurance Scheme', *Research and Practice in Intellectual and Developmental Disabilities*, vol. 1, no. 1, pp. 6–16, DOI: doi:10.1080/23297018.2014.906050.

Spade, D 2011, *Normal life: administrative violence, critical trans politics, and the limits of law*, South End Press, Brooklyn.

Spade, D 2015, *Normal life: administrative violence, critical trans politics, and the limits of law*, revised and expanded edition, South End Press, Brooklyn.

Spade, D & Rohlfs, R 'Legal equality, gay numbers and the (after?)math of eugenics', *Scholar and Feminist Online*, vol. 13, no. 2, online: http://sfonline.barnard.edu/navigating-neoliberalism-in-the-academy-nonprofits-and-beyond/dean-spade-rori-rohlfs-legal-equality-gay-numbers-and-the-aftermath-of-eugenics/.

Spagnuolo, N 2016, 'Building back wards in a "post" institutional era: hospital confinement, group home eviction, and Ontario's treatment of people labelled with intellectual disabilities', *Disability Studies Quarterly*, vol. 36, no. 4, online: http://dsq-sds.org/article/view/5279/4480.

Spiers, M 2004, 'Summary disposal of criminal offences under s 32 Mental Health (Criminal Procedure) Act 1990: diversion of cognitively impaired or mentally-ill defendants', *Judicial Officers' Bulletin*, vol. 16, no. 2, pp. 9–11.

Spivakovsky, C 2014a, 'From punishment to protection: containing and controlling the lives of people with disabilities in human rights', *Punishment & Society*, vol. 16, no. 5, pp. 560–577, DOI: doi:10.1177/1462474514548805.

Spivakovsky, C 2014b, 'Making dangerousness intelligible in intellectual disability', *Griffith Law Review*, vol. 23, no. 3, pp. 389–404, DOI: doi:10.1080/10383441.2014.979463.

Spivakovsky, C 2017, 'Governing freedom through risk: locating the group home in the archipelago of confinement and control', *Punishment & Society*, vol. 19, no. 3, pp. 366–383, DOI: doi:10.1177/1462474517703968.

Spivakovsky, C 2018, 'The impossibilities of "bearing witness" to the violence of coercive interventions in the disability sector', in C Spivakovsky, K Seear & A Carter (eds), *Critical perspectives on coercive interventions: law, medicine and society*, Routledge, Abingdon & New York, pp. 97–113.

Spivakovsky, C & Seear K 2017, 'Making the abject: problem solving courts, addiction, mental illness and impairment', *Continuum*, vol. 31, no. 3, pp. 458–469, DOI: doi:10.1080/10304312.2016.1275152.

Stanev, R & Wildeman, S 2018, 'Freedom: a work in progress', in E Flynn, A Arstein-Kerslake, C de Bhalis & ML Serra (eds), *Global perspectives on legal capacity reform: our voices, our stories*, Routledge, Abingdon & New York, pp. 197–212.

Stathopoulos, M 2012, 'Addressing women's victimisation histories in custodial settings', ACSSA Issues No 13, Australian Centre for the Study of Sexual Assault, https://aifs.gov.au/sites/default/files/publication documents/i13.pdf.

Steadman, HJ, Redlich, AD, Griffin, P, Petrila, J & Monahan, J 2005,'From referral to disposition: case processing in seven mental health courts', *Behavioral Sciences and the Law*, vol. 23, pp. 215–226, DOI: doi:10.1002/bsl.641.

Steele, L 2014, 'Disability, abnormality and criminal law: sterilisation as lawful and good violence', *Griffith Law Review*, vol. 23, no. 3, pp. 467–497, DOI: doi:10.1080/10383441.2014.1000223.

Steele, L 2016, 'Court-authorised sterilisation and human rights: inequality, discrimination and violence against women and girls with disability?', *UNSW Law Journal*, vol. 39, no. 3, pp. 1002–1037, online: http://classic.austlii.edu.au/au/journals/UTSLRS/2016/32.html.

Steele, L 2017a, 'Disabling forensic mental health detention: the carcerality of the disabled body', *Punishment & Society*, vol. 19, no. 3, pp. 327–347, DOI: doi:10.1177/1462474516680204.

Steele, L 2017b, 'Lawful institutional violence against disabled people', *Precedent*, no. 143 (November/December), pp. 4–7.

Steele, L 2017c, 'Policing normalcy: sexual violence against women offenders with disability', *Continuum*, vol. 31, no. 3, pp. 422–435, DOI: doi:10.1080/10304312.2016.1275144.

Steele, L 2017d, 'Temporality, disability and institutional violence: revisiting In Re F', *Griffith Law Review*, vol. 26, no. 3, pp. 378–400, DOI: doi:10.1080/10383441.2017.1436368.

Steele L 2018a, 'Activating Parramatta Female Factory Precinct as a site of conscience', paper presented at Co.Lab18, LandCom and Urban Growth NSW, Parramatta, Australia, 22 November 2018.

Steele, L 2018b, 'Restrictive practices in Australian schools: institutional violence, disability and law', in R Dixon, K Trimmer & YS Findlay (eds), *The Palgrave handbook of education law for schools*, Palgrave Macmillan, Cham, pp. 533–552.

Steele, L 2018c, 'Sterilisation, disability and wellbeing: the curative imaginary of the "welfare jurisdiction"', in C Spivakovsky, K Seear & A Carter (eds), *Critical perspectives on coercive interventions: law, medicine and society*, Routledge, Abingdon, pp. 149–163.

Steele, L 2018d, 'Troubling law's indefinite detention: disability, the carceral body and institutional injustice', *Social & Legal Studies*, online first, DOI: doi:10.1177/0964663918769478.

Steele, L, Djuric, B, Hibberd, L & Yeh, F 2020 (forthcoming), 'Parramatta Female Factory Precinct as a site of conscience: using institutional pasts to shape just legal futures', *UNSW Law Journal*, vol. 43, no. 2.

Steele, L, Dowse, L & Trofimovs, J 2016, 'Who is diverted? Moving beyond diagnosed impairment towards a social and political analysis of diversion', *Sydney Law Review*, vol. 38, no. 2, pp. 179–206, online: http://classic.austlii.edu.au/au/journals/SydLawRw/2016/8.html.

Stefan, S & Winick, BJ 2005, 'Foreword: a dialogue on mental health courts', *Psychology, Public Policy and Law*, vol. 11, no. 4, pp. 507–526, DOI: doi:10.1037/1076-8971.11.4.507.

Steinberg, D, Mills, D, & Romano, M 2015, *When did prisons become acceptable mental healthcare facilities?*, Stanford Law School Three Strikes Project, online: https://law.stanfordedu/publications/when-did-prisons-become-acceptable-mental-healthcare-facilities-2/.

TallBear, K 2013, *Native American DNA: tribal belonging and the false promise of genetic science*, University of Minnesota Press, Minneapolis.

Tam, L 2013, 'Whither Indigenizing the mad movement?: theorizing the social relations of race and madness through conviviality', in B Lefrancois, R Menzies & G Reaume (eds), *Mad matters: a critical reader in Canadian mad studies*, Canadian Scholars Press, Toronto, pp. 281–297.

Tam, L 2017, 'Agitation and sudden death: containing black detainee affect', *American Quarterly*, vol. 69, no. 2, pp. 339–345, DOI: doi:10.1353/aq.2017.0030.

Taylor, A 2015, 'Expressions of "lives worth living" and their foreclosure through philosophical theorizing on moral status and intellectual disability', in S Tremain (ed), *Foucault and the government of disability*, revised and expanded edition, University of Michigan Press, Ann Arbor, pp. 372–395.

Ticktin, M 2011, *Casualties of care: immigration and the politics of humanitarianism in France*, University of California Press, Berkeley.

Ticktin, M 2017, 'A world without innocence', *American Ethnologist*, vol. 44, no. 4, pp. 577–590, DOI: doi:10.1111/amet.12558.

Toki, V 2010, 'Therapeutic jurisprudence and mental health courts for Maori', *International Journal of Law and Psychiatry*, vol. 33, no. 5–6, pp. 440–447, DOI: doi:10.1016/j.ijlp.2010.09.014.

Tremain, S 2002, 'On the subject of impairment', in M Corker & T Shakespeare (eds), *Disability/postmodernity: embodying disability theory*, Continuum, London, pp. 32–47.

Tremain, S 2005, 'Foucault, governmentality, and critical disability theory: an introduction', in S Tremain (ed), *Foucault and the government of disability*, University of Michigan Press, Ann Arbor, pp. 1–24.

Unsworth, C 1991, 'Mental disorder and the tutelary relationship: from pre- to post-carceral legal order', *Journal of Law and Society*, vol. 18, no. 2, pp. 254–278.

Valverde, M 2015, *Chronotopes of law: jurisdiction, scale and governance*, Routledge, Abingdon.

Van Veen, C, Teghtsoonian, K & Morrow, M 2019, 'Enacting violence and care: neo-liberalism, knowledge claims and resistance', in A Daley, L Costa & P Beresford (eds), *Madness, violence and power: a critical collection*, University of Toronto Press, Toronto, pp. 63–79.

Veitch, S 2007, *Law and irresponsibility: on the legitimation of human suffering*, Routledge-Cavendish, Abingdon & New York.

Veracini, L 2010, *Settler colonialism: a theoretical overview*, Palgrave Macmillan, Basingstoke.

Voronka, J 2003, *The race to space madness: making respectability through mad sites in Ontario*, Masters thesis submitted to University of Toronto, Toronto.

Voronka, J 2013, 'Rerouting the weeds: the move from criminalizing to pathologizing "troubled youth" in *The Review of the Roots of Youth Violence*', in B Lefrancois, R Menzies & G Reaume (eds), *Mad matters: a critical reader in Canadian mad studies*, Canadian Scholars Press, Toronto, pp. 309–322.

Voronka, J 2016, 'Inclusion interrupted', *Asylum*, vol. 23, no. 4, p. 6.

Voronka, J 2019, 'Slow death through evidence-based research', in A Daley, L Costa & P Beresford (eds), *Madness, violence and power: a critical collection*, University of Toronto Press, Toronto, pp. 80–96.

Wadiwel, D 2017, 'Disability and torture: exception, epistemology and "black sites"', *Continuum*, vol. 31, no. 3, pp. 388–399, DOI: doi:10.1080/10304312.2016.1275134.

Ware, S, Ruzsa, J & Dias, G 0214, 'It can't be fixed because it's not broken: racism and disability in the prison industrial complex', in L Ben-Moshe, C Chapman & AC Carey (eds), *Disability incarcerated: imprisonment and disability in the United States and Canada*, Palgrave Macmillan, New York, pp. 163–184.

Watson, I 2015, *Aboriginal peoples, colonialism and international law: raw law*, Routledge, Abingdon & New York.

Watts, IE &Erevelles, N 2004, 'These deadly times: reconceptualizing school violence by using critical race theory and disability studies', *American Educational Research Journal*, vol. 41, no. 2, pp. 271–299, DOI: doi:10.3102/00028312041002271.

Wexler, DB 1991, 'Putting mental health into mental health law: therapeutic jurisprudence', in DB Wexler & BJ Winick, *Essays in therapeutic jurisprudence*, Carolina Academic Press, Durham, pp. 3–15.

Wildeman, S 2016, 'Agonizing identity in mental health law and policy (part II): a political taxonomy of psychiatric subjectification', *Dalhousie Law Journal*, vol. 39, no. 1, pp. 147–193.

Wildeman, S 2018a, 'Disabling solitary: a cautious appraisal of mental disability discrimination as prison justice strategy', paper presented at The Canadian Prison Law Conference, Schulich School of Law, Dalhousie University, Halifax, Nova Scotia, 21–23 September 2018.

Wildeman, S 2018b, 'Anti-carceral disability rights litigation in Canada: pathways to substantive equality informed by the CRPD', paper presented at Disability and (virtual) institutions? Interventions, integration and inclusion, International Institute for the Sociology of Law, Onati, Spain, 21–22 June 2018.

Withers, AJ 2012a, *Disability politics and theory*, Fernwood Publishing, Halifax, Nova Scotia & Winnipeg.

Wolfe, P 2006, 'Settler colonialism and the elimination of the Indigenous', *Journal of Genocide Research*, vol. 8, no. 4, pp. 387–409.

Wolff, N 2002, 'Courts as therapeutic agents: thinking past the novelty of mental health courts', *The Journal of the American Academy of Psychiatry and the Law*, vol. 30, no. 3, pp. 431–437.

Wynter, S 1994, 'No humans involved: an open letter to my colleagues', *Forum NHI: Knowledge for the 21st Century*, vol. 1, no. 1, pp. 42–73, online: http://carmenkynard.org/wp-content/uploads/2013/07/No-Humans-Involved-An-Open-Letter-to-My-Colleagues-by-SYLVIA-WYNTER.pdf.

Yates, S 2005, 'Truth, power, and ethics in care services for people with learning difficulties', in S Tremain (ed), *Foucault and the government of disability*, University of Michigan Press, Ann Arbor, pp. 65–77.

Other sources

Cases

Broome v Liristis [2011] NSWDC 40 (15 June 2011).

R v Birch (1989) 11 Cr App R(S) 202 (CA).

DPP (NSW) v El Mawas (2006) 66 NSWLR 93.

DPP (NSW) v Lopez-Aguilar [2013] NSWSC 1019 (5 August 2013).

DPP (NSW) v Saunders [2017] NSWSC 760 (16 June 2017).

DPP (NSW) v Soliman [2013] NSWSC 346 (16 April 2013).

He Kaw Teh v The Queen (1985) 157 CLR 523.

Mantell v Molyneux (2006) 68 NSWLR 46.

Minister for Corrective Services v Harris (Unreported), Supreme Court of New South Wales, Brownie J, 10 July 1987.

Police v Deng [2008] NSWLC 2 (30 January 2008).

Police v Goodworth [2007] NSWLC 2 (28 March 2007).

Police v Winter [2008] NSWLC 15 (22 August 2008).
Presser v R [1958] VR 45.
Ryan v The Queen (1967) 121 CLR 205.

Legislation

Civil Liability Act 2002 (New South Wales, Australia).
Crimes (Administration of Sentences) Act 1999 (New South Wales, Australia).
Crimes (Mental Disorder) Amendment Act 1983 (New South Wales, Australia).
Crimes (Sentencing Procedure) Act 1999 (New South Wales, Australia).
Crimes Act 1900 (New South Wales, Australia).
Crimes Act 1914 (Commonwealth of Australia).
Crimes (Domestic and Personal) Violence Act 2007 (New South Wales, Australia).
Criminal Procedure (Mentally Impaired Persons) Act 2003 (New Zealand).
Criminal Procedure (Scotland) Act 1995 (Scotland).
Felons (Civil Proceedings) Act 1981 (NSW).
Intellectual Disability (Compulsory Care and Rehabilitation) Act 2003 (New Zealand).
Magistrates' Court Act 1989 (Victoria, Australia).
Mental Health (Care and Treatment) (Scotland) Act 2003 (Scotland).
Mental Health (Compulsory Assessment and Treatment) Act 1992 (New Zealand).
Mental Health (Criminal Procedure) Act 1990 (New South Wales, Australia).
Mental Health (Forensic Provisions) Act 1990 (New South Wales, Australia).
Mental Health Act 1983 (England and Wales).
Mental Health and Related Services Act1998 (Northern Territory, Australia).
Mental Health Legislation Amendment (Forensic Provisions) Act 2008 (New South Wales, Australia).
Mentally Impaired Defendants Act 1996 (Western Australia, Australia).
National Disability Insurance Scheme Act 2013 (Commonwealth of Australia).
The Mental Health (Northern Ireland) Order 1986 (Northern Ireland).
Sentencing Act 2017 (South Australia, Australia).

Other legislative

Explanatory Notes, Crimes Legislation Amendment Bill 2002 (New South Wales, Australia).
Explanatory Notes, Mental Health (Criminal Procedure) Amendment Bill 2005 (New South Wales, Australia)

Parliamentary debates

New South Wales (Australia), *Parliamentary Debates*, Legislative Assembly, 22 November 1983.
New South Wales (Australia), *Parliamentary Debates*, Legislative Assembly, 8 November 2005.

UN treaties and other documents

United Nations2008, *Convention on the Rights of Persons with Disabilities*, 2515 UNTS 3, opened for signature 13 December 2006, entered into force 3 May 2008.

UNDisability Committee 2013, Concluding observations on the initial report of Australia, 10th session: 2–13 September 2013, UN Doc CRPD/C/AUS/CO/1, 21 October 2013.

UNDisability Committee 2014a, Concluding observations on the initial report of New Zealand, 12th session: 15 September - 3 October 2014,CRPD/C/NZL/CO/1, 31 October 2014.

UNDisabilityCommittee 2014b, General Comment No 1 on Article 1: Equal Recognition Before the Law, 19 May 2014.

UNDisability Committee 2014c, General Comment 2 on Article 9: Accessibility, 22 May 2014.

UNDisability Committee 2015, Guidelines on Article 14 of the Convention on the Rights of Persons with Disabilities: The right to liberty and security of persons with disabilities, 14th session: 17 August – 4 September 2015, https://www.ohchr.org/EN/HRBodies/CRPD/Pages/Guidelines.aspx.

UNDisability Committee 2016, Noble v Australia (Communication No 7/2012), CRPD/C/16/D/7/2012, 16th session: 15 August – 2 September 2016, published 10 October 2016.

UNDisability Committee 2018a, General Comment No 5 on Article 19: Living Independently and Being Included in the Community, 26 April 2018.

UNDisability Committee 2018b, General Comment 6 on Article 5: Equality and Non-Discrimination, 26 April 2018.

UN Office of the High Commissioner for Human Rights 2009, Thematic study by the Office of the United Nations High Commissioner for Human Rights on enhancing awareness and understanding of the Convention on the Rights of Persons with Disabilities, Human Rights Council, 10th session: 2–27 March 2009, UN Doc A/HRC/10/48, 26 January 2009.

UN Office of the High Commissioner for Human Rights 2014, Statement on article 14 of the Convention on the Rights of Persons with Disabilities, https://www.ohchr.org/EN/NewsEvents/Pages/DisplayNews.aspx?NewsID=15183&LangID=E.

UN Special Rapporteur on the Rights of Persons with Disabilities, Report of the Special Rapporteur on the Rights of Persons with Disabilities: rights of persons with disabilities, 40th session Human Rights Council, 25 February – 22 March 2019, UN Doc A/HRC/40/54, 11 January 2019.

Media

Allam, L, Wahlquist, C & Evershed, N 2018, 'The 147 dead: terrible toll of Indigenous deaths in custody spurs calls for reform', *The Guardian*, 28 August 2018, www.theguardian.com/australia-news/2018/aug/28/the-147-dead-indigenous-leaders-demand-action-over-unacceptable-deaths-in-custody.

BBC News 2012, 'Timeline: Winterbourne View abuse scandal', *BBC News*, 10 December 2012, www.bbc.com/news/uk-england-bristol-20078999.

BBC News 2019, 'Winterbourne View abuse whistleblower speaks out', *BBC News*, 23 May 2019, www.bbc.com/news/uk-england-bristol-48381550.

Maqbool, A 2018, 'Don't shoot, I'm disabled', *BBC News*, 4 October 2018, www.bbc.com/news/stories-45739335.

McKenzie, N 2014, 'In our care', *Four Corners, ABC Television*, 24 November 2014, www.abc.net.au/4corners/in-our-care/5916148.

Nicholson, K & Marcoux, J 2018, 'Most Canadians killed in police encounters since 2000 had mental health or substance abuse issues', *CBC News*, 4 April 2018, online: www.cbc.ca/news/investigates/most-canadians-killed-in-police-encounters-since-2000-had-mental-health-or-substance-abuse-issues-1.4602916.

Perkel, C 2013, 'Ashley Smith inquest: psychologist describes "reign of terror" at prison', *CTV News*, 25 June 2013, online: www.ctvnews.ca/canada/ashley-smith-inquest-psychologist-describes-reign-of-terror-at-prison-1.1341342.

Perry, D 2017, 'Police killings: the price of being disabled and black in America', *The Guardian*, 22 June 2017, online: www.theguardian.com/us-news/2017/jun/22/police-killings-disabled-black-people-mental-illness.

Pidd, H & Wolfe-Robinson, M 2019, 'Care homes accused of being too quick to call police on children', *The Guardian*, 6 November 2019, online: https://www.theguardian.com/society/2019/nov/06/care-homes-accused-quick-police-children.

Pilkington, E 2018, '"It's torture": critics step up bid to stop US school using electric shocks on children', *The Guardian*, 16 November 2018, www.theguardian.com/us-news/2018/nov/16/judge-rotenberg-center-massachusetts-electric-shocks.

Plomin, J 2019, 'Whorlton Hall hospital abuse and how it was uncovered', *BBC News*, 22 May 2019, www.bbc.com/news/health-48369500.

Qadar, S 2020, 'Why we need more Indigenous psychologists', *All in the Mind*, ABC Radio National (16 February 2020), https://www.abc.net.au/radionational/programs/allinthemind/why-we-need-more-indigenous-psychologists/11954110

Zhou, N 2018, 'Police tactics "entirely inappropriate" in shooting death of Courtney Topic, coroner says', 30 July 2018, *The Guardian*, online: www.theguardian.com/australia-news/2018/jul/30/police-tactics-entirely-inappropriate-in-shooting-death-of-courtney-topic-says-coroner.

Law reform submissions

Beveridge, MC 1994, Submission to New South Wales Law Reform Commission, People with an Intellectual Disability and the Criminal Justice System, 5 April 1994.

Cleary, TG 1995, Submission to New South Wales Law Reform Commission, People with an Intellectual Disability and the Criminal Justice System, 7 February 1995.

Ierace, M 1992, Submission to the New South Wales Law Reform Commission, *People with an Intellectual Disability in the Criminal Justice System*, 16 December 1992.

Rowe, S, Simpson, J, Baldry E & McGee, P 2017, 'The provision of services under the NDIS for people with disabilities who are in contact with the criminal justice system: submission to the joint standing committee on the NDIS', Submission to the Joint Standing Committee on the National Disability Insurance Scheme, submission no 121, www.crcnsw.org.au/wp-content/uploads/2017/08/Submission-NDIS-Joint-Standing-Committee-Final.pdf.

Steele, L 2011, Submission to the NSW Law Reform Commission project on people with cognitive and mental health impairment in the NSW criminal justice system, www.lawreform.justice.nsw.gov.au/Documents/Completed-projects/2010-onwards/Mental-health/Submissions/crefl20_mh45lsteele.pdf.

Steele, L 2013, Submission to the Senate Community Affairs References Committee Inquiry into the involuntary or coerced sterilisation of people with disabilities in Australia, https://www.aph.gov.au/Parliamentary_Business/Committees/Senate/Community_Affairs/Involuntary_Sterilisation/Submissions.

Steele, L 2015, Submission to the Senate Community Affairs References Committee Inquiry into violence, abuse and neglect against people with disability in institutional and residential settings, including the gender and age related dimensions, and the particular situation of Aboriginal and Torres Strait Islander people with disability, and culturally and linguistically diverse people with disability, https://www.aph.gov.au/Parliamentary_Business/Committees/Senate/Community_Affairs/Violence_abuse_neglect/Submissions?main_0_content_1_RadGrid1ChangePage=5_20.

Blogposts

Bjornsdottir, B 2017, '"I've always had a yearning for justice"', Gay Iceland, 28 February 2017, https://gayiceland.is/2017/ive-always-yearning-justice/.

Bond, C 2017, 'We just Black matter: Australia's indifference to Aboriginal lives and land', The Conversation, 16 October 2017, https://theconversation.com/we-just-black-matter-australias-indifference-to-aboriginal-lives-and-land-85168.

Dehm, S 2019, 'The evidence is clear: the medevac law saves lives. But even this isn't enough to alleviate refugee suffering', *The Conversation*, 22 October 2019, www.theconversation/the-evidence-is-clear-the-medevac-law-saves-lives-but-even-this-isnt-enough-to-alleviate-refugee-suffering-125308.

Guenther, L 2018, 'Healing and haunting at Kingston's Prison for Women', Hidden Persuaders, 8 August 2018, http://www.bbk.ac.uk/hiddenpersuaders/blog/healing-and-haunting-at-kingstons-prison-for-women/.

Krishnarayan, V 2017, 'Mental health policy reform: time to decolonise our minds', Commonwealth Foundation, 20 November 2017, https://commonwealthfoundation.com/mental-health-policy-reform-time-decolonise-minds/.

Malaquias, C 2019, 'Ethical supply chains, disability, sheltered workshops, segregation and exploitation', Starting with julius, www.startingwithjulius.org.au/ethical-supply-chains-disability-sheltered-workshops-segregation-and-exploitation/.

McCausland, R 2018, 'Dharriwaa Elders Group launches a vision for young people in Walgett', Croakey, https://croakey.org/dharriwaa-elders-group-launches-a-vision-for-young-people-in-walgett/.

Mingus, M 2011, 'Changing the framework: disability justice', Leaving evidence, 12 February 2011, https://leavingevidence.wordpress.com/2011/02/12/changing-the-framework-disability-justice/.

Mingus, M 2015, 'Medical industrial complex visual', Leaving evidence, 6 February 2015, https://leavingevidence.wordpress.com/2015/02/.

Mingus, M 2017, 'Access intimacy, interdependence and disability justice', Leaving evidence, 20 April 2017, https://leavingevidence.wordpress.com/2017/04/.

Mingus, M 2019, 'Transformative justice: a brief description', Leaving evidence, 9 January 2019, https://leavingevidence.wordpress.com/2019/01/09/transformative-justice-a-brief-description/.

Parker, L 2017, '"Disability justice is the art and the practice of honouring the body": an interview with Lydia XZ', Sideways time, 2 April 2017, https://sidewaystimesblog.wordpress.com/2017/04/02/disability-justice-is-the-art-and-the-practice-of-honouring-the-body-an-interview-with-lydia-x-z-brown/.

Porter, A 2016, 'Why we should honour the humanity of every person who dies in custody', The Conversation, 15 April 2016, https://theconversation.com/why-we-should-honour-the-humanity-of-every-person-who-dies-in-custody-57272.

Withers, AJ 2012b; 'Incarceration and institutionalization: disability and imprisonment', Stillmyrevolution, 1 January 2012, https://stillmyrevolution.org/2012/01/01/incarceration-and-institutionalization-disability-and-imprisonment/.

Zehr, H 2011, 'Restorative or transformative justice?', Zehr Institute for Restorative Justice, 10 March 2011, https://emu.edu/now/restorative-justice/2011/03/10/restorative-or-transformative-justice/.

Webpages

Aboriginal Legal Service (NSW/ACT)n.d., Custody Notification Service, www.alsnswact.org.au/our-work/custody-notification-service/

Ageing, Disability and Home Care, Department of Family and Community Services NSWn.d., Transfer of New South Wales disability services, https://ndis.nsw.gov.au/about-ndis-nsw/transfer-of-nsw-disability-services/

Brown, LXZn.d., 'Definitions', Autistic Hoya, http://www.autistichoya.com/p/definitions.html

Council of State Governments Justice Centern.d., Mental health courts, https://csgjusticecenter.org/mental-health-court-project/.

Courts Administration Authority of South Australian.d., Magistrates Court diversion program, http://www.courts.sa.gov.au/OurCourts/MagistratesCourt/InterventionPrograms/Pages/Magistrates-Court-Diversion-Program.aspx.

Djirran.d., https://djirra.org.au/.

Harvard Project on American Indian Economic Developmentn.d., https://hpaied.org/.

Jumbunna Institute for Indigenous Education and Researchn.d., Nation Building Project, www.uts.edu.au/research-and-teaching/our-research/jumbunna-institute-indigenous-education-and-research.

Justice Health and Forensic Mental Health Network, Department of Health (NSW)n.d., Courts, www.justicehealth.nsw.gov.au/about-us/health-care-locations/courts.

Murri Watchn.d., Cell Visitor Service, http://murriwatch.org.au/services/cell-visitor/.

People with Disability Australian.d., Royal Commission into Violence, Abuse, Neglect and Exploitation of People with Disability, https://pwd.org.au/royal-commission-now/.

Prison Reform Trustn.d., Care Not Custody, http://www.prisonreformtrust.org.uk/WhatWeDo/Projectsresearch/Mentalhealth/CarenotCustody.

Sins Invalidn.d., www.sinsinvalid.org/.

The Icarus Projectn.d., https://theicarusproject.net/.

Wellness Network for Lawn.d., http://wellnessforlaw.com/.

Other

Department of Justice (New South Wales)n.d., 'Cognitive Impairment Diversion Program factsheet', http://www.localcourt.justice.nsw.gov.au/Documents/Facts%20Sheets/Cognitive%20Impairment%20Diversion%20Program/CIDP-factsheet-stakeholders.pdf.

Dharriwaa Elders Group2018, 'Yuwaya Ngarra-li action plan for children and young people, Walgett', http://www.dharriwaaeldersgroup.org.au/images/downloads/Walgett-Action-Plan-for-Children-and-Young-People-June18.pdf.

Hunter, C 2014, 'Effects of child abuse and neglect for adult survivors', CFCA Resource Sheet, January 2014, Australian Institute of Family Studies, https://aifs.gov.au/cfca/publications/effects-child-abuse-and-neglect-adult-survivors.

NSW Government 2017, Department of Justice / Request for Tender for the provision of Cognitive Impairment Diversion Program – NGO Support role - DJ 2017–2055, 16 May 2017, https://tenders.nsw.gov.au/justice/?event=public.rft.showArchived&RFTUUID=994A404F-A2E9-4C49-8059624FD24CDF75.

NSW Bureau of Crime Statistics and Research 2019a, NSW Local and Children's Court Statistics Jan 2008 to Sep 2018: number of charges finalised in the Local and Children's Court under Section 32/33 of the Mental Health (Forensic Provisions) Act, Reference: jh18–17356, 15 March 2019.

NSW Bureau of Crime Statistics and Research 2019b, NSW Local and Children's Court Statistics Jan 2008 to Sep 2018: number of finalised charges for offences under 32(3A) of the Mental Health (Forensic Provisions) Act (Failure to comply with S32(3) order - Lawpart 53959) in Penrith and Gosford Local Courts by court outcome (Forensic Provisions) Act, Reference: sr19–17496, 30 April 2019.

Yukon Community Wellness Court 2009, Yukon community wellness court: court process, http://www.yukoncourts.ca/pdf/cwc_legal_process.pdf.

Index

accountability 201, 204–206
Altermark, N 83, 128, 187, 188, 190, 191, 217, 218
assertive community treatment 36
Australia 14, 43, 111; death-in-custody cases 9; diversion schemes 31–32; forensic mental health laws 11; institutional racism 7; *Marlon Noble v Australia* 70–72; mental health courts 34–35; New South Wales 19–20, 31, 35, 43, 119–128; overrepresentation of disabled people 24; South Australia 32, 35; Victoria 34–35, 43; *see also* New South Wales Law Reform Commission (NSWLRC)
Avery, S 202

back-end net widening 40
Baldry, E 41, 43, 67, 68, 138
Balint, J 208
Bartlett, P 37, 42, 44, 68
Bazelon Center for Mental Health Law 41, 43
Beaupert, F 173
Ben-Moshe, Liat 100, 102, 162, 201, 226
Berlant, L 85, 87
Berne, Patty 215
Beveridge, MC 125
biopower 74, 76–81, 83–84, 86, 87, 95
Blagg, H 203
Bloom, H 33, 35
Bond, C 8, 111
Boon-Kuo, L 52
Bradley, K 26
Bush, George W 33
Button, Judge 158

Canada 9, 14, 89, 110, 207; colonial violence in 8; mental health courts 34; overrepresentation of disabled people 24
carceral archipelago 99
carceral continuum 18, 98, 195
carceral control 17, 20, 98, 101, 103, 110; alternative ways of knowing criminalised disabled individuals 170–176; appropriateness of diversion 165–167; choosing legal domain 176–184; competing ways of knowing 173–176; criminal legal domain as residual domain of 195–196; criminal responsibility, absence of 176–179; fitness and trial 182–183; ineffective sentencing 179–182; isotopic and legitimating relationship between legal domains 167–169; non-colonial 159–160; police documents and criminal legal subject 171–172; practicality and efficacy of diversion 184–186, 187; and psychological abnormality 168, 169; psy professional reports and doubling 172–173; *see also* disability services
carcerality 17–18, 97, 98–104, 224, 227; noncolonial, diversion as 110–111; retrieving excess through diversion 104–106
Carey, AC 100
Carney, T 67
Carter, D 105
challenging behaviour 160, 172, 173
Chapman, Chris 88, 89, 100, 102, 110, 138, 147, 161, 205, 210, 212, 223, 224, 227
child welfare 134, 137, 138, 147
Chunn DE 144

citizenship, and diversion 37, 49, 50, 75–76
civil commitment laws, reform of 24
civil mental health legislation, policing through 143–145
Cleary, TG 125
Clinton, Bill 33
coercion 2–3, 4–5, 29, 46, 47–48, 166; compulsion orders 31; and criminal courts 37; and disability services 54–55, 85, 103, 105; intervention of only criminalised disabled people 50–57; intervention without conviction and sentence 48–50; legal basis for 27; and mental health courts 39, 40, 42; and section 32 (NSW, Australia) 122, 124, 126, 128, 159, 163, 166, 185; and violence 13, 84, 85, 86, 87; voluntary 34
cognitive impairment 2, 32, 82, 128
Cohen, Stanley 40
colonialism 6–8, 9, 10–11, 18, 156, 181, 224; and carcerality 110–111; and CRPD 64; and jurisdiction 160, 163; and legality 117–118; logic of elimination 7; and oppression 54; and social disadvantage 135; violence 8, 16, 53, 72, 84–85, 88–89, 207, 208
community-led support 201–204
community orders 30
compulsion orders 31
Convention on the Rights of Persons with Disabilities (CRPD) 20–21, 47, 59, 95–96, 103, 147, 214–215, 216, 225; accessibility 66; access to justice 62, 71; ambivalence towards criminal justice 63–70; and court diversion 60–61; disability-based discrimination 61–62, 63; and disability criminal justice 61–63; discrimination against disabled people on all grounds 61, 63–64; equality and non-discrimination 61, 63–64, 71; fitness 67; freedom from torture or cruel/inhuman/degrading treatment or punishment 71; independent living and inclusion in community 68–69, 70; liberty and security of person 60, 61, 65–66, 71; *Marlon Noble v Australia* 70–72; right to equal recognition before law 62, 68, 71
Correctional Service Canada (CSC) 24
corrosive social disadvantage 16, 54, 63, 89, 130, 132–135
Corston, J 26
court liaison and diversion schemes (CLDSs) 30
Cover, R 212
Crimes Act 1900 (NSW), section 428W 124
criminal courts, legislated powers to 29–32, 36–38
criminalisation 38, 40, 41, 67, 72, 135–140, 204
criminal justice system 1, 3, 5, 30, 88; disability overrepresentation 3, 24–26, 54, 67, 72, 106–109, 116–117; and immigration 10; institutional archipelago 18, 84, 98, 100–101, 102, 103, 104, 105, 106, 109, 110, 134, 139, 143, 147, 162, 167, 196, 221; and mental health system, convergence of 44; and mental health system, movement between 11, 100, 103, 144; net widening 39, 40; police 11, 103, 129, 134, 137, 138, 139, 143–147, 171–172; prison 6, 7, 11, 24–25, 37, 57; and settler colonialism 7–8, 16; social control 40; structural problems in 41–42, 110, 169
criminal law 51, 55–56, 58, 105, 186, 222, 225; actus reus 168, 170, 171; completeness of 114–115, 139; conviction 50–51, 176–179; fitness 122, 168, 182–183; legality 109–118; liberal protections of 50; and liberty 66; mens rea 168, 170, 171, 183; not guilty by reason of mental illness 11, 62, 113; positivist view of 49, 50; preventive turn of 50; psychological individualism 111–114, 168, 225
criminal legal liberal citizenship 49, 50, 54, 87, 156, 162
criminal responsibility, absence of 176–179
critical disability legal pedagogy 209–212
critical disability studies 10–11, 15, 16, 75, 81, 88, 90
cross-system collaboration, and diversion schemes 29
Cruikshank, Barbara 188
Cunneen, C 7, 8
Custody Notification Service (CNS) 202–203

Davis, LJ 160
Day, Tanya 10
Dean, A 208
death in custody 9, 10, 117, 139, 142
debility 16–17, 75, 92, 93–96, 102, 162
degeneracy 79, 90–92, 94, 217–218, 219
Dharriwaa Elders Group 203–204
disability 2, 15–16, 226; as absolute category 160; bifurcation of 16–17, 90, 92–93, 94; as biopolitical category 16; biopower 80–81, 83–84, 86, 87; capacity 92; carcerality 17–18, 97, 98–109, 110–111, 227; critical jurisprudence of 217–219; curative imaginary 85; debility 16–17, 92, 93–96, 102; degeneracy 90–92, 94, 217–218, 219; diagnostic labels of 8–9, 155; disadvantage 16, 54, 63, 89, 130, 132–135; distress, criminalisation of 139; eugenics 53, 54, 87, 90, 217; inclusionism 92, 93, 152, 162; indigeneity 13, 51, 53, 89, 117; injustices, and diversion 6–15, 52; institution 217–219; and legality 51–52, 109–118, 155; non-normative 90; overrepresentation in criminal justice system 3, 24–26, 54, 67, 72, 106–109, 116–117; race 13, 37, 51, 53; temporality 83–84, 85, 115–118; victimisation 145–147
disability carceral scholarship 100, 102, 109, 221
Disability Justice movement 21
Disability Rights Movement 215
disability services 4, 5, 14, 16, 20, 26, 182; access to 4, 5, 25, 28, 35, 52, 106–107, 222; and coercion 48, 52, 54–55, 60, 61, 85, 103, 105, 223; community access 191; and conditionality of diversion orders 184, 185–186, 195–196; and control 83, 94, 103, 164–165, 167, 186, 189; court diversion and liaison scheme (England) 26; and criminalisation 41, 138–139; distribution in space 190–192; forensic disability services 127; group homes 14, 69, 83, 188, 192, 193; humane and therapeutic framing of 186–187; legally ordered services 27, 47, 82, 84, 103; National Disability Insurance Scheme (Australia) 127, 128; and overrepresentation of disabled people 3, 24; and prison, relationship between 103–104; restriction of choices 188–190; skills development 188; structuring time and activity 192–195; treatment plans 187, 188–195
discipline 77–78, 79–80, 81, 84, 99–100, 104, 167
diversion 1–2, 3, 14, 23, 26, 27–29, 220; acute problems with 4–5; alternatives to 198–200; appropriateness of 95, 108, 165–167, 183; Australia 31–32, 34–35, 43, 129–148; benefits 35–38; breach aspects of 58; Canada 34, 89, 110, 207; coercion 39, 40, 42, 46, 47–58, 84; court diversion 2, 23; and criminal legal intervention 18, 95, 111, 112–113, 166–167, 168, 225; criticisms 39–45; definition of 2; diagnostic frameworks and expert knowledge 53; and disability injustices 6–15, 52; disability justice beyond 20–22; effects at population level 94; England 2, 29–31, 39, 42, 43; human rights and 59–73; and legal considerations 28–29; as a legal process 27; legislated powers to criminal courts 29–32, 36–38; mechanisms, underuse of 44; mental health courts 32–35, 36, 37, 39, 40, 41, 42–43; of minority of criminalised disabled people 57–58, 226; net widening 39, 40; New South Wales 31, 129–148; New Zealand 32; of non-convicted people 49; Northern Ireland 31; police diversion 134, 137, 138, 139, 143–145, 171–172; practicality and efficacy of 184–186, 187; Republic of Ireland 31; schemes, features of 28–29, 57–58; Scotland 31; section 32 (NSW, Australia) 119, 120–128; social control impacts of 40; South Australia 32, 35; subjectification of disabled people 74, 81–82, 94, 151–152, 153–154, 168, 170–173; as subsidiary to criminal legal intervention 57, 68, 104–105, 221; theorising 74–76; as therapeutic solution 2–4; United States of America 33–34, 43; Victoria 34–35; and violence 84–89; Wales 29–31, 39
Djirra 203
Dorsett, S 152, 153
doubling 104, 106–107, 171, 172–173
Dowse, Leanne 16, 54, 89, 90, 94, 102, 134, 138

DPP (NSW) v El Mawas (2006) 121, 123, 149, 155, 156, 163, 164, 165–166, 167, 170, 184–185, 187
DPP (NSW) v Lopez-Aguilar (2013) 158
DPP (NSW) v Saunders (2017) 122–123
DPP (NSW) v Soliman (2013) 158
Drinkwater, C 83
Dudgeon, P 202

England 2, 10, 14; diversion schemes in 26, 29–31, 39, 42, 43; mental health courts 35
epistemic violence 83, 130
eugenics 53, 54, 87, 90, 217
Evans, J 208

Fabris, E 101
Faraci, SM 40, 41
Fennell, P 39
First Nations people 222, 224; alternatives to court diversion for 202; and colonialism 6–8, 9, 53, 64, 88–89, 110–111, 207; and CRPD 64–65; death in custody 142; degeneracy 91; and diagnostic labels of disability 8–9; human rights 216; overrepresentation of 24, 110, 117–118; state violence against 9–10; subjectification of 88
First People's Disability Network 202
Fitzpatrick P 115
Fontaine, Tina 134
formal diversion 27
Foucault, Michel 75, 86–87, 98–100, 161, 166, 194; biopower 74, 76–80, 81, 83–84, 86, 87; carceral archipelago 99; carceral control 17; degeneracy 79, 91; discipline 77–78, 79–80, 81, 84, 99–100, 104, 167; doubling 106–107; human rights 215–216; isotopy 167; law 115; massification 106–109; regulatory controls 78–80; scientific racism 79, 84, 86, 87, 91
Fritsch, K 90, 95, 96, 223
front-end net widening 40

Generation Five 205
Gillman, M 155, 160
Gilmore, RW 85, 141
Godden, L 152
Goffman, E 17
Golder, Ben 103, 109, 115, 213, 215–216
Goldson, B 137–138
governmentality 192
guardianship orders 30, 31, 191, 194

Harcourt, BE 18, 100
Harrison, Judge 158
Hatch, A 101
Haydon-Laurelut, M 173, 190
Hazen, D 227
Heerema, M 33, 35
Heyman, B 155, 160
Hickey, H 64
hospital orders 30, 31, 39, 43
humanitarian intervention, diversion as 36–37
human rights 20–21, 59, 103; Convention on the Rights of Persons with Disabilities 20–21, 47, 59, 60–73, 126, 214–215, 216, 225; and criminal justice 61–63; institutionalisation 69–70; legal capacity 62, 65, 67–68, 71–72, 96; *Marlon Noble v Australia* 70–72; prisons 66, 69–70, 72; strategic engagement with 214–216
Human Rights Watch 6
Hume, RA 122–123

Icarus Project 201
identity politics 90–91
immigration, and mental health system 10
inclusionism 92, 93, 152, 162
Indigenous Australians 7, 43, 131, 156–157, 160–161, 177–178, 180; carceral control 194, 196; colonialism 7–8, 111, 135, 138, 142, 143, 207; community-led support 202–203; criminalisation 72, 135–136, 137–139; death-in-custody cases 9, 10, 142; incarceration 72, 140–143, 204; and jurisdiction 159–160, 163; *Marlon Noble v Australia* 70–72; overrepresentation of 24; self-determination 72, 141, 202; social disadvantage 132, 133, 134, 135; subjectification of 172–173; as victims of crime 145–147; violence 8, 11, 141–142, 146, 147
Indigenous people 222, 224; alternatives to court diversion for 202; and colonialism 6–8, 9, 53, 64, 88–89, 110–111; and CRPD 64–65; degeneracy 91; and diagnostic labels of disability 8–9; human rights 216; overrepresentation of 24,

117–118; state violence against 9–10; subjectification of 88
informal diversion 27
inheritance, and disability injustices 208–209
institutionalisation 14, 69, 83, 100, 102, 187, 217–218; deinstitutionalisation 14, 17, 25, 35, 54, 69, 83–84, 102, 124; institutional archipelago 18, 84, 98, 100–101, 102, 103, 104, 105, 106, 109, 110, 134, 139, 143, 147, 162, 167, 196, 221; transinstitutionalisation 25, 101
institutional racism 7
Intellectual Disability (Compulsory Care and Rehabilitation) Act 2003, New Zealand 32
Intellectual Disability Rights Service 193
interlocutory orders 120
isotopy 104, 167

James, DV 30, 34
Joseph, AJ 91, 110, 218
juridical individualism 112
jurisdiction 149, 162, 169, 183; alternative legal subjectivity 151–157; apolitical and non-colonial lawful relations 157–163; critical approaches to 152–154; diagnosed disability and lawful authority 154–157; effects at systemic/population level 153, 154; jurisdictional fact 149–150; and subjectification 153–154

Kafer, A 85, 87, 116
Kaiser, HA 39, 40, 41
Kim, E 85–86, 87, 116, 208

Laing, J 42
Lamble S 205
lawful authority 150, 151–152, 154–157, 159, 162
law reform 25, 26, 126, 127, 167, 213–214
Law Reform Commission (NSW) 26
Leeming, M 150
legal domains 150, 153–154, 155–156, 170–171, 221–222; of carceral control, choosing 176–184; isotopic and legitimating relationship between 167–169; police documents and criminal legal subject 171–172; psy professional reports and doubling 172–173
legal education 209–212
legality 18–19, 51–52, 109, 155, 224; definition of 109; and jurisdiction 156, 163, 169; noncolonial carcerality, diversion as 110–111; and psychological individualism 111–114; and temporality 115–118
legal safeguards to disabled people 42
Levinson, J 83, 192
Linton, S 155
logic of elimination 7

MacGillivray, P 203, 204
Maher, Rebecca 10
Maori, overrepresentation of 24
Marlon Noble v Australia 70–72
massification 106–109
Mawani 116
McCausland, R 41, 43, 203, 204
McColl, Ruth 121, 123, 149, 164, 165, 170, 185
McLoughlin, D 109
McMillan, N 208
McSherry, B 39, 41, 200
McVeigh, S 152, 153
McWhorter, L 90, 91, 218, 219
medical industrial complex (MIC) 101–102
medical model of disability 15, 75, 80–81, 82, 154–155
Mental Health Act 1983 (England and Wales) 30
Mental Health (Compulsory Assessment and Treatment) Act 1992, New Zealand 32
Mental Health (Forensic Provisions) Act 1990 (NSW), section 32 19, 119, 120–122, 149, 164, 170; alternative legal subjectivities 173–176; amendments 125–126; conditionality of orders 184, 185–186, 195–196; Court Data 151, 160; critical concerns with 122–123; final order 184–185; interim order 184; jurisdiction 149–150, 154, 158, 159, 162; lawful authority 156–157; legal domains of carceral control, choosing 176–184; NSWLRC recommendations 126–127; police documents 171; tensions in 123–128; treatment plans 187, 188
mental health courts 32–35, 36, 37, 82, 200; and coercion 39, 40, 42; informal process of 42; segregating and

discriminatory effects of 42–43; use of incarceration 41; and voluntariness 42
mental health law 2, 11, 39, 71, 124, 201–202, 218, 224
Mental Health Legislation Amendment (Forensic Provisions) Act 2008 (NSW) 124
mental health services *see* disability services
Mentally Impaired Defendants Act 1996 (WA) 70, 71, 72
Menzies, RJ 144
Mettray, France 98–99
Million, Dian 9, 53, 88, 222
Mills, C 110, 163
Mingus, Mia 101, 204, 205–206
Minkowitz, T 227
Mitchell, DT 12, 93, 162
Ms Dhu 142
Murri Watch 203
Mustill, LJ 30

National Disability Insurance Scheme (NDIS) 127, 128
National Inquiry into Missing and Murdered Indigenous Women and Girls 8
neoliberalism 13, 52, 93, 223
net widening 39, 40
New South Wales, Australia 19–20, 43, 119, 149; Cognitive Impairment Diversion Program 128; diversion 31, 129–148; Law Reform Commission 26; mental health courts 35; *see also* Mental Health (Forensic Provisions) Act 1990 (NSW), section 32
New South Wales Law Reform Commission (NSWLRC) 122, 124–125, 126–127
New Zealand: diversion schemes 32; mental health courts 35; over-representation of disabled people 24
Nixon, R 87
Noble v Australia 70–72
Norrie, Alan 112–113, 168
Northern Ireland 31
Northern Territory, Australia: diversion schemes 32; mental health courts 35
Nunkoosing, K 173, 190

O'Mahony, C 3, 37
out-of-home care (OOHC) 130, 134, 135, 137–138, 139

Pasternak, S 162
Peay, J 30
Perlin, M 37, 39
place-conscious legal pedagogy 211–212
poetics of law reform 213
police documents and criminal legal subject 171–172
Porter, A 142
positivist view of criminal law 49, 50
postadjudication 33
postcode justice 43
preadjudication 33
prisons 11, 37, 85, 108, 221; as asylums 24; and control 18; disability services in 24; failure of 100, 102; high profile deaths in 6; and human rights 66, 69–70, 72; incarceration 140–143; and mental health systems, movement between 11, 100, 103, 144; transinstitutionalisation 25; *see also* carcerality
problem-solving courts 32, 200
Psychiatric Disabilities Anti-violence Coalition 207
psychiatric survivor anti-violence framework 207
psychiatry 79, 82
psychological individualism 111–114, 168, 225
psycho-pharmaceuticals 101
psychosocial disability 2
psy knowledge 82, 83, 105, 157, 161, 170
psy professionals 150, 151, 154, 160, 171, 172–173
Puar, Jasbir 87, 91, 92, 93, 94, 102, 116, 162

racism 85, 141; institutional 7; scientific 79, 84, 86, 87, 91; and violence 86–87
Razack, Sherene 88, 91, 117, 142, 181, 233
Reed, Sarah 6
regulatory controls 78–80
Republic of Ireland 31
restorative justice 205
restriction orders 30–31
restrictive practices 56, 194
Richards, K 4
Richardson, E 40, 41, 200
Rigg, Marcia 10
Rigg, Sean 10
Rinaldi, J 207
risk management, and self-realisation 189

Rose, N 82
Rossiter, K 207
Royal Commission and Board of Inquiry into the Protection and Detention of Children in the Northern Territory 8
Royal Commission into Aboriginal Deaths in Custody 8
Rule, Latoya 10
Rutherford, M 44

Sandland, R 37, 42, 44
Schneider, RD 33, 35
Schweik, SM 218
scientific racism 79, 84, 86, 87, 91
Scotland 31
Seear, K 43, 44, 82, 213
segregation 42–43, 52, 69, 101, 134
self-determination 8, 53, 64, 201, 203, 211; collective 9, 21, 65, 204; of Indigenous Australians 72, 141, 202
Seltzer, T 41
settler colonialism *see* colonialism
Shildrick, M 226
Sites of Conscience 209, 212, 214
slow death 85, 87, 95, 98, 102, 116, 141
slow violence 87–88, 130, 141, 142
Smith, Ashley 6, 139
Snedker, S 37
Snyder SL 12, 93, 162
social and emotional wellbeing 9
social control 40
social inequalities, and diversion 43
Soteria houses 201
South Australia 32, 35
South Australian Magistrates Court Diversion Program 35
sovereign power 76–77
Spade, D 162, 199, 213–214, 221
Spiers, M 125
Spivakovsky, C 43, 44, 82, 213
Stefan, S 39, 41–42, 43
stigmatisation 43, 52–53
strengths-based approach to wellbeing 9
structural justice 208
Swain, J 155, 160

Tam, L 10, 201
temporality 83–84, 85, 115–118, 192–193
therapeutic jurisprudence (TJ) 32, 36
Ticktin, Miriam 226
total institutions 17
trans disabled people 6
transformative justice 204–206
transinstitutionalisation 25, 101
treatment 3, 25–26, 28–29; assertive community treatment 36; compulsory 32; plans 34, 41, 120, 126, 185, 186, 187, 188–195; shift from punishment to 40
Tulich, T 203

United Kingdom: duration of interventions 48; overrepresentation of disabled people 24
United States of America 14, 18, 100; due process 42; mental health courts 33–34, 42, 43; overrepresentation of disabled people 24
universal legal individualism 112

Valverde, M 152, 153, 155
Veitch, S 116
Victoria, Australia 34–35, 43
violence 12–13, 75; colonial 8, 53, 84–85, 88–89, 110; curative 85–86, 87; and diversion 84–89, 181; epistemic 83, 130; interpersonal 205, 206; and legal education 210–211; legal 5, 13, 55, 56, 72, 210, 212; ontological 86, 223; prison 6, 11, 57, 103–104; rate, of disabled people 13; redress for 206–209; sexual 145–147; slow death 85, 87, 95, 98, 102, 116, 141; slow 87–88, 130, 141, 142; state 9–10; unlawful 5, 13, 55–56
voluntariness, and mental health courts 42
Voronka, J 110, 168–169, 180, 218, 223

Wales 26, 42; diversion schemes 29–31, 39, 43; mental health courts 35
welfare state 13
Wellness Network for Law 211
Wildeman, S 108, 201–202
Winick, BJ 36, 37
Withers, AJ 88, 138, 147, 159, 161, 205, 210, 212, 215
Wolfe, P 7

Yuwaya Ngarra-li project 203–204

For Product Safety Concerns and Information please contact our EU representative GPSR@taylorandfrancis.com
Taylor & Francis Verlag GmbH, Kaufingerstraße 24, 80331 München, Germany

www.ingramcontent.com/pod-product-compliance
Ingram Content Group UK Ltd.
Pitfield, Milton Keynes, MK11 3LW, UK
UKHW022022180926
475701UK00005B/976

9780367498078